> # computing
ESSENTIALS

introductory
2008

The O'Leary Series

Computing Concepts

- *Computing Essentials 2006* Introductory & Complete Editions
- *Computing Essentials 2007* Introductory & Complete Editions
- *Computing Essentials 2008* Introductory & Complete Editions

Microsoft Office Applications

- *Microsoft Office 2007*
- *Microsoft Office Word 2007* Introductory & Brief Editions
- *Microsoft Office Excel 2007* Introductory & Brief Editions
- *Microsoft Office Access 2007* Introductory & Brief Editions
- *Microsoft Office PowerPoint 2007* Brief Edition

>computing

ESSENTIALS

TIMOTHY J. O'LEARY
Professor Emeritus
Arizona State University

LINDA I. O'LEARY

introductory

2008

McGraw-Hill
Irwin

Boston   Burr Ridge, IL   Dubuque, IA   Madison, WI   New York   San Francisco   St. Louis
Bangkok   Bogotá   Caracas   Kuala Lumpur   Lisbon   London   Madrid   Mexico City
Milan   Montreal   New Delhi   Santiago   Seoul   Singapore   Sydney   Taipei   Toronto

 **McGraw-Hill**
Irwin

COMPUTING ESSENTIALS 2008: INTRODUCTORY EDITION

Published by McGraw-Hill/Irwin, a business unit of The McGraw-Hill Companies, Inc., 1221 Avenue of the Americas, New York, NY, 10020. Copyright © 2008 by The McGraw-Hill Companies, Inc. All rights reserved. No part of this publication may be reproduced or distributed in any form or by any means, or stored in a database or retrieval system, without the prior written consent of The McGraw-Hill Companies, Inc., including, but not limited to, in any network or other electronic storage or transmission, or broadcast for distance learning.

Some ancillaries, including electronic and print components, may not be available to customers outside the United States.

This book is printed on acid-free paper.

3 4 5 6 7 8 9 0 WCK/WCK 0 9 8

ISBN-13: 978-0-07-329468-1
MHID: 0-07-329468-3

Editorial director: *John E. Biernat*
Publisher: *Linda Schreiber*
Associate sponsoring editor: *Janna Martin*
Developmental editor: *Kelly L. Delso*
Developmental editor I: *Alaina Grayson*
Marketing manager: *Sarah Wood*
Media producer: *Greg Bates*
Lead project manager: *Lori Koetters*
Lead production supervisor: *Michael R. McCormick*
Senior designer: *Artemio Ortiz Jr.*
Senior photo research coordinator: *Jeremy Cheshareck*
Photo researcher: *Keri Johnson*
Lead media project manager: *Cathy L. Tepper*
Cover design: *Asylum Studios*
Typeface: *10/12 New Aster*
Compositor: *Laserwords Private Limited*
Printer: *Quebecor World Versailles Inc.*

Library of Congress Cataloging-in-Publication Data

O'Leary, Timothy J., 1947-
    Computing essentials 2008 / Timothy J. O'Leary, Linda I. O'Leary.—Introductory ed., 19th ed.
        p. cm.—(The O'Leary series)
    Includes index.
    ISBN-13: 978-0-07-329468-1 (alk. paper)
    ISBN-10: 0-07-329468-3 (alk. paper)
    1. Computers. 2. Electronic data processing. I. O'Leary, Linda I. II. Title.
QA76.O4282 2008
004—dc22
                                                    2006100097

www.mhhe.com

DEDICATION

We dedicate this edition to Nicole and Katie who have brought love and joy to our lives.

Brief Contents

Contents

4

SPECIALIZED APPLICATION SOFTWARE *92*

5

SYSTEM SOFTWARE *120*

6

THE SYSTEM UNIT   148

7

INPUT AND OUTPUT   180

PREFACE

The 20th century brought us the dawn of the digital information age and unprecedented changes in information technology. There is no indication that this rapid rate of change will be slowing—it may even be increasing. As we begin the 21st century, computer literacy is undoubtedly becoming a prerequisite in whatever career you choose.

The goal of *Computing Essentials* is to provide you with the basis for understanding the concepts necessary for success. *Computing Essentials* also endeavors to instill an appreciation for the effect of information technology on people and our environment and to give you a basis for building the necessary skill set to succeed in this the 21st century.

Times are changing, technology is changing, and this text is changing too. As students of today, you are different from those of yesterday. You put much effort toward the things that interest you and the things that are relevant to you. Your efforts directed at learning application programs and exploring the Web seem, at times, limitless. On the other hand, it is sometimes difficult to engage in other equally important topics such as personal privacy and technological advances.

In this text, we present practical tips related to key concepts through the demonstration of interesting applications that are relevant to your lives and by focusing on outputs rather than processes. Then, we discuss the concepts and processes.

Motivation and relevance are the keys. This text has several features specifically designed to engage and demonstrate the relevance of technology in your lives. These elements are combined with a thorough coverage of the concepts and sound pedagogical devices.

We have specifically designed the end-of-chapter materials to this text to meet the different needs of students and instructors. In addition to the traditional end-of-chapter review materials, you will find three unique categories: (1) Applying Technology is designed to help students gain a better understanding of how the technology covered in a particular chapter is used today, (2) Expanding Your Knowledge offers a deeper understanding to topics covered in that particular chapter, and (3) Writing About Technology provides the opportunity to hone essential writing skills while learning about technology issues relating to privacy, security, and ethics.

This table offers a glimpse of the unique coverage you can find at the end of each chapter.

END-OF-CHAPTER COVERAGE

Chapter	Applying Technology	Expanding Your Knowledge	Writing About Technology
1	TV Tuner Cards and Video Clips (p. 176) Digital Video Editing (p. 98) Home Networking (p. 273) Job Opportunities (p. 331)	How Virus Protection Programs Work (p. 146) How Digital Cameras Work (p. 210) How Internet Telephones Work (p. 210) How Wireless Home Networks Work (p. 274)	HTML Source Code (p. 119) Antitrust (p. 147) Electronic Monitoring (p. 275) Processor Serial Numbers (p. 178)
2	Blocking Spam (p. 57) Online Shopping (p. 57) Web Auctions (p. 57)	How Spam Filters Work (p. 58) How Instant Messaging Works (p. 58) Domain Registrations (p. 58)	Free Speech Online (p. 59) Dot-Bombs (p. 59)
3	Speech Recognition (p. 89) Presentation Graphics (p. 89) Corel WordPerfect Office Suite (p. 89)	How Speech Recognition Works (p. 90) Sharing Data between Applications (p. 90) Shareware (p. 90)	Acquiring Software (p. 91) Software Standards (p. 91)
4	Digital Video Editing (p. 117) Shockwave (p. 117) Streaming Multimedia Players (p. 117)	How Digital Video Editing Works (p. 118) Personal Web Site (p. 118) Streaming Multimedia (p. 118)	HTML Source Code (p. 119) Online Expert Systems (p. 119)
5	Virus Protection (p. 145) Windows Update (p. 145) WinZip (p. 145)	How Virus Protection Programs Work (p. 146) Booting and POST (p. 146) Customized Desktop (p. 146)	Antitrust (p. 147) Online Backup (p. 147)
6	TV Tuner Cards and Video Clips (p. 176) Desktop and Notebook Computers (p. 176) Custom System Units (p. 176)	How TV Tuner Cards Work (p. 177) How Virtual Memory Works (p. 177) Binary Numbers (p. 177)	Processor Serial Numbers (p. 178) Smart Cards (p. 178)
7	WebCams and Instant Messaging (p. 209) Internet Telephones (p. 209) Voice Recognition (p. 209)	How Digital Cameras Work (p. 210) How Internet Telephones Work (p. 210) Handwriting Recognition (p. 210)	WebCams (p. 211) Electronic Security (p. 211)
8	iPods and Music from the Internet (p. 237) iPod (p. 237) USB Storage Devices (p. 237)	How Music is Downloaded from the Internet (p. 238) File Compression (p. 238) Internet Hard Drives (p. 238)	CD-R and Music Files (p. 239) Storage Trade-offs (p. 239)
9	Home Networking (p. 273) Distributed Computing (p. 273) Palm (p. 273)	How Wireless Home Networks Work (p. 274) How Napster and Gnutella Work (p. 274) Hotspots (p. 274)	Electronic Monitoring (p. 275) Digital Rights Management (p. 275)
10	Spyware (p. 307) Personal Firewalls (p. 307) Ergonomic Workstations (p. 307)	How Web Bugs Work (p. 308) Mistaken Identity (p. 308) Air Travel Database (p. 308)	Facial Recognition (p. 309) Plagiarism (p. 309)
11	Jobs Online (p. 331) Maintain Computer Competence (p. 331)	Your Career (p. 332) Resume Advice (p. 332)	Writing about Privacy and Ethics (p. 333) Writing about Security (p. 333)

Before beginning this new edition, an extensive review process was completed. Many of the reviewers were current users of *Computing Essentials* and many were users of other textbooks. A clear message was sent: More is not better . . . better is better. One reviewer succinctly stated: "Determine what is most important and focus on that."

As an educator myself, I knew exactly what the reviewer meant. Today, so many textbooks on information technology have way too much detail and too many technical terms. The density of the information can become overwhelming. To help ease this, many textbooks add relief by inserting numerous photographs that, while attractive to the eye, have little or no informational content.

The result is that our students have difficulty determining what is most important. Too many details tend to hide what is most important. As authors add more and more detail to textbooks, students have greater and greater challenges discerning what is really important—what are the key concepts. More is not better . . . better is better.

Fresh from reading the reviewer comments, I carefully reread *Computing Essentials 2007*. From this new perspective, it was clear what needed to be done. So, the focus of *Computing Essentials 2008* is not to just cover the newest material but to refocus on what are the most important concepts. I have carefully reviewed every figure, photograph, and table. If it lacked informational content, the figure, photograph, or table was dropped. I reexamined every key term. If the term was outdated or not essential, I dropped it. My objective was to return to the roots of *Computing Essentials*—focusing on the most important and essential concepts of information technology.

VISUAL LEARNING

VISUAL CHAPTER OPENERS

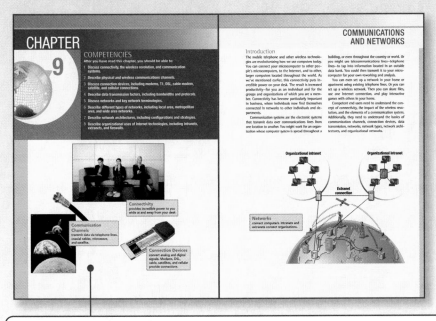

Each chapter begins with a list of chapter competencies or objectives and provides a brief introduction to what will be covered in the chapter. Graphics in the chapter opener demonstrate how the chapter is organized, while text callouts provide a glimpse of topical coverage.

VISUAL SUMMARIES

Visual summaries appear at the end of every chapter and summarize major concepts covered throughout the chapter. Like the chapter openers, these summaries use graphics to reinforce key concepts in an engaging and meaningful way.

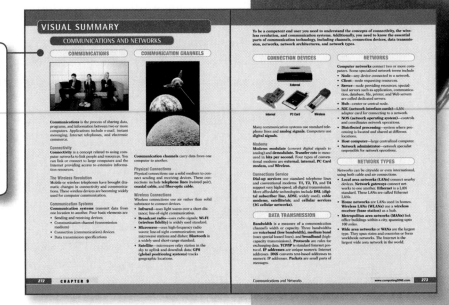

HANDS-ON

ON THE WEB EXPLORATIONS

Figure 4-17 Virtual reality

At least two On the Web Explorations appear within the margins of nearly every chapter. These explorations ask you to search specific Web sites for additional information on key topics, encouraging you to expand your knowledge through Web resources.

TIPS

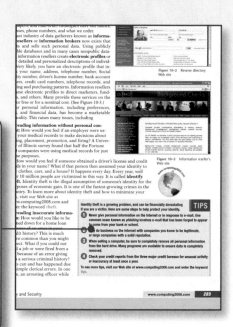

Tips appear within nearly every chapter and provide advice on chapter-related issues, such as how to efficiently locate information on the Web, how to speed up computer operations, and how to protect against computer viruses. Tips assist you with common technology-related problems or issues and motivate you by showing the relevance of concepts presented in the chapter to everyday life. Additional tips can be found on the O'Leary Web site at www. computing2008.com by entering the keyword **tips**.

MAKING IT WORK FOR YOU

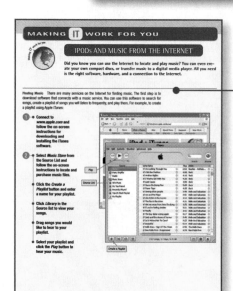

Special interest topics are presented in the Making IT Work for You section found within nearly every chapter. These topics include protecting against computer viruses, downloading music from the Internet, and using the Internet to place free long-distance telephone calls.

LEARNING TOOLS

MAKING IT WORK FOR YOU

The Making IT Work for You icon appears throughout the chapter to show you which topics in the chapter are expanding upon the Making IT Work for You section.

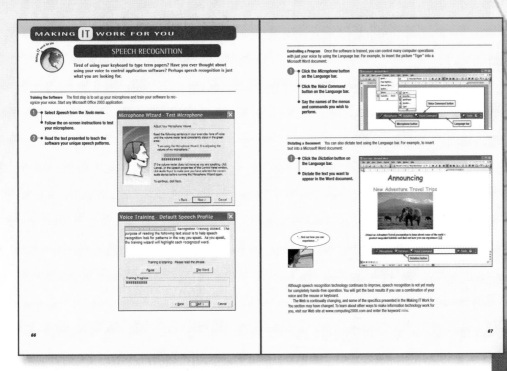

MAKING IT WORK FOR YOU FIGURES

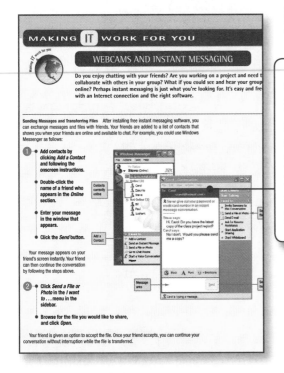

Critical technologies are presented to show how technologies work and how they are used. These animated figures include such topics as How Digital Cameras Work, How Instant Messaging Works, and How Home Networks Work. Additionally, several other topics are animated and presented on the book's Web site.

REINFORCING KEY CONCEPTS

CONCEPT CHECKS

Located at points throughout each chapter, the Concept Check cues you to note which topics have been covered and to self-test your understanding of the material already discussed.

systems. Windows, Mac OS, and Linux are operating systems commonly used by individuals.

▼ **CONCEPT CHECK**

▶ What is system software? What are the four kinds of system software programs?

▶ What is an operating system? Discuss operating system functions and features.

▶ Describe each of the three categories of operating systems.

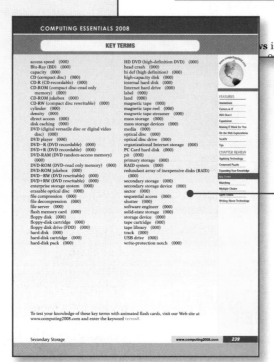

vs is by far the most popular microcomputer operating sys-

KEY TERMS

Throughout the text, the most important terms are presented in bold and are defined within the text. You will also find a list of key terms at the end of each chapter and in the glossary at the end of the book.

CHAPTER REVIEW

Following the Visual Summary, the chapter review includes material designed to review and reinforce chapter content. It includes a Key Terms list that reiterates the terms presented in the chapter, a Crossword Puzzle to challenge your understanding of the chapter material, Multiple Choice questions to help test your understanding of information presented in the chapter, Matching exercises to test your recall of terminology presented in the chapter, and Open-Ended questions or statements to help review your understanding of the key concepts presented in the chapter.

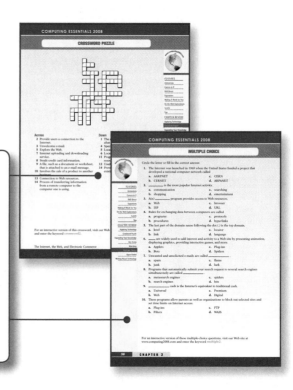

THE FUTURE OF INFORMATION TECHNOLOGY

CAREERS IN IT

Some of the fastest-growing career opportunities are in information technology. Each chapter highlights one of the most promising careers in IT by presenting job titles, responsibilities, educational requirements, and salary ranges. Among the careers covered are Webmaster, software engineer, and database administrator. You will learn how the material you are studying relates directly to a potential career path.

CAREERS IN IT

Webmasters develop and maintain Web sites and Web resources. (See Figure 2-29.) The job may include backup of the company Web site, updating resources, or development of new resources. Webmasters are often involved in the design and development of the Web site. Part of their job also may include monitoring and updating the interface design. Some Webmasters monitor traffic on the site and take steps to improve the publicity of the site. Webmasters also may work with marketing personnel to increase site traffic and may be involved in development of Web promotions.

Employers look for candidates with a bachelor's degree in computer science or information systems and knowledge of common programming languages and Web development software. Knowledge of HTML is considered essential. Those with experience using Web authoring software and programs like Adobe Illustrator and Adobe Flash are often preferred. Webmasters often work in conjunction with many other departments and employees. Good communication and organizational skills are vital in this position.

Webmasters can expect to earn an annual salary of $48,000 to $73,000. This position is relatively new in many corporations and tends to have fluid responsibilities. With technological advances and increasing corporate emphasis on a Web presence, experience in this field could lead to managerial opportunities. To learn about other careers in IT, visit us at www.computing 2008.com and enter the keyword careers.

Figure 2-29 Webmasters

The Internet, the Web, and Electronic Commerce   www.computing2008.com   **49**

A LOOK TO THE FUTURE

Each chapter concludes with a brief discussion of a recent technological advancement related to the chapter material, reinforcing the importance of staying informed.

A Look to the Future

Robots Can Look, Act, and Think Like Us

Would you like to voice conference with your mom through robots that resemble you both and demonstrate your emotions on their rubber faces? What if you received a companion robot with a set of moral values? Would you trust a robot to trade the stocks in your portfolio? Researchers are currently at work on robots with the artificial intelligence needed to perform these tasks and more.

The Saya robot, with its artificial skin and muscles, is currently under development in Tokyo. Researchers hope that eventually it will be used as a communication device similar to a current Web cam. For example, you could connect to a robot that resembles you at your mother's house and communicate through it with her. You would see your mother through the robot's visual system. Your mother would hear your voice come from the robot and your emotions would be displayed on its face.

Other research is being conducted that will give robots a sense of values. It is hoped that these robots will be able to make decisions independently based on this set of values. Researchers in California are creating robots that act as surveillance instruments, capable of following a target without direction from a human. The robots can predict potential escape routes and pursue a subject through crowded areas.

At the Sociable Machines Project at MIT, students are working on a robot named Kismet that detects human emotions through social and audio cues and responds with emotions of its own. Kismet recognizes faces and responds to stimuli like an infant would with emotions ranging from surprise to disgust. Researchers believe that robots such as Kismet can interact with and learn from humans better than traditional computer interfaces.

All of these projects are designed to move beyond simple computing and into a decidedly human realm of emotional intelligence. Some experts have even suggested that human intelligence relies on emotional input for all important decision making. Thus, by definition, for a machine to approximate human intelligence, it would have to understand and rely on emotions. If computers could read human emotions, and had emotional intelligence of their own, it could be possible for your computer to act as a stress counselor when you stay up all night working on a project.

Computers with their own emotional intelligence could be the ultimate human companions. Computer scientists have suggested they may read your mood and play music accordingly. Or they could search through audio and video files for media you would find moving, funny, or dramatic. If computers had their own emotional sense, it is possible that they, like the humans they emulate, would require interaction for mental health.

Would you use a robot as a communication device? Do you think we should build robots with a sense of moral values? Some researchers have suggested that robots with artificial intelligence could serve as ideal supervisors and managers. What do you think? Would you like to have an "emotional" robot for a boss?

114   CHAPTER 4

APPLYING TECHNOLOGY

In each chapter, Applying Technology presents questions designed to help you gain a better understanding of how technology is being used today. One question typically relates to the chapter's Making IT Work for You topic. Other questions focus on interesting applications of technology that relate directly to you. Topics include online auctions, online Personal Information Managers, and desktop and notebook computers.

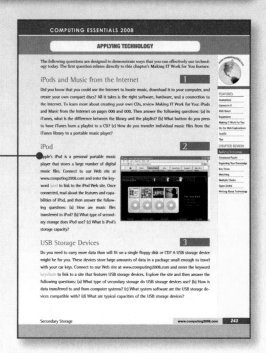

EXPANDING YOUR KNOWLEDGE

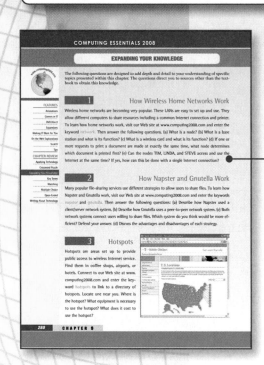

In each chapter, Expanding Your Knowledge presents questions that help you gain a deeper understanding of select topics. Typically, one question relates to a topic presented at the book's Web site, www.computing2008.com, such as How Instant Messaging Works, How Streaming Media Works, and How Virus Protection Works. Other questions in Expanding Your Knowledge typically require Web research into carefully selected topics including robotics, multimedia, HDTV, and Internet hard drives.

WRITING ABOUT TECHNOLOGY

In each chapter, Writing About Technology presents questions relating to security, privacy, and ethical issues. The issues presented include HTML source code, antitrust legislation, processor serial numbers, CD-R and music files, and electronic monitoring. One objective of the Writing About Technology feature is to help you develop critical thinking and writing skills. Another objective is to help you recognize, understand, and analyze key privacy, security, and ethical issues relating to technology.

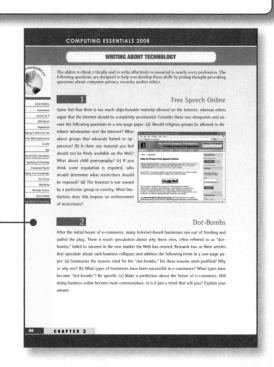

SUPPORT MATERIALS

IR CD-ROM

Instructor's Resource CD-ROM (ISBN: 9780073294698; MHID: 0073294691) contains the Instructor's Manual, PowerPoint slides, an EZ Test generation software with accompanying test item files for each chapter, and 20 video clips (with summaries) from G4techTV.

The Instructor's Manual, prepared by Ann Mauss of Loras College, offers lecture outlines with teaching notes and page references. It provides definitions of key terms and solutions to the end-of-chapter material, including multiple-choice, matching, and open-ended questions. It also offers summaries of the concept checks in each chapter. A selection of G4techTV video clips accompany this text, as do summaries for each clip.

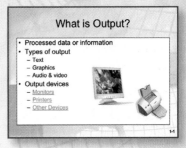

The PowerPoint slides, prepared by Brenda Nielsen of Mesa Community College–Red Mountain, are designed to provide instructors with a comprehensive resource for lecture use. The slides include a review of key terms and definitions, artwork taken from the text, as well as new illustrations to further explain concepts covered in each chapter. Comprehensive teaching notes are provided for each slide.

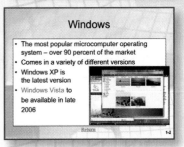

The testbank, prepared by Rajiv D. Narayana, senior editor, and Flevy Crasto, group manager–operations, of Info Data Systems (India) Pvt. Ltd., contains over 2,200 questions categorized by level of learning (definition, concept, and application). This is the same learning scheme that is introduced in the text to provide a valuable testing and reinforcement tool. Text page references have been provided for all questions, including a level-of-difficulty rating. Additional quizzes are provided on the Online Learning Center at www.computing2008.com. These can be used by students to help them prepare for classroom testing. The testbank is offered in Word files, as well as in EZ Test format.

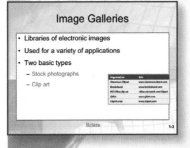

G4TECHTV VIDEOS

G4techTV videos offer instructors and students video content directly related to computing that enhances the classroom or lab experience with technology programming from business and society. Video selections include "The Screen Savers" and "Pulse," which provide edgy and informative discussion. Use of these videos will help students understand how computing interacts with and contributes to business and society and will also offer an advance look at emerging technology and devices.

THE O'LEARY WEB SITE

The O'Leary Web site can be found at www.computing 2008.com. Students can find a host of additional resources on the Web site, including animations of key concepts, videos relating to select Making IT Work for You applications, and in-depth coverage of select topics. Look for the Web icon throughout the text to indicate where additional related materials can be found on the Web site. Throughout the end-of-chapter material for the text, marginal lists, denoted by the Web icon, alert students that expanded coverage of the material in the text can be found on the Web site.

OLC

The text's Online Learning Center can be found at www.mhhe.com/ce2008. Instructors can find support materials to accompany the text on the OLC and can link directly to the OLC from the text's Web site.

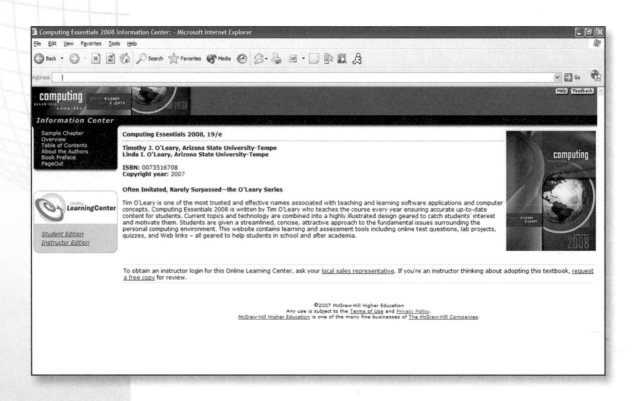

O'LEARY SERIES

The O'Leary Application Series for Microsoft Office is available separately or packaged with *Computing Essentials*. The O'Leary Application Series offers a step-by-step approach to learning computer applications and is available in both brief and introductory versions. The introductory books are MCAS Certified and prepare students for the Microsoft Office User Certification Exam.

SIMNET ASSESSMENT FOR OFFICE APPLICATIONS

SimNet Assessment for Office Applications provides a way for you to test students' software skills in a simulated environment. Simnet is available for Microsoft Office 2007 and provides flexibility for you in your applications course by offering:

Pre-testing options

Post-testing options

Course placement testing

Diagnostic capabilities to reinforce skills

Web delivery of test

MCAS preparation exams

Learning verification reports

For more information on skills assessment software, please contact your local sales representative, or visit us at www.mhhe.com.

ACKNOWLEDGMENTS

We would like to extend our thanks to the professors who took time out of their busy schedules to provide us with the feedback necessary to develop the 2008 edition of this text. The following professors offered valuable suggestions on revising the text:

Scott Russell,
Eastern Arizona College

Mark Bomgardner,
Hutchinson Community College

Louis Voit,
McMurry University

Lou Berzai,
Notre Dame University

Susan Grapevine,
Northwest Iowa Community College

Trissa Cox,
Howard Payne University

Morgan Shepherd,
University of Colorado at Colorado Springs

Bernice Eng,
Brookdale Community College

Karen Sturm,
Loras College

Robert Caruso,
Sonoma State University

Kathy Harvey,
Butte College

Sita Moripara,
Skyline College

Mike Moore,
Eastern Arizona College

Lloyd Sandmann,
Pima Community College

Judy Dunn,
Laramie County Community College

Michael Gowin,
Lincoln Christian College

Ravinder S. Kang BSc(Hon) MSc,
Highline Community College

Lester Towell,
Howard Payne University

Brian L. Rodehaver,
Ashland Community & Technical College

Christopher M. Jay Hopper,
Highline Community College

Marcel Marie Robles,
Eastern Kentucky University

Dr. Michael T. Marsh,
Shippensburg University

Neil Dunlop,
Vista Community College

Daniel Gant,
Savannah River College

Steve St. John,
Tulsa Community College

Laura Marshall,
Northern Oklahoma College

Gary Armstrong,
Shippensburg University

Linda Bettinger,
Southeast Community College

Dr. Marcel M. Robles,
Eastern Kentucky University

Theresa Allyn,
Edmonds Community College

Jerry Humphrey,
Tulsa Community College

Stephen Juaire,
Winona State University Memorial Hall

Barry Andrews,
Mt. San Antonio Community College

Jeff Brown,
Montana State University–Great Falls

Dick Winslow,
Central Wyoming College

John Haney,
Snead State Community College

Becky Cunningham,
Arkansas Tech University

Richard B. Wilkerson,
Dyersburg State Community College

Thomas R. Russell,
Cameron University

Kelli Cross,
Harrisburg Area Community College

John Haney,
Snead State Community College

Robert Molnar,
Indiana University–Purdue University

Gina Bowers-Miller,
Harrisburg Area Community College

Annie Brown,
Hawaii Community College

Bill Flechtner,
Warner Pacific College

Diane Anderson,
Big Sandy Community & Technical College

Jason Livey Ed. S.,
Howard Payne University

Robert Terrell,
Carson-Newman College

Thomas Whisenand,
Shippensburg University

Michelle Todd,
Hannibal LaGrange College

Karen Stanton,
Los Medanos College

Ramana M. Gosukonda,
Fort Valley State University

David Childress,
Ashland Community & Technical College

Catherine Stoughton,
Laramie County Community College

Steven J. Hicks,
Palo Alto College

Jeff Watson,
Walla Walla Community College

Dr. Bill Hammerschlag,
Brookhaven College

Neil Dunlop,
Vista Community College

William J. Hitchcock,
Loras College

Our thanks also go to Brenda Nielsen of Mesa Community College–Red Mountain for all her work on creating the PowerPoint presentations to accompany the text. We are grateful to Ann Mauss of Loras College, the author of the Instructor's Manual, for her revision of this valuable resource, and to Rajiv D. Narayana and Flevy Crasto of Info Data Systems for their careful revision of the testbank materials and creation of quizzing materials.

ABOUT THE AUTHORS

Tim and Linda O'Leary live in the American Southwest and spend much of their time engaging instructors and students in conversation about learning. In fact, they have been talking about learning for over 25 years. Something in those early conversations convinced them to write a book, to bring their interest in the learning process to the printed page. Today, they are as concerned as ever about learning, about technology, and about the challenges of presenting material in new ways, in terms of both content and method of delivery.

A powerful and creative team, Tim combines his 25 years of classroom teaching experience with Linda's background as a consultant and corporate trainer. Tim has taught courses at Stark Technical College in Canton, Ohio, and at Rochester Institute of Technology in upstate New York, and is currently a professor emeritus at Arizona State University in Tempe, Arizona. Linda offered her expertise at ASU for several years as an academic advisor. She also presented and developed materials for major corporations such as Motorola, Intel, Honeywell, and AT&T, as well as various community colleges in the Phoenix area.

Tim and Linda have talked to and taught numerous students, all of them with a desire to learn something about computers and applications that make their lives easier, more interesting, and more productive.

Each new edition of an O'Leary text, supplement, or learning aid has benefited from these students and their instructors who daily stand in front of them (or over their shoulders). *Computing Essentials* is no exception.

> **computing**

ESSENTIALS

introductory

2008

CHAPTER

1

COMPETENCIES

After you have read this chapter, you should be able to:

1 Explain the five parts of an information system: people, procedures, software, hardware, and data.

2 Distinguish between system software and application software.

3 Discuss the three kinds of system software programs.

4 Distinguish between basic and specialized application software.

5 Identify the four types of computers and the four types of microcomputers.

6 Describe the different types of computer hardware including the system unit, input, output, storage, and communication devices.

7 Define data and describe document, worksheet, database, and presentation files.

8 Explain computer connectivity, the wireless revolution, and the Internet.

Information Systems
consist of people, procedures, software, hardware, and data

Software
or programs control
computer operations

Hardware
includes system unit, input,
output, and secondary
storage devices

INFORMATION TECHNOLOGY, THE INTERNET, AND YOU

Introduction

The purpose of this book is to help you become competent with computer technology. **Computer competency** refers to acquiring computer-related skills—indispensable tools for today. They include how to effectively use popular application packages and the Internet.

In this chapter, we present an overview of an information system: people, procedures, software, hardware, and data. It is essential to understand these basic parts and how connectivity through the Internet and the Web expands the role of information technology in our lives. Later, we will describe these parts of an information system in detail. Fifteen years ago, most people had little to do with computers, at least directly. Of course, they filled out computerized forms, took computerized tests, and paid computerized bills. But the real work was handled by specialists. Then microcomputers came along and changed everything. Today it is easy for nearly everybody to use a computer.

- Microcomputers are common tools in all areas of life. Writers write, artists draw, engineers and scientists calculate—all on microcomputers. Students and businesspeople do all this, and more.
- New forms of learning have developed. People who are homebound, who work odd hours, or who travel frequently may take Web courses. A college course need not fit within a quarter or a semester.
- New ways to communicate, to find people with similar interests, and to buy goods are available. People use electronic mail, electronic commerce, and the Internet to meet and to share ideas and products.

To be competent with computer technology, you need to know the five parts of an information system: people, procedures, software, hardware, and data. You also need to understand connectivity, the wireless revolution, the Internet, and the Web and to recognize the role of information technology in your personal and professional life.

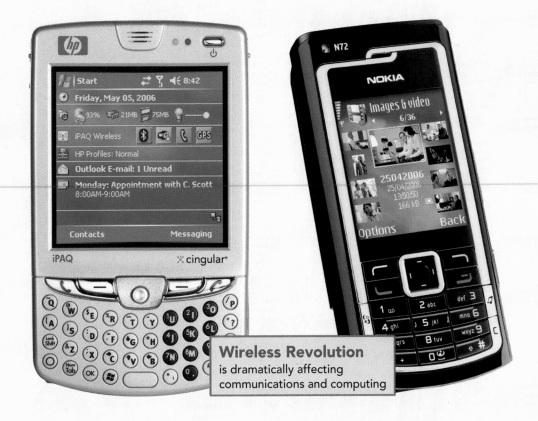

Wireless Revolution is dramatically affecting communications and computing

INFORMATION SYSTEMS

When you think of a microcomputer, perhaps you think of just the equipment itself. That is, you think of the monitor or the keyboard. Yet, there is more to it than that. The way to think about a microcomputer is as part of an information system. An **information system** has five parts: *people, procedures, software, hardware,* and *data.* (See Figure 1-1.)

- **People:** It is easy to overlook people as one of the five parts of an information system. Yet this is what microcomputers are all about—making **people, end users** like you, more productive.
- **Procedures:** The rules or guidelines for people to follow when using software, hardware, and data are **procedures.** These procedures are typically documented in manuals written by computer specialists. Software and hardware manufacturers provide manuals with their products. These manuals are provided either in printed or electronic form.
- **Software:** A **program** consists of the step-by-step instructions that tell the computer how to do its work. **Software** is another name for a program or programs. The purpose of software is to convert **data** (unprocessed facts) into **information** (processed facts). For example, a payroll program would instruct the computer to take the number of hours you worked in a week (data) and multiply it by your pay rate (data) to determine how much you are paid for the week (information).

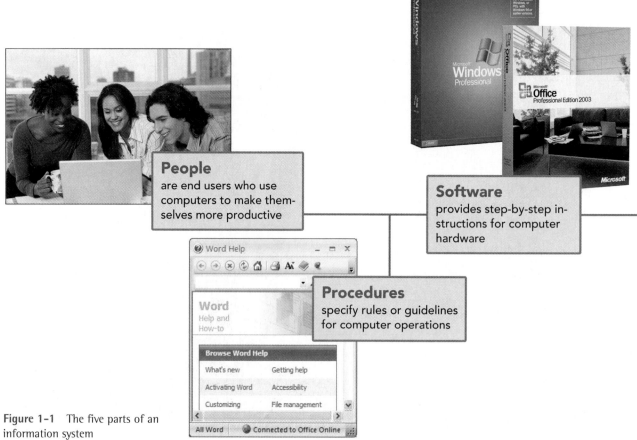

People
are end users who use computers to make themselves more productive

Software
provides step-by-step instructions for computer hardware

Procedures
specify rules or guidelines for computer operations

Figure 1-1 The five parts of an information system

- **Hardware:** The equipment that processes the data to create information is called **hardware.** It includes the keyboard, mouse, monitor, system unit, and other devices. Hardware is controlled by software.
- **Data:** The raw, unprocessed facts, including text, numbers, images, and sounds, are called data. Processed data yields information. Using the previous example of a payroll program, the data (number of hours worked and pay rate) is processed (multiplied) to yield information (weekly pay).

Almost all of today's computer systems add an additional part to the information system. This part, called **connectivity,** allows computers to connect and to share information. These connections, including Internet connections, can be by telephone lines, by cable, or through the air. Connectivity allows users to greatly expand the capability and usefulness of their information systems.

In large computer systems, there are specialists who write procedures, develop software, and capture data. In microcomputer systems, however, end users often perform these operations. To be a competent end user, you must understand the essentials of **information technology (IT),** including software, hardware, and data.

▼ CONCEPT CHECK

▶ What are the five parts of an information system?

▶ What is the difference between data and information?

▶ What is connectivity?

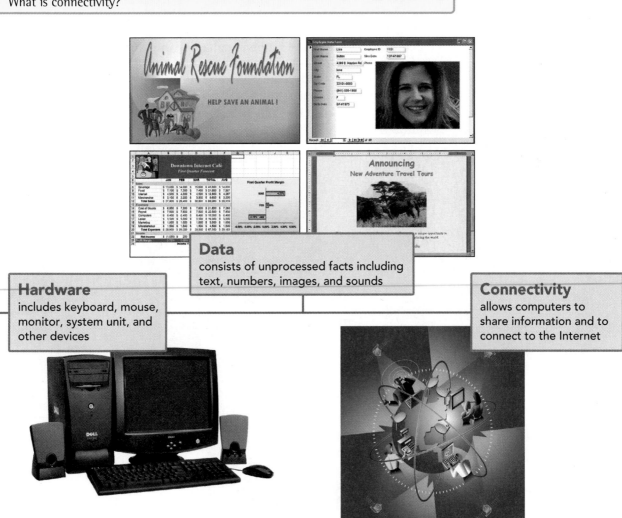

Data
consists of unprocessed facts including text, numbers, images, and sounds

Hardware
includes keyboard, mouse, monitor, system unit, and other devices

Connectivity
allows computers to share information and to connect to the Internet

Although easy to overlook, people are surely the most important part of any information system. Our lives are touched every day by computers and information systems. Many times the contact is direct and obvious, such as when we create documents using a word processing program or when we connect to the Internet. Other times, the contact is not as obvious. Consider just the four examples in Figure 1-2.

Throughout this book you will find a variety of features designed to help you become computer competent and knowledgeable. These features include Making IT Work for You, Tips, Careers in IT, and the Computing Essentials Web site.

- **Making IT Work for You.** In the chapters that follow, you will find Making IT Work for You features that present interesting and practical IT applications. Using a step-by-step procedure, you are provided with specific instructions on how to use each application. Figure 1-3 presents a list of these applications.

- **Tips.** We all can benefit from a few tips or suggestions. Throughout this book you will find numerous Tips ranging from the basics of keeping your computer system running smoothly to how to protect your privacy while surfing the Web. For a partial list of the Tips presented in the following chapters, see Figure 1-4.

- **Careers in IT.** One of the most important decisions of your life is to decide upon your life's work or career. Perhaps you are planning to be a writer, an artist, or an engineer. Or you might become a professional in information technology. Each of the following chapters highlights a specific career in information technology. This feature provides job descriptions, projected employment demands, educational requirements, current salary ranges, and advancement opportunities.

- **Computing Essentials Web site.** Throughout the text you will find numerous text references to the Computing Essentials Web site at

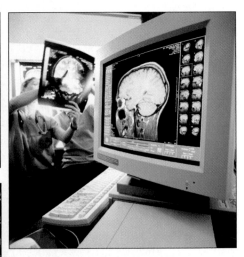

Figure 1-2 Computers in entertainment, business, education, and medicine

Topic	Description
Blocking Spam	Are you tired of unwanted e-mail in your Inbox? Do you frequently spend valuable time sorting through junk e-mail? Installing spam blocking software can help. Some e-mail programs include spam blocking software. See page 36.
Speech Recognition	Tired of using your keyboard to type term papers? Have you ever thought about using your voice to control application software? Perhaps speech recognition is just what you are looking for. See page 64.
Digital Video Editing	Do you want to make your own movie? Would you like to edit some home movies and distribute them to family and friends on DVDs? It's easy with the right equipment and software. See page 98.
Virus Protection and Internet Security	Worried about computer viruses? Did you know that others could be intercepting your private e-mail? It is even possible for them to gain access and control of your computer system. Fortunately, Internet security suites are available to help ensure your safety while you are on the Internet. See page 134.
TV Tuner Cards and Video Clips	Want to watch your favorite television program while you work? Perhaps you would like to include a video clip from a television program or from a DVD in a class presentation. It's easy using a TV tuner card. See page 162.
Web Cams and Instant Messaging	Do you enjoy chatting with your friends? Are you working on a project and need to collaborate with others in your group? What if you could see and hear your group online? Perhaps instant messaging is just what you're looking for. See page 190.
Music from the Internet	Did you know that you can use the Internet to locate music, download it to your computer, create your own custom CD, and upload to a portable music player? All it takes is the right software, hardware, and a connection to the Internet. See page 224.
Home Networking	Computer networks are not just for corporations and schools anymore. If you have more than one computer, you can use a wireless home network to share files and printers, to allow multiple users access to the Internet at the same time, and to play interactive computer games. See page 256.
Spyware Removal	Are you concerned about maintaining your privacy while you are surfing the Web? Did you know that programs known as spyware could be monitoring your every move? Fortunately, these programs are relatively easy to detect and remove. See page 284.
Job Opportunities	Did you know that you can use the Internet to find a job? You can browse through job openings, post your resume, and even use special programs that will search for the job that's just right for you. See page 440.

Figure 1-3   Making IT Work for You applications

www.computing2008.com. These references are easily recognized by this graphic. They carefully integrate the textbook with information presented on the Web. At the site, you'll find videos, animations, career information, tips, crosswords, test review materials, and much more.

SOFTWARE

Software, as we mentioned, is another name for programs. Programs are the instructions that tell the computer how to process data into the form you want. In most cases, the words *software* and *programs* are interchangeable. There are two major kinds of software: *system software* and *application software.* You can think of application software as the kind you use. Think of system software as the kind the computer uses.

1 Controlling spam. Do you get a lot of unwanted e-mail advertisements? Americans receive over 200 billion spam e-mails every year. There are some basic steps that you can take to keep your inbox spam-free. See page 35.

2 Online shopping. Have you ever bought anything online? If not, it's likely that in the future you will join the millions who have. Consider a few guidelines to make your shopping easier and safer. See page 43.

3 Creating and updating Web sites. Are you thinking about creating your own Web site? Perhaps you already have one and would like to spruce it up a bit. Here are a few suggestions that might help. See page 105.

4 Improving slow computer operations. Does your computer seem to be getting slower and slower? Consider a few suggestions that might add a little zip to your current system. See page 159.

5 Improving hard disk performance. Does your internal hard-disk drive run a lot and seem slow? Are you having problems with lost or corrupted files? To clean up the disk and speed up access, consider defragging. See page 217.

6 Protecting your privacy. Are you concerned about your privacy while on the Web? Consider some suggestions for protecting your identity online. See page 283.

To see additional tips, visit our Web site at www.computing2008.com and enter the keyword tips.

Figure 1-4   Selected tips

SYSTEM SOFTWARE

The user interacts primarily with application software. **System software** enables the application software to interact with the computer hardware. System software is "background" software that helps the computer manage its own internal resources.

System software is not a single program. Rather it is a collection of programs, including the following:

- **Operating systems** are programs that coordinate computer resources, provide an interface between users and the computer, and run applications. Windows XP, Windows Vista, and the Mac OS X are three of the best-known operating systems for today's microcomputer users. (See Figure 1-5.)
- **Utilities** perform specific tasks related to managing computer resources. For example, the Windows utility called Disk Defragmenter locates and eliminates unnecessary file fragments and rearranges files and unused disk space to optimize computer operations.
- **Device drivers** are specialized programs designed to allow particular input or output devices to communicate with the rest of the computer system.

Figure 1-5   Windows XP, Windows Vista, and Mac operating systems

APPLICATION SOFTWARE

Application software might be described as end user software. These programs can be categorized as either *basic* or *specialized applications*.

Basic applications, are widely used in nearly all career areas. They are the kinds of programs you have to know to be considered computer competent. One of these basic applications is a browser to navigate, explore, and find information on the Internet. (See Figure 1-6.) The two most widely used browsers are Microsoft's Internet Explorer and Netscape's Navigator. For a summary of the basic applications, see Figure 1-7.

Have you used the Internet? If so, then you probably already know how to use a browser. For those of you who do not, here are a few tips to get you started. **TIPS**

1 **Start browser.** Typically, all you need to do is double-click the browser's icon on the desktop.

2 **Enter URL.** In the browser's location box, type the URL (uniform resource locator, or address) of the Internet or Web location (site) that you want to visit.

3 **Press ENTER.** On your keyboard, press the ENTER key to connect to the site.

4 **Read and explore.** Once connected to the site, read the information displayed on your monitor. Using the mouse, move the pointer on the monitor. When the pointer changes from an arrow to a hand, click the mouse button to explore other locations.

5 **Close browser.** Once you are done exploring, click on your browser's CLOSE button.

To see additional tips, visit our Web site at www.computing2008.com and enter the keyword tips.

Figure 1-6   Internet Explorer browser

Type	Description
Browser	Connect to Web sites and display Web pages
Word processor	Prepare written documents
Spreadsheet	Analyze and summarize numerical data
Database management system	Organize and manage data and information
Presentation graphics	Communicate a message or persuade other people

Figure 1-7 Basic applications

Specialized applications include thousands of other programs that are more narrowly focused on specific disciplines and occupations. Some of the best known are graphics, audio, video, multimedia, Web authoring, and artificial intelligence programs.

HARDWARE

Computers are electronic devices that can follow instructions to accept input, process that input, and produce information. This book focuses principally on microcomputers. However, it is almost certain that you will come in contact, at least indirectly, with other types of computers.

TYPES OF COMPUTERS

There are four types of computers: supercomputers, mainframe computers, minicomputers, and microcomputers.

- **Supercomputers** are the most powerful type of computer. These machines are special high-capacity computers used by very large organizations. IBM's Blue Gene is considered by many to be the fastest computer in the world. (See Figure 1-8.)
- **Mainframe computers** occupy specially wired, air-conditioned rooms. Although not nearly as powerful as supercomputers, mainframe computers are capable of great processing speeds and data storage. For example, insurance companies use mainframes to process information about millions of policyholders.

- **Minicomputers,** also known as **midrange computers,** are refrigerator-sized machines. Medium-sized companies or departments of large companies typically use them for specific purposes. For example, production departments use minicomputers to monitor certain manufacturing processes and assembly-line operations.
- **Microcomputers** are the least powerful, yet the most widely used and fastest-growing, type of computer. There are four types of microcomputers: *desktop, notebook,*

Figure 1-8   IBM's Blue Gene supercomputer

tablet PC, and *handheld computers.* (See Figure 1-9.) **Desktop computers** are small enough to fit on top of or alongside a desk yet are too big to carry around. **Notebook computers,** also known as *laptop computers,* are portable, lightweight, and fit into most briefcases. A **tablet PC** is a type of notebook computer that accepts your handwriting. This input is digitized and converted to standard text that can be further processed by programs such as a word processor. **Handheld computers** are the smallest and are designed to fit into the palm of one hand. Also known as **palm computers,** these systems typically combine pen input, writing recognition, personal organizational tools, and communications capabilities in a very small package. **Personal digital assistants (PDAs)** are the most widely used handheld computer.

Desktop

Notebook

Tablet PC

Handheld

Figure 1-9   Microcomputers

MICROCOMPUTER HARDWARE

Hardware for a microcomputer system consists of a variety of different devices. See Figure 1-10 for a typical desktop system. This physical equipment falls into four basic categories: system unit, input/output, secondary storage, and communication. Because we discuss hardware in detail later in this book, here we will present just a quick overview of the four basic categories.

- **System unit:** The **system unit** is a container that houses most of the electronic components that make up a computer system. Two important components of the system unit are the *microprocessor* and *memory.* (See Figure 1-11.) The **microprocessor** controls and manipulates data to produce information. Many times the microprocessor is contained within a protective cartridge. **Memory,** also known as **primary storage** or **random access memory (RAM),** holds data and program instructions for processing the data. It also holds the processed information before it is output. Memory is sometimes referred to as *temporary storage* because its contents will typically be lost if the electrical power to the computer is disrupted.

- **Input/output: Input devices** translate data and programs that humans can understand into a form that the computer can process. The most common input devices are the **keyboard** and the **mouse. Output devices** translate

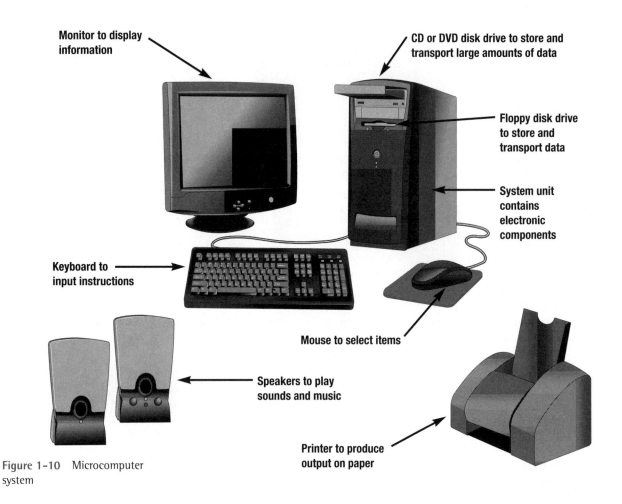

Monitor to display
information

CD or DVD disk drive to store and
transport large amounts of data

Floppy disk drive
to store and
transport data

System unit
contains
electronic
components

Keyboard to
input instructions

Mouse to select items

Speakers to play
sounds and music

Printer to produce
output on paper

Figure 1-10   Microcomputer
system

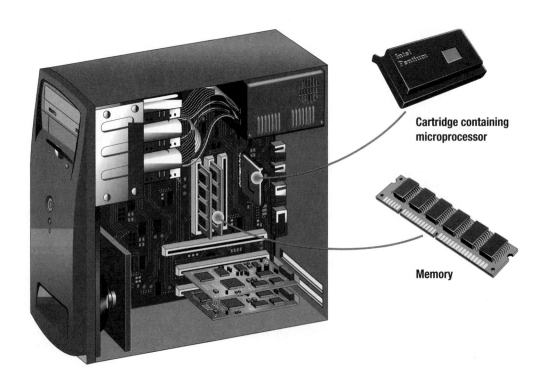

Cartridge containing
microprocessor

Memory

Figure 1-11   System unit

the processed information from the computer into a form that humans can understand. The most common output devices are **monitors** (see Figure 1-12) and **printers.**

- **Secondary storage:** Unlike memory, **secondary storage** holds data and programs even after electrical power to the computer system has been turned off. The most important kinds of secondary media are *floppy, hard,* and *optical disks.* **Floppy disks** are often used to store and transport data from one computer to another. They are called floppy because data is stored on a very thin flexible, or floppy, plastic disk. **Hard disks** are typically used to store programs and very large data files. Using a rigid metallic platter, hard disks have a much greater capacity and are able to access information much faster than floppy disks. **Optical discs** use laser technology and have the greatest capacity. (See Figure 1-13.) Three types of optical discs are **compact discs (CDs), digital versatile** (or **video**) **discs (DVDs),** and **high-definition (hi def)** discs.

- **Communication:** At one time, it was uncommon for a microcomputer system to communicate with other computer systems. Now, using **communication devices,** a microcomputer can communicate with other computer systems located as near as the next office or as far away as halfway around the world using the Internet. The most widely used communication device is a **modem,** which modifies telephone communications into a form that can be processed by a computer. Modems also modify computer output into a form that can be transmitted across standard telephone lines.

Figure 1-12 Monitor

Figure 1-13 Optical disc

Information Technology, the Internet, and You

DATA

Data is raw, unprocessed facts, including text, numbers, images, and sounds. As we have mentioned earlier, processed data becomes information. When stored electronically in files, data can be used directly as input for the system unit.

Four common types of files (see Figure 1-14) are

- **Document files,** created by word processors to save documents such as memos, term papers, and letters.
- **Worksheet files,** created by electronic spreadsheets to analyze things like budgets and to predict sales.
- **Database files,** typically created by database management programs to contain highly structured and organized data. For example, an employee database file might contain all the workers' names, social security numbers, job titles, and other related pieces of information.

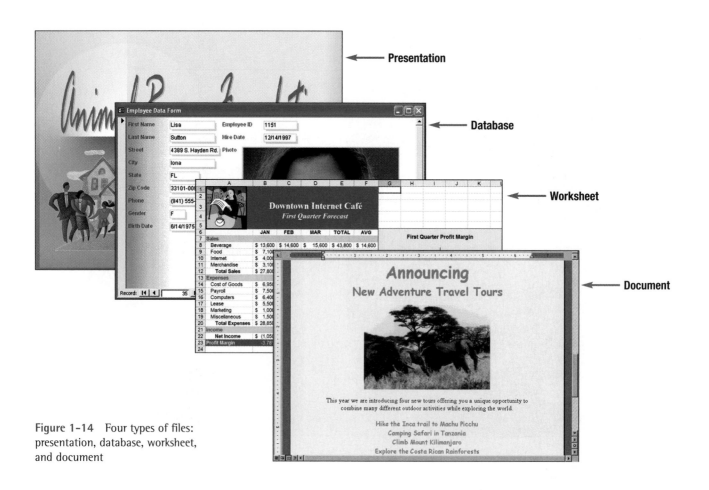

Figure 1-14 Four types of files: presentation, database, worksheet, and document

- **Presentation files,** created by presentation graphics programs to save presentation materials. For example, a file might contain audience hand-outs, speaker notes, and electronic slides.

CONNECTIVITY, THE WIRELESS REVOLUTION, AND THE INTERNET

Connectivity is the capability of your microcomputer to share information with other computers. The single most dramatic change in connectivity in the past five years has been the widespread use of mobile or wireless communication devices. For just a few of these devices, see Figure 1-15. Many experts predict that these wireless applications are just the beginning of the **wireless revolution,** a revolution that is expected to dramatically affect the way we communicate and use computer technology.

Figure 1-15   Wireless communication devices

Central to the concept of connectivity is the **network.** A network is a communications system connecting two or more computers. The largest network in the world is the **Internet.** It is like a giant highway that connects you to millions of other people and organizations located throughout the world. The **Web** provides a multimedia interface to the numerous resources available on the Internet.

▼ CONCEPT CHECK

▶ Define data. List four common types of files.

▶ Define connectivity and the wireless revolution.

▶ What is a network? Describe the Internet. What is the Web?

CAREERS IN IT

As mentioned previously, each of the following chapters highlights a specific career in information technology. (See Figure 1-16.) Each provides specific job descriptions, salary ranges, advancement opportunities, and more. For a partial list of these careers, see Figure 1-17. For a complete list, visit our Web site at www.computing2008.com and enter the keyword careers.

Figure 1-16   Software engineer

Career	Description
Webmaster	Develops and maintains Web sites and Web resources. See page 48.
Computer support specialist	Provides technical support to customers and other users. See page 137.
Technical writer	Prepares instruction manuals, technical reports, and other scientific or technical documents. See page 200.
Software engineer	Analyzes users' needs and creates application software. See page 228.
Network administrator	Creates and maintains computer networks. See page 264.
Database administrator	Uses database management software to determine the most efficient ways to organize and access data. See page 353.
Systems analyst	Plans, designs, and maintains information systems. See page 385.
Programmer	Creates, tests, and troubleshoots computer programs. See page 418.

Figure 1-17   Careers in information technology

A Look to the Future

Using and Understanding Information Technology Means Being Computer Competent

The purpose of this book is to help you use and understand information technology. We want to help you become computer competent in today's world and to provide you with a foundation of knowledge so that you can understand how technology is being used today and anticipate how technology will be used in the future. This will enable you to benefit from six important information technology developments.

THE INTERNET AND THE WEB

The Internet and the Web are considered by most to be the two most important technologies for the 21st century. Understanding how to efficiently and effectively use the Internet to browse the Web, communicate with others, and locate information are indispensable computer competencies. These issues are presented in Chapter 2, The Internet, the Web, and Electronic Commerce.

POWERFUL SOFTWARE

The software now available can do an extraordinary number of tasks and help you in an endless number of ways. You can create professional-looking documents, analyze massive amounts of data, create dynamic multimedia Web pages, and much more. Today's employers are expecting the people they hire to be able to effectively and efficiently use a variety of different types of software. Basic and specialized applications are presented in Chapters 3 and 4. System software is presented in Chapter 5.

POWERFUL HARDWARE

Microcomputers are now much more powerful than they used to be. New communication technologies such as wireless networks are dramatically changing the ways to connect to other computers, networks, and the Internet. However, despite the rapid change of specific equipment, their essential features remain unchanged. Thus, the competent end user should focus on these features. Chapters 6 through 9 explain what you need to know about hardware. A Buyer's Guide and an Upgrader's Guide are presented at the end of this book for those considering the purchase or upgrade of a microcomputer system.

SECURITY AND PRIVACY

What about people? Experts agree that we as a society must be careful about the potential of technology to negatively impact our personal privacy and security. Additionally, we need to be aware of potential physical and mental health risks associated with using technology. Finally, we need to be aware of negative effects on our environment caused by the manufacture of computer-related products. Thus, Chapter 10 explores each of these critical issues in detail.

ORGANIZATIONS

Almost all organizations rely on the quality and flexibility of their information systems to stay competitive. As a member or employee of an organization, you will undoubtedly be involved in these information systems. Therefore, you need to be knowledgeable about the different types of organizational information systems and how they are used. Accordingly, we devote Chapters 11 through 14 to detail what you need to know about information systems and how to develop, modify, and maintain these systems.

CHANGING TIMES

Are the times changing any faster now than they ever have? Most people think so. Whatever the answer, it is clear we live in a fast-paced age. The Evolution of the Computer Age section presented at the end of this book tracks the major developments since computers were first introduced.

After reading this book, you will be in a very favorable position compared with many other people in industry today. You not only will learn the basics of hardware, software, connectivity, the Internet, and the Web, but you also will learn the most current technology. You will be able to use these tools to your advantage.

INFORMATION TECHNOLOGY, THE INTERNET, AND YOU

INFORMATION SYSTEMS

The way to think about a microcomputer is to realize that it is one part of an **information system.** There are five parts of an information system:

1. **People** are an essential part of the system. The purpose of information systems is to make people, or **end users** like you, more productive.
2. **Procedures** are rules or guidelines to follow when using software, hardware, and data. They are typically documented in manuals written by computer professionals.
3. **Software (programs)** provides step-by-step instructions to control the computer to convert data into information.
4. **Hardware** consists of the physical equipment. It is controlled by software and processes data to create information.
5. **Data** consists of unprocessed facts including text, numbers, images, and sound. **Information** is data that has been processed by the computer.

Connectivity is an additional part to today's information systems. It allows computers to connect and share information. To be **computer competent,** end users need to understand **information technology (IT).**

PEOPLE

People are the most important part of an information system. People are touched hundreds of times daily by computers. This book contains several features to demonstrate how people just like you use computers. These features include the following:

- **Making IT Work for You** presents several interesting and practical applications. Topics include creating personal Web sites, using digital photography, and searching for job opportunities.
- **Tips** offer a variety of suggestions on such practical matters as how to improve slow computer performance and how to protect your privacy while on the Web.
- **Careers in IT** presents job descriptions, employment demands, educational requirements, salary ranges, and advancement opportunities.
- **Computing Essentials Web site** integrates the textbook with information on the Web including videos, animations, career information, tips, crosswords, test review materials, and much more.

www.computing2008.com

To prepare for your future as a competent end user, you need to understand the basic parts of an information system: people, procedures, software, hardware, and data. Also you need to understand connectivity through the Internet and the Web and to recognize the role of technology in your professional and personal life.

SOFTWARE

Software, or **programs,** consists of system and application software.

System Software
System software enables application software to interact with computer hardware. It consists of a variety of programs:

- **Operating systems** coordinate resources, provide an interface for users and computer hardware, and run applications. Windows XP, Windows Vista, and Mac OS X are operating systems.
- **Utilities** perform specific tasks to manage computer resources.
- **Device drivers** are specialized programs to allow input and output devices to communicate with the rest of the computer system.

Application Software
Application software includes basic and specialized applications.

- **Basic applications** are widely used in nearly all career areas. Programs include browsers, word processors, spreadsheets, database management systems, and presentation graphics.
- **Specialized applications** focus on specific disciplines and occupations. These programs include graphics, audio, video, multimedia, Web authoring, and artificial intelligence programs.

HARDWARE

Hardware is the physical equipment in an information system.

Types of Computers
Supercomputer, mainframe, minicomputer (midrange), and **microcomputer** are four types of computers. Microcomputers can be **desktop, notebook, tablet PC,** or **handheld (palm). PDAs** are the most widely used handheld computer.

Microcomputer Hardware
There are four basic categories of hardware devices.

- **System unit** contains the electronic circuitry, including the **microprocessor** and **memory (primary storage, random access memory [RAM],** temporary storage**).**
- **Input/output devices** are translators between humans and computers. **Input devices** include the **keyboard** and **mouse. Output devices** include **monitors** and **printers.**
- **Secondary storage** holds data and programs. Typical media include **floppy disks, hard disks,** and **optical discs** (**CD, DVD,** and **hi def**).
- **Communication devices** connect the system unit to other computers and the Internet. A **modem** modifies signals for processing and communication.

DATA

Data is the raw facts unprocessed about something. Common file types include

- **Document files** created by word processors.

- **Worksheet files** created by spreadsheet programs.

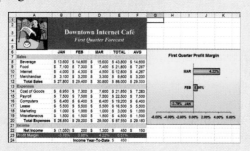

- **Database files** created by database management programs.

- **Presentation files** created by presentation graphics programs.

CONNECTIVITY AND THE INTERNET

Connectivity

Connectivity is a concept describing the ability of end users to tap into resources well beyond their desktops. **Networks** are connected computers that share data and resources.

The Wireless Revolution

The **wireless revolution** is the widespread and increasing use of mobile (wireless) communication devices.

Internet

The **Internet** is the world's largest computer network. The **Web** provides a multimedia interface to resources available on the Internet.

CAREERS IN IT

Career	Description
Webmaster	Develops and maintains Web sites and Web resources. See page 48.
Computer support specialist	Provides technical support to customers and other users. See page 137.
Technical writer	Prepares instruction manuals, technical reports, and other scientific or technical documents. See page 200.
Software engineer	Analyzes users' needs and creates application software. See page 228.
Network administrator	Creates and maintains computer networks. See page 264.
Database administrator	Uses database management software to determine the most efficient ways to organize and access data. See page 353.
Systems analyst	Plans, designs, and maintains information systems. See page 385.
Programmer	Creates, tests, and troubleshoots computer programs. See page 418.

KEY TERMS

www.computing2008.com

application software   (9)
basic application   (9)
communication device   (13)
compact disc (CD)   (13)
computer competency   (3)
connectivity   (5, 15)
data   (4)
database file   (14)
desktop computer   (11)
device driver   (8)
digital versatile disc (DVD)   (13)
digital video disc (DVD)   (13)
document file   (14)
end user   (4)
floppy disk   (13)
handheld computer   (11)
hard disk   (13)
hardware   (5)
high definition (hi def)   (13)
information   (4)
information system   (4)
information technology (IT)   (5)
input device   (11)
Internet   (16)
keyboard   (11)
mainframe computer   (10)
memory   (11)
microcomputer   (10)
microprocessor   (11)
midrange computer   (10)

minicomputer   (10)
modem   (13)
monitor   (13)
mouse   (11)
network   (16)
notebook computer   (11)
operating system   (8)
optical disc   (13)
output device   (11)
palm computer   (11)
people   (4)
personal digital assistant (PDA)   (11)
presentation file   (15)
primary storage   (11)
printer   (13)
procedures   (4)
program   (4)
random access memory (RAM)   (11)
secondary storage   (13)
software   (4)
specialized application   (10)
supercomputer   (10)
system software   (8)
system unit   (11)
tablet PC   (11)
utility   (8)
Web   (16)
wireless revolution   (15)
worksheet file   (14)

FEATURES

Animations

Careers in IT

DVD Direct

Expansions

Making IT Work for You

On the Web Explorations

TechTV

Tips

CHAPTER REVIEW

Applying Technology

Crossword Puzzle

Expanding Your Knowledge

Key Terms

Matching

Multiple Choice

Open-Ended

Writing About Technology

To test your knowledge of these key terms with animated flash cards, visit our Web site at www.computing2008.com and enter the keyword terms1.

CROSSWORD PUZZLE

www.computing2008.com

Across

1 The most essential part of an information system.
7 Coordinates computer resources.
10 Modifies signals for processing.
12 Data that has been processed by the computer.
13 Unprocessed facts.
14 Notebook computer that accepts handwritten input.

Down

2 Uses computers to become more productive.
3 Rules or guidelines to follow when using software, hardware, and data.
4 Created by word processors.
5 Specialized program that allows input and output devices to communicate.
6 Created by database management programs.
8 The physical equipment of a microcomputer.
9 The world's largest computer network.
11 Provides step-by-step instructions to the computer.

For an interactive version of this crossword, visit our Web site at www.computing2008.com and enter the keyword **crossword1**.

MULTIPLE CHOICE

Circle the letter or fill in the correct answer.

1. A common term that describes the combination of traditional computer and communication technologies is
   a. management of information systems
   b. information technology
   c. information superhighway
   d. computer competency

2. Procedures are typically documented in manuals written by
   a. end users
   b. computer specialists
   c. Microsoft
   d. service providers

3. Which of the following is an example of connectivity?
   a. Internet
   b. floppy disk
   c. power cord
   d. data

4. Windows XP, Windows Vista, and Macintosh OS X are all examples of
   a. application software
   b. operating systems
   c. browsers
   d. shareware

5. Because of their size and cost, these computers are relatively rare.
   a. minicomputers
   b. mainframe computers
   c. microcomputers
   d. supercomputers

6. The system component that controls and manipulates data in order to produce information is called the
   a. monitor
   b. mouse
   c. keyboard
   d. microprocessor

7. A system component that translates data and programs that humans can understand into a form that the computer can process is called a(n)
   a. input device
   b. pointer
   c. output device
   d. display

8. A CD is an example of a(n)
   a. output device
   b. floppy disk
   c. optical disc
   d. hard disk

9. If you want to communicate a message or persuade other people, you would typically use this type of software.
   a. worksheet
   b. document
   c. database
   d. presentation

10. Many experts are predicting that this revolution is expected to dramatically affect the way we communicate and use computer technology.
    a. FTP
    b. World Wide Web
    c. Telnet
    d. wireless

For an interactive version of multiple-choice questions, visit our Web site at www.computing2008.com and enter the keyword multiple1.

MATCHING

www.computing2008.com

Match each numbered item with the most closely related lettered item. Write your answers in the spaces provided.

a. microcomputers
b. optical discs
c. input device
d. primary storage
e. procedures
f. program
g. secondary storage
h. supercomputers
i. system software
j. the Internet

1. Guidelines people follow when using software. _____
2. Consists of the step-by-step instructions that tell the computer how to do its work. _____
3. Software that enables the application software to interact with the computer hardware. _____
4. The most powerful type of computer. _____
5. The least powerful and most widely used type of computer. _____
6. Translates data and programs that humans can understand into a form that the computer can process. _____
7. Holds data and programs even after electrical power to the system has been turned off. _____
8. Uses laser technology. _____
9. Holds data and program instructions for processing data. _____
10. The largest network in the world. _____

For an interactive version of this matching exercise, visit our Web site at www.computing2008.com and enter the keyword **matching1**.

OPEN-ENDED

On a separate sheet of paper, respond to each question or statement.

1. Explain the five parts of an information system. What part do people play in this system?
2. What is system software? What kinds of programs are included in system software?
3. Define and compare basic and specialized application software. Describe some different types of basic applications. Describe some types of specialized applications.
4. Describe the different types of computers. What is the most common type? What are the types of microcomputers?
5. What is connectivity? How are the wireless revolution and connectivity related? What is a computer network? What is the Internet? What is the Web?

APPLYING TECHNOLOGY

Applying Technology questions are designed to demonstrate ways that you can effectively use technology today.

Making a habit of keeping current with technology trends is a key to your success with information technology. In each of this book's chapters, the Applying Technology feature will present questions designed to help you gain a better understanding of how technology is being used today.

The first question typically relates to one of the Making IT Work for You topics. Some of these topics are listed below. Select the two that you find the most interesting and then describe why they are of interest to you and how you might use (or are using) those applications.

TV Tuner Cards and Video Clips

Want to watch your favorite television program while you work? Perhaps you would like to include a video clip from a television program or from a VHS tape in a class presentation. It's easy using a TV tuner card. See page 162.

Digital Video Editing

Want to make your own movie? Would you like to edit and distribute home movies to friends and family? It's easy with the right equipment and software. See page 98.

Home Networking

Computer networks are not just for corporations and schools anymore. If you have more than one computer, you can use a wireless home network to share files and printers, to allow multiple users access to the Internet at the same time, and to play interactive computer games. See page 273.

Job Opportunities

Did you know that you can use the Internet to find a job? You can browse through job openings, post your resume, and even use special programs that will search for the job that's just right for you. See page 453.

EXPANDING YOUR KNOWLEDGE

Expanding Your Knowledge questions are designed to add depth and detail to your understanding of specific topics presented within this chapter. The questions direct you to sources other than the textbook to obtain this knowledge.

A deeper knowledge of select topics can greatly enhance your understanding of information technology. In each of the following chapters, the Expanding Your Knowledge feature presents questions designed to help you gain a deeper understanding of select topics.

The first question typically relates to a topic presented at our Web site at www.computing2008.com. Some of those topics are listed below. Select the two that you find the most interesting and then describe why they are of interest to you and why they are important.

How Computer Virus Protection Programs Work

Computer viruses are destructive and dangerous programs that can migrate through networks and operating systems. They often attach themselves to other programs, e-mail messages, and databases. It is essential to protect your computer systems from computer viruses. See page 146.

How Digital Cameras Work

While traditional cameras capture images on film, digital cameras capture images and convert them into a digital form. These images can be viewed immediately and saved to a disk or into the camera's memory. See page 210.

How Internet Telephones Work

Internet telephones offer a low-cost alternative to making long-distance calls. Using the Internet telephone (or other appropriate audio input and output devices), the Internet, a special service provider, a sound card, and special software, you can place long-distance calls to almost anywhere in the world. See page 210.

How Wireless Home Networks Work

Wireless home networks are becoming very popular. They are easy to set up and use. They allow different computers to share resources including a common Internet connection and printer. See page 274.

WRITING ABOUT TECHNOLOGY

The ability to think critically and to write effectively is essential to nearly every profession. Writing About Technology questions are designed to help you develop these skills by posing thought-provoking questions about computer privacy, security, and/or ethics.

Regardless of your career path, critical thinking, analysis, and writing are essential skills. In each of the following chapters, the Writing About Technology feature presents questions about privacy, security, and ethics. These questions are designed to help you develop critical thinking, analysis, and writing skills. Some of the topics are listed below. Select two that you find the most interesting and then describe why they are of interest to you.

HTML Source Code

A common way to create interesting and dynamic Web pages is to examine how professionals create their sites. Once connected to most Web sites, you can display the HTML source code used to create that site. Additionally, you can make a copy of the code and save it on your computer system. Some argue that this is unethical and illegal. Others argue that this is an acceptable way to create personal and professional sites. See page 119.

Antitrust

Much attention has been focused on Microsoft's legal battles over antitrust issues. At the core of these battles is the Microsoft Windows operating system, which controls over 90 percent of today's microcomputers. Microsoft's opponents claim that recent versions of Windows have been tailored to work specifically with Microsoft's applications, thus giving them an unfair advantage. See page 147.

Electronic Monitoring

Surveillance of individuals occurs more frequently today than ever before. For example, the FBI has proposed the widespread use of a technology known as Carnivore to help them track terrorists. This technology supports widespread monitoring of individual Internet activity and e-mail. Privacy advocates claim that this would be an unnecessary and unneeded invasion of personal privacy. Others believe electronic surveillance is essential to protect national security. See page 275.

CHAPTER

2

COMPETENCIES

After you have read this chapter, you should be able to:

1 Discuss the origins of the Internet and the Web.

2 Describe how to access the Web using providers and browsers.

3 Discuss Internet communications, including e-mail, instant messaging, and social networking.

4 Describe search tools, including search engines, metasearch engines, and specialized search engines.

5 Evaluate the accuracy of information presented on the Web.

6 Discuss electronic commerce, including B2C, C2C, B2B, and security issues.

7 Describe these Web utilities: Web-based applications, FTP, plug-ins, and filters.

Browsers
connect to Web sites and display Web pages

Communication
includes e-mail, instant messaging, and social networking

THE INTERNET, THE WEB, AND ELECTRONIC COMMERCE

Introduction

Want to communicate with a friend across town, in another state, or even in another country? Perhaps you would like to send a drawing, a photo, or just a letter. Looking for a long-list friend? Looking for travel or entertainment information? Perhaps you're researching a term paper or exploring different career paths. Where do you start? For these and other information-related activities, most people use the Internet and the Web.

The Internet is often referred to as the Information Superhighway. In a sense, it is like a highway that connects you to millions of other people and organizations. Unlike typical highways that move people and things from one location to another, the Internet moves your ideas and information. The Web provides an easy-to-use, intuitive, multimedia interface to resources available on the Internet. It has become an everyday tool for all of us to use. For example, you can create personal Web sites to share information with others and use instant messaging to chat with friends and collaborate on group projects.

Competent end users need to be aware of the resources available on the Internet and the Web. Additionally, they need to know how to access these resources, to effectively communicate electronically, to efficiently locate information, to understand electronic commerce, and to use Web utilities.

Search assists in locating Web resources

E-Commerce involves the buying and selling of goods over the Internet

Web Utilities are programs that make using the Web easier

THE INTERNET AND THE WEB

The **Internet** was launched in 1969 when the United States funded a project that developed a national computer network called **Advanced Research Project Agency Network (ARPANET).** The Internet is a large network that connects together smaller networks all over the globe. The **Web** was introduced in 1992 at the **Center for European Nuclear Research (CERN)** in Switzerland. Prior to the Web, the Internet was all text—no graphics, animations, sound, or video. The Web made it possible to include these elements. It provided a multimedia interface to resources available on the Internet. From these early research beginnings, the Internet and the Web have evolved into one of the most powerful tools of the 21st century.

It is easy to get the Internet and the Web confused, but they are not the same thing. The Internet is the actual physical network. It is made up of wires, cables, and satellites. Being connected to this network is often described as being **online.** The Internet connects millions of computers and resources throughout the world. The Web is a multimedia interface to the resources available on the Internet. Every day over a billion users from nearly every country in the world use the Internet and the Web. What are they doing? The most common uses are the following:

- **Communicating** is by far the most popular Internet activity. You can exchange e-mail with your family and friends almost anywhere in the world. You can join and listen to discussions and debates on a wide variety of special-interest topics.

- **Shopping** is one of the fastest-growing Internet applications. You can window shop, look for the latest fashions, search for bargains, and make purchases.

- **Searching** for information has never been more convenient. You can access some of the world's largest libraries directly from your home computer. You can find the latest local, national, and international news.

- **Entertainment** options are nearly endless. You can find music, movies, magazines, and computer games. You will find live concerts, movie previews, book clubs, and interactive live games. (See Figure 2-1.)

Figure 2–1   Entertainment site

- **Education** or **e-learning** is another rapidly emerging Web application. You can take classes on almost any subject. There are courses just for fun and there are courses for high school, college, and graduate school credit. Some cost nothing to take and others cost a lot.

The first step to using the Internet and Web is to get connected, or to gain access to the Internet.

▼ CONCEPT CHECK

▶ Describe how the Internet and the Web started.

▶ What is the difference between the Internet and the Web?

▶ List and describe five of the most common uses of the Internet and the Web.

ACCESS

The Internet and the telephone system are similar—you can connect a computer to the Internet much like you connect a phone to the telephone system. Once you are on the Internet, your computer becomes an extension of what seems like a giant computer—a computer that branches all over the world. When provided with a connection to the Internet, you can use a browser program to search the Web.

PROVIDERS

The most common way to access the Internet is through an **Internet service provider (ISP).** The providers are already connected to the Internet and provide a path or connection for individuals to access the Internet. Your college or university most likely provides you with free access to the Internet either through its local area networks or through a dial-up or telephone connection. There are also some companies that offer free Internet access.

The most widely used commercial Internet service providers are national and wireless providers.

- **National service providers** like America Online (AOL) are the most widely used. They provide access through standard telephone or cable connections. Users can access the Internet from almost anywhere within the country for a standard fee without incurring long-distance telephone charges. (See Figure 2-2.)

- **Wireless service providers** do not use telephone or cable lines. They provide Internet connections for computers with wireless modems and a wide array of wireless devices.

As we will discuss in Chapter 9, users connect to ISPs using one of a variety of connection technologies including **dial-up, DSL, cable,** and **wireless modems.**

BROWSERS

Browsers are programs that provide access to Web resources. This software connects you to remote computers, opens and transfers files, displays text and images, and provides in one tool an uncomplicated interface to the Internet and Web documents. Browsers allow you to explore, or to **surf,** the Web by easily

Figure 2-2   America Online ISP

Figure 2-3   Internet Explorer

moving from one Web site to another. Three well-known browsers are Mozilla Firefox, Netscape Communications, and Microsoft Internet Explorer. (See Figure 2-3.)

For browsers to connect to resources, the **location** or **address** of the resources must be specified. These addresses are called **uniform resource locators (URLs).** All URLs have at least two basic parts. (See Figure 2-4.) The first part presents the protocol used to connect to the resource. As we will discuss in Chapter 9, **protocols** are rules for exchanging data between computers. The protocol *http://* is the most widely used Web protocol. The second part presents the **domain name.** It is the name of the server where the resource is located. In Figure 2-4 the server is identified as www.mtv. com. (Many URLs have additional parts specifying directory paths, file names, and pointers.) The last part of the domain name following the dot (.) is the **top-level domain (TLD).** It identifies the type of organization. For example, *.com* indicates a commercial site. The URL *http://www.mtv.com* connects your computer to a computer that provides information about MTV.

Once the browser has connected to the Web site, a document file is sent back to your computer. This document typically contains **Hypertext Markup Language (HTML)** commands. The browser interprets the HTML commands and displays the document as a **Web page.** For example, when your browser first connects to the Internet, it opens up to a Web page specified in the browser settings. This page presents information about the site along with references and **hyperlinks** or **links** that

Figure 2-4   Two basic parts of a URL

connect to other documents containing related information—text files, graphic images, audio, and video clips. (See Figure 2-5.)

These documents may be located on a nearby computer system or on one halfway around the world. The links typically appear on the Web page as underlined and colored text and/or images. To access the referenced material, all you do is click on the highlighted text or image. A connection is automatically made to the computer containing the material, and the referenced material appears on your display screen.

Web pages also can contain special programs called **applets** that are typically written in a programming language such as **Java.** (Java and other programming languages will be presented in Chapter 14.) These programs can be downloaded quickly and run by most browsers. Java applets are widely used to add interest and activity to a Web site by presenting animation, displaying graphics, providing interactive games, and much more.

To learn more about browsers, visit our Web site at www.computing2008.com and enter the keyword browsers.

Figure 2–5 MTV Web site

▼ CONCEPT CHECK

▶ What is the function of an ISP? Describe two types of ISPs.

▶ What is the function of a browser?

▶ What are URLs, HTML, Web pages, hyperlinks, applets, and Java?

COMMUNICATION

As previously mentioned, communication is the most popular Internet activity, and its impact cannot be overestimated. At a personal level, friends and family can stay in contact with one another even when separated by thousands of miles. At a business level, electronic communication has become a standard, and many times preferred, way to stay in touch with suppliers, employees, and customers. The three most popular types of Internet communication are e-mail, instant messaging, and discussion groups.

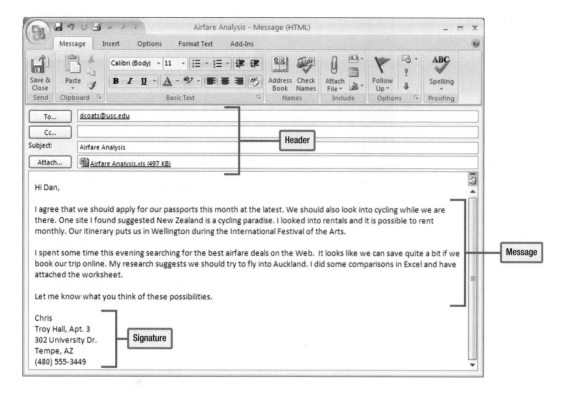

Figure 2-6 Basic elements of an e-mail message

E-MAIL

E-mail or **electronic mail** is the transmission of electronic messages over the Internet. At one time, e-mail consisted only of basic text messages. Now e-mail routinely includes graphics, photos, and many different types of file attachments. People all over the world send e-mail to each other. You can e-mail your family, your co-workers, and even your senator. All you need to send and receive e-mail is an e-mail account, access to the Internet, and an e-mail program. Two of the most widely used e-mail programs are Microsoft's Outlook Express and Mozilla Thunderbird.

A typical e-mail message has three basic elements: header, message, and signature. (See Figure 2-6.) The **header** appears first and typically includes the following information:

- **Addresses:** Addresses of the persons sending, receiving, and, optionally, anyone else who is to receive copies. E-mail addresses have two basic parts. (See Figure 2-7.) The first part is the user's name and the second part is the domain name, which includes the top-level domain. In our example e-mail, *dcoats* is Dan's user name. The server providing e-mail service for Dan is *usc.edu*. The top-level domain indicates that the provider is an educational institution.

Figure 2-7 Two parts of an e-mail address

- **Subject:** A one-line description, used to present the topic of the message. Subject lines typically are displayed when a person checks his or her mailbox.
- **Attachments:** Many e-mail programs allow you to attach files such as documents and worksheets. If a message has an attachment, the file name appears on the attachment line.

The letter or **message** comes next. It is typically short and to the point. Finally, the **signature line** provides additional information about the sender. Typically, this information includes the sender's name, address, and telephone number.

E-mail can be a valuable asset in your personal and professional life. However, like many other valuable technologies, there are drawbacks too. Americans receive billions of unwanted and unsolicited e-mails every year. This unwelcome mail is called **spam.** While spam is indeed a distraction and nuisance, it also can be dangerous. For example, **computer viruses** or destructive programs are often attached to unsolicited e-mail. Computer viruses and ways to protect against them will be discussed in Chapter 5.

In an attempt to control spam, anti-spam laws have been added to our legal system. For example, the recently enacted CAN-SPAM Act requires that every marketing-related e-mail provide an opt-out option. When the option is selected, the recipient's e-mail address is to be removed from future mailing lists. Failure to do so results in heavy fines. This approach, however, has had minimal impact since over 50 percent of all spam originates from servers outside the United States. A more effective approach has been the development and use of **spam blockers.** (See Figure 2-8.) These programs use a variety of different approaches to identify and eliminate spam. To learn about these approaches, visit our Web site at www.computing2008.com and enter the keyword spam. To learn how to block spam from your inbox, see Making IT Work for You: Blocking Spam on pages 36 and 37.

On the Web Explorations

Almost all ISPs and online service providers offer e-mail service to their customers. But you can get this service for free from several sources. To learn more about these free services, visit our site at www.computing2008.com and enter the keyword freemail.

INSTANT MESSAGING

Instant messaging (IM) is an extension of e-mail that allows two or more people to contact each other via direct, live communication. To use instant messaging, you specify a list of **friends** and register with an instant messaging server. Whenever you connect to the Internet, special software informs your messaging server that you are online. In response, the server will notify you if any of your contacts are online. At the same time, it notifies your friends that you are online. You can then send messages directly back and forth to one another. Most instant messaging programs also include video conferencing features, file sharing, and remote assistance. Many businesses routinely use these instant messaging features. To see how instant messaging works, visit our Web site at www.computing2008.com and enter the keyword im.

Spam Blocker	Site
InBoxer	www.inboxer.com
OnlyMyEmailPersonal	www.onlymymail.com
Qurb	www.qurb.com
Vanquish vqME	www.vanquish.com

Figure 2-8 Spam blockers

BLOCKING SPAM

Do you get a lot of junk e-mail? Are you tired of locating and deleting spam from your inbox? Installing special spam-blocking software can help. Some e-mail programs include spam-blocking software. For example, the Mozilla Thunderbird e-mail program, available free of charge from www.mozilla.org, comes with spam-blocking software built in.

Training the Software   After downloading and installing Mozilla Thunderbird, you need to train it to recognize unwanted messages. After following the steps below for several weeks, Mozilla Thunderbird will become more and more efficient at recognizing spam and automatically moving it to an appropriate folder.

1
- Select each spam message in your inbox and click the *Junk* button.

- Open the Junk folder and review any new messages. If a message is not spam, click the *Not Junk* button and return it to your inbox.

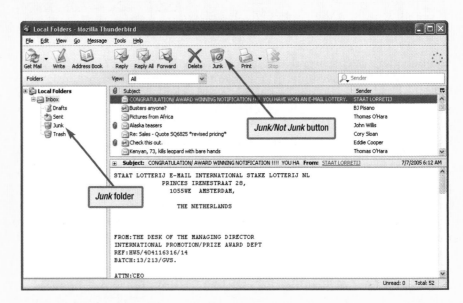

Creating a White List   A *white list* is a list of e-mail addresses that should never be blocked, such as addresses of friends and family. Mozilla Thunderbird can use your personal address book as a white list.

1
- Click *Tools* from the menu.

- Select *Junk Mail Controls . . .*

- Ensure the box labeled *Do not mark messages as junk mail if the sender is in my address book* is checked, then click OK.

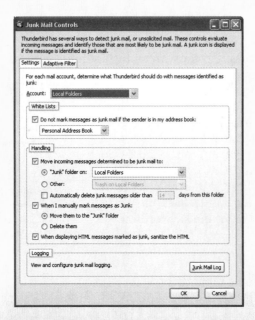

Blocking Images   Some e-mail messages contain special images that let spammers know that you have received them. Once spammers know your e-mail address is valid, you can be sure they will send more. Mozilla Thunderbird can help protect you by blocking images in new e-mail messages.

 ● Click *Tools* from the menu.

● Select *Options.*

● Select the Advanced category.

● Ensure that the box labeled *Block loading of remote images in mail messages* is checked and click *OK.*

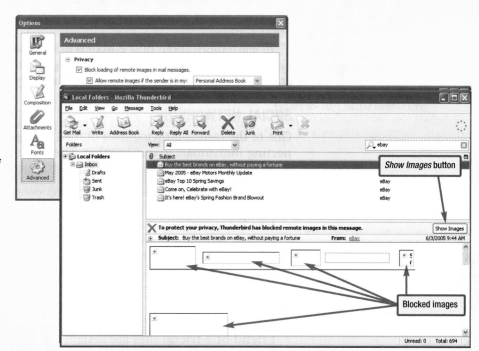

Images are now blocked from view in e-mail messages.

2 ● To view the images in an e-mail message from a sender you trust, click the *Show Images* button.

Spam-blocking programs are continually changing and some of the specifics presented in this Making IT Work for You may have changed. To learn about other ways to make information technology work for you, visit our Web site at www.computing2008.com and enter the keyword miw.

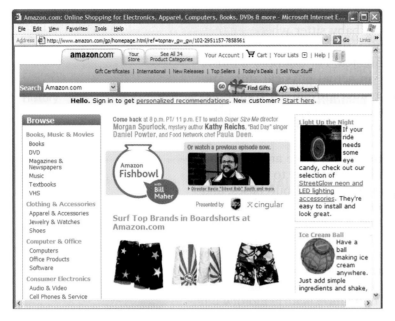

Figure 2-16 Online shopping

Support	Site
Product comparisons	www.shopping.com
Locating closeouts	www.overstock.com
Finding coupons	www.ebates.com
Reviewing classifieds	www.craigslist.org

Figure 2-17 Consumer support

banking operations. These online operations include accessing account information, balancing check books, transferring funds, paying bills, and applying for loans.

- **Online stock trading** allows investors to research, buy, and sell stocks and bonds over the Internet. While e-trading is more convenient than using a traditional full-service broker, the greatest advantage is cost.

- **Online shopping** includes the buying and selling of a wide range of consumer goods over the Internet. (See Figure 2-16.) There are thousands of e-commerce applications in this area. Fortunately, there are numerous Web sites that provide support for consumers looking to compare products and to locate bargains. (See Figure 2-17.)

To learn how online stores are created, visit our Web site at www.computing2008.com and enter the keyword **storefront**.

CONSUMER-TO-CONSUMER E-COMMERCE

A recent trend in C2C e-commerce is the growing popularity of Web auctions. **Web auctions** are similar to traditional auctions except that buyers and sellers seldom, if ever, meet face-to-face. Sellers post descriptions of products at a Web site and buyers submit bids electronically. Like traditional auctions, sometimes the bidding becomes highly competitive and enthusiastic. There are two basic types of Web auction sites:

- **Auction house sites** sell a wide range of merchandise directly to bidders. The auction house owner presents merchandise that is typically from a company's surplus stock. These sites operate like a traditional auction, and bargain prices are not uncommon. Auction house sites are generally considered safe places to shop.

- **Person-to-person auction sites** operate more like flea markets. The owner of the site provides a forum for numerous buyers and sellers to gather. While the owners of these sites typically facilitate the bidding process, they are not involved in completing transactions or in verifying the authenticity of the goods sold. (See Figure 2-18.) As with purchases at a flea market, buyers and sellers need to be cautious.

For a list of the most popular Web auction sites, see Figure 2-19.

SECURITY

The single greatest challenge for e-commerce is the development of fast, secure, and reliable payment methods for purchased goods. The three basic payment options are check, credit card, and electronic cash.

- Checks are the most traditional. Unfortunately, check purchases require the longest time to complete. After selecting an item, the buyer sends a check through the mail. Upon receipt of the check, the seller verifies that the check is good. If it is good, then the purchased item is sent out.

- Credit card purchases are faster and more convenient than check purchases. Credit card fraud, however, is a major concern for both buyers and sellers. Criminals known as **carders** specialize in stealing, trading, and using stolen credit cards over the Internet. We will discuss this and other privacy and security issues related to the Internet in Chapter 10.

- **Digital cash** is the Internet's equivalent to traditional cash. Buyers purchase digital cash from a third party (a bank that specializes in electronic currency) and use it (see Figure 2-20) to purchase goods. Sellers convert the digital cash to traditional currency through the third party. Although not as convenient as credit card purchases, digital cash is more secure. For a list of digital cash providers, see Figure 2-21.

Figure 2-18   Person-to-person Web auction site

Organization	Site
Amazon	www.auctions.amazon.com
Bidz	www.bidz.com
eBay	www.ebay.com
Sotheby's	www.searchsothebys.com
Yahoo!	www.auctions.yahoo.com

Figure 2-19   Auction sites

Organization	Site
ECash	www.ecash.com
Google	checkout.google.com
Internet Cash	www.internetcash.com
PayPal	www.paypal.com

Figure 2-21   Digital cash providers

Figure 2-20   PayPal offers digital cash

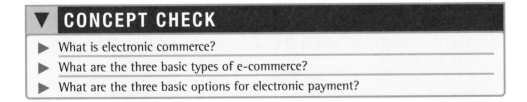

▼ CONCEPT CHECK

► What is electronic commerce?

► What are the three basic types of e-commerce?

► What are the three basic options for electronic payment?

The Internet, the Web, and Electronic Commerce

WEB UTILITIES

Utilities are programs that make computing easier. **Web utilities** are specialized utility programs that make using the Internet and the Web easier and safer. Some of these utilities are Internet services for connecting and sharing resources over the Internet. Others are browser-related programs that either become part of your browser or are executed from your browser.

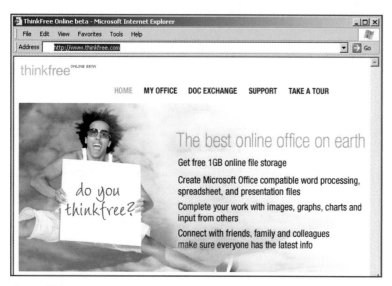

Figure 2-22 ThinkFree offers Web-based applications

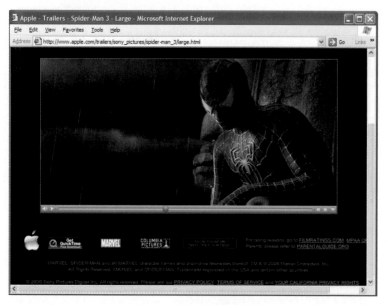

Figure 2-23 QuickTime movie at Apple.com

WEB-BASED APPLICATIONS

Typically, application programs are owned by individuals or organizations and stored on their computer system's hard disks. An emerging trend, however, is to free users from owning and storing applications by using **Web-based services** such as Think-Free. (See Figure 2-22.) This free service provides access to programs with capabilities similar to Microsoft's Word, Excel, and PowerPoint.

To use one of these **Web-based applications,** you connect to the Web site of the application service provider, copy the application program to your computer system's memory, and then run the application. To see how Web-based applications work, visit our Web site at www.computing2008.com and enter the keyword **asp.**

FTP

File transfer protocol (FTP) is an Internet standard for transferring files. Many computers on the Internet allow you to copy files to your computer. This is called **downloading.** You also can use FTP to copy files from your computer to another computer on the Internet. This is called **uploading.**

PLUG-INS

Plug-ins are programs that are automatically started and operate as a part of your browser. Many Web sites require you to have one or more plug-ins to fully experience their content. Some widely used plug-ins include

- Acrobat Reader from Adobe—for viewing and printing a variety of standard forms and other documents saved in a special format called PDF.
- Windows Media Player from Microsoft—for playing audio files, video files, and much more.
- QuickTime from Apple—for playing audio and video files. (See Figure 2-23.)
- RealPlayer from RealNetworks—for playing audio and video files.
- Shockwave from Adobe—for playing Web-based games and viewing concerts and dynamic animations.

Some of these utilities are included in many of today's browsers and operating systems. Others must be installed before they can be used by your browser. To learn more about plug-ins and how to download them, visit some of the sites listed in Figure 2-24.

Plug-in	Source
Acrobat Reader	www.adobe.com
Media Player	www.microsoft.com
QuickTime	www.apple.com
RealPlayer	www.service.real.com
Shockwave	www.adobe.com

Figure 2-24 Plug-in sites

FILTERS

Filters block access to selected sites. The Internet is an interesting and multifaceted arena. But one of those facets is a dark and seamy one. Parents, in particular, are concerned about children roaming unrestricted across the Internet. (See Figure 2-25.) Filter programs allow parents as well as organizations to block out selected sites and set time limits. (See Figure 2-26.) Additionally, these programs can monitor use and generate reports detailing the total time spent on the Internet and the time spent at individual Web sites, chat groups, and newsgroups. For a list of some of the best-known filters, see Figure 2-27.

Figure 2-25 Parents play an important role in Internet supervision

Figure 2-26 CyberPatrol is a Web filter

Filter	Site
CyberPatrol	www.cyberpatrol.com
Cybersitter	www.cybersitter.com
iProtectYou Pro Web Filter	www.softforyou.com
Net Nanny	www.netnanny.com
Safe Eyes Platinum	www.safeeyes.com

Figure 2-27 Filters

The Internet, the Web, and Electronic Commerce

Figure 2-28   Symantec's Norton Internet Security

INTERNET SECURITY SUITES

An **Internet security suite** is a collection of utility programs designed to maintain your security and privacy while you are on the Web. These programs control spam, protect against computer viruses, provide filters, and much more. You could buy each program separately; however, the cost of the suite is typically much less. Two of the best-known Internet security suites are McAfee's Internet Security and Symantec's Norton Internet Security. (See Figure 2-28.)

▼ CONCEPT CHECK

▶ What are Web utilities? Web-based applications? FTP?

▶ What are plug-ins and filters used for?

▶ Describe Internet security suites.

CAREERS IN IT

Webmasters develop and maintain Web sites and Web resources. (See Figure 2-29.) The job may include backup of the company Web site, updating resources, or development of new resources. Webmasters are often involved in the design and development of the Web site. Some Webmasters monitor traffic on the site and take steps to improve the publicity of the site. Webmasters also may work with marketing personnel to increase site traffic and may be involved in development of Web promotions.

Employers look for candidates with a bachelor's degree in computer science or information systems and knowledge of common programming languages and Web development software. Knowledge of HTML is considered essential. Those with experience using Web authoring software and programs like Adobe Illustrator and Adobe Flash are often preferred. Good communication and organizational skills are vital in this position.

Webmasters can expect to earn an annual salary of $48,000 to $73,000. This position is relatively new in many corporations and tends to have fluid responsibilities. With technological advances and increasing corporate emphasis on a Web presence, experience in this field could lead to managerial opportunities. To learn about other careers in IT, visit us at www.computing 2008.com and enter the keyword careers.

Figure 2-29   Webmaster

Web-Accessible Refrigerators Will Automatically Restock Themselves

What if you could virtually tour your home from anywhere using the Web? What if your refrigerator knew what it contained and could create a grocery list to restock itself? What if you could remotely check to see if you left your wallet on the bedside table or make sure you remembered to turn the oven off? In the future, this will almost certainly be the case, as every aspect of the modern home becomes Web accessible.

Web-accessible home appliances are not a new idea. Several companies offer kitchen appliances that connect to the Internet. At present these appliances are passive, meaning that they do not have any knowledge of what food items they contain and are therefore not able to actively act to restock. In the future, however, appliances will be much more active. Refrigerators will know what food they contain and what food is needed to be fully stocked and automatically will place orders over the Internet to restock missing items. Also, every appliance in your home will have its own Web page. Through such a Web page, you will be able to actively interact and control these appliances.

The home of the future will include more than just smart appliances. Internet cameras, high-speed Internet, and wireless technologies are converging to offer an inexpensive way to virtually visit your home from anywhere with Internet access. You will be able to follow pets to make sure they stay off the couch or search for a missing wallet you may have left on the nightstand. Coupled with Internet appliances, you could review your pantry using Internet cameras and your refrigerator's Web site to create a grocery list. You could have this list e-mailed to your grocery store and then pick up the groceries on the way home.

Could there be a downside to all this? Currently, many people's computers are infested with Internet viruses and spyware. What could happen if these malicious programs infested your home's appliances? Would it be possible that your every move in your own home could be broadcast to others over the Internet?

THE INTERNET, THE WEB, AND ELECTRONIC COMMERCE

INTERNET AND WEB

ACCESS

Internet

Launched in 1969 with **ARPANET,** the **Internet** consists of the actual physical network made up of wires, cables, and satellites. Being connected to this network is often described as being **online.**

Web

Introduced in 1992 at **CERN,** the **Web** provides a multimedia interface to Internet resources.

Common Uses

The most common uses of the Internet and Web include

- Communication—the most popular Internet activity.
- Shopping—one of the fastest-growing Internet activities.
- Searching—access libraries and local, national, and, international news.
- Entertainment—music, movies, magazines, and computer games.
- Education—**e-learning** or taking online courses.

Once connected to the Internet, our computer seemingly becomes an extension of a giant computer that branches all over the world.

Providers

Internet service providers are connected to the Internet. The most widely used **ISPs** are **national** and **wireless.**

Connection technologies include **dial-up, DSL, cable,** and **wireless modems.**

Browsers

Browsers access the Web allowing you to **surf** or explore. Some related terms are

- **URLs**—**locations** or **addresses** to Web resources; two parts are **protocol** and **domain name; top-level domain (TLD)** identifies type of organization.
- **HTML**—commands to display **Web pages; hyperlinks (links)** are connections.
- **Applets**—special programs linked to Web pages; typically written in **Java.**

To be a competent end user, you need to be aware of resources available on the Internet and Web, to be able to access these resources, to effectively communicate electronically, to efficiently locate information, to understand electronic commerce, and to use Web utilities.

COMMUNICATION

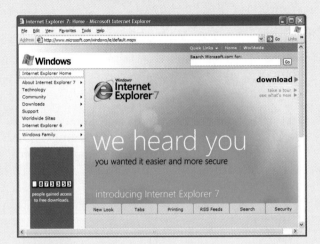

SEARCH TOOLS

E-mail

E-mail (electronic mail) is the transmission of electronic messages. Basic elements: **header** (including **addresses, subject,** and **attachments**), **message,** and **signature line. Spam** is unwanted and unsolicited e-mail that may include a **computer virus. Spam blockers** are programs that identify and eliminate spam.

Instant Messaging

Instant messaging (IM) extends e-mail to support live communication with **friends. Universal instant messengers** support communication with other services.

Social Networking

Social networks connect individuals to one another. Three types are

- Reuniting sites connect people who have lost touch with one another.
- Friend-of-a-friend sites bring together two people who share a common friend.
- Common interest sites connect individuals, who share common interests or hobbies.

Search services maintain huge databases relating to Web site content. **Spiders** are programs that update these databases.

Search Engines

Search engines locate information on the Web. Two approaches are **keyword search** (enter keyword, and it returns a list of **hits;** good for locating specific information) and **directory search** (select from a list of topics, good for locating general information).

Metasearch Engines

Metasearch engines submit to several search engines simultaneously. Duplicate sites are eliminated, hits are ordered, and composite hits are presented.

Specialized Search Engines

Specialized search engines focus on subject-specific Web sites.

Content Evaluation

Consider the following criteria to evaluate the accuracy of information on the Web: authority, accuracy, objectivity, and currency.

Electronic commerce, or **e-commerce,** is the buying and selling of goods over the Internet. Three basic types of e-commerce are **business-to-consumer (B2C), business-to-business,** and **consumer-to-consumer.**

Business-to-Business E-Commerce

Most widely used **business-to-business** (**B2B**) applications are **online banking, online stock trading,** and **online shopping.**

Consumer-to-Consumer E-Commerce

Web auctions are a growing **consumer-to-consumer (C2C)** application. Two basic types are **auction house sites** and **person-to-person auction sites.**

Security

Security is the greatest challenge for e-commerce development. Three basic payment options are **check, credit card,** and **digital cash.**

Organization	Site
ECash	www.ecash.com
Google	checkout.google.com
Internet Cash	www.internetcash.com
PayPal	www.paypal.com

Web utilities are specialized utility programs that make using the Internet and the Web easier and safer.

Web-Based Applications

Web-based Applications free users from owning and storing applications. The programs are accessed from a Web site, copied to the user's computer memory, and run.

FTP

FTP (file transfer protocol) is an Internet standard for transferring files. **Downloading** is the process of receiving a file from another computer. **Uploading** is the process of sending a file to another computer.

Plug-ins

Plug-ins are automatically loaded and operate as part of a browser. Many Web sites require specific plug-ins to fully experience their content. Some plug-ins are included in many of today's browsers; others must be installed.

Filters

Filters are used by parents and organizations to block certain sites and to monitor use of the Internet and the Web.

Internet Security Suite

An **Internet security suite** is a collection of utility programs designed to protect your privacy and security on the Internet.

Webmasters develop and maintain Web sites and Web resources. Bachelor's degree in computer science or information systems and knowledge of common programming languages and Web development software required. Salary range $48,000 to $73,000.

KEY TERMS

address (32, 34)
Advanced Research Project Agency
  Network (ARPANET) (30)
applets (33)
attachment (35)
auction house site (44)
browser (31)
business-to-
  business (B2B) (43)
business-to-consumer (B2C) (43)
cable (31)
carder (45)
Center for European Nuclear
  Research (CERN) (30)
computer virus (35)
consumer-to-consumer (C2C) (43)
dial-up (31)
digital cash (45)
directory search (40)
domain name (32)
downloading (46)
DSL (31)
e-commerce (42)
e-learning (31)
electronic commerce (42)
electronic mail (34)
e-mail (34)
file transfer
  protocol (FTP) (46)
filter (47)
friend (35)
header (34)
hit (40)
hyperlink (32)
Hypertext Markup Language (HTML) (32)
instant messaging (IM) (35)
Internet (30)
Internet security
  suite (48)
Internet service provider (ISP) (31)
Java (33)
keyword search (40)

link (32)
location (32)
message (35)
metasearch engine (41)
national service
  provider (31)
online (30)
online banking (43)
online shopping (44)
online stock trading (44)
person-to-person auction
  site (44)
plug-in (46)
protocol (32)
search engine (40)
search service (39)
signature line (35)
social networking (38)
spam (35)
spam blocker (35)
specialized search
  engine (42)
spider (39)
subject (35)
surf (31)
top-level domain (TLD) (32)
uniform resource locator (URL) (32)
universal instant
  messenger (38)
uploading (46)
Web (30)
Web auction (44)
Web-based application (46)
Web-based services (46)
Webmaster (48)
Web page (32)
Web utility (46)
wireless modem (31)
wireless service
  provider (31)

FEATURES

Animations

Careers in IT

DVD Direct

Expansions

Making IT Work for You

On the Web Explorations

TechTV

Tips

CHAPTER REVIEW

Applying Technology

Crossword Puzzle

Expanding Your Knowledge

Key Terms

Matching

Multiple Choice

Open-Ended

Writing About Technology

To test your knowledge of these key terms with animated flash cards, visit our Web site at
www.computing2008.com and enter the keyword terms2.

CROSSWORD PUZZLE

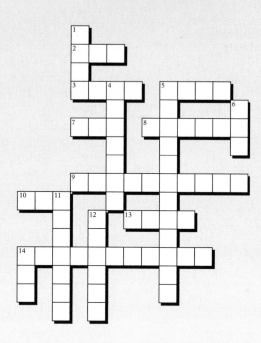

Across

2 Provide users a connection to the Internet.

3 Unwelcome e-mail.

5 Explore the Web.

7 Internet uploading and downloading service.

8 Steals credit card information.

9 A file, such as a document or worksheet, that is attached to an e-mail message.

10 Involves the sale of a product to another business.

13 Connection to Web resources.

14 Process of transferring information from a remote computer to the computer one is using.

Down

1 The sites that a search engine returns after running a keyword search.

4 Special programs written in Java.

5 Locates information online.

6 Location of Web resource.

11 Program that provides access to Web resources.

12 Used to block certain sites.

14 Provides high-speed connection using existing telephone lines.

For an interactive version of this crossword, visit our Web site at www.computing2008.com and enter the keyword **crossword2**.

MULTIPLE CHOICE

Circle the letter or fill in the correct answer.

1. The Internet was launched in 1969 when the United States funded a project that developed a national computer network called

   a. AARPNET   **c.** CERN

   b. CERNET   **d.** ARPANET

2. _____ is the most popular Internet activity.

   a. communication   **c.** searching

   b. shopping   **d.** entertainment

3. A(n) _____ program provides access to Web resources.

   a. Web   **c.** browser

   b. ISP   **d.** URL

4. Rules for exchanging data between computers are called

   a. programs   **c.** protocols

   b. procedures   **d.** hyperlinks

5. The last part of the domain name following the dot (.) is the top _____ domain.

   a. level   **c.** locator

   b. link   **d.** language

6. ____ are widely used to add interest and activity to a Web site by presenting animation, displaying graphics, providing interactive games, and more.

   a. Applets   **c.** Plug-ins

   b. Bots   **d.** Spiders

7. Unwanted and unsolicited e-mails are called _____ .

   a. spam   **c.** flame

   b. junk   **d.** lurk

8. Programs that automatically submit your search request to several search engines simultaneously are called _____ .

   a. metasearch engines   **c.** spiders

   b. search engines   **d.** hits

9. _____ cash is the Internet's equivalent to traditional cash.

   a. Universal   **c.** Premium

   b. Web   **d.** Digital

10. These programs allow parents as well as organizations to block out selected sites and set time limits on Internet access.

    a. plug-ins   **c.** FTP

    b. filters   **d.** WAIS

For an interactive version of these multiple-choice questions, visit our Web site at www.computing2008.com and enter the keyword **multiple2**.

MATCHING

www.computing2008.com

Match each numbered item with the most closely related lettered item. Write your answers in the spaces provided.

a. carders
b. digital cash
c. e-commerce
d. header
e. hits
f. metasearch engine
g. plug-in
h. reuniting
i. URLs
j. Web auction

1. Addresses of Web resources. _____
2. Part of an e-mail message that includes the subject, address, and attachments. _____
3. Program that starts and operates as part of a browser. _____
4. The list of sites that contain the keywords of a keyword search. _____
5. Program that automatically submits a search request to several search engines simultaneously. _____
6. Buying and selling goods over the Internet. _____
7. Type of social networking site that reconnects people who have lost touch with one another. _____
8. Similar to a traditional auction, but buyers and sellers typically interact only on the Web. _____
9. Criminals that specialize in stealing, trading, and using stolen credit cards over the Internet. _____
10. Internet equivalent to traditional cash. _____

For an interactive version of this matching exercise, visit our Web site at www.computing2008.com and enter the keyword **matching2**.

OPEN-ENDED

On a separate sheet of paper, respond to each question or statement.

1. Discuss the uses of the Internet. Which activities have you participated in? Which one do you think is the most popular?
2. Explain the differences between the two most common types of providers.
3. What are the basic elements of an e-mail message?
4. What is social networking? Describe the three types of social networking sites.
5. Describe the different types of search engines. Give an example of the type of search each engine is best for.

APPLYING TECHNOLOGY

The following questions are designed to demonstrate ways that you can effectively use technology today. The first question relates directly to this chapter's Making IT Work for You feature.

Blocking Spam

1

Are you tired of unwanted e-mail in your inbox? Do you frequently spend valuable time sorting through junk e-mail? Spam can mean anything from a minor annoyance to a serious loss of productivity. Installing spam-blocking software can help. To learn more about how to block spam, review Making IT Work for You: Blocking Spam, on pages 36 and 37. Then complete the following questions: (a) Describe how Mozilla Thunderbird can be used to block spam e-mail messages. (b) What is the name for the list of e-mail addresses that should never be considered spammers? (c) Why is it important to block images in new e-mail messages?

Online Shopping

2

Connect to our Web site at www.computing2008.com and enter the keyword shopping to link to a popular shopping site. Once there, try shopping for one or two products, and answer the following questions: (a) What product(s) did you shop for? Could you find the product(s) at the site? If not, then search for another product that you can locate at the site. (b) Describe your experience. Was the site easy to use? Did you find it easy to locate the product(s)? What are the pros and cons of shopping online versus at a traditional store?

Web Auctions

3

Connect to our Web site at www.computing2008.com and enter the keyword auction to link to a popular online auction. Once there, read about how the auction works and check out a few of the items up for bid. Answer the following questions: (a) What are the advantages of using a Web auction to purchase items? What are the disadvantages? (b) What are the advantages and disadvantages to selling an item on an online auction, as opposed to a traditional method (such as a classified ad in the newspaper)? (c) Have you ever bought or sold an item at an online auction? If you have, describe what you bought and how you bought it. If you have not, do you think that you will in the near future? Why or why not?

EXPANDING YOUR KNOWLEDGE

The following questions are designed to add depth and detail to your understanding of specific topics presented within this chapter. The questions direct you to sources other than the textbook to obtain this knowledge.

1   How Spam Filters Work

Spam is an ongoing problem for e-mail users everywhere. Spam is cheap, easy to send, and difficult to track, so the problem is unlikely to disappear soon. Fortunately, spam-blocking software is available. To learn "How Spam Filters Work," visit our Web site at www.computing2008.com and enter the keyword spam. Then answer the following questions: (a) Briefly describe an advantage and a disadvantage to using each of the three types of filters to stop spam. (b) Choose one of the filters and draw a diagram depicting a spam e-mail going through this filter. Be sure to label each step. (c) Modify the diagram to show an e-mail from a friend.

2   How Instant Messaging Works

One of the fastest-growing applications on the Internet is instant messaging. This extension to e-mail provides a way for friends and colleagues to communicate and share information from almost anywhere in the world. To learn "How Instant Messaging Works," visit our Web site at www.computing2008.com and enter the keyword im. Then answer the following:

As described in Step 4: Communicate, Linda, Steve, and Chris agree to meet for a movie. Then Chris tells them that he has to leave for school and disconnects. Linda and Steve continue talking with Linda asking Steve, "Have you seen any good movies lately?" On a single page of paper, create a drawing based on the animation that describes these events beginning with Step 5 when Chris says, "Bye for now—I have to leave for school."

3   Domain Registration

Individuals and businesses do not *own* domain names. Instead, names such as "yahoo.com" are *registered* with a domain name registrar for an annual fee. Conduct a Web search to locate a domain name registrar site. Review the process for registering a domain name and address the following questions: (a) List the steps involved in registering a domain name. (b) What is the cost for registering a domain name? (c) How long can a domain name be registered for?

WRITING ABOUT TECHNOLOGY

The ability to think critically and to write effectively is essential to nearly every profession. The following questions are designed to help you develop these skills by posing thought-provoking questions about computer privacy, security, and/or ethics.

www.computing2008.com

Free Speech Online

1

Some feel that there is too much objectionable material allowed on the Internet, whereas others argue that the Internet should be completely uncensored. Consider these two viewpoints and answer the following questions in a one-page paper: (a) Should religious groups be allowed to distribute information over the Internet? What about groups that advocate hatred or oppression? (b) Is there any material you feel should not be freely available on the Web? What about child pornography? (c) If you think some regulation is required, who should determine what restrictions should be imposed? (d) The Internet is not owned by a particular group or country. What limitations does this impose on enforcement of restrictions?

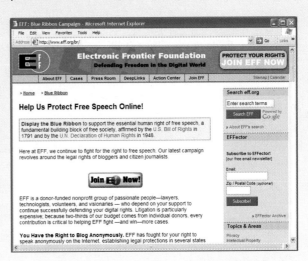

Dot-Bombs

2

After the initial boom of e-commerce, many Internet-based businesses ran out of funding and pulled the plug. There is much speculation about why these sites, often referred to as "dot-bombs," failed to succeed in the new market the Web has created. Research two or three articles that speculate about such business collapses and address the following items in a one-page paper: (a) Summarize the reasons cited for the "dot-bombs." Do these reasons seem justified? Why or why not? (b) What types of businesses have been successful in e-commerce? What types have become "dot-bombs"? Be specific. (c) Make a prediction about the future of e-commerce. Will doing business online become more commonplace, or is it just a trend that will pass? Explain your answer.

CHAPTER

3

COMPETENCIES

After you have read this chapter, you should be able to:

1 **Discuss common features of most software applications.**

2 **Discuss word processors and word processing features.**

3 **Describe spreadsheets and spreadsheet features.**

4 **Discuss database management systems and database management features.**

5 **Describe presentation graphics and presentation graphics features.**

6 **Discuss integrated software.**

7 **Describe software suites and the different types of suites.**

Announcing

New Adventure Travel Trips

Attend an Adventure Travel presentation to learn about some of the earth's greatest unspoiled habitats and find out how you can experience the adventure of a lifetime. This year we are introducing four new tours and offering you a unique opportunity to combine many different outdoor activities while exploring the world.

Hike the Inca trail to Machu Picchu
Camp on safari in Tanzania
Climb Mt. Kilimanjaro
Explore the Costa Rican rain forests

Presentation dates and times are January 5 at 7 PM, February 3 at 7:30 PM, and March 8 at 7 PM. All presentations are held at convenient hotel locations. The hotels are located in downtown Los Angeles, Santa Clara and at the airport.

Call 1-800-777-0004 for presentation locations, a full color brochure, and itinerary information, costs, and trip dates.

Word Processing Software
create text-based documents

Database Management Systems
organize data for efficient retrieval

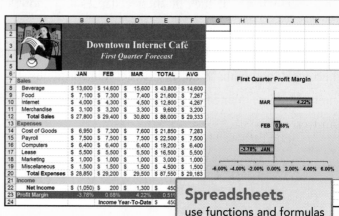

Spreadsheets
use functions and formulas to analyze numeric data

BASIC APPLICATION SOFTWARE

Introduction

Not long ago, trained specialists were required to perform many of the operations you can now do with a microcomputer. Secretaries used typewriters to create business correspondence. Market analysts used calculators to project sales. Graphic artists created designs by hand. Data processing clerks created electronic files to be stored on large computers. Now you can do all these tasks—and many others—with a microcomputer and the appropriate application software.

Think of the microcomputer as an electronic tool.

You may not consider yourself very good at typing, calculating, organizing, presenting, or managing information. However, a microcomputer can help you do all these things and much more. All it takes is the right kinds of software.

Competent end users need to understand the capabilities of basic application software, which includes word processors, spreadsheets, database management systems, and presentation programs. They need to know about integrated packages and software suites.

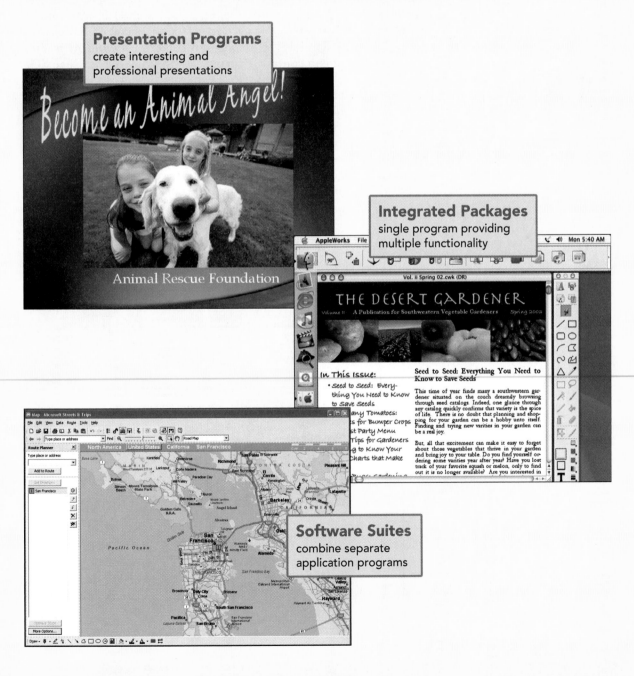

Presentation Programs
create interesting and professional presentations

Integrated Packages
single program providing multiple functionality

Software Suites
combine separate application programs

APPLICATION SOFTWARE

As we discussed in Chapter 1, there are two kinds of software. **System software** works with end users, application software, and computer hardware to handle the majority of technical details. **Application software** can be described as end-user software and is used to accomplish a variety of tasks.

Application software, in turn, can be divided into two categories. One category, **basic applications,** is the focus of this chapter. These programs are widely used in nearly every discipline and occupation. They include word processors, spreadsheets, database management systems, and presentation graphics. The other category, **specialized applications** includes thousands of other programs that are more narrowly focused on specific disciplines and occupations. Specialized applications are presented in Chapter 4.

COMMON FEATURES

A **user interface** is the portion of the application that you work with. Most applications use a **graphical user interface (GUI)** that displays graphical elements called **icons** to represent familiar objects and a mouse. The mouse controls a **pointer** on the screen that is used to select items such as icons. Another feature is the use of windows to display information. A **window** is simply a rectangular area that can contain a document, program, or message. (Do not confuse the term *window* with the various versions of Microsoft's Windows operating systems, which are programs.) More than one window can be opened and displayed on the computer screen at one time.

Most software programs including Microsoft Office 2003, have menus, dialog boxes, toolbars, and buttons. (See Figure 3-1.) **Menus** present commands that are typically displayed in a **menu bar** at the top of the screen. When one of the menu items is selected, an additional list of menu options or a **dialog box** that provides additional information and requests user input may appear.

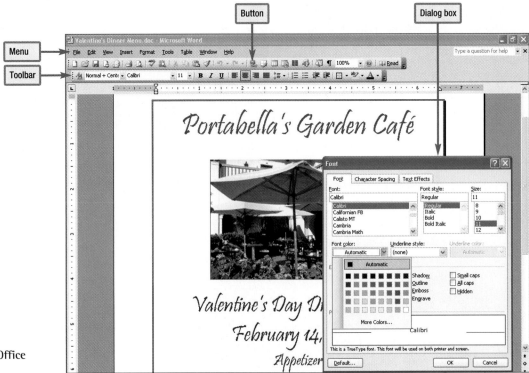

Figure 3–1   Microsoft Office Word 2003

Toolbars typically are below the menu bar. They contain small graphic elements called **buttons** that provide shortcuts for quick access to commonly used commands.

The newest Office version, 2007 Microsoft Office, has a redesigned interface that is intended to make it easier for users to find and use all the features of an application. This new design introduces ribbons, contextual tabs, galleries, and more. (See Figure 3-2.)

- **Ribbons** replace menus and toolbars by organizing commonly used commands into a set of tabs. These tabs display command buttons that are the most relevant to the tasks being performed by the user.

- **Contextual tabs** are tabs that appear automatically. These tabs only appear when they are needed and anticipate the next operations to be preformed by the user.

- **Galleries** simplify the process of making a selection from a list of alternatives. This is accomplished by replacing many dialog boxes with visual presentations of potential results.

This new interface is the first major change in over a decade and promises to greatly improve user functionality and efficiency.

Some applications support **speech recognition**, the ability to accept voice input to select menu options and dictate text. See Making IT Work for You: Speech Recognition on pages 64 and 65. To learn more about how speech recognition works, visit our Web site at www.computing2008.com and enter the keyword speech.

Figure 3-2   Microsoft Office
Word 2007

▼ CONCEPT CHECK

▶ What is the difference between basic and specialized applications?

▶ List some common features of programs in Microsoft Office 2003.

▶ Describe some of the features introduced in 2007 Microsoft Office.

Word **processors** create text-based **documents** and are one of the most flexible and widely used software tools. All types of people and organizations use word processors to create memos, letters, and faxes. Organizations create newsletters, manuals, and brochures to provide information to their customers. Students and researchers use word processors to create reports. Word processors can even be used to create personalized Web pages.

The three most widely used word processing programs are Microsoft Word, Corel WordPerfect, and Lotus Word Pro.

FEATURES

Word processors provide a variety of features to make entering, editing, and formatting documents easy. One of the most basic features for entering text is **word wrap.** This feature automatically moves the insertion point to the next line once the current line is full. As you type, the words wrap around to the next line.

There are numerous features designed to support **editing** or modifying a document. One of these is a **thesaurus** that provides synonyms, antonyms, and related words for a selected word or phrase. You can quickly locate and replace selected words using the **find and replace** feature. **Spelling** and **grammar checkers** look for misspelled words and problems with capitalization, punctuation, and sentence structure. Other features are designed to improve the **format** or appearance of a document. One of the most basic is the **font** or design of the characters. (See Figure 3-3.) The height of a character is its **font size.** The appearance of characters can be enhanced using such **character effects** as **bold,** *italic,* **shadow,** and colors. **Bulleted** and **numbered lists** can make a sequence of topics easy to read.

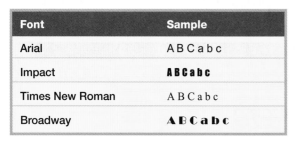

Font	Sample
Arial	A B C a b c
Impact	**ABCabc**
Times New Roman	A B C a b c
Broadway	**A B C a b c**

Figure 3–3   Sample fonts

CASE

Assume that you have accepted a job as an advertising coordinator for Adventure Travel Tours, a travel agency specializing in active adventure vacations. Your primary responsibilities are to create and coordinate the company's promotional materials, including flyers and travel reports. To see how you could use Microsoft Word, the most widely used word processing program, as the advertising coordinator for the Adventure Travel Tours, see Figures 3-4 and 3-5.

▼ CONCEPT CHECK

▶ What do word processors do? What is word wrap?

▶ Describe the following editing features: thesaurus, find and replace, spelling and grammar checkers.

▶ Describe the following formatting features: font, font size, character effects, numbered and bulleted lists.

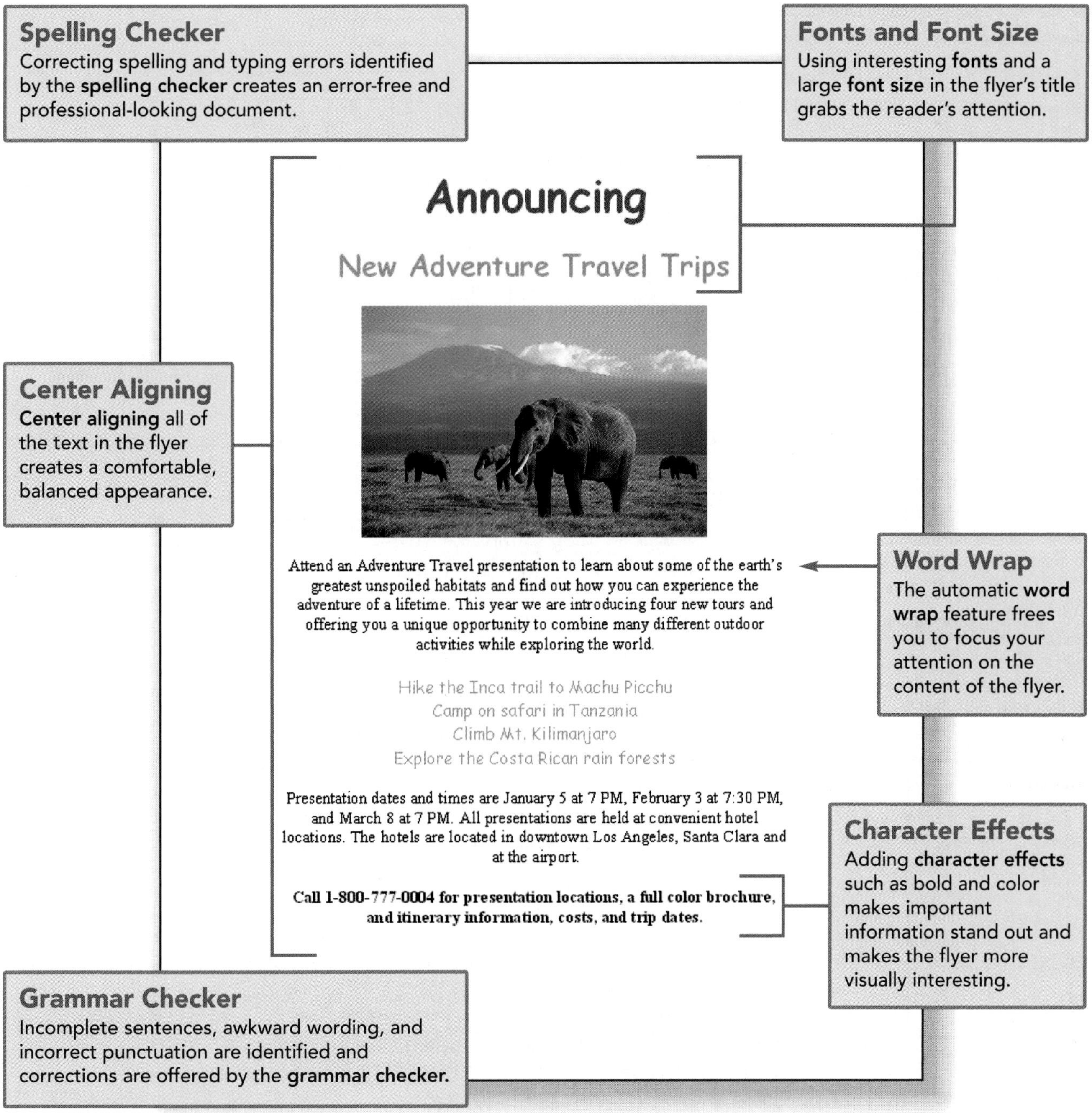

Spelling Checker
Correcting spelling and typing errors identified by the **spelling checker** creates an error-free and professional-looking document.

Fonts and Font Size
Using interesting **fonts** and a large **font size** in the flyer's title grabs the reader's attention.

Announcing

New Adventure Travel Trips

Center Aligning
Center aligning all of the text in the flyer creates a comfortable, balanced appearance.

Attend an Adventure Travel presentation to learn about some of the earth's greatest unspoiled habitats and find out how you can experience the adventure of a lifetime. This year we are introducing four new tours and offering you a unique opportunity to combine many different outdoor activities while exploring the world.

Hike the Inca trail to Machu Picchu
Camp on safari in Tanzania
Climb Mt. Kilimanjaro
Explore the Costa Rican rain forests

Presentation dates and times are January 5 at 7 PM, February 3 at 7:30 PM, and March 8 at 7 PM. All presentations are held at convenient hotel locations. The hotels are located in downtown Los Angeles, Santa Clara and at the airport.

Call 1-800-777-0004 for presentation locations, a full color brochure, and itinerary information, costs, and trip dates.

Word Wrap
The automatic **word wrap** feature frees you to focus your attention on the content of the flyer.

Character Effects
Adding **character effects** such as bold and color makes important information stand out and makes the flyer more visually interesting.

Grammar Checker
Incomplete sentences, awkward wording, and incorrect punctuation are identified and corrections are offered by the **grammar checker**.

Figure 3–4   Flyer

CREATING A FLYER

You have been asked to create an advertising flyer for upcoming promotional presentations. After discussing the flyer's contents and basic structure with your supervisor, you start to enter the flyer's text. As you enter the text, *words wrap* automatically at the end of each line. Also, while entering the text, the *spelling checker* and *grammar checker* catch spelling and grammatical errors. Once the text has been entered, you focus your attention on enhancing the visual aspects of the flyer. You add an interesting graphic and experiment with different character and paragraph formats including *fonts, font sizes, colors,* and *alignments.*

CREATING A REPORT

Your next assignment is to create a report on Tanzania and Peru. After conducting your research, you start writing your paper. As you enter the text for the report, you notice that the *AutoCorrect* feature automatically corrects some grammar and punctuation errors. Your report includes several figures and *tables*. You use the *captions* feature to keep track of figure and table numbers, to enter the caption text, and to position the captions. When referencing figures or tables from the text, you use the *cross reference* feature. You then carefully document your sources using *footnotes*. Finally, you prepare the report for printing by adding *header* and *footer* information.

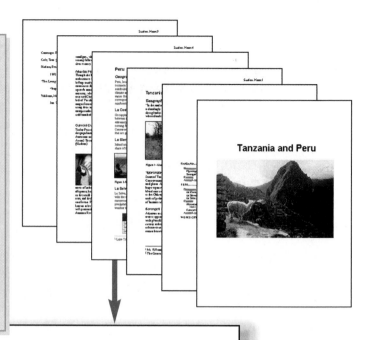

AutoCorrect
As you enter text, you occasionally forget to capitalize the first word in a sentence. Fortunately, **AutoCorrect** recognizes the error and automatically capitalizes the word.

Footnote
To include a note about Lake Titicaca, you use the **footnote** feature. This feature inserts the footnote superscript number and automatically formats the bottom of the page to contain the footnote text.

Header or Footer
Page numbers and other document-related information can be included in a **header** or **footer**.

Captions and Cross References
Identifying figures with **captions** and using **cross references** in a report makes the report easier to read and more professional.

Table
To concisely present and organize the weather information, you use a **table**.

- 1 -

Peru

Geography and Climate

Peru, located in South America, borders the Pacific Ocean on its west and shares common borders with the countries of Ecuador, Colombia, Brazil, and Bolivia. Peru is subdivided into three regions – La Costa, La Sierra, and La Selva — based on differing climate and geographical features. Though entirely within the tropics, Peru's climate varies from region to region, ranging from tropical to arctic. Its varied climate corresponds to the sharply contrasting geographical features of seafront, mountains, and rainforests.

La Costa

Occupying the slender area along Peru's western coastline, La Costa, provides a division between the mountains and sea. Although some of this area is fertile, mostly it is extremely dry and arid. The Andes Mountains prevent greater annual precipitation coming from the east. Some areas in the south are considered drier than the Sahara. Conversely, there are a few areas in this region where mountain rivers meet the ocean that are green with life and do not give the impression of being in a desert at all.

La Sierra

Inland and to the east is the mountainous region called La Sierra, encompassing Peru's share of the Andes mountain range. The southern portion of this region is prone to  volcanic activity, and some volcanoes are active today. La Sierra is subject to a dry season from May to September, which is winter in that part of the world. The weather is typically sunny, with moderate annual precipitation. The former Incan capital Cuzco is in this region, as well as the Sacred Valley of the Incas. This region also contains Lake Titicaca, the world's highest navigable lake.[1]

Figure 1-Sacred Valley

La Selva

La Selva, a region of tropical rainforest, is the easternmost region in Peru. This region, with the eastern foot of the Andes Mountains, forms the Amazon Basin, into which numerous rivers flow. La Selva is extremely wet, with some areas exceeding an annual precipitation of 137 inches. Its wettest season occurs from November to April. The weather here is humid and extremely hot.

Region	Annual Rainfall (Inches)	Average Temperature (Fahrenheit)
La Costa	2	68
La Sierra	35	54
La Selva	137	80

[1] Lake Titicaca is 12,507 feet above sea level.

Figure 3–5   Report

Spreadsheet programs organize, analyze, and graph numeric data such as budgets and financial reports. Once used exclusively by accountants, spreadsheets are widely used by nearly every profession. Marketing professionals analyze sales trends. Financial analysts evaluate and graph stock market trends. Students and teachers record grades and calculate grade point averages.

The three most widely used spreadsheet programs are Microsoft Excel, Corel Quattro Pro, and Lotus 1-2-3.

FEATURES

Unlike word processors, which manipulate text and create text documents, spreadsheet programs manipulate numeric data and create workbook files. **Workbook files** consist of one or more related worksheets. A **worksheet,** also known as a **spreadsheet** or **sheet,** is a rectangular grid of **rows** and **columns.** For example, in Figure 3-6, the columns are identified by letters and the rows are identified by numbers. The intersection of a row and column creates a **cell.** For example, the cell D8 is formed by the intersection of column D and row 8.

A cell can contain text or numeric entries. **Text entries** or **labels** provide structure to a worksheet by describing the contents of rows and columns. For example, in Figure 3-6, cell B8 contains the label Food. The cell D8 contains a number identified as the food expense.

A **numeric entry** can be a number or a formula. A **formula** is an instruction to calculate or process. For example, the cell F15 contains the formula = E5−E13. This formula will calculate a value and display that value in cell F15 (Net). The value is calculated by taking the value in cell E5 (Wages) and subtracting the value in cell E13 (Total Expenses). **Functions** are prewritten formulas provided by the spreadsheet program that perform calculations such as adding a series of cells. For example, the cell E13 contains the function SUM(D8:D12), which adds the values in the range from D8 to D12. A **range** is a series of continuous cells. In this case, the range includes D8, D9, D10, D11, and D12. The sum of the values in this range is displayed in cell E13.

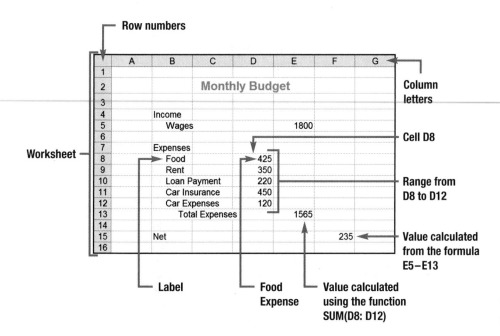

Figure 3-6 Monthly budget worksheet

Spreadsheet programs typically provide a variety of different types of functions, including financial, mathematical, statistical, and logical functions. Some of these functions are presented in Figure 3-7.

Analytical graphs or **charts** are visual representations of data in a worksheet. You can readily create graphs in a spreadsheet program by selecting the cells containing the data to be charted and then selecting the type of chart to display. If you change one or more numbers in your spreadsheet, all related formulas will automatically recalculate and charts will be recreated. This is called **recalculation.** The process of observing the effect of changing one or more cells is often referred to as **what-if analysis.** For example, to analyze the effect of a rent increase in the Monthly Budget worksheet in Figure 3-6, all you would need to do is replace the contents in cell D9. The entire worksheet, including any charts that had been created, would be recalculated automatically.

CASE

Assume that you have just accepted a job as manager of the Downtown Internet Café. This cafe provides a variety of flavored coffees as well as Internet access. One of your responsibilities is to create a financial plan for the next year. To see how you could use Microsoft Excel, the most widely used spreadsheet program, as the manager for the Downtown Internet Café, see Figures 3-8 through 3-10.

▼ CONCEPT CHECK

► What are spreadsheets used for? What is a workbook? What is a worksheet?

► Define rows, columns, cells, ranges, text, and numeric entries.

► Describe the following spreadsheet features: formulas, functions, charts, recalculation, and what-if analysis.

Type	Function	Calculates
Financial	PMT	Size of loan payments
	PV	Present value for an investment
Mathematical	SUM	Sum of the numbers in a range of cells
	ABS	Absolute value of a number
Statistical	AVERAGE	Average or mean of the numbers in a range of cells
	MAX	Largest number in a range of cells
Logical	IF	Whether a condition is true; if true, a specified value is displayed; if not true, then a different specified value is displayed
	AND	Whether two conditions are true; if both are true, then a specified value is displayed, if either one or both are not true, then a different specified value is displayed

Figure 3-7 Selected spreadsheet functions

CREATING A SALES FORECAST

Your first project is to develop a first-quarter sales forecast for the cafe. You begin by studying the sales at the Downtown Internet Café and talking with several managers. After obtaining sales and expense estimates, you are ready to create the first-quarter forecast. You start structuring the *worksheet* by inserting descriptive *text entries* for the row and column headings. Next, you insert *numeric entries,* including *formulas* and *functions* to perform calculations. To test the accuracy of the worksheet, you change the values in some cells and compare the recalculated spreadsheet results with hand calculations.

Worksheets

Worksheets are used for a wide range of different applications. One of the most common uses is to create, analyze, and forecast budgets.

Text Entries

Text entries provide meaning to the values in the worksheet. The rows are labeled to identify the various sales and expense items. The columns are labeled to specify the months.

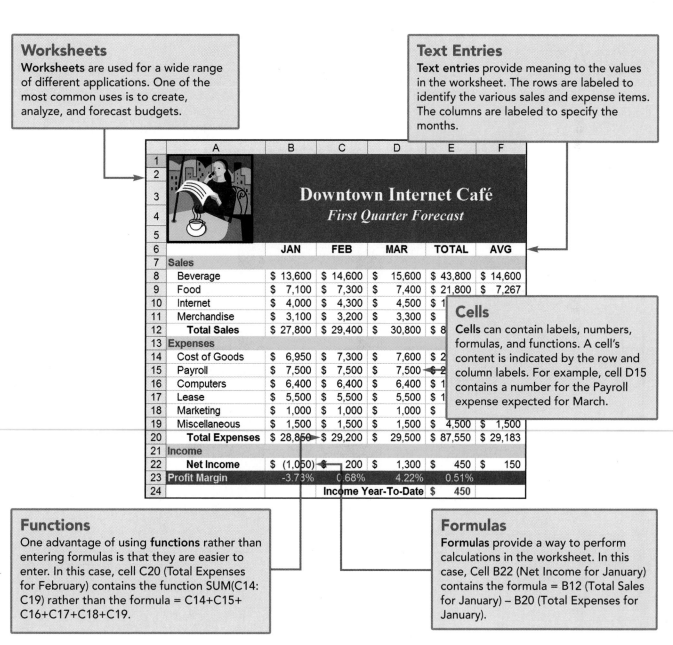

Cells

Cells can contain labels, numbers, formulas, and functions. A cell's content is indicated by the row and column labels. For example, cell D15 contains a number for the Payroll expense expected for March.

Functions

One advantage of using **functions** rather than entering formulas is that they are easier to enter. In this case, cell C20 (Total Expenses for February) contains the function SUM(C14:C19) rather than the formula = C14+C15+C16+C17+C18+C19.

Formulas

Formulas provide a way to perform calculations in the worksheet. In this case, Cell B22 (Net Income for January) contains the formula = B12 (Total Sales for January) – B20 (Total Expenses for January).

Figure 3–8   Worksheet

CREATING A CHART

After completing the First-Quarter Forecast for the Downtown Internet Café, you decide to *chart* the sales data to better visualize the projected growth in sales. You select the 3D column *chart type* to show each month's projected sales category. Using a variety of chart options, you enter descriptive *titles* for the chart, the x-axis, and the y-axis. Then you use *data labels* to focus attention on the growing Internet sales. Finally, you insert a *legend* to define the chart's different columns.

Chart Types
To display the monthly expenses over the quarter, you consider several different **chart types** before selecting the 3D column chart. The 3D variation of the chart provides an interesting depth perception to the columns.

Chart
Once data is in the worksheet, it is very easy to **chart** the data. All you need to do is to select the data to chart, select the chart types, and add some descriptive text.

Titling
Clearly **titling** the chart as well as the x-axis and y-axis makes the chart easier to read and understand.

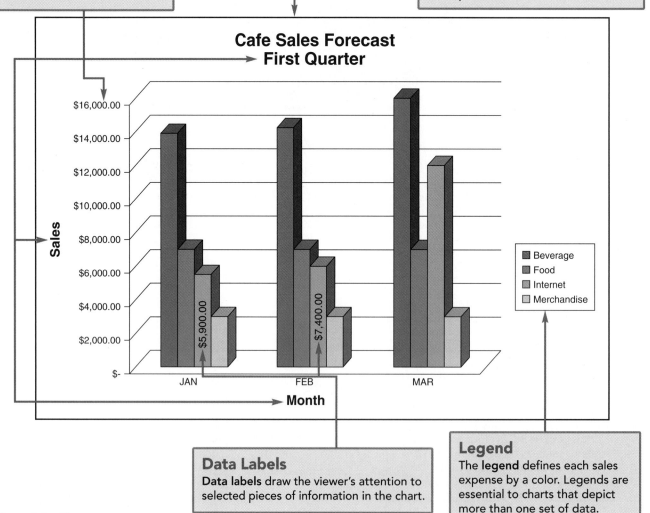

Data Labels
Data labels draw the viewer's attention to selected pieces of information in the chart.

Legend
The **legend** defines each sales expense by a color. Legends are essential to charts that depict more than one set of data.

Figure 3–9   Chart

ANALYZING YOUR DATA

After presenting the First-Quarter Forecast to the owner, you revise the format and expand the *workbook* to include worksheets for each quarter and an annual forecast summary. You give each worksheet a descriptive *sheet name*. At the request of the owner, you perform a *what-if analysis* to test the effect of different estimates for payroll, and you use *Goal Seek* to determine how much Internet Sales would have to increase to produce a profit margin of 5.00 percent for January.

Workbook

The first worksheet in a **workbook** is often a summary of the following worksheets. In this case, the first worksheet presents the entire year's forecast. The subsequent worksheets provide the details.

Sheet Name

Each worksheet has a unique **sheet name**. To make the workbook easy to navigate, it is a good practice to always use simple yet descriptive names for each worksheet.

What-If Analysis

What-if analysis is a very powerful and simple tool to test the effects of different assumptions in a spreadsheet.

Goal Seek

A common goal in many financial workbooks is to achieve a certain level of profit. **Goal seek** allows you to set a goal and then will analyze other parts of the workbook that would need to be adjusted to meet that goal.

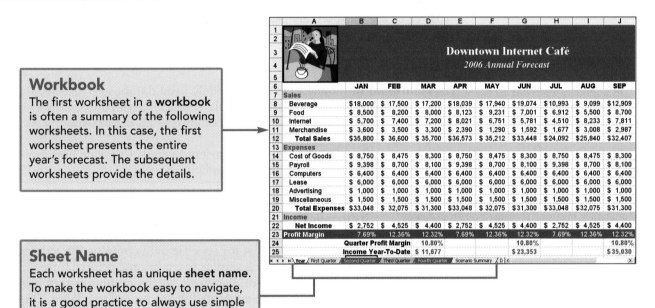

Figure 3-10   Workbook

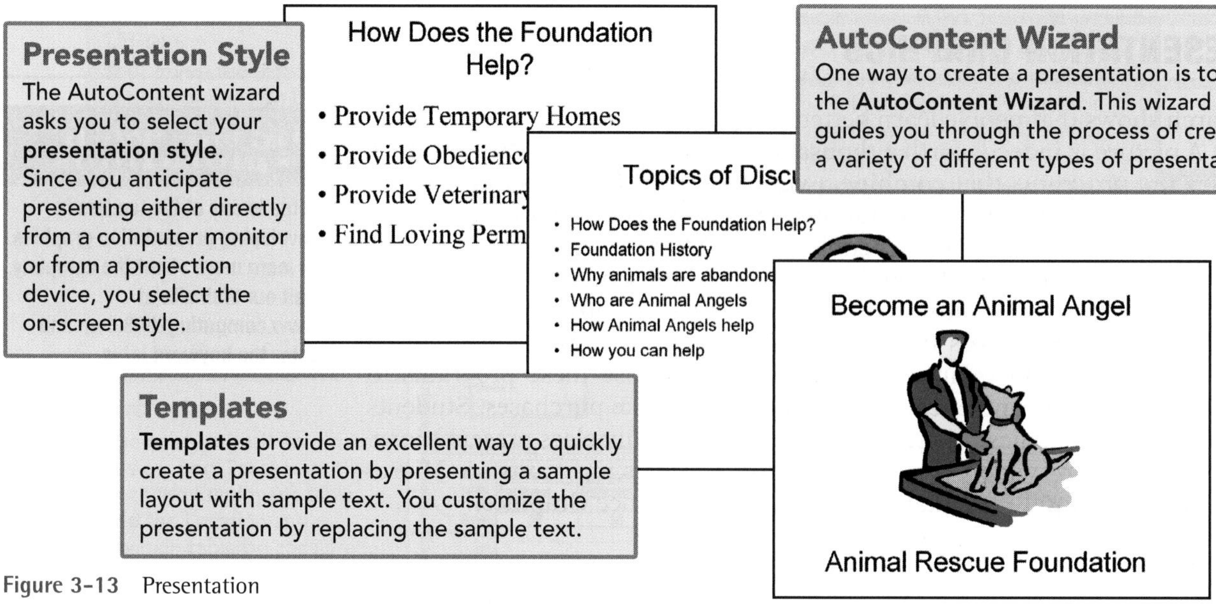

Presentation Style

The AutoContent wizard asks you to select your **presentation style**. Since you anticipate presenting either directly from a computer monitor or from a projection device, you select the on-screen style.

How Does the Foundation Help?

• Provide Temporary Homes
• Provide Obedience
• Provide Veterinary
• Find Loving Perm

AutoContent Wizard

One way to create a presentation is to use the **AutoContent Wizard**. This wizard guides you through the process of creating a variety of different types of presentations.

Topics of Disc

• How Does the Foundation Help?
• Foundation History
• Why animals are abandone
• Who are Animal Angels
• How Animal Angels help
• How you can help

Become an Animal Angel

Animal Rescue Foundation

Templates

Templates provide an excellent way to quickly create a presentation by presenting a sample layout with sample text. You customize the presentation by replacing the sample text.

Figure 3–13   Presentation

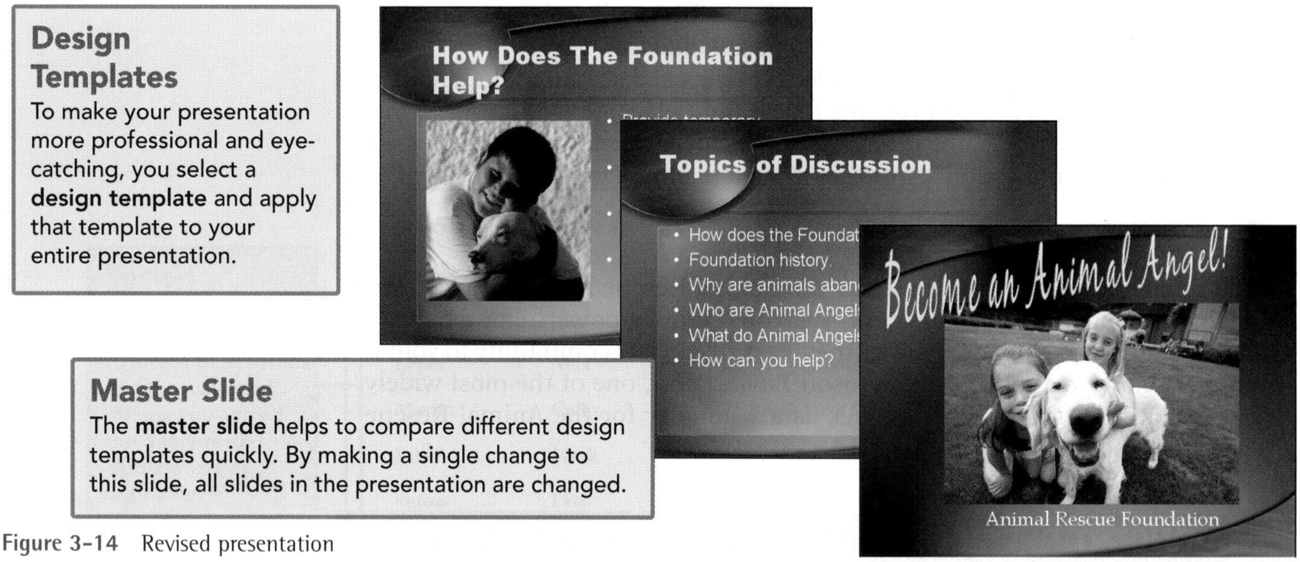

Design Templates

To make your presentation more professional and eye-catching, you select a **design template** and apply that template to your entire presentation.

How Does The Foundation Help?

• Provide temporary

Topics of Discussion

• How does the Foundat
• Foundation history
• Why are animals aban
• Who are Animal Angel
• What do Animal Angel
• How can you help?

Become an Animal Angel!

Animal Rescue Foundation

Master Slide

The **master slide** helps to compare different design templates quickly. By making a single change to this slide, all slides in the presentation are changed.

Figure 3–14   Revised presentation

UPDATING A PRESENTATION

After discussing the presentation with the director, you have some ideas to enhance the effectiveness of the message. First, you improve the color of selected items and add more graphics. Next, you select one of the *design templates* and make some other changes. You apply these changes to all the slides by simply adjusting the *master slide.* Finally, you practice or rehearse the presentation, create speaker notes, and print out audience handouts. You're ready to give a professionally designed, dynamic presentation.

INTEGRATED PACKAGES

An **integrated package** is a single program that provides the *functionality* of a word processor, spreadsheet, database manager, and more. The primary disadvantage of an integrated package is that the capabilities of each function (such as word processing) are not as extensive as in the individual programs (such as Microsoft Word). The primary advantages are cost and simplicity. The cost of an integrated package is much less than the cost of the individual powerful, professional-grade application programs discussed thus far in this chapter.

Integrated packages are popular with many home users and are sometimes classified as **personal** or **home software.** The most widely used integrated packages are Microsoft Works and AppleWorks. See Figure 3-15.

Figure 3-15   AppleWorks

CASE

Assume that you publish a gardening newsletter that you distribute to members of the Desert Gardening Club. Using the word processing function, you entered text, formatted titles and subtitles, and inserted several photographs. (See Figure 3-16.) Using the spreadsheet function, you analyzed daily rainfall for the feature article and included a chart. After completing the newsletter, you will use the database function and the membership database to print mailing labels.

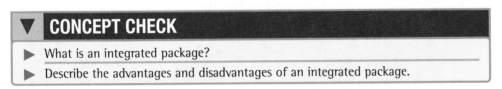

▼ CONCEPT CHECK

▶ What is an integrated package?

▶ Describe the advantages and disadvantages of an integrated package.

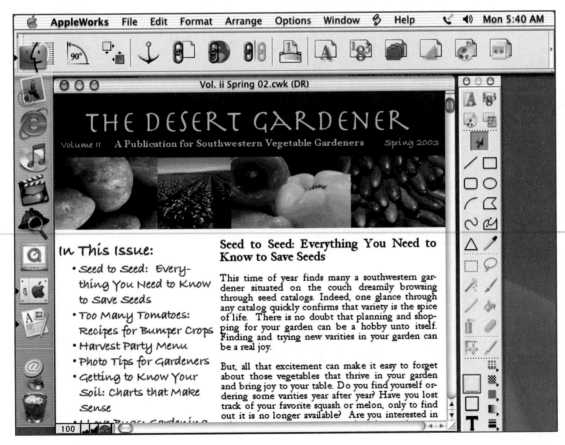

Figure 3-16   Integrated package (AppleWorks)

SOFTWARE SUITES

A **software suite** is a collection of separate application programs bundled together and sold as a group. While the applications function exactly the same whether purchased in a suite or separately, it is significantly less expensive to buy a suite of applications than to buy each application separately. There are four types of suites:

* **Productivity suite.** Productivity suites, also known as **business suites,** contain professional-grade application programs, including a word processor, spreadsheet, database manager, and more. The best known is Microsoft Office. (See Figure 3-17.) Other well-known productivity suites are Apple iWork, Sun StarOffice, Corel WordPerfect Office Suite, and Lotus SmartSuite.

* **Personal suite.** Also known as **home suites,** these contain personal software applications or programs intended for home use. The best known is Microsoft Works Suite, which includes the Works integrated package along with Works Calendar, Streets & Trips, and more. (See Figure 3-18.)

* **Specialized suite.** Specialized suites focus on specific applications. These include graphics suites, financial planning suites, and many others. (Graphics suites will be discussed in Chapter 4.)

Figure 3-17   Microsoft Office

* **Utility suite.** These suites include a variety of programs designed to make computing easier and safer. Two of the best known are Norton System-Works and Norton Internet Security Suite. (Utility suites will be discussed in detail in Chapter 5.)

Many times it is convenient to share data between applications. For example, when writing a report, it may be useful to include a chart from a spreadsheet or data from a database. Data created by one application can be shared with another application in a variety of differ-

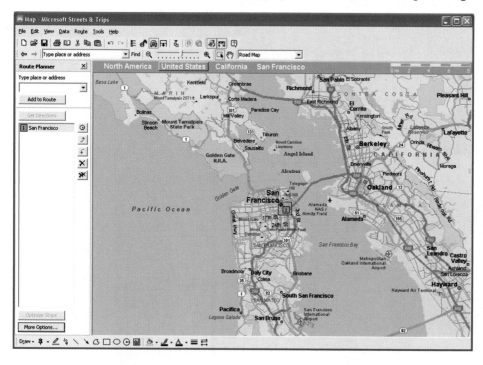

Figure 3-18   Streets & Trips from Microsoft Works Suite

ent ways, including copying and pasting, object linking, and object embedding. To learn more about sharing data between applications, visit us on the Web at www.computing2008.com and enter the keyword sharing.

▼ **CONCEPT CHECK**

▶ What is a software suite? What are the advantages of purchasing a suite?

▶ What are the four types of software suites?

▶ What is the best-known productivity suite? What is the best-known personal suite?

Computer trainers instruct new users on the latest software or hardware. (See Figure 3.19.) Many computer training positions are offered to those with experience with the most popular business software.

Employers look for good communication skills and teaching experience. Though a teaching degree may not be required, it may be preferred. Experience with the latest software and/or hardware is essential, but this varies depending on the position. Employers often seek detail-oriented individuals with IT experience.

Computer trainers can expect to earn an annual salary of $26,000 to $54,000. However, salary is dependent on experience and may vary drastically. Responsibilities typically include preparation of course materials, grading coursework, and continuing education in the field. Opportunities for advancement include management of other trainers and consulting

Figure 3-19   Computer trainer

work. To learn more about other careers in information technology, visit us at www.computing2008.com and enter the keyword careers.

A Look to the Future

Agents Will Help Write Papers, Pay Bills, and Shop on the Internet

Wouldn't it be great to have your own personal assistant? Your assistant could research topics for a term paper, collect relevant information, and even suggest famous quotes that apply to your topic. Your assistant could monitor your personal budget using a spreadsheet and even evaluate the impact of a rental income. Or your assistant could punch up a classroom presentation by suggesting and locating relevant photos and videos. All this is likely with special programs called *agents.*

An agent is an intelligent program that can understand your needs and act to fulfill those needs. Today, primitive agents already exist in many help tools to interpret user questions and to formulate appropriate responses. Computer scientists at the University of Maryland are working on the next-generation agents that may provide the most efficient way to locate information on the Web. These agents promise to understand words and the context in which they are used. They will locate Web sites that not only have the *words* you are looking for but also the *meaning.* This future is not far off, but as agent technology improves, it is only a matter of time until agents act in more autonomous ways and can help you use basic applications to do complex tasks, like prepare an essay, a budget, or a presentation.

What do you think? Should we all have our own personal agent to help us write papers, pay bills, and shop on the Internet?

BASIC APPLICATION SOFTWARE

APPLICATION SOFTWARE

There are two basic types of software. **System software** focuses on handling technical details. **Application software** focuses on completing specific tasks or applications. Two categories are **basic applications** and **specialized applications.**

Common Features

Common features of most application programs including Microsoft Office 2003 are

- **User interface**—most have **graphical user interfaces (GUI)** that display **icons.**
- **Windows**—rectangular areas that can contain documents, programs, and messages.
- **Menus**—present commands listed on the **menu bar.**
- **Dialog box**—provides additional information or requests user input.
- **Toolbars**—contain **buttons** for quick access to commonly used commands.

2007 Microsoft Office has a new interface designed to make it easier to find and use application features. This interface introduces

- **Ribbons** replace menus and toolbars; use tabs to organize commands.
- **Contextual tabs** automatically appear when needed.
- **Galleries** replace many dialog boxes with visual presentations of potential results.

Some applications support **speech recognition** by allowing voice input.

WORD PROCESSORS

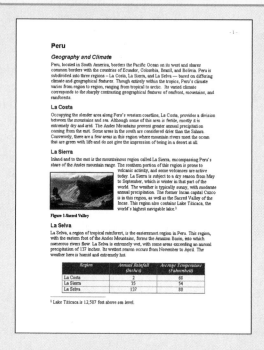

Word processors allow you to create, edit, save, and print text-based **documents,** including flyers, reports, newsletters, and Web pages.

Features

Word wrap is a basic feature that automatically moves the insertion point to the next line.
    Editing features include

- **Thesaurus,** which provides synonyms, antonyms, and related words.
- **Find and replace,** which locates (finds), removes, and inserts (replaces) another word(s).
- **Spelling** and **grammar checkers**, which automatically locate misspelled words and grammatical problems.

Formatting features include

- **Font**—design of characters. **Font size** is the height of characters.
- **Character effects**—include **bold,** *italic,* **shadow**, and colors.
- **Bulleted** and **numbered lists**—used to present sequences of topics or steps.

To be a competent end user, you need to understand the capabilities of basic application software, which includes word processors, spreadsheets, database management systems, and presentation programs. You need to know how to use these applications and how data can be shared between them.

SPREADSHEET

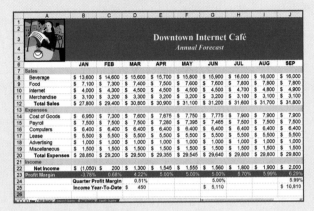

Spreadsheet programs are used to organize, analyze, and graph numeric data.

Features
Principal spreadsheet features include the following

- **Workbook files** consist of one or more related worksheets.
- **Worksheets,** also known as **spreadsheets** or **sheets,** are rectangular grids of **rows** and **columns.** Rows are identified by numbers, columns by letters.
- **Cells** are formed by the intersection of a row and column; used to hold text and numeric entries.
- **Text entries (labels)** provide structure and **numeric entries** can be numbers or formulas.
- **Formulas** are instructions for calculations. **Functions** are prewritten formulas.
- **Range** is a series of cells.
- **Analytical graphs (charts)** represent data visually.
- **Recalculation** occurs whenever a value changes in one cell that affects another cell(s).
- **What-if analysis** is the process of observing the effect of changing one or more values.

DATABASE MANAGEMENT SYSTEMS

A **database** is a collection of related data. A **database management system (DBMS),** also known as a **database manager,** structures a database and provides tools for entering, editing, and retrieving data.

Features
Principal database management system features include the following

- **Relational database** organizes data into related tables.
- **Tables** have rows (**records**) and columns (**fields**).
- **Sort** is a tool to rearrange records using a particular field.
- **Query** is a question or request for specific data contained in a database.
- **Forms** are used to enter new records or edit existing records.
- **Reports** are printed output in a variety of forms.

PRESENTATION GRAPHICS

Presentation graphics combine a variety of visual objects to create attractive, visually interesting presentations. They are excellent tools to communicate a message and to persuade people.

Features
Principal presentation graphics features include the following:

- **Slides**—individual page or screen of a presentation.
- **AutoContent wizard**—steps you through the process of creating a presentation.
- **Design templates**—professionally selected combination of color schemes, slide layouts, and special effects.
- **Master slide**—does not appear in presentation; controls format and placement of all slides in a presentation.

INTEGRATED PACKAGES

An **integrated package,** also known as **personal** or **home software,** is a single program that provides the functionality of several application packages. Some important characteristics include

- Functions that typically include word processing, spreadsheet, database manager, and more. Each function is not as extensive or powerful as a single-function application program.
- Less expensive than purchasing several individual application programs.
- Simple to use and switch between functions.
- Popular with home users who are willing to sacrifice some advanced features for cost and simplicity.

SOFTWARE SUITES

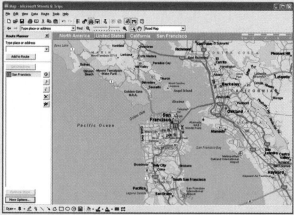

A **software suite** is a collection of individual application packages sold together.

- **Productivity suites (business suites)** contain professional-grade application programs.
- **Personal suites (home suites)** contain personal software applications or programs intended for home use.
- **Specialized suites** focus on specific applications such as graphics.
- **Utility suites** include a variety of programs designed to make computing easier and safer.

CAREERS IN IT

Computer trainers instruct new users on the latest software or hardware. Teaching degree is preferred and experience with latest software and/or hardware is essential. Salary range $26,000 to $54,000.

KEY TERMS

analytical graph   (70)
application software   (62)
AutoContent wizard   (77)
basic application   (62)
bulleted list   (66)
business suite   (80)
button   (63)
cell   (69)
character effect   (66)
chart   (70)
column   (69)
computer trainer   (81)
contextual tab   (63)
database   (74)
database management system (DBMS)   (74)
database manager   (74)
design template   (77)
dialog box   (62)
document   (66)
editing   (66)
field   (74)
find and replace   (66)
font   (66)
font size   (66)
form   (74)
format   (66)
formula   (69)
function   (69)
galleries   (63)
grammar checker   (66)
graphical user interface (GUI)   (62)
home software   (79)
home suite   (80)
icons   (62)
integrated package   (79)
label   (69)
master slide   (77)
menu   (62)

menu bar   (62)
numbered list   (66)
numeric entry   (69)
personal software   (79)
personal suite   (80)
pointer   (62)
presentation graphics   (77)
productivity suite   (80)
query   (74)
range   (69)
recalculation   (70)
record   (76)
relational database   (74)
report   (74)
ribbons   (63)
row   (69)
sheet   (69)
slide   (77)
software suite   (80)
sort   (74)
specialized application   (62)
specialized suite   (80)
speech recognition   (63)
spelling checker   (66)
spreadsheet   (69)
system software   (62)
table   (74)
text entry   (69)
thesaurus   (66)
toolbar   (63)
user interface   (62)
utility suite   (80)
what-if analysis   (70)
window   (62)
word processor   (66)
word wrap   (66)
workbook file   (69)
worksheet   (69)

FEATURES

Animations

Careers in IT

DVD Direct

Expansions

Making IT Work for You

On the Web Explorations

TechTV

Tips

CHAPTER REVIEW

Applying Technology

Crossword Puzzle

Expanding Your Knowledge

Key Terms

Matching

Multiple Choice

Open-Ended

Writing About Technology

To test your knowledge of these key terms with animated flash cards, visit our Web site at www.computing2008.com and enter the keyword terms3.

CROSSWORD PUZZLE

Across

4 Rectangular area that contains messages.
5 System to organize and retrieve data.
8 Collection of individual applications.
10 Rearrange records using a field.
11 Formed by intersection of row and column.
14 Collection of related data.
16 Flyer, report, newsletter, Web page.
17 These make up a presentation.
18 Question or request for data in a database.

Down

1 List of commands.
2 Rectangular grid of rows and columns used in programs like Excel.
3 Has records and fields.
6 Controls format and placement of slides.
7 Requests user input.
9 Moves insertion point to next line.
12 Series of cells.
13 A vertical block of cells one cell wide.
15 Contains buttons and menus.

For an interactive version of this crossword, visit our Web site at www.computing2008.com and enter the keyword **crossword3**.

MULTIPLE CHOICE

Circle the letter or fill in the correct answer.

1. This type of software works with end users, application software, and computer hardware to handle the majority of technical details.
    a. communications software
    b. application software
    c. Web software
    d. system software

2. _____ are narrowly focused on specific disciplines and occupations.
    a. Basic applications
    b. Utility programs
    c. Specialized applications
    d. Business suites

3. The primary purpose of this type of software is to create text-based documents.
    a. Web development
    b. word processing
    c. spreadsheet
    d. presentation

4. Organizations create newsletters, manuals, and brochures with this type of software.
    a. presentation
    b. graphics
    c. spreadsheet
    d. word processing

5. Letters, memos, term papers, reports, and contracts are all examples of
    a. menus
    b. models
    c. spreadsheets
    d. documents

6. Numbers and formulas entered in a cell are called
    a. numeric entries
    b. intersection
    c. labels
    d. text

7. The acronym DBMS stands for what?
    a. document binder management system
    b. database management system
    c. double-blind management setup
    d. data binding and marketing structure

8. Database _____ are primarily used to enter new records and to make changes to existing records.
    a. table
    b. forms
    c. queries
    d. reports

9. A file that includes predefined settings that can be used to create many common types of presentations is called a
    a. pattern
    b. model
    c. template
    d. blueprint

10. A(n) _____ is a single program that provides the functionality of a word processor, spreadsheet, database manager, and more.
    a. software suite
    b. integrated package
    c. specialized application
    d. basic application

For an interactive version of these multiple-choice questions, visit our Web site at www.computing2008.com and enter the keyword multiple3.

MATCHING

Match each numbered item with the most closely related lettered item. Write your answers in the spaces provided.

a. analytical
b. cell
c. integrated package
d. range
e. relational database
f. software suite
g. sort
h. spelling checker
i. what-if analysis
j. window

1. Area that contains a document, program, or message. _____
2. Type of graph or chart. _____
3. Includes the functionality of a word processor, spreadsheet, database manager, and more. _____
4. Identifies incorrectly spelled words and suggests alternatives. _____
5. The intersection of a row and column in a spreadsheet. _____
6. A collection of two or more cells in a spreadsheet. _____
7. Spreadsheet feature in which changing one or more numbers results in the automatic recalculation of all related fields. _____
8. Database structure that organizes data into related tables. _____
9. Arranging objects numerically or alphabetically. _____
10. Individual applications that are sold as a group. _____

For an interactive version of this matching exercise, visit our Web site at www.computing2008.com and enter the keyword matching3.

OPEN-ENDED

On a separate sheet of paper, respond to each question or statement.

1. Explain the difference between general-purpose and special-purpose applications.
2. Discuss the common features of most software programs. Describe the new interface introduced with 2007 Microsoft Office.
3. What is the difference between a function and a formula? How is a formula related to what-if analysis?
4. What are presentation graphics programs? How are they used?
5. What is the difference between an integrated package and a software suite? What are the advantages and disadvantages of each?

APPLYING TECHNOLOGY

The following questions are designed to demonstrate ways that you can effectively use technology today. The first question relates directly to this chapter's Making IT Work for You feature.

Speech Recognition

1

Tired of using your keyboard? Have you ever thought about speaking to your computer? Perhaps speech recognition is for you. To learn more about speech recognition, review Making IT Work for You: Speech Recognition on pages 64 and 65. Then answer the following questions: (a) What menu item is selected to begin training the software? (b) What are the verbal commands to insert a picture into a Microsoft Word document? (c) Have you ever used speech recognition? If you have, describe how you used it and discuss how effective it was for you. If you have not, discuss how you might use it in the future. Be specific.

Presentation Graphics

2

For presentations, having the right software can help grab your audience's attention. Connect to our Web site at www.computing2008.com and enter the keyword presentation to link to a presentation

graphics software package. Once connected, review the product's features and answer the following questions: (a) What computer hardware and software are required to use the presentation graphics product? (b) List and describe three features that could help you organize or present your ideas. (c) What types of files can be embedded with a presentation using this software?

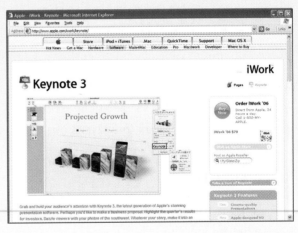

Corel WordPerfect Office Suite

3

Microsoft's major competitor in the office suite market is Corel. Visit our site at www.computing 2008.com and enter the keyword corel to connect to Corel's Web site. Review the site, and then answer the following questions: (a) What applications are provided in Corel's WordPerfect Office Suite? (b) What are the similarities and differences between the Microsoft and Corel office suites? (c) Which suite would you choose? Why?

FEATURES

Animations

Careers in IT

DVD Direct

Expansions

Making IT Work for You

On the Web Explorations

TechTV

Tips

CHAPTER REVIEW

Applying Technology

Crossword Puzzle

Expanding Your Knowledge

Key Terms

Matching

Multiple Choice

Open-Ended

Writing About Technology

EXPANDING YOUR KNOWLEDGE

The following questions are designed to add depth and detail to your understanding of specific topics presented within this chapter. The questions direct you to sources other than the textbook to obtain this knowledge.

1   How Speech Recognition Works

Speech recognition is an emerging technology. To learn how speech recognition works, visit our Web site at www.computing2008.com and enter the keyword speech. Then answer the following: (a) Create a drawing similar to the one on our Web site that would represent dictating a mailing address for an address label. (b) What hardware is required to use voice recognition software? (c) Describe how speech recognition could enhance your use of each of the following types of applications: word processing, spreadsheet, and presentation. (d) Describe a profession that could benefit from speech recognition software. Be specific.

2   Sharing Data between Applications

Sharing data between applications can be very convenient and can greatly increase your productivity. The three most common ways to share information are copy and paste, object linking, and object embedding. To learn more about sharing data between applications, visit out Web site at www.computing2008.com and enter the keyword sharing. Then respond to the folowing: (a) Discuss how copy and paste works. Provide a specific example. (b) What is the difference between object linkling and object embedding? Provide specific examples. (c) Describe a specific situation in which you might use all three types of sharing data between applications.

3   Shareware

One way to acquire new application software is by downloading shareware. Conduct a Web search for shareware programs. Connect to and explore a shareware site offering a program that might interest you. Then respond to the following: (a) What is shareware? Who creates it? (b) What does shareware cost to use? What about support if you have a problem using it? (c) What are the risks of using shareware? Be thorough. (d) Would you use shareware? Why or why not?

WRITING ABOUT TECHNOLOGY

The ability to think critically and to write effectively is essential to nearly every profession. The following questions are designed to help you develop these skills by posing thought-provoking questions about computer privacy, security, and/or ethics.

Acquiring Software

1

There are three common ways to obtain new software: use public domain software, use shareware, buy commercial software. In addition to these three ways, two others are to copy programs from a friend or to purchase unauthorized copies of programs. Investigate each of these five options, and then answer the following in a one-page paper: (a) Define and discuss each option. Be sure to discuss both the advantages and disadvantages of each. (b) Which seems like the best method to you? Why? (c) Do you think there is anything wrong with obtaining and using unauthorized software? Identify and explore the key issues.

Software Standards

2

Most of the products you encounter every day, such as cars, electronics, and food, are required by law to meet certain conditions to ensure your safety and a minimum level of quality. Software, however, can be written by anyone with few of these constraints. Fortunately, some standards of certification do exist. Research a certification program for software vendors. Write a one-page paper to answer the following: (a) Describe the certification program you selected. What type of software is it intended for? (b) What requirements must software meet to receive certification? (c) Who performs the software tests to ensure compliance? (d) As a consumer of software, what additional certification requirements would you like to see? Explain your answer.

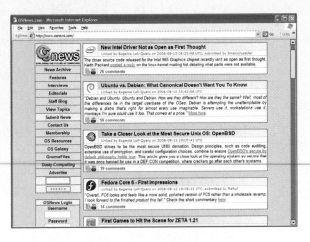

CHAPTER

4

COMPETENCIES

After you have read this chapter, you should be able to:

1 Describe graphics software, including desktop publishing, image editors, illustration programs, image galleries, and graphics suites.

2 Discuss audio and video editing software.

3 Describe multimedia, including story boards and multimedia authoring programs.

4 Explain Web authoring, Web site design, and Web authoring programs.

5 Describe virtual reality and VRML.

6 Discuss knowledge-based (expert) systems.

7 Describe robotics including perception systems, industrial robots, and mobile robots.

Graphics Programs include desktop publishing, image editors, and illustration programs

Video Editing Software reorganizes and adds special effects and music to digitized video

SPECIALIZED APPLICATION SOFTWARE

Introduction

Expect surprises—exciting and positive opportunities. The latest technological developments offer you new opportunities to extend your range of computer competency. As we show in this chapter, software that for years was available only for mainframes has recently become available for microcomputers. This new generation of software, called specialized applications, now makes it possible to perform advanced tasks at home.

The latest technological developments have created an opportunity for home users to take advantage of software previously used only in professional environments. For example, it is now possible, and quite common, for people to create their own Web sites. Home users also have access to software that helps manipulate and create graphic images. Many musicians and artists work from home to create complex and beautiful work using specialized applications.

Some of these same technological advances have allowed researchers and computer scientists to make advances in the field of artificial intelligence that previously were envisioned only in science fiction. Robots now provide security and assistance in homes. Virtual reality is providing opportunities in the fields of medicine and science but also commonly appears in video games.

Competent end users need to be aware of specialized applications. They need to know who uses them, what they are used for, and how they are used. These advanced applications include graphics programs, audio and video editing software, multimedia, Web authoring, and artificial intelligence, including virtual reality, knowledge-based systems, and robotics.

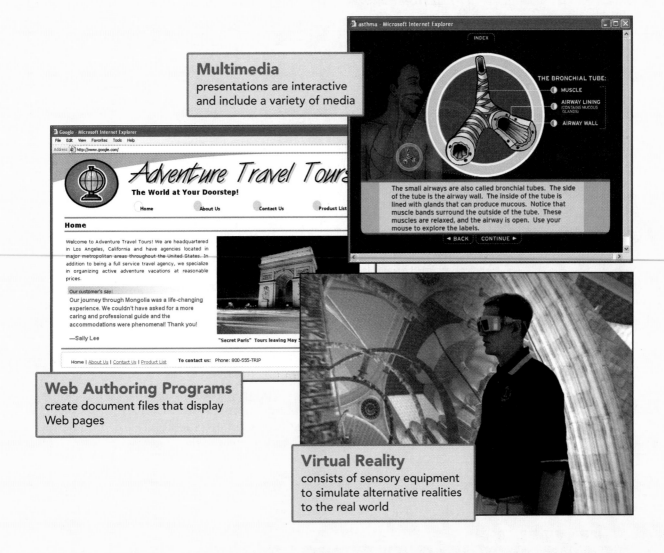

Multimedia
presentations are interactive and include a variety of media

Web Authoring Programs
create document files that display Web pages

Virtual Reality
consists of sensory equipment to simulate alternative realities to the real world

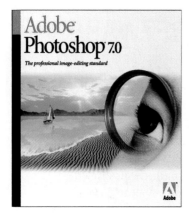

In the previous chapter, we discussed basic applications that are widely used in nearly every profession. This chapter focuses on specialized applications that are widely used within specific professions. (See Figure 4-1.) Specifically, we will examine

- Graphics programs for creating professional-looking published documents, for creating and editing images, and for locating and inserting graphics.
- Audio and video software to create, edit, and play music and videos.
- Multimedia programs to create dynamic interactive presentations.
- Web authoring programs to create, edit, and design Web sites.
- Artificial intelligence, including virtual reality, knowledge-based systems, and robotics.

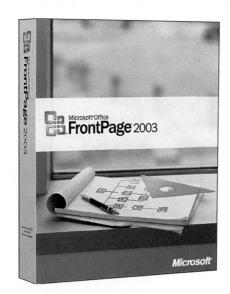

Figure 4–1 Specialized applications

GRAPHICS

In Chapter 3, we discussed analytical and presentation graphics, which are widely used to analyze data and to create professional-looking presentations. Here we focus on more specialized graphics programs used by professionals in the graphic arts profession.

DESKTOP PUBLISHING

Desktop publishing programs, or **page layout programs,** allow you to mix text and graphics to create publications of professional quality. While word processors focus on creating text and have the ability to combine text and graphics, desktop publishers focus on page design and layout and provide greater flexibility. Professional graphic artists use desktop publishing programs to create documents such as brochures, newsletters, newspapers, and textbooks.

Popular desktop publishing programs include Adobe PageMaker, Microsoft Publisher, and QuarkXPress. While these programs provide the capability to create text and graphics, typically graphic artists import these elements from other sources, including word processors, digital cameras, scanners, image editors, illustration programs, and image galleries.

IMAGE EDITORS

One of the most common types of graphic files is bitmap. **Bitmap images,** also known as **raster images,** use thousands of dots or **pixels** to represent images. Each dot has a specific location, color, and shade. One limitation of bitmap images, however, is that when they are expanded, the images can become pixilated, or jagged on the edges. For example, when the letter A in Figure 4-2 is expanded, the borders of the letter appear jagged, as indicated by the expanded view.

Image editors, also known as **photo editors,** are specialized graphics programs for editing or modifying digital photographs. Popular professional image editors include Microsoft Paint, Adobe Photoshop, Corel PhotoPaint, and Paint Shop Pro. (See Figure 4-3.)

Letter A

Expanded view

Figure 4-2 Bitmap image

Figure 4-3 Adobe Photoshop

ILLUSTRATION PROGRAMS

Vector is another common type of graphic file. While bitmap images use pixels to represent images, **vector images,** also known as **vector illustrations,** use geometric shapes or objects. (See Figure 4-4.) These objects are created by connecting lines and curves. Because these objects can be defined by mathematical equations, they can be rapidly and easily resized, colored, textured, and manipulated. An image is a combination of several objects. **Illustration programs,** also known as **drawing programs,** are used to create and edit vector images.

Popular professional illustration programs include Adobe Illustrator, CorelDraw, Macromedia FreeHand, and Micrografx Designer. (See Figure 4-5.)

IMAGE GALLERIES

Image galleries are libraries of electronic images. These images are used for a wide variety of applications from illustrating textbooks to providing visual interest to presentations. There are two basic types of electronic images in these galleries:

- **Stock photographs**—photographs on a variety of subject material from professional models to natural landscapes.
- **Clip art**—graphic illustrations representing a wide range of topics. Most applications provide access to a limited selection of free clip art. For example, in Microsoft Word, you can gain access to several pieces of clip art by issuing the command Insert>Pictures>Clip Art.

There are numerous Web image galleries. (See Figure 4-6.) Some of these sites offer free images and clip art while others charge a fee.

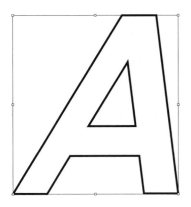

Figure 4-4   Vector image

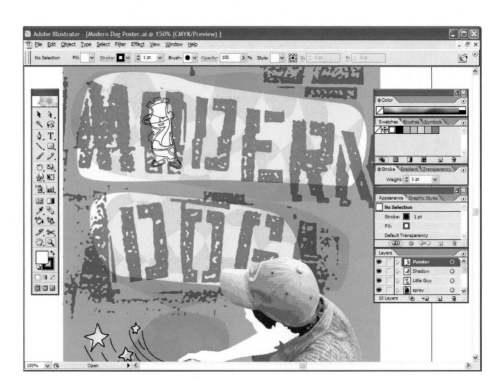

Figure 4-5   Adobe Illustrator

GRAPHICS SUITES

Some companies are combining or bundling their separate graphics programs in groups called **graphics suites.** The advantage of the graphics suites is that you can buy a larger variety of graphics programs at a lower cost than if purchased separately.

One of the most popular suites is from the Corel Corporation. The suite, called CorelDraw Graphics Suite, includes five individual Corel graphics programs plus a large library of clip art, media clips, and fonts. (See Figure 4-7.) Two other popular suites are Adobe's Creative Suites and Macromedia's Studio.

Organization	Site
Classroom Clipart	www.classroomclipart.com
ClipArt.com	www.clipart.com
Free Clip-art	www.free-graphics.com
Graphics Factory	www.graphicsfactory.com
MS Office clip art	office.microsoft.com/clipart

Figure 4-6 Selected Web image galleries

▼ CONCEPT CHECK

▶ What is desktop publishing?

▶ What is the difference between an image editor and an illustration program?

▶ Describe image galleries. What are graphics suites?

Figure 4-7 CorelDraw Graphics Suite

AUDIO AND VIDEO

In the past, professional-quality editing of home audio and video was a job for professional photo labs or studios. For example, if you wanted to assemble footage from all your Fourth of July picnics, you sent all the tapes to a lab and waited for a compilation tape. Now, using audio and video editing software, you can create your own compilation movies.

- **Video editing software** allows you to reorganize, add effects, and more to your digital video footage. Two commonly used video editing software programs are Apple's iMovie and Windows Movie Maker. (See Figure 4-8.) These programs are designed to allow you to assemble and edit new home videos and movies from raw digital video footage. To see how digital video editors work, visit our Web site at www.computing2008. com and enter the keyword video. To learn how to use a digital video editor, see Making IT Work for You: Digital Video Editing on pages 98 and 99.

- **Audio editing software** allows you to create and edit audio clips. Most audio editing software also has features that allow you to add audio effects, like filters, to your tracks. For example, you can use this type of software to filter out pops or scratches in an old recording. You can even use this software to create your own MP3s. Some commonly used audio editing software programs are Apple's GarageBand and Sony's ACID. (See Figure 4-9.)

DIGITAL VIDEO EDITING

Do you want to make your own movie? Would you like to edit some home movies and distribute them to family and friends on DVDs? It's easy with the right equipment and software.

Capturing Video   You can capture video to your computer from a device such as a digital camcorder. Once captured, the video can be edited using digital video editing software. Follow the steps below to capture video from a digital camcorder using Windows Movie Maker.

1 ● Connect the digital camcorder to your computer. The *Video Capture Wizard* starts automatically.

   ● Enter a file name for your captured video and select a location to save it to.

2 ● Follow the on-screen instructions to select a video setting and capture method for your video.

3 ● Preview the video as it is captured from your camera to the file you specified.

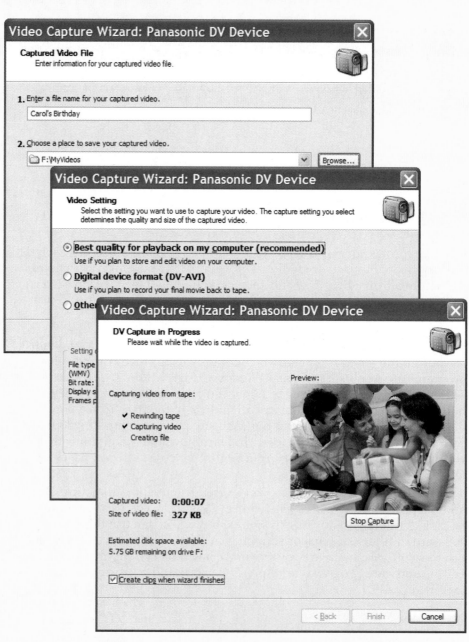

Editing a Movie   Windows Movie Maker divides your captured video into *clips,* or scenes that make up your movie. Follow the steps below to create a movie by arranging clips and adding special effects.

1.
- **Drag movie clips from the Collection Pane and arrange them in the Timeline.**
- **Use the options in the Movie Tasks Pane to add a soundtrack to your movie.**
- **Use the options in the Movie Tasks Pane to add effects, titles, and credits.**
- **Use the Monitor to preview your movie.**

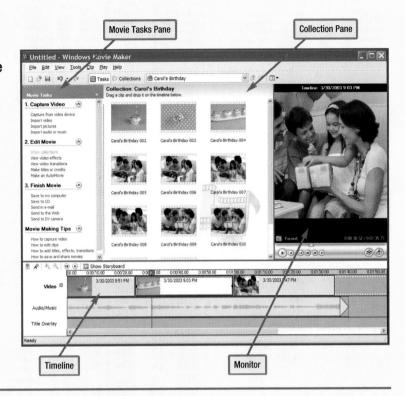

Creating a DVD   Once you have edited your movies, you can create a DVD to share with friends and family. You will need a DVD writer and some special software, such as Sonic MyDVD. Follow the steps below to design a menu, add movies, and create your DVD.

1.
- **Open Sonic MyDVD and select *Create or Modify a DVD-Video Project.***

2.
- **Click the title text to change the title of your DVD menu.**
- **Click *Get Movies* to add your movie files.**
- **Click the Burn button to create your DVD.**

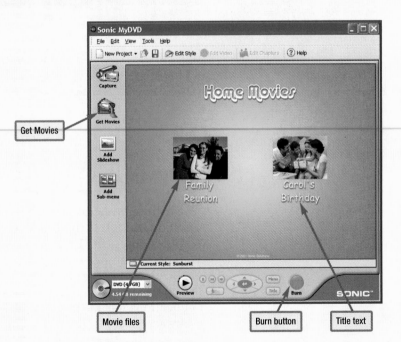

The Web is continually changing, and some of the specifics presented in this Making IT Work for You may have changed. To learn about other ways to make information technology work for you, visit our website at www.computing2008.com and enter the keyword miw.

Figure 4-8 Apple iMovie

Figure 4-9 Apple GarageBand

MULTIMEDIA

Multimedia is the integration of all sorts of media into one presentation. For example, a multimedia presentation may include video, music, voice, graphics, and text. You may have seen multimedia applied in video games, Web presentations, or even a word processing document. Many of the basic application software programs you learned about in Chapter 3 include features that make the incorporation of multimedia in documents easy. Although these applications include multimedia features, they create documents that are generally accessed in a linear fashion and provide very limited user interaction.

Effective multimedia presentations incorporate user participation or interactivity. **Interactivity** allows the user to choose the information to view, to control the pace and flow of information, and to respond to items and receive feedback. When experiencing an interactive multimedia presentation, users customize the presentation to their needs. For example, Figure 4-10 presents an opening page of a multimedia presentation titled "About Asthma." Users are able to select the language to be used and decide whether to include sound.

Once used almost exclusively for computer games, interactive multimedia is now widely used in business, education, and the home. Business uses include high-quality interactive presentations, product demonstrations, and Web page design. In education, interactive multimedia is used for in-class presentations and demonstrations, long-distance learning, and online testing over the Internet. In the home, multimedia is primarily used for entertainment.

LINKS AND BUTTONS

An interactive multimedia presentation is typically organized as a series of related pages. Each page presents information and provides **links,** or connections, to related information. These links can be to video, sound, graphics, and text files, and to other pages and resources. By clicking special areas called **buttons** on a page, you can make appropriate links and navigate through a presentation to locate and discover information. Typically, there are several buttons on a page. You can select one, several, or none of them. You are in control. You direct the flow and content of the presentation. (See Figure 4-11.)

DEVELOPING MULTIMEDIA PRESENTATIONS

To create interactive multimedia presentations, follow these steps: plan and analyze, design, create, and support. Follow the same development process regardless of the complexity and size of the project.

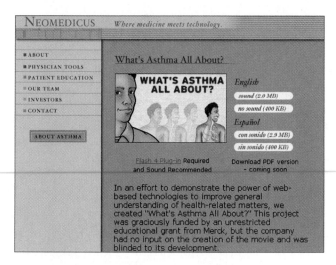

Figure 4-10   Opening page of a multimedia presentation "About Asthma"

Figure 4-11   Links and buttons are used to navigate the "About Asthma" multimedia presentation

On the Web Explorations

A final version of the multimedia presentation "About Asthma" is available on the Web. For a link to this presentation, visit our Web site at www.computing2008.com and enter the keyword asthma.

On the Web Explorations

To learn more about some of the leading companies that develop multimedia authoring programs, visit our Web site at www.computing2008.com and enter the keyword multimedia.

- **Plan and analyze:** Determine the overall objective of the project, the resources required, and the person or team of people who will work on the project.
- **Design:** The creation of a story board is essential to the development of the project. A **story board** is a design tool used to record the intended overall logic, flow, and structure of a multimedia presentation. Figure 4-12 presents a partial overall story board. The highlighted path indicates just one of the many different paths a user could take. Each rectangle represents a single page in the presentation. Each page has a detailed story board associated with it that specifies the content, style, and design along with the links to video, audio, graphics, text, or any other media for that particular page.
- **Create:** Use a multimedia authoring program to create the interactive multimedia presentation. For example, see a selection of pages from "About Asthma" in Figure 4-13. This sequence of pages matches the highlighted story board elements in Figure 4-12 and represents just one possible path through the presentation.
- **Support:** Evaluate effectiveness, identify errors, and revise as needed.

MULTIMEDIA AUTHORING PROGRAMS

Multimedia authoring programs are special programs used to create multimedia presentations. They bring together all the video, audio, graphics, and text elements into an interactive framework. Widely used authoring programs include Macromedia Director, Authorware, and Toolbook.

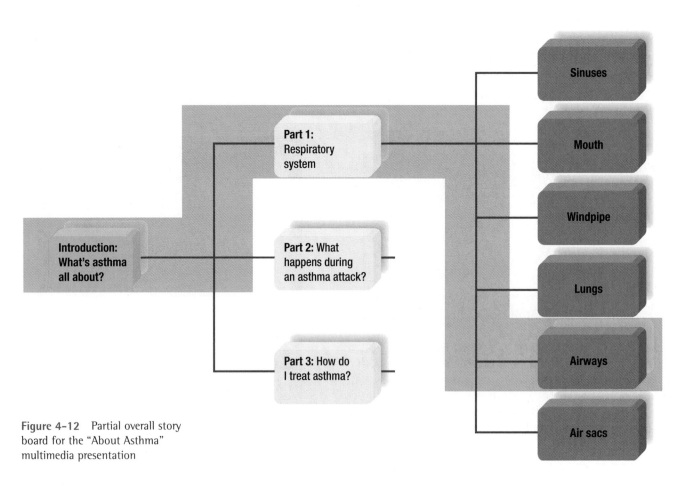

Figure 4-12 Partial overall story board for the "About Asthma" multimedia presentation

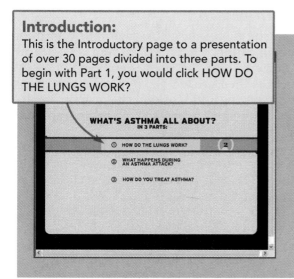

Introduction:
This is the Introductory page to a presentation of over 30 pages divided into three parts. To begin with Part 1, you would click HOW DO THE LUNGS WORK?

WHAT'S ASTHMA ALL ABOUT?
IN 3 PARTS:

① HOW DO THE LUNGS WORK? ②

② WHAT HAPPENS DURING AN ASTHMA ATTACK?

③ HOW DO YOU TREAT ASTHMA?

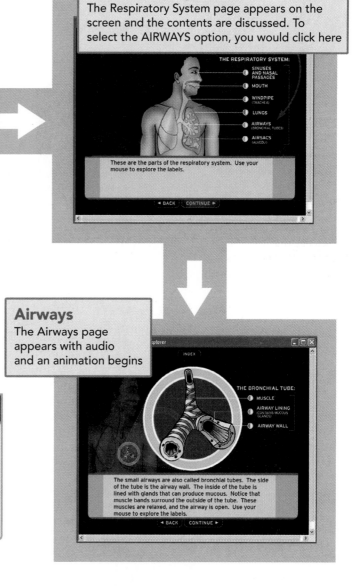

Respiratory System
The Respiratory System page appears on the screen and the contents are discussed. To select the AIRWAYS option, you would click here

THE RESPIRATORY SYSTEM:
SINUSES AND NASAL PASSAGES
MOUTH
WINDPIPE (TRACHEA)
LUNGS
AIRWAYS (BRONCHIAL TUBES)
AIRSACS (ALVEOLI)

These are the parts of the respiratory system. Use your mouse to explore the labels.

◄ BACK   CONTINUE ►

Figure 4-13 One path through the "About Asthma" multimedia presentation

Airways
The Airways page appears with audio and an animation begins

INDEX

THE BRONCHIAL TUBE:
MUSCLE
AIRWAY LINING (CONTAINS MUCOUS GLANDS)
AIRWAY WALL

The small airways are also called bronchial tubes. The side of the tube is the airway wall. The inside of the tube is lined with glands that can produce mucous. Notice that muscle bands surround the outside of the tube. These muscles are relaxed, and the airway is open. Use your mouse to explore the labels.

◄ BACK   CONTINUE ►

▼ CONCEPT CHECK

► What is digital video editing software? What is audio editing software?

► What are multimedia and interactivity? What are multimedia authoring programs?

► Describe the steps to create an interactive multimedia presentation.

WEB AUTHORING

You have probably interacted with a multimedia presentation on a Web site. There are over half a million commercial Web sites on the Internet, and hundreds more are being added every day. Corporations use the Web to reach new customers and to promote their products. (See Figure 4-14.) Many individuals create their own personal sites, called **Web logs** or **blogs,** to keep in touch with friends and family. Creating a site is called **Web authoring.** It begins with site design followed by creation of a document file that displays the Web site's content.

Figure 4-14 Adventure Travel Tours Web site

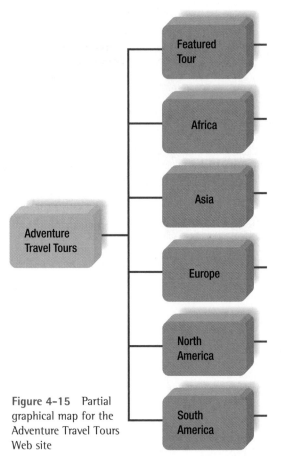

Figure 4-15 Partial graphical map for the Adventure Travel Tours Web site

WEB SITE DESIGN

A Web site is an interactive multimedia form of communication. Designing a Web site begins with determining the site's overall content. The content is then broken down into a series of related pieces of information. The overall site design is commonly represented in a **graphical map.** (See Figure 4-15.)

Notice that the graphical map shown in Figure 4-15 is very similar to the story board depicted in Figure 4-12. In this case, however, each block in the map represents a Web page. Lines joining the blocks represent links to related pages of information that make up the Web site. The first page typically serves as an introduction and supplies a table of contents. The following pages present the specific pieces or blocks of information.

Multimedia elements are added to individual pages to enhance interest and interactivity. One common multimedia element found on most Web sites is moving graphics called **animations.** These animations can be simple moving text or complicated interactive features. There are many specialized programs available to aid in the creation of animation. One type of interactive animation is produced using software from Adobe. This type of animation, called **Flash,** is usually full-screen, highly dynamic, and interactive. Another common visual effect found on the Web is morphing. **Morphing** is a special effect in which one image seems to melt into another.

WEB AUTHORING PROGRAMS

As we mentioned in Chapter 2, Web pages are displayed using HTML documents. With knowledge of HTML and a simple text editor, you can create Web pages. Even without knowledge of HTML, you can create Web pages using a word processing package like Microsoft Word.

More specialized and powerful programs, called **Web authoring programs,** are typically used to create sophisticated commercial sites. Also known as **Web page editors** and **HTML editors,** these programs provide support for Web site design and HTML coding. Widely used Web authoring programs include Macromedia Dreamweaver, NetObjects Fusion, and Microsoft FrontPage. The Web site depicted in Figures 4-14 and 4-15 was created using Microsoft FrontPage. (See Figure 4-16.)

To learn more about creating your own personal Web site, visit us at www.computing2008.com and enter the keyword blog.

▼ CONCEPT CHECK

▶ Describe Web authoring.

▶ What are graphical maps, animation, Flash, and morphing?

▶ What are Web authoring programs?

Graphical Map
FrontPage provides tools to create a graphical map for the entire site. This is part of the site map for the Adventure Travel Tours site

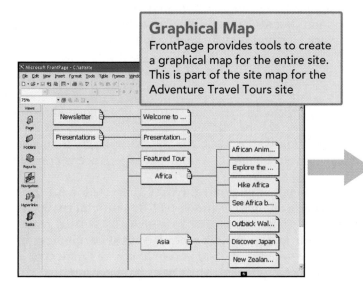

HTML Coding
Using descriptions of each Web page, Microsoft FrontPage creates HTML code for the entire site

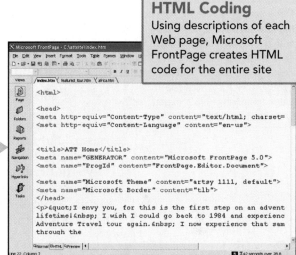

Figure 4-16 Microsoft FrontPage and the Adventure Travel Tours

Web Page
Using a browser, the completed HTML document can be displayed. This is the first page of the Adventure Travel Tours Web site

ARTIFICIAL INTELLIGENCE

The field of computer science known as **artificial intelligence (AI)** attempts to develop computer systems that can mimic or simulate human senses, thought processes, and actions. These include reasoning, learning from past actions, and using senses such as vision and touch. Artificial intelligence that corresponds to human intelligence is still a long way off. However, several tools that emulate human senses, problem solving, and information processing have been developed.

These modern applications of artificial intelligence are designed to help people and organizations become more productive. Many of these tools have practical applications for business, medicine, law, and so on. In the past, computers used calculating power to solve structured problems, which can be broken down into a series of well-defined steps. People—using intuition, reasoning, and memory—were better at solving unstructured problems, whether building a product or approving a loan. Organizations have long been able to computerize the tasks once performed by clerks. Now knowledge-intensive work and unstructured problems, such as activities performed by many managers, are being automated. Let us now consider three areas in which human talents and abilities have been enhanced with "computerized intelligence": virtual reality, knowledge-based systems, and robotics.

VIRTUAL REALITY

Suppose you could create and virtually experience any new form of reality you wished. You could see the world through the eyes of a child, a robot—or even a lobster. You could explore faraway resorts, the moon, or inside a nuclear waste dump without leaving your chair. This simulated experience is possible with virtual reality.

Virtual reality is an artificial, or simulated, reality generated in 3-D by a computer. Virtual reality is also commonly known as **VR, artificial reality,** or **virtual environments.** To navigate in a virtual space, you use virtual reality hardware including headgear and gloves. The headgear has earphones and three-dimensional stereoscopic screens (one type is called Eyephones). The gloves have sensors that collect data about your hand movements (one type is called DataGlove). Coupled with software (such as a program called Body Electric), this interactive sensory equipment lets you immerse yourself in a computer-generated world. See Figure 4-17.

Virtual reality modeling language (VRML) is used to create real-time animated 3-D scenes. Hundreds of sites exist on the Web with virtual reality applications. Users are able to experience these applications with browsers that support VRML.

Creating virtual reality programs once required very-high-end software costing several thousands of dollars. Recently, several lower-cost yet powerful authoring programs have been introduced. These programs utilize VRML and are widely used to create

Figure 4–17 Virtual reality

Web-based virtual reality applications. One of the best known is Cosmo Worlds from Cosmo Software.

There are any number of possible applications for virtual reality. The ultimate recreational use might be something resembling a giant virtual amusement park. More serious applications can simulate important experiences or training environments such as in aviation, surgical operations, spaceship repair, or nuclear disaster cleanup. Modern virtual reality strives to be an **immersive experience,** allowing a user to walk into a virtual reality room or view simulations on a **virtual reality wall.** (See Figure 4-18.)

Figure 4-18 Virtual reality wall

KNOWLEDGE-BASED (EXPERT) SYSTEMS

People who are expert in a particular area—certain kinds of law, medicine, accounting, engineering, and so on—are generally well paid for their specialized knowledge. Unfortunately for their clients and customers, these experts are expensive, not always available, and hard to replace when they move on.

What if you were to somehow capture the knowledge of a human expert and make it accessible to everyone through a computer program? This is exactly what is being done with so-called knowledge-based or expert systems. **Knowledge-based systems,** also known as **expert systems,** are a type of artificial intelligence that uses a database to provide assistance to users. These systems use a database, or **knowledge base,** that contains specific facts, rules to relate these facts, and user input to formulate recommendations and decisions. The sequence of processing is determined by the interaction of the user and the knowledge base. Many expert systems use so-called **fuzzy logic,** which allows users to respond to questions in a very humanlike way. For example, if an expert system asked how your classes were going, you could respond, "great," "OK," "terrible," and so on.

Over the past decade, expert systems have been developed in areas such as medicine, geology, architecture, and nature. There are expert systems with such names as Oil Spill Advisor, Bird Species Identification, and even Midwives Assistant. A system called Grain Marketing Advisor helps farmers select the best way to market their grain.

Figure 4-19 Asimo

ROBOTICS

Robotics is the field of study concerned with developing and using robots. **Robots** are computer-controlled machines that mimic the motor activities of living things. For example, Honda's Asimo robot resembles a human and is capable of walking upstairs, dancing, shaking hands, and much more. (See Figure 4-19.) Some robots can even solve unstructured problems using artificial intelligence.

Robots are used in factories, manufacturing, home security, the military, and many other fields of human endeavor. They differ from other assembly-line machines because they can be reprogrammed to do more than one task. Robots often are used to handle dangerous, repetitive tasks. There are three types of robots.

Specialized Application Software

Figure 4-20   Industrial robot

- **Perception systems: Perception system robots** imitate some of the human senses. For example, robots with television-camera vision systems are particularly useful. They can guide machine tools, inspect products, and secure homes.
- **Industrial robots: Industrial robots** are used to perform a variety of tasks. Examples are machines used in automobile plants to do welding, polishing, and painting. Some types of robots have claws for picking up objects and handling dangerous materials. (See Figure 4-20.)
- **Mobile robots: Mobile robots** act as transports and are widely used for a variety of different tasks. For example, the police and military use them to locate and disarm explosive devices. Mobile robots have entered the world of entertainment with their own television program called *Battlebots*. You can even build your own personal robot using special robot building kits.

▼ CONCEPT CHECK

▶ Define artificial intelligence. What is virtual reality? What is VRML?

▶ Describe knowledge-based systems and fuzzy logic.

▶ Describe three types of robots.

CAREERS IN IT

Desktop publishers use computers to format and create publication-ready material. (See Figure 4-21.) They may create books, magazines, newsletters, and newspapers on home computers using special application software. A large part of the job is designing page layout, importing text, and manipulating graphics. Most desktop publishers work for companies that handle commercial printing accounts. However, there are also many independent contractors.

Desktop publishing positions usually require completion of a program at a vocational school or a university. Internships and part-time work can be a valuable asset to someone pursuing this career. Employers typically look for individuals with good communication skills and artistic ability.

Desktop publishers can expect to earn an annual salary of $25,000 to $42,000. Advancement opportunities include management positions or independent

contracting. To learn about other careers in information technology, visit us at www.computing2008.com and enter the keyword careers.

Figure 4-21   Desktop publisher

Robots Can Look, Act, and Think Like Us

Would you like to voice conference with your mom through robots that both resemble you and demonstrate your emotions on their rubber faces? What if you received a companion robot with a set of moral values? Would you trust a robot to trade the stocks in your portfolio? Researchers are currently at work on robots with the artificial intelligence needed to perform these tasks and more.

The Saya robot, with its artificial skin and muscles, is currently under development in Tokyo. Researchers hope that eventually it will be used as a communication device similar to a current Web cam. For example, you could connect to a robot that resembles you at your mother's house and communicate through it with her. You would see your mother through the robot's visual system. Your mother would hear your voice come from the robot and your emotions would be displayed on its face.

Other research is being conducted that will give robots a sense of values. It is hoped that these robots will be able to make decisions independently based on this set of values. Researchers in California are creating robots that act as surveillance instruments, capable of following a target without direction from a human. The robots can predict potential escape routes and pursue a subject through crowded areas.

At the Sociable Machines Project at MIT, students are working on a robot named Kismet that detects human emotions through social and audio cues and responds with emotions of its own. Kismet recognizes faces and responds to stimuli like an infant would with emotions ranging from surprise to disgust. Researchers believe that robots such as Kismet can interact with and learn from humans better than traditional computer interfaces.

All of these projects are designed to move beyond simple computing and into a decidedly human realm of emotional intelligence. Some experts have even suggested that human intelligence relies on emotional input for all important decision-making. Thus, by definition, for a machine to approximate human intelligence, it would have to understand and rely on emotions. If computers could read human emotions, and had emotional intelligence of their own, it could be possible for your computer to act as a stress counselor when you stay up all night working on a project.

Computers with their own emotional intelligence could be the ultimate human companions. Computer scientists have suggested they may read your mood and play music accordingly. Or they could search through audio and video files for media you would find moving, funny, or dramatic. If computers had their own emotional sense, it is possible that they, like the humans they emulate, would require interaction for mental health.

Would you use a robot as a communication device? Do you think we should build robots with a sense of moral values? Some researchers have suggested that robots with artificial intelligence could serve as ideal supervisors and managers. What do you think? Would you like to have an "emotional" robot for a boss?

SPECIALIZED APPLICATION SOFTWARE

GRAPHICS

Professionals in graphic arts use specialized graphics programs.

Desktop Publishing
Desktop publishing programs (page layout programs) mix text and graphics to create professional publications.

Image Editors
Image editors (photo editors) create and modify **bitmap (raster) image** files. Images are recorded as dots or **pixels.**

Illustration Programs
Illustration programs, also known as **drawing programs,** modify **vector images (vector illustrations).** In a vector file, images are recorded as a collection of objects such as lines, rectangles, and ovals.

Image Galleries
Image galleries are libraries of electronic images, widely available from the Web. Two types are **stock photographs** and **clip art.**

Graphics Suites
A **graphics suite** is a collection of individual graphics programs sold as a unit.

AUDIO AND VIDEO

Recent advances in video and audio technology allow individuals to assemble near-professional-quality video and audio footage.

Video Software
Video editing software allows you to reorganize, add effects, and more to digital video.

Audio Software
Audio editing software allows you to create and edit audio clips. You can add audio effects, like filters, to your tracks. You can create MP3s.

To be a competent end user, you need to be aware of specialized applications. You need to know who uses them, what they are used for, and how they are used. Specialized applications include graphics programs, audio and video editing software, multimedia, Web authoring, and the field of artificial intelligence.

MULTIMEDIA

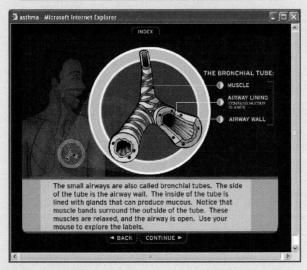

Multimedia integrates all sorts of media, including video, music, voice, graphics, and text, into one presentation. An essential feature is user participation or **interactivity.**

Links and Buttons
A multimedia presentation is organized as a series of related pages. Pages are **linked,** or connected, by clicking **buttons.**

Developing Multimedia Presentations
The creation of multimedia presentations involves four steps:

- **Plan and analyze**—determine objectives, resources required, and project team.
- **Design**—use **story boards** to record the intended overall logic, flow, and structure.
- **Create**—use multimedia authoring programs to create a presentation and integrate various media elements.
- **Support**—identify errors, evaluate effectiveness, and revise as needed.

Multimedia Authoring Programs
Multimedia authoring programs are special programs to create multimedia presentations. They bring together video, audio, graphics, and text elements in an interactive framework.

WEB AUTHORING

Web logs (blogs) are personal Web sites. Creating Web sites is called **Web authoring.** It begins with Web site design, followed by creating a document file that displays the Web site content.

Web Site Design
Web sites are an interactive multimedia form of communication.

Graphical maps use linked blocks to represent a Web site's overall content. Typically, blocks represent individual Web pages and links indicate relationships between related pages.

The first Web page usually introduces the site and supplies a table of contents. Multimedia elements are added to pages. **Animations** are moving graphics. **Flash** is a widely used type of Web animation. **Morphing** is a special effect that seems to melt one image into another.

Web Authoring Programs
Web sites can be created using a simple text editor or word processor. **Web authoring programs,** also known as **Web page editors** or **HTML editors,** are specifically designed to create Web sites. They provide support for Web site design and HTML coding.

Artificial intelligence (AI) attempts to develop computer systems that mimic human senses, thought processes, and actions. Three areas are virtual reality, knowledge-based systems, and robotics.

Virtual Reality

Virtual reality (VR, artificial reality, or **virtual environments)** creates computer-generated simulated environments. It involves the use of interactive sensory equipment, including head gear and gloves. **VRML (virtual reality modeling language)** is used to create or program real-time virtual reality applications.

Applications include recreational and other areas such as aviation, surgical operations, spaceship repair, and nuclear disaster cleanup. Modern applications strive for **immersive experiences** and can be viewed on **virtual reality walls.**

Knowlege-Based (Expert) Systems

Knowledge-based (expert) systems are programs that duplicate the knowledge that humans use to perform specific tasks. **Knowledge bases** are databases containing facts and rules. **Fuzzy logic** allows users to respond to questions in a very humanlike way.

Robotics

Robotics is concerned with developing and using robots. **Robots** are computer-controlled machines that mimic the motor activities of living things. Three types of robots are **perception system, industrial,** and **mobile.**

Desktop publishers use computers to format and create publication-ready material. Vocational or university degree is preferred plus good communication skills and artistic ability. Salary range $25,000 to $42,000.

KEY TERMS

animation   (104)
artificial intelligence (AI)   (106)
artificial reality   (106)
audio editing software   (97)
bitmap image   (95)
blog   (103)
button   (101)
clip art   (96)
desktop publisher   (108)
desktop publishing program   (94)
drawing program   (96)
expert system   (107)
Flash   (104)
fuzzy logic   (107)
graphical map   (104)
graphics suite   (97)
HTML editor   (104)
illustration program   (96)
image editors   (95)
image gallery   (96)
immersive experience   (107)
industrial robot   (108)
interactivity   (101)
knowledge base   (107)
knowledge-based system   (107)
link   (101)
mobile robot   (108)

morphing   (104)
multimedia   (100)
multimedia authoring program   (102)
page layout program   (94)
perception system robot   (108)
photo editors   (95)
pixel   (95)
raster image   (95)
robot   (107)
robotics   (107)
stock photograph   (96)
story board   (102)
vector   (96)
vector illustration   (96)
vector image   (96)
video editing software   (97)
virtual environment   (106)
virtual reality   (106)
virtual reality modeling language (VRML)
   (106)
virtual reality wall   (107)
VR   (106)
Web authoring   (103)
Web authoring program   (104)
Web log   (103)
Web page editor   (104)

To test your knowledge of these key terms with animated flash cards, visit our Web site at www.computing2008.com and enter the keyword terms4.

CROSSWORD PUZZLE

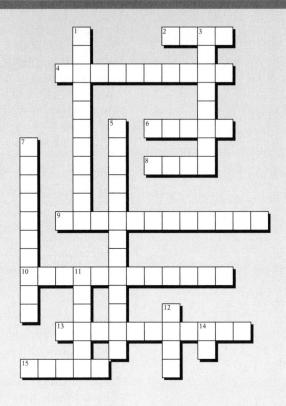

Across

2 Used to create real-time 3D animation.
4 Design tool used to plan multimedia presentations.
6 Editing software used to create MP3s.
8 A type of personal Web site where articles are regularly posted.
9 Creating a site.
10 Representation of overall site design.
13 Image recorded as a collection of objects.
15 Widely used type of Web animation.

Down

1 Composed of thousands of pixels.
3 Special effect that blends images together.
5 User participation.
7 Allows responses like OK and Great.
11 Dots that make up an image.
12 Connection between pages in a multimedia presentation.
14 Attempt to develop computers that mimic human senses.

For an interactive version of this crossword, visit our Web site at www.computing2008.com and enter the keyword **crossword4**.

MULTIPLE CHOICE

Circle the letter or fill in the correct answer.

1. Graphic programs widely used in the graphic arts profession include ____.
   a. desktop publishing programs, image editors, and illustration programs
   b. artificial intelligence, virtual reality, and illustration programs
   c. megamedia programs, image editors, and desktop publishing programs
   d. virtual reality, desktop publishing programs, and illustration programs

2. Image editors are used for creating and editing ____.
   a. bitmap images
   b. vector images
   c. text
   d. HTML codes

3. Programs used to create or modify vector images are called ____.
   a. illustration programs
   b. image editors
   c. graphical modifiers
   d. bit publishing packages

4. Pages in a multimedia presentation typically provide ____ or connections to related information.
   a. blogs
   b. links
   c. logs
   d. maps

5. When determining the overall objective of a multimedia project, the resources required, and the people who will work on the project, you are in the ____ step.
   a. planning
   b. designing
   c. creating
   d. supporting

6. Many individuals create their own personal sites called Web logs, or
   a. flobs
   b. blogs
   c. buds
   d. fellows

7. A special effect in which one image seems to melt into another is referred to as
   a. drifting
   b. flashing
   c. morphing
   d. polling

8. Users can interact in a fully immersed 3-D environment using ____.
   a. unstructured problems
   b. virtual reality
   c. VRML
   d. robotics

9. Fuzzy logic is
   a. used to respond to questions in a humanlike way
   b. a new programming language used to program animation
   c. the result of fuzzy thinking
   d. a term that indicates logical values greater than one

10. Robots used in automobile plants would be classified as
    a. perception system robots
    b. industrial robots
    c. mobile robots
    d. knowledge robots

For an interactive version of these multiple-choice questions, visit our Web site at www.computing2008.com and enter the keyword multiple4.

EXPANDING YOUR KNOWLEDGE

The following questions are designed to add depth and detail to your understanding of specific topics presented within this chapter. The questions direct you to sources other than the textbook to obtain this knowledge.

1   How Digital Video Editing Works

The falling prices of digital camcorders and improvements in computer technology have made digital video editing affordable for individuals. To learn more about digital video editing, visit our Web site at www.computing2008.com and enter the keyword *video*. Then answer the following questions: (a) What hardware is needed to capture video from a VCR tape? Why is this hardware necessary? (b) How can video editing software be used to improve a video? (c) What are some common ways to share videos?

2   Personal Web Site

Would you like a personal Web site but don't want to deal with learning HTML? There are many services available to get you started. To learn more about personal Web sites, visit our Web site at www.computing2008.com and enter the keyword *blog*. Then answer the following questions: (a) What are Web logs? What are they used for? (b) What is Blogger.com? Describe the following features provided by Blogger.com: templates, upload file, hyperlink, post, publish, and view Web page. (c) Have you ever created a Web log or other types of personal Web site? If you have, describe how you created it and what you used it for. If you have not, discuss why and how you might use one.

3   Streaming Multimedia

Many Web sites are now enhanced with streaming multimedia. Some sites offer streaming audio or video to augment text, such as news sites with file footage. For others, the content *is* the streaming multimedia, such as Internet radio or animation sites. Locate several Web sites that offer streaming multimedia and pick one to review. Then answer the following: (a) Define "streaming multimedia." (b) What type of streaming multimedia did the site offer?

Who is the intended audience? (c) In what ways was the experience limited? Be specific.

WRITING ABOUT TECHNOLOGY

The ability to think critically and to write effectively is essential to nearly every profession. The following questions are designed to help you develop these skills by posing thought-provoking questions about computer privacy, security, and/or ethics.

HTML Source Code

1

One way to learn how to create interesting and dynamic Web sites is to examine how professionals create their sites. Once connected to a Web site, you can typically display the HTML source code used to create that site. With Internet Explorer, for example, select Source from the View submenu. Try this out on your own for your favorite Web site and then answer the following questions in a one-page paper: (a) Do you see any ethical issues that relate to examining the HTML code? (b) What about copying parts of the code for your own Web site? (c) What about copying all the code? Defend your answers.

Online Expert Systems

2

Expert systems have been integrated into many Web sites for consumers. For example, health-related Web sites help patients "self-diagnose" illnesses before seeing a physician. Research Web sites that make expert systems available and address the following items in a one-page paper: (a) Define "expert system." (b) What benefits do these expert systems offer the user? (c) Are there ways these systems could be harmful? What responsibilities do users of online expert systems have? (d) What responsibilities do providers of online expert systems have?

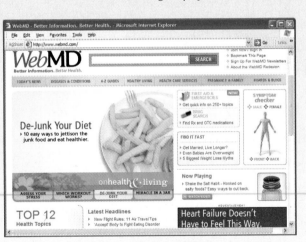

CHAPTER

5

COMPETENCIES

After you have read this chapter, you should be able to:

1   Describe the differences between system software and application software.

2   Discuss the four types of system software.

3   Discuss the basic functions, features, and categories of operating systems.

4   Describe the Windows, Mac OS, UNIX, and Linux operating systems.

5   Describe the purpose of utilities and utility suites.

6   Identify the five most essential utilities.

7   Discuss Windows utility programs.

8   Describe device drivers, including printer drivers.

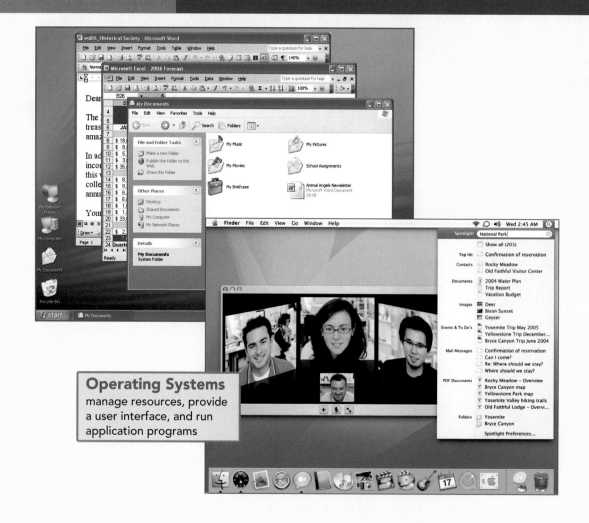

Operating Systems
manage resources, provide a user interface, and run application programs

Introduction

When most people think about computers, they think about surfing the Web, creating reports, analyzing data, storing information, making presentations, and any number of other valuable applications. We typically think about applications and application software. Computers and computer applications have become a part of the fabric of our everyday lives. Most of us agree that they are great . . . as long as they are working.

We usually do not think about the more mundane and behind-the-scenes computer activities: loading and running programs, coordinating networks that share resources, organizing files, protecting our computers from viruses, performing periodic maintenance to avoid problems, and controlling hardware devices so that they can communicate with one another. Typically, these activities go on behind the scenes without our help.

That is the way it should be, and the way it is, as long as everything is working perfectly. But what if new application programs are not compatible and will not run on our current computer system? What if we get a computer virus? What if our hard disk fails? What if we buy a new digital video camera and can't store and edit the images on our computer system? What if our computer starts to run slower and slower?

These issues may seem mundane, but they are critical. This chapter covers the vital activities that go on behind the scenes. A little knowledge about these activities can go a long way to making your computing life easier. To effectively use computers, competent end users need to understand the functionality of system software, including operating systems, utility programs, and device drivers.

Utilities
make computing easier by providing tools to correct problems and to avoid problems

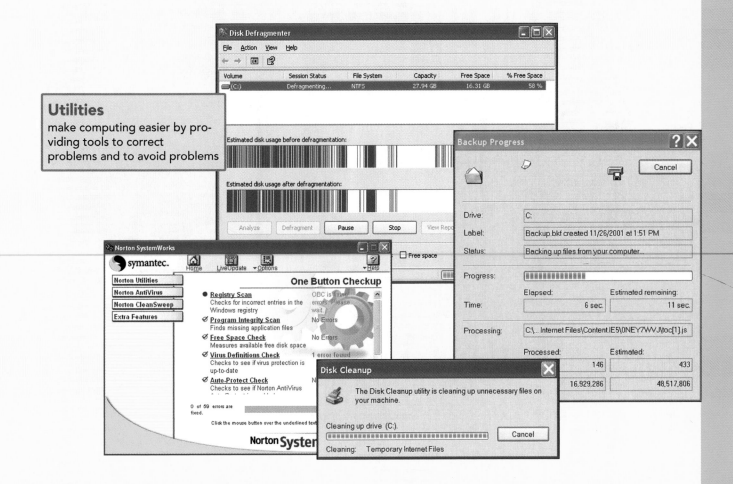

SYSTEM SOFTWARE

End users use application software to accomplish specific tasks. For example, we use word processors to create brochures, letters, and reports. However, end users also use system software. **System software** works with end users, application software, and computer hardware to handle the majority of technical details. For example, system software controls where a word processing program is stored in memory, how commands are converted so that the system unit can process them, and where a completed document or file is saved. See Figure 5-1.

System software is not a single program. Rather it is a collection or a system of programs that handle hundreds of technical details with little or no user intervention. System software consists of four types of programs:

- **Operating systems** coordinate computer resources, provide an interface between users and the computer, and run applications.
- **Utilities** perform specific tasks related to managing computer resources.
- **Device drivers** are specialized programs that allow particular input or output devices to communicate with the rest of the computer system.
- **Language translators** convert the programming instructions written by programmers into a language that computers understand and process.

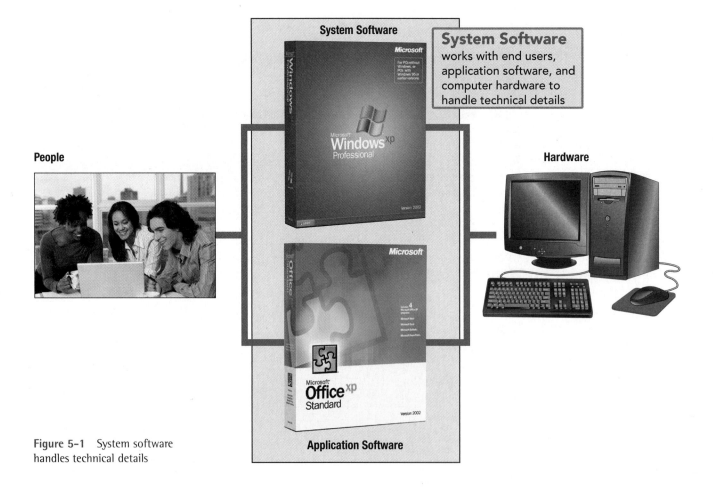

System Software works with end users, application software, and computer hardware to handle technical details

Figure 5-1 System software handles technical details

OPERATING SYSTEMS

An **operating system** is a collection of programs that handle many of the technical details related to using a computer. In many ways, an operating system is the most important type of computer program. Without it your computer would be useless.

FUNCTIONS

Every computer has an operating system and every operating system performs a variety of functions. These functions can be classified into three groups:

- **Managing resources:** These programs coordinate all the computer's resources including memory, processing, storage, and devices such as printers and monitors. They also monitor system performance, schedule jobs, provide security, and start up the computer.

- **Providing user interface:** Users interact with application programs and computer hardware through a **user interface.** Many older operating systems used a character-based interface in which users communicated with the operating system through written commands such as "Copy A: assign.doc to C:". Almost all newer operating systems use a **graphical user interface (GUI).** As we discussed in Chapter 3, a graphical user interface uses graphical elements such as icons and windows.

- **Running applications:** These programs load and run applications such as word processors and spreadsheets. Most operating systems support **multitasking,** or the ability to switch between different applications stored in memory. With multitasking, you could have Word and Excel running at the same time and switch easily between the two applications.

FEATURES

Starting or restarting a computer is called **booting** the system. There are two ways to boot a computer: a warm boot and a cold boot. A **warm boot** occurs when the computer is already on and you restart it without turning off the power. A warm boot can be accomplished in several ways. For example, in Windows XP, a running computer can be restarted by pressing a sequence of keys. Starting a computer that has been turned off is called a **cold boot.** To learn more about booting your computer system and POST, visit our Web site at www.computing2008.com and enter the keyword boot.

You typically interact with the operating system through the graphical user interface. Most provide a place, called the **desktop,** which provides access to computer resources. (See Figure 5-2.) Operating systems have several features in common with application programs, including

- **Icons**—graphic representations for a program or function.
- **Pointer**—controlled by a mouse and changes shape depending upon its current function. For example, when shaped like an arrow, the pointer can be used to select items such as an icon.
- **Windows**—rectangular areas for displaying information and running programs.
- **Menus**—provide a list of options or commands.
- **Dialog boxes**—provide information or request input.
- **Help**—provides online assistance for operating system functions and procedures.

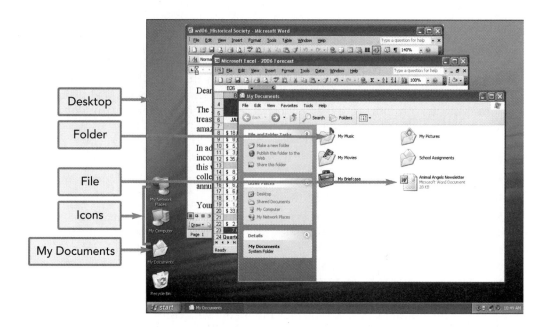

Figure 5-2   Desktop

Most operating systems store data and programs in a system of files and folders. Unlike the traditional filing cabinet, computer files and folders are stored on a secondary storage device such as your hard disk. **Files** are used to store data and programs. Related files are stored within a **folder,** and for organizational purposes, a folder can contain other folders. For example, you might organize your electronic files in the *My Documents* folder on your hard disk. This folder could contain other folders, each named to indicate their contents. One might be "Computers" and could contain all the files you have created (or will create) for this course.

CATEGORIES

While there are hundreds of different operating systems, there are only three basic categories: embedded, network, or stand-alone.

Figure 5-3   PDAs have embedded operating systems

- **Embedded operating systems** are used for handheld computers and smaller devices like PDAs. (See Figure 5-3.) The entire operating system is stored within or embedded in the device. The operating system programs are permanently stored on ROM, or read-only memory, chips. Popular embedded operating systems include Windows CE and windows XP Embedded.

- **Network operating systems (NOS)** are used to control and coordinate computers that are networked or linked together. Many networks are small and connect only a limited number of microcomputers. Other networks, like those at colleges and universities, are very large and complex. These networks may include other smaller networks and typically connect a variety of different types of computers.

  Network operating systems are typically located on one of the connected computers' hard disks. Called the **network server,** this computer coordinates all communication between the other computers. Popular network operating systems include NetWare, Windows NT Server, Windows XP Server, and UNIX.

- **Stand-alone operating systems,** also called **desktop operating systems,** control a single desktop or notebook computer. (See Figure 5-4.) These operating systems are located on the computer's hard disk. Often desktop

Windows operating system

Figure 5-4 Stand-alone operating system

computers and notebooks are part of a network. In these cases, the desktop operating system works with the network's NOS to share and coordinate resources. In these situations, the desktop operating system is referred to as the *client operating system*. Popular desktop operating systems include Windows, Mac OS, and some versions of UNIX.

The operating system is often referred to as the **software environment** or **platform.** Almost all application programs are designed to run with a specific platform. For example, the standard version of AppleWorks is designed to run with the Mac OS environment. There are many different types of operating systems. Windows, Mac OS, and Linux are operating systems commonly used by individuals.

▼ CONCEPT CHECK

▶ What is system software? What are the four kinds of system software programs?

▶ What is an operating system? Discuss operating system functions and features.

▶ Describe each of the three categories of operating systems.

WINDOWS

Microsoft's **Windows** is by far the most popular microcomputer operating system today with over 90 percent of the market. Because its market share is so large, more application programs are developed to run under Windows than any other operating system. Windows comes in a variety of different versions and is designed to run with Intel and Intel-compatible microprocessors such as the Pentium IV. For a summary of Microsoft's desktop operating systems, see Figure 5-5.

The most widely used version of Windows, **Windows XP,** was introduced in 2001. The next major version, **Windows Vista,** is scheduled to be released in 2007. (See Figure 5-6.) Compared to Windows XP, Windows Vista promises to provide several improvements:

• Advanced system security to guard against malicious files and programs, including spyware.

Name	Description
Windows NT Workstation	Client operating system designed to work with the Windows NT Server
Windows 98	Stand-alone operating system
Windows 2000 Professional	Upgrade to Windows NT Workstation
Windows ME	Upgrade to Windows 98 specifically designed for home users
Windows XP	Upgrade to Windows 2000 with improved interface, stability, and reliability
Windows Vista	Microsoft's newest operating system with improved security, three-dimensional workspace, and filtering capabilities.

Figure 5-5 Microsoft desktop operating systems

- Three-dimensional workspace capable of displaying transparent cascading windows.
- Filtering capabilities to provide convenient parentel controls by blocking access of objectionable Web sites.

Figure 5-6 Windows Vista

MAC OS

Macintosh introduced its first operating system and microcomputer in 1984. It provided one of the first GUIs, making it easy even for novice computer users to move and delete files. Designed to run with Apple computers, **Mac OS** is not nearly as widely used as the Windows operating system. As a result, fewer application programs have been written for it. Nonetheless, Mac OS is considered to be one of the most innovative operating systems. It is a powerful, easy-to-use operating system that is popular with professional graphic designers, desktop publishers, and many home users.

One of the latest versions of the Macintosh operating system is **Mac OS X,** also known as **Tiger.** This operating system provides a wide array of powerful features including Spotlight and Dashboard Widgets. **Spotlight** is an advanced search tool that can rapidly locate files, folders, e-mail messages, addresses, and much more. **Dashboard Widgets** are a collection of specialized programs that will constantly update and display information. (See Figure 5-7.) The next version of Mac OS, **Leopard** includes **Boot Camp**, which allows appropriately equipped Apple computers to use both Mac OS and Windows XP.

Figure 5-7 Mac OS X

UNIX AND LINUX

The **UNIX** operating system was originally designed to run on minicomputers in network environments. Now, it is also used by powerful microcomputers and by servers on the Web. There are a large number of different versions of UNIX. One receiving a great deal of attention today is **Linux.**

Linux was originally developed by a graduate student at the University of Helsinki, Linus Torvalds, in 1991. He allowed free distribution of the operating system code and encouraged others to modify and further develop the code. Linux is one of the most popular and powerful alternatives to the Windows operating system. (See Figure 5-8.)

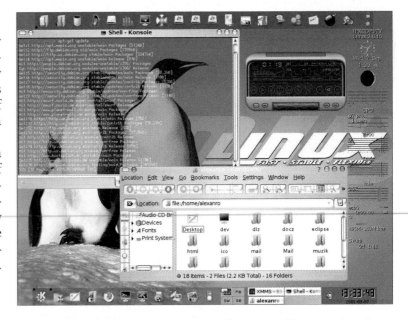

Figure 5-8 Recent version of Linux

▼ CONCEPT CHECK

▶ What is Windows? What is Windows XP? What is Windows Vista?

▶ What is Mac OS? What is Tiger? Spotlight? Dashboard Widgets? Boot Camp?

▶ What is UNIX? What is Linux?

System Software

Ideally, microcomputers continuously run without problems. However, that simply is not the case. All kinds of things can happen—internal hard disks can crash, computers can freeze up, operations can slow down, and so on. These events can make computing very frustrating. That's where utilities come in. **Utilities** are specialized programs designed to make computing easier. There are hundreds of different utility programs. The most essential are

- **Troubleshooting** or **diagnostic programs** that recognize and correct problems, ideally before they become serious.

- **Antivirus programs** that guard your computer system against viruses or other damaging programs that can invade your computer system.

- **Uninstall programs** that allow you to safely and completely remove unneeded programs and related files from your hard disk.

- **Backup programs** that make copies of files to be used in case the originals are lost or damaged.

- **File compression programs** that reduce the size of files so they require less storage space and can be sent more efficiently over the Internet.

Most operating systems provide some utility programs. Even more powerful utility programs can be purchased separately or in utility suites.

WINDOWS UTILITIES

The Windows operating systems are accompanied by several utility programs, including Backup, Disk CleanUp, and Disk Defragmenter. These utilities can be accessed from the System Tools menu. (See Figure 5-9.)

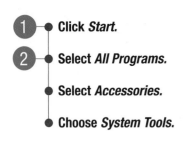

1. Click *Start.*
2. Select *All Programs.*
   - Select *Accessories.*
   - Choose *System Tools.*

Figure 5-9 Accessing Windows XP utilities

Backup is a utility program included with the many versions of Windows that makes a copy of all files or selected files that have been saved onto a disk. It helps to protect you from the effects of a disk failure. For example, using the Professional edition of XP, you can select Backup from the Windows XP System Tools menu to create a backup for your hard disk as shown in Figure 5-10. (While most versions of XP include the Backup utility, the XP Home edition does not.)

When you surf the Web, a variety of programs and files are saved on your hard disk. Many of these and other files are not essential. **Disk Cleanup** is a troubleshooting utility that identifies and eliminates nonessential files. This frees up valuable disk space and improves system performance.

1 ● Click *Start.*

● Select *Accessories* from the *All Programs* menu.

● Select *Backup* from the *System Tools* menu.

2 ● Run the Backup or Restore Wizard and specify your settings.

● Choose *Backup* and choose the files you want to include.

● Choose the destination for the backup.

3 ● Finish the Backup or Restore Wizard to back up the selected drive.

● Close the *Backup Progress* window or view the report.

Figure 5-10   Backup utility

including by opening attachments to e-mail messages and downloading software from the Internet. (We will discuss computer viruses in detail in Chapter 10.)

To learn more about virus protection, visit our Web site at www.computing 2008.com and enter the keyword virus. Also see Making IT Work for You: Virus Protection and Internet Security on pages 134 and 135.

Norton SystemWorks is one of the most widely used utility suites. It includes the following:

- **Norton AntiVirus** is a collection of antivirus programs that can protect your system from over 21,000 different viruses, quarantine or delete existing viruses, and automatically update its virus list to check for the newest viruses.
- **Norton CleanSweep** is a collection of programs that guide you through the process of safely removing programs and files you no longer need. Additionally, they will archive, move, and make backups of programs as well as clean up your hard disk. They also can protect your existing files from damage when you install new programs.
- **Web CleanUp** is a collection of programs that check your computer system for unnecessary files, including temporary files created by application programs, cache files, history files, and cookies. You can then eliminate these files with a click of a button.
- **GoBack Personal Edition** will restore system configurations, help to locate lost files, and repair damaged files.
- **Norton Utilities** is a collection of several separate troubleshooting utilities. These programs can be used to find and fix problems, improve system performance, prevent problems from occurring, and troubleshoot a variety of other problems. One of the programs, **One Button Checkup,** integrates several of the separate troubleshooting utilities. (See Figure 5-14.)

On the Web Explorations

Utility software can make your computer faster, safer, and more productive. To learn more about a market leader of utility software, visit our Web site at www. computing2008.com and enter the keyword utility.

▼ CONCEPT CHECK

▶ What is the difference between a utility and a utility suite?

▶ Describe Backup, Disk Cleanup, and Disk Defragmenter.

▶ What is a computer virus? How can you protect yourself against them?

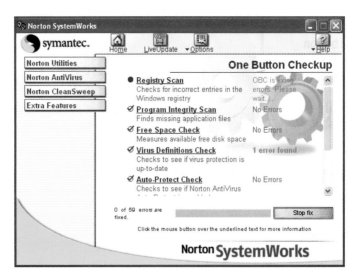

Figure 5-14 Norton SystemWorks' One Button Checkup

Every device, such as a mouse or printer, that is connected to a computer system has a special program associated with it. This program, called a **device driver** or simply a **driver,** works with the operating system to allow communication between the device and the rest of the computer system. Each time the computer system is started, the operating system loads all of the device drivers into memory.

Whenever a new device is added to a computer system, a new device driver must be installed before the device can be used. Windows supplies hundreds of different device drivers with its system software. For many devices, the appropriate drivers are automatically selected and installed when the device is first connected to the computer system. For others, the device driver must be manually installed. Fortunately, Windows provides wizards to assist in this process. For example, Windows' **Add Printer Wizard** provides step-by-step guidance for selecting the appropriate printer driver and installing that driver. (See Figure 5-15.) If a particular device driver is not included with the Windows system software, the product's manufacturer will supply one. Many times these drivers are available directly from the manufacturer's Web site.

You probably never think about the device drivers in your computer. However, when your computer behaves unpredictably, you may find reinstalling or updating your device drivers solves your problems. Windows makes it easy to update the drivers on your computer using **Windows Update,** as shown in Figure 5-16.

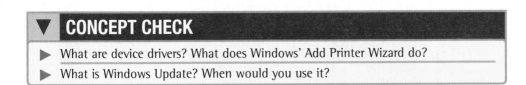

▼ CONCEPT CHECK

▶ What are device drivers? What does Windows' Add Printer Wizard do?

▶ What is Windows Update? When would you use it?

To access the Add Printer Wizard

- Select *Control Panel* from the *Start* menu.

- Click *Printers and faxes.*

- Click *Add a printer.*

Figure 5-15 Add Printer Wizard

VIRUS PROTECTION AND INTERNET SECURITY

Are you worried that a computer virus will erase your personal files? Did you know that others could be intercepting your private e-mail? It is even possible for others to gain access to and control over your computer system. Fortunately, Internet security suites are available to help ensure your safety while you are on the Internet.

Getting Started   The first step is to install an Internet security suite. Once installed, the software will continually work to ensure security and privacy. For example, to install McAfee Internet Security Suite follow the instructions below.

1 ● **Connect to *www.mcafee.com* and follow the on-screen instructions to subscribe to this Internet security suite.**

2 ● **The security suite is downloaded and installed to your computer directly from the Web site.**

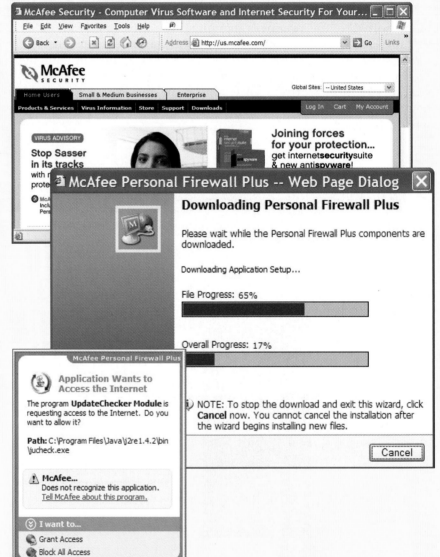

Once installed, the security suite will automatically be activated each time you start your computer. An alert similar to the one on the right is displayed when any privacy or security vulnerabilities are detected.

Internet Security Suite Internet Security Suite runs a number of programs continually to monitor your computer. Some of Internet Security Suite's most powerful programs include VirusScan, PersonalFirewall, and PrivacyService. You can modify the way these programs run with the McAfee SecurityCenter.

VirusScan controls how frequently the computer system is searched for computer viruses. When a file is checked, it is compared to the profile of known viruses. Once a virus is detected, the infected file is quarantined or deleted.

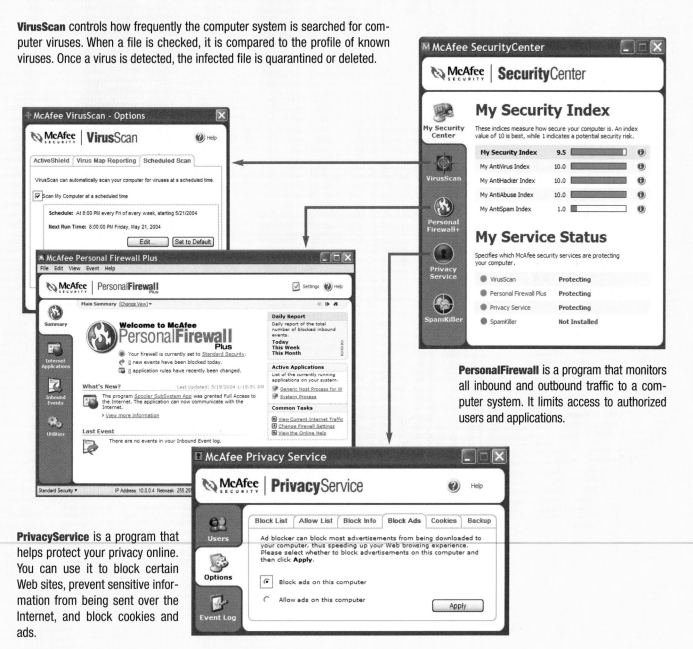

PersonalFirewall is a program that monitors all inbound and outbound traffic to a computer system. It limits access to authorized users and applications.

PrivacyService is a program that helps protect your privacy online. You can use it to block certain Web sites, prevent sensitive information from being sent over the Internet, and block cookies and ads.

The Web is continually changing, and some of the specifics presented in this Making IT Work for You may have changed. To learn about other ways to make information technology work for you, visit our Web site at www.computing2008.com and enter the keyword miw.

1 ● Access *Windows Update* from the *All Programs* list of the *Start* menu.

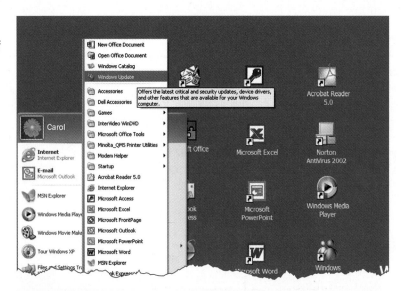

2 ● Click *Scan for updates.*

● Click *Driver Updates.*

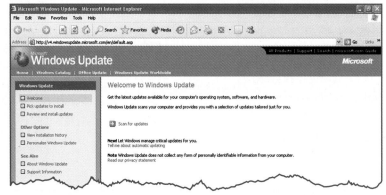

3 ● Click *Add.*

● Click *Review and Install Drivers.*

● Click *Install Now* and *Accept* the license agreement.

● Click *OK* to restart the computer.

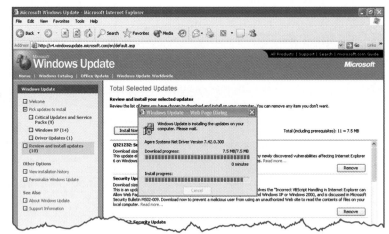

Figure 5-16   Using Windows Update

Computer support specialists provide technical support to customers and other users. (See Figure 5.17.) They also may be called technical support specialists or help-desk technicians. Computer support specialists manage the everyday technical problems faced by computer users. They resolve common networking problems and may use troubleshooting programs to diagnose problems. Most computer support specialists are hired to work within a company and provide technical support for other employees and divisions. However, it is increasingly common for companies to provide technical support as an outsourced service.

Employers generally look for individuals with a bachelor's degree to fill computer support specialist positions. Degrees in computer science or information systems may be preferred. However, because demand for qualified applicants is so high, those with practical experience and certification from a training program increasingly fill these positions. Employers seek individuals with good analytical and communication skills. Those with good people skills and customer service experience have an advantage in this field.

Figure 5-17   Computer support specialists

Computer support specialists can expect to earn an annual salary of $31,000 to $53,000. Opportunities for advancement are very good and may involve design and implementation of new systems. Some computer support specialists become software engineers. To learn about other careers in information systems, visit us at www.computing2008.com and enter the keyword careers.

A Look to the Future

Self-Healing Computers Could Mean an End to Computer Crashes and Performance Problems

Wouldn't it be nice if computers could fix themselves? What if you never had to worry about installing or updating software? What if your computer could continually fine-tune its operations to maintain peak performance? What if your computer could fight off viruses and malicious attacks from outsiders? For many people, this sounds too good to be true. Maintenance and security tasks like these can be time-consuming and frustrating.

Now imagine you run a business and unless these tasks are performed, you will lose valuable time and money. It is not a pleasant daydream and it quickly becomes a nightmare without properly trained systems administrators to keep servers running smoothly. Yet many experts predict that supercomputers and business systems are not far from becoming too complex for humans to oversee. Recent news from IBM makes the dream of a self-repairing, self-updating, and self-protecting server seem ever closer.

IBM has announced plans to concentrate research efforts on developing just such a server. The project, called the Autonomic Computing Initiative (ACI), hopes to free businesses from the time-consuming maintenance and the complexity of business infrastructure. IBM hopes the new system will be self-regulating and virtually invisible. They believe ACI has the potential to revolutionize the way businesses run.

Autonomic computing is a system that allows machines to run with little human intervention. Such computers would not have self-awareness, but rather would be self-correcting. Autonomic processes in machines are modeled after autonomic processes in the human body. For example, you are not consciously breathing as you read this. Instead, your body monitors and maintains your respiration without your constant input. Scientists hope autonomic computing will behave in a similar manner and maintain self-regulating systems without intervention.

Autonomic machines would be able to sense security flaws and repair them. They would be able to sense slow operations' programs and take corrective action. They would be able to sense new equipment, format it, and test it. These goals are impressive and the autonomic computer is still in development.

As technology continues to develop, many computer systems have become too complex for human maintenance. This progress makes autonomic computing more valuable now than ever. However, it is important to note that autonomic computing is not artificial intelligence, because autonomic machines do not have human cognitive abilities or intelligence. Instead, these machines have knowledge of their own systems and the capability to learn from experiences to correct errors in such systems.

Given the potential for a self-maintaining server, the possibility of a similar system designed for a microcomputer seems less like a dream and more like a reality. What do you think—will microcomputers someday care for themselves?

SYSTEM SOFTWARE

SYSTEM SOFTWARE

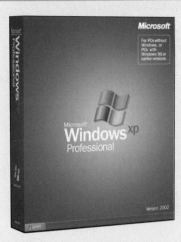

System software works with end users, application programs, and computer hardware to handle many details relating to computer operations.

Not a single program but a collection or system of programs, these programs handle hundreds of technical details with little or no user intervention.

Four kinds of systems programs are operating systems, utilities, device drivers, and language translators.

- **Operating systems** coordinate resources, provide an interface between users and the computer, and run programs.
- **Utilities** perform specific tasks related to managing computer resources.
- **Device drivers** allow particular input or output devices to communicate with the rest of the computer system.
- **Language translators** convert programming instructions written by programmers into a language that computers can understand and process.

OPERATING SYSTEMS

Operating systems (software environments, platforms) handle technical details.

Functions

Functions include managing resources, providing a **user interface** (most newer operating systems use a **graphical user interface,** or **GUI**), and running applications (**multitasking** allows switching between different applications stored in memory).

Features

Booting starts (**cold**) or restarts (**warm**) a computer system. The **desktop** provides access to computer resources. Common features include **icons, pointers, windows, menus, dialog boxes,** and **Help.** Data and programs are stored in a system of **files** and **folders.**

Categories

Three categories of operating systems are

- **Embedded**—used with handheld computers; operating system stored within device.
- **Network (NOS)**—controls and coordinates networked computers; located on the **network server.**
- **Stand-alone (desktop)**—controls a single computer; located on the hard disk.

Operating systems are often called **software environments** or **platforms.**

To effectively use computers, competent end users need to understand the functionality of system software, including operating systems, utility programs, and device drivers.

OPERATING SYSTEMS

Windows

Windows is the most widely used operating system with over 90 percent of the market. It is designed to run with Intel and Intel-compatible microprocessors. There are numerous versions of Windows. **Windows XP** is the most widely used. **Windows Vista** is the next major version of Windows. It promises advanced system security, a three-dimensional workspace, and filtering capability.

Mac OS

Mac OS is an innovative, powerful, easy-to-use operating system; designed to run with Macintosh computers. One of the latest versions, **Tiger,** has many powerful features including **Spotlight,** an advanced search tool, and **Dashboard Widgets,** a collection of specialized programs. The next version is **Leopard,** with **Boot Camp,** which allows appropriately equipped Apple computers to run both Mac OS and Windows XP.

UNIX and Linux

UNIX was originally designed to run on minicomputers in network environments. Now, it is used by powerful microcomputers and servers on the Web. There are many different versions of UNIX. One version, **Linux,** is one of the most popular and powerful alternatives to the Windows operating system.

UTILITIES

Utilities make computing easier. The most essential are **troubleshooting (diagnostic), antivirus, uninstall, backup,** and **file compression.**

Windows Utilities

Several utility programs are accessible from the System Tools menu including **Backup, Disk Cleanup,** and **Disk Defragmenter** (eliminates unnecessary **fragments; tracks** are concentric rings; **sectors** are wedge-shaped).

Utility Suites

Utility suites combine several programs into one package. Computer **viruses** are dangerous programs. **One Button Checkup** integrates several Norton utilities.

DEVICE DRIVERS

Device drivers (drivers) allow communication between hardware devices. **Add Printer Wizard** gives step-by-step guidance to install printer drivers. **Windows Update** automates the process of updating device drivers.

CAREERS IN IT

Computer support specialists provide technical support to customers and other users. Degrees in computer science or information systems preferred plus good analytical and communication skills. Salary range $31,000 to $53,000.

KEY TERMS

Add Printer Wizard   (133)
antivirus program   (128)
Backup   (129)
backup program   (128)
Boot Camp   (127)
booting   (123)
cold boot   (123)
computer support specialist   (137)
Dashboard Widgets   (127)
desktop   (123)
desktop operating system   (124)
device driver   (122, 133)
diagnostic program   (128)
dialog box   (123)
Disk Cleanup   (129)
Disk Defragmenter   (131)
driver   (133)
embedded operating systems   (124)
file   (124)
file compression program   (128)
folder   (124)
fragmented   (130)
graphical user interface (GUI)   (123)
Help   (123)
icon   (123)
language translator   (122)
Leopard   (127)
Linux   (127)
Mac OS   (127)

Mac OS X   (127)
menu   (123)
multitasking   (123)
network operating systems (NOS)   (124)
network server   (124)
One Button Checkup   (132)
operating system   (122, 123)
platform   (125)
pointer   (123)
sectors   (130)
software environment   (125)
Spotlight   (127)
stand-alone operating system   (124)
system software   (122)
Tiger   (127)
tracks   (130)
troubleshooting program   (128)
uninstall program   (128)
UNIX   (127)
user interface   (123)
utility   (122, 128)
utility suite   (131)
virus   (131)
warm boot   (123)
window   (123)
Windows   (125)
Windows Update   (133)
Windows Vista   (125)
Windows XP   (125)

FEATURES

Animations

Careers in IT

DVD Direct

Expansions

Making IT Work for You

On the Web Explorations

TechTV

Tips

CHAPTER REVIEW

Applying Technology

Crossword Puzzle

Expanding Your Knowledge

Key Terms

Matching

Multiple Choice

Open-Ended

Writing About Technology

To test your knowledge of these key terms with animated flash cards, visit our Web site at www.computing2008.com and enter the keyword **terms5**.

CROSSWORD PUZZLE

www.computing2008.com

Across

5 Program that makes copies of files in case of damage or loss.

6 Boot that occurs when the computer is already on.

8 Combination of several utility programs in one package.

9 Allows communication between devices and the operating system.

11 Concentric rings on a disk.

12 Used to control and coordinate networked computers.

Down

1 Location to store related files.

2 Computer that coordinates all communication between other computers.

3 Uses graphical elements to communicate with the operating system.

4 Broken-up file stored in different sectors.

5 Starting or restarting a computer.

7 Operating system with over 80 percent of the market.

10 Graphic objects on the desktop used to represent programs and other files.

For an interactive version of this crossword, visit our Web site at www.computing2008.com and enter the keyword **crossword5**.

MULTIPLE CHOICE

Circle the letter or fill in the correct answer.

1. Software that allows your computer to interact with the user, applications, and hardware is called
   a. application software
   b. word processor
   c. system software
   d. database software

2. In order for a computer to understand a program, it must be converted into machine language by a(n) ____.
   a. operating system
   b. utility
   c. device driver
   d. language translator

3. "GUI" stands for
   a. gnutella universal interface
   b. graphic uninstall/install
   c. graphical user interface
   d. general utility interface

4. To connect several computers together, one generally needs to be running a(n) ____ operating system.
   a. network
   b. Internet
   c. stand-alone
   d. embedded

5. _____ is the most widely used operating system.
   a. Windows
   b. Mac OS
   c. UNIX
   d. Linux

6. This operating system is most popular with graphic designers and those who work in multimedia.
   a. Windows XP
   b. Linux
   c. Mac OS
   d. UNIX

7. This operating system was originally designed to run on minicomputers used in a network environment.
   a. Linux
   b. UNIX
   c. Windows
   d. Mac OS

8. These programs guard your computer against malicious programs that may invade your computer system.
   a. file compression program
   b. antivirus program
   c. backup program
   d. troubleshooting program

9. A concentric ring on a hard disk is referred to as a
   a. track
   b. sector
   c. table
   d. segment

10. Every time the computer system is started, the operating system loads these into memory.
    a. driver updates
    b. device managers
    c. device drivers
    d. Windows updates

For an interactive version of these multiple-choice questions, visit our Web site at www.computing2008.com and enter the keyword **multiple5**.

MATCHING

Match each numbered item with the most closely related lettered item. Write your answers in the spaces provided.

a. desktop OS

b. embedded OS

c. file compression program

d. Leopard

e. Linux

f. multitasking

g. NOS

h. platform

i. system software

j. track

1. Concentric ring on a disk.____

2. A version of Mac Os X.____

3. A computer's ability to run more than one application at a time.____

4. Operating systems completely stored within ROM.____

5. Operating system used to control and coordinate computers that are linked together.____

6. Another name for software environment.____

7. An operating system located on a single stand-alone hard disk.____

8. One popular, and free, version of the UNIX operating system.____

9. Collection of programs that handle technical details.____

10. Program that reduces the size of files for efficient storage.____

For an interactive version of this matching exercise, visit our Web site at www.computing2008.com and enter the keyword **matching5**.

OPEN-ENDED

On a separate sheet of paper, respond to each question or statement.

1. Describe system software. What are the four types of system programs?

2. What are the basic functions of every operating system? What are the three basic operating system categories?

3. Explain the differences and similarities between Windows, Mac OS, and Linux.

4. Discuss utilities. What are the five most essential utilities? What is a utility suite?

5. Explain the role of device drivers. Discuss the Add Printer Wizard and Windows Update.

APPLYING TECHNOLOGY

The following questions are designed to demonstrate ways that you can effectively use technology today. The first question relates directly to this chapter's Making IT Work for You feature.

Virus Protection 1

Worried about computer viruses? Did you know that others could be intercepting your private e-mail? It is even possible for them to gain access and control over your computer systems. Fortunately, Internet security suites are available to help ensure your safety while you are on the Internet. To learn more about virus protection, review Making IT Work for You: Virus Protection and Internet Security on pages 134 and 135. Then answer the following questions: (a) What are viruses? What are Internet security suites? What do they do? (b) Have you ever experienced a computer virus? If you have, describe the virus, how you got it, and what you did to get rid of it. If you have not, have you taken any special precautions? Discuss the precautions. Do you think it's possible that you may have one now and not know it, or do you think that you have just been lucky? (c) What is a personal firewall? What does it do?

Windows Update 2

Windows Update is a utility built into Windows that monitors and controls the process of keeping the computer up to date. Connect to our Web site at www.computing2008.com and enter the keyword update to link to the Windows Update Web site. Read the information about Windows Update. Then answer the following questions: (a) How does Windows Update work? (b) How does a user know when he or she requires an update? (c) What is the process for initiating an update using Windows Update? (d) In what ways can Windows Update be automated?

WinZip 3

WinZip is one of the most popular file compression utilities available. Visit our Web site at www.computing2008.com and enter the keyword winzip for a link to the WinZip Web site. Once there, read about this utility, and then answer the following: (a) What is WinZip? What does it do? (b) What is a Zip file? (c) List the most common uses for Zip files. (d) Describe in detail the procedure for creating a Zip file with WinZip.

EXPANDING YOUR KNOWLEDGE

www.computing2008.com

The following questions are designed to add depth and detail to your understanding of specific topics presented within this chapter. The questions direct you to sources other than the textbook to obtain this knowledge.

1   How Virus Protection Programs Work

Computer viruses are destructive and dangerous programs that can migrate through networks and operating systems. They often attach themselves to other programs, e-mail messages, and databases. It is essential to protect your computer system from computer viruses. To learn how virus protection programs work, visit our Web site at www.computing2008.com and enter the keyword virus. Then answer the following: (a) Briefly describe the four steps taken by virus protection programs. (b) What is signature scanning? (c) What is heuristic detection and how is it different from signature scanning? (d) Do you use a virus protection program? If yes, what program(s) do you use and has it been effective? If no, do you plan to in the near future? Why or why not?

2   Booting and POST

Computers do a considerable amount of work before a user even hits a key. Knowing how a computer starts up can be an invaluable tool for fixing a broken computer or getting working computers to run at peak efficiency. To learn how a computer starts up, visit our Web site at www.computing2008.com and enter the keyword boot. Then answer the following: (a) Briefly describe the four steps of a cold boot. (b) When booting up, what does the microprocessor do first? (c) What does BIOS stand for? (d) Advanced users often customize their BIOS and POST. What benefits can users achieve by modifying their BIOS or POST?

3   Customized Desktop

There are several ways to customize your computer's desktop to make it more interesting, informative, or efficient. To learn about customizations, connect to the Yahoo site at www.yahoo.com and look at the subject area "Computers and Internet: Desktop Customization" or search the Web using the keywords "desktop customization." Then address the following: (a) Summarize some of the customizations you found. (b) Briefly explain how these customizations are added to a user's computer. (c) Explain how customization could make your computing experience more enjoyable or productive.

WRITING ABOUT TECHNOLOGY

The ability to think critically and to write effectively is essential to nearly every profession. The following questions are designed to help you develop these skills by posing thought-provoking questions about computer privacy, security, and/or ethics.

Antitrust

1

Much attention has been focused on Microsoft's legal battles over antitrust issues. It has been argued that Microsoft has an unfair market advantage because its Windows operating system has been tailored to use Microsoft applications. Write a one-page paper responding to the following questions: (a) Do you think Microsoft has an unfair advantage in the software market? (b) How can the decisions in the Microsoft antitrust case affect the software available for consumers to buy? (c) What ethical obligations do you think Microsoft has to other software developers? (d) What ethical obligations does it have to the consumer? Explain your answer.

Online Backup

2

One of the best ways to safeguard important personal or corporate data is to use an online backup service. Research three or four online backup services and then answer the following questions in a one-page paper: (a) What are the general features of online backup services? (b) What types of emergencies do online backups help with that other backup methods do not? (c) How are backups scheduled? (d) Is this service a replacement for making backups locally? Why or why not?

CHAPTER

6

COMPETENCIES

After you have read this chapter, you should be able to:

1 Describe the four basic types of system units.

2 Discuss how a computer uses binary codes to represent data in electronic form.

3 Describe each of the major system unit components.

4 Discuss microprocessors, including specialty processors.

5 Describe the different types of memory.

6 Discuss expansion slots and boards.

7 Describe the five principal types of expansion buses.

8 Discuss the four standard ports.

Disk Drives
are secondary storage devices for saving data, programs, and information

Power Supply Unit
converts AC to DC, providing power to the system unit

System Board
connects all system components to one another

System Unit
contains most of the computer's electronic components

Bus Lines
provide data pathways that connect various system components

Introduction

Why are some microcomputers more powerful than others? The answer lies in three words: speed, capacity, and flexibility. After reading this chapter, you will be able to judge how fast, powerful, and versatile a particular microcomputer is. As you might expect, this knowledge is valuable if you are planning to buy a new microcomputer system or to upgrade an existing system. (The Buyer's Guide and the Upgrader's Guide at the end of this book provide additional information.) It also will help you to evaluate whether or not an existing microcomputer system is powerful enough for today's new and exciting applications. For example, with the right hardware, you can use your computer to watch TV while you work and to capture video clips for class presentations.

Sometime you may get the chance to watch when a technician opens up a microcomputer. You will see that it is basically a collection of electronic circuitry. While there is no need to understand how all these components work, it is important to understand the principles. Once you do, you will be able to determine how powerful a particular microcomputer is. This will help you judge whether it can run particular kinds of programs and can meet your needs as a user.

Competent end users need to understand the functionality of the basic components in the system unit, including the system board, microprocessor, memory, system clock, expansion slots and cards, bus lines, ports, cables, and power supply units.

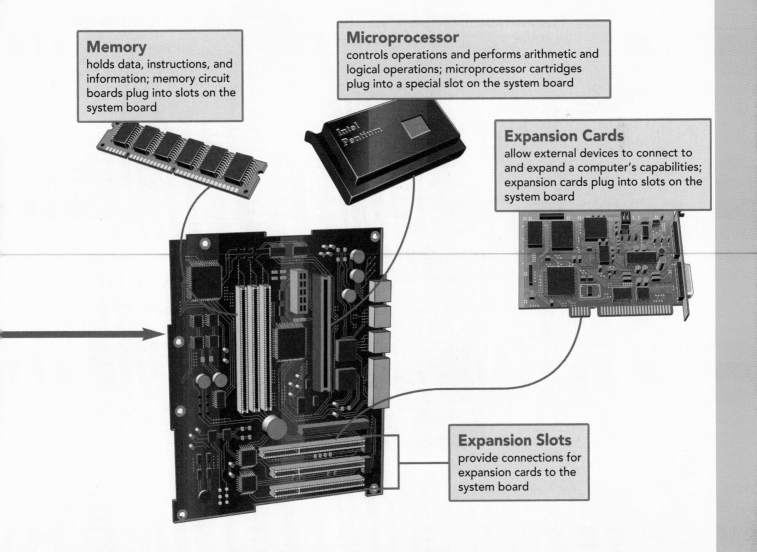

Memory
holds data, instructions, and information; memory circuit boards plug into slots on the system board

Microprocessor
controls operations and performs arithmetic and logical operations; microprocessor cartridges plug into a special slot on the system board

Expansion Cards
allow external devices to connect to and expand a computer's capabilities; expansion cards plug into slots on the system board

Expansion Slots
provide connections for expansion cards to the system board

SYSTEM UNIT

The **system unit,** also known as the **system cabinet,** is a container that houses most of the electronic components that make up a computer system. All computer systems have a system unit. For microcomputers, there are four basic types (see Figure 6-1):

- **Desktop system units** typically contain the system's electronic components and selected secondary storage devices. Input and output devices, such as a mouse, keyboard, and monitor, are located outside the system unit. This type of system unit is designed to be placed either horizontally or vertically.

- **Notebook system units** are portable and much smaller. These system units contain the electronic components, selected secondary storage devices, and input devices (keyboard and pointing device). Located outside the system unit, the monitor is attached by hinges. Notebook system units are often called **laptops.**

- **Tablet PC system units** are similar to notebook system units. **Tablet PCs** are highly portable devices that support the use of a stylus or pen to input commands and data. There are two basic types. One type is effectively a notebook computer with a monitor that swivels and folds onto its keyboard. The other type is similar to a notebook computer except that its

Desktop

Notebook

Tablet PC

PDA

Figure 6-1 Basic types of system units

Swivel screen

Without keyboard

Figure 6–2   Tablet PCs

monitor is attached to the system unit and does not have a keyboard integrated into the system unit. (See Figure 6-2.)

- **Handheld computer system units** are the smallest and are designed to fit into the palm of one hand. These systems contain an entire computer system, including the electronic components, secondary storage, and input and output devices. **Personal digital assistants (PDAs)** are the most widely used handheld computers.

While the actual size may vary, each type of system unit has the same basic system components including system board, microprocessor, and memory. Before considering these components, however, a more basic issue must be addressed. How do we as human beings communicate with and control all this electronic circuitry?

▼ CONCEPT CHECK

▶ What is the system unit?

▶ Describe the four basic types of microcomputer system units.

▶ What is a tablet PC? Describe the two basic types.

ELECTRONIC DATA AND INSTRUCTIONS

Have you ever wondered why it is said that we live in a digital world? It's because computers cannot recognize information the same way you and I can. People follow instructions and process data using letters, numbers, and special characters. For example, if we wanted someone to add the numbers 3 and 5 together and record the answer, we might say "please add 3 and 5." The system unit, however, is electronic circuitry and cannot directly process such a request.

The System Unit

Our voices create **analog,** or continuous, signals that vary to represent different tones, pitches, and volume. Computers, however, can recognize only **digital** electronic signals. Before any processing can occur within the system unit, a conversion must occur from what we understand to what the system unit can electronically process.

What is the most fundamental statement you can make about electricity? It is simply this: It can be either on or off. Indeed, there are many forms of technology that can make use of this two-state on/off, yes/no, present/absent arrangement. For instance, a light switch may be on or off, or an electric circuit open or closed. A specific location on a tape or disk may have a positive charge or a negative charge. This is the reason, then, that a two-state or binary system is used to represent data and instructions.

The decimal system that we are all familiar with has 10 digits (0, 1, 2, 3, 4, 5, 6, 7, 8, 9). The **binary system,** however, consists of only two digits—0 and 1. Each 0 or 1 is called a **bit**—short for binary digit. In the system unit, the 0 can be represented by electricity being off, and the 1 by electricity being on. In order to represent numbers, letters, and special characters, bits are combined into groups of eight called **bytes.** Each byte typically represents one character. To learn more about binary systems and binary arithmetic, visit our Web site at www.computing2008.com and enter the keyword binary.

BINARY CODING SCHEMES

Code	Uses
ASCII	Microcomputers
EBCDIC	Large computers
Unicode	International languages

Figure 6-3   Binary codes

Now let us consider an important question. How are characters represented as 0s and 1s ("off" and "on" electrical states) in the computer? The answer is in the use of **binary coding schemes.** A binary coding scheme assigns a unique binary number to each character. (See Figure 6-3.) Two of the most popular binary coding schemes use eight bits or one byte. These two codes are ASCII and EBCDIC. (See Figure 6-4.) A recently developed code, unicode, uses 16 bits.

- **ASCII,** pronounced "as-key," stands for **A**merican **S**tandard **C**ode for **I**nformation **I**nterchange. This is the most widely used binary code for microcomputers. For example, the number 3 is represented in ASCII code as 0011 0011.

- **EBCDIC,** pronounced "eb-see-dick," stands for **E**xtended **B**inary **C**oded **D**ecimal **I**nterchange **C**ode. It was developed by IBM and is used primarily for large computers. For example, the number 3 is represented in EBCDIC code as 1111 0011.

- **Unicode** is a 16-bit code originally designed to support international languages like Chinese and Japanese. These languages have too many characters to be represented by the eight-bit ASCII and EBCDIC codes.

When you press a key on the keyboard, a character is automatically converted into a series of electronic pulses that the system can recognize. For example, pressing the number 3 on a keyboard causes an electronic signal to be sent to the microcomputer's system unit where it is converted to the ASCII code of 0011 0011.

Coding schemes are particularly important to hardware designers and computer programmers for tracking down errors and other types of problems. But why are coding schemes important to end users? There are several reasons. One of the most important is that data created by one computer system using one coding scheme cannot be directly accessed and used by another computer system using a different coding scheme. Generally, this is not a problem if both computers are microcomputers since both would most likely use ASCII code. And most microcomputer applications store data using this code. However, problems occur when data is shared between microcomputers and larger computers that use EBCDIC code. The data must be translated from one coding scheme to the other before processing can begin. Fortunately, special conversion programs are available to help with this translation.

Symbol	ASCII	EBCDIC	Symbol	ASCII	EBCDIC
A	0100 0001	1100 0001	X	0101 1000	1110 0111
B	0100 0010	1100 0010	Y	0101 1001	1110 1000
C	0100 0011	1100 0011	Z	0101 1010	1110 1001
D	0100 0100	1100 0100	!	0010 0001	0101 1010
E	0100 0101	1100 0101	ì	0010 0010	0111 1111
F	0100 0110	1100 0110	#	0010 0011	0111 1011
G	0100 0111	1100 0111	$	0010 0100	0101 1011
H	0100 1000	1100 1000	%	0010 0101	0110 1100
I	0100 1001	1100 1001	&	0010 0110	0101 0000
J	0100 1010	1101 0001	(	0010 1000	0100 1101
K	0100 1011	1101 0010	)	0010 1001	0101 1101
L	0100 1100	1101 0011	*	0010 1010	0101 1100
M	0100 1101	1101 0100	+	0010 1011	0100 1110
N	0100 1110	1101 0101	0	0011 0000	1111 0000
O	0100 1111	1101 0110	1	0011 0001	1111 0001
P	0101 0000	1101 0111	2	0011 0010	1111 0010
Q	0101 0001	1101 1000	3	0011 0011	1111 0011
R	0101 0010	1101 1001	4	0011 0100	1111 0100
S	0101 0011	1110 0010	5	0011 0101	1111 0101
T	0101 0100	1110 0011	6	0011 0110	1111 0110
U	0101 0101	1110 0100	7	0011 0111	1111 0111
V	0101 0110	1110 0101	8	0011 1000	1111 1000
W	0101 0111	1110 0110	9	0011 1001	1111 1001

ASCII code for +

ASCII code for 3

ASCII code for 5

Figure 6-4 ASCII and EBCDIC binary coding schemes

CONCEPT CHECK

- What are decimal and binary systems? How are they different?
- What are binary coding schemes? Name and describe three.
- Describe how ASCII code is used to represent numbers and letters.

SYSTEM BOARD

The **system board** is also known as the **motherboard.** The system board is the communications medium for the entire computer system. Every component of the system unit connects to the system board. It acts as a data path allowing the various components to communicate with one another. External devices such as the keyboard, mouse, and monitor could not communicate with the system unit without the system board.

On a desktop computer, the system board is located at the bottom of the system unit or along one side. It is a large flat circuit board covered with a variety

On the Web Explorations

Improvements in system unit components are being made every day. To learn more about a company on the forefront of these technologies, visit our Web site at www.computing2008.com and enter the keyword component.

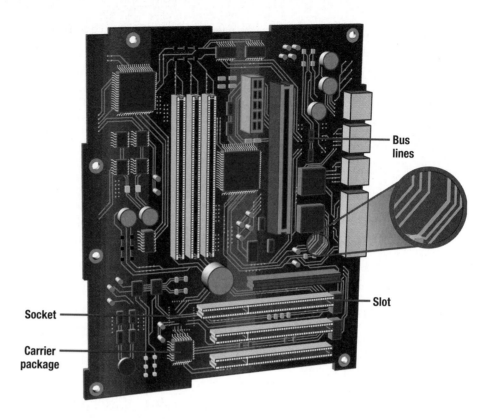

Figure 6–5 System board

of different electronic components including sockets, slots, and bus lines. (See Figure 6-5.)

- **Sockets** provide a connection point for small specialized electronic parts called chips. **Chips** consist of tiny circuit boards etched onto squares of sandlike material called silicon. These circuit boards can be smaller than the tip of your finger. (See Figure 6-6.) A chip is also called a **silicon chip, semiconductor,** or **integrated circuit.** Chips are mounted on **carrier packages.** (See Figure 6-7.) These packages either plug directly into sockets on the system board or onto cards that are then plugged into slots on the system board. Sockets are used to connect the system board to a variety of different types of chips, including microprocessor and memory chips.
- **Slots** provide a connection point for specialized cards or circuit boards. These cards provide expansion capability for a computer system. For

Figure 6-6 Chip

Figure 6-7 Chip mounted onto a carrier package

example, a modem card plugs into a slot on the system board to provide a connection to the Internet.

- Connecting lines called **bus lines** provide pathways that support communication among the various electronic components that are either located on the system board or attached to the system board. (See Figure 6-8.)

Notebook, tablet PC, and handheld system boards are smaller than desktop system boards. However, they perform the same functions as desktop system boards.

Figure 6-8 Bus lines

▼ CONCEPT CHECK

▶ What is the system board and what does it do?

▶ Define and describe sockets, slots, and bus lines.

▶ What are chips? How are chips attached to the system board?

MICROPROCESSOR

In a microcomputer system, the **central processing unit (CPU)** or **processor** is contained on a single chip called the **microprocessor.** The microprocessor is either mounted onto a carrier package that plugs into the system board or contained within a cartridge that plugs into a special slot on the system board. (See Figure 6-9.) The microprocessor is the "brains" of the computer system. It has two basic components: the control unit and the arithmetic-logic unit.

- **Control unit:** The **control unit** tells the rest of the computer system how to carry out a program's instructions. It directs the movement of electronic signals between memory, which temporarily holds data, instructions, and processed information, and the arithmetic-logic unit. It also directs these control signals between the CPU and input and output devices.

- **Arithmetic-logic unit:** The **arithmetic-logic unit,** usually called the **ALU,** performs two types of operations: arithmetic and logical. **Arithmetic**

Carrier package

Cartridge

Figure 6-9 Microprocessor carrier package and cartridge

operations are, as you might expect, the fundamental math operations: addition, subtraction, multiplication, and division. **Logical operations** consist of comparisons. That is, two pieces of data are compared to see whether one is equal to (=), less than (<), or greater than (>) the other.

MICROPROCESSOR CHIPS

Chip capacities are often expressed in word sizes. A **word** is the number of bits (such as 16, 32, or 64) that can be accessed at one time by the CPU. The more bits in a word, the more powerful—and the faster—the computer is. As mentioned previously, eight bits group together to form a byte. A 32-bit-word computer can access 4 bytes at a time. A 64-bit-word computer can access 8 bytes at a time. Therefore, the computer designed to process 64-bit words is faster.

Unit	Speed
Microsecond	Millionth of a second
Nanosecond	Billionth of a second
Picosecond	Trillionth of a second

Figure 6-10 Processing speeds

Older microcomputers typically process data and instructions in millionths of a second, or microseconds. Newer microcomputers are much faster and process data and instructions in billionths of a second, or nanoseconds. Supercomputers, by contrast, operate at speeds measured in picoseconds—1,000 times as fast as microcomputers. (See Figure 6-10)

The two most significant recent developments in microprocessors are the 64-bit processor and the dual-core chip. Until recently, 64-bit processors were only used in large mainframe and supercomputers. All of that is changing as 64-bit processors are becoming commonplace in today's more powerful microcomputers.

The other recent development is the dual-core chip. As mentioned previously, a traditional microcomputer's CPU is typically contained on a single microprocessor chip. A new type of chip, the **dual-core chip,** can provide two separate and independent CPUs. These chips allow a single computer to run two programs at the same time. For example, Access could be searching a large database while the end user is creating a multimedia presentation with PowerPoint. More significantly, however, is the potential for microcomputers to run very large complex programs that previously were run only on mainframe and supercomputers. This requires specifically designed programs that are divided into parts that each CPU could process independently. This approach is called **parallel processing.** While some of these programs currently exist, many more are expected in the near future.

See Figure 6-11 for a table of popular microprocessors.

On the Web Explorations

The most powerful microprocessors are capable of dual-core and 64-bit processing. To learn more about one of the manufacturers of these chips, visit our Web site at www.computing2008.com and enter the keyword dual.

Processor	Manufacturer	Description
Pentium 4	Intel	32-bit
Core 2	Intel	64-bit, dual-core
Xeon	Intel	64-bit, dual-core
Athlon 64	AMD	64-bit, dual-core
Opteron	AMD	64-bit, dual-core
PowerPC	IBM	64-bit, dual-core

Figure 6-11 Popular microprocessors

SPECIALTY PROCESSORS

In addition to microprocessor chips, a variety of more specialized processing chips have been developed.

- **Coprocessors** are specialty chips designed to improve specific computing operations. One of the most widely used is the **graphics coprocessor** designed to handle the processing requirements related to 3-D images.

- **Smart cards** are plastic cards the size of a regular credit card that have an embedded specialty chip. Many colleges and universities provide smart cards to their students for identfication. (see Figure 6-12.)

- Many cars have as many as 70 separate specialty processors to control nearly everything from fuel efficiency to satellite entertainment and tracking systems.

- **RFID tags** are specialty chips embedded in merchandise to track their location. The Civil Aviation Orginization has proposed inserting RFID chips in over a billion passports to track visitors to the United States.

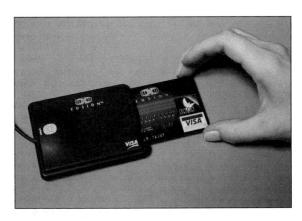

Figure 6-12   Smart card

▼ CONCEPT CHECK

▶ Name and describe the two components of a microprocessor.

▶ Discuss the two most significant developments in microprocessor chips.

▶ What are specialty chips? Describe coprocessors smart cards, and RFID tags.

MEMORY

Memory is a holding area for data, instructions, and information. Like microprocessors, **memory** is contained on chips connected to the system board. There are three well-known types of memory chips: random-access memory (RAM), read-only memory (ROM), and complementary metal-oxide semiconductor (CMOS).

RAM

Random-access memory (RAM) chips hold the program (sequence of instructions) and data that the CPU is presently processing. (See Figure 6-13.) RAM is called temporary or volatile storage because everything in most types of RAM is lost as soon as the microcomputer is turned off. It is also lost if there is a power failure or other disruption of the electric current going to the microcomputer. Secondary storage, which we shall describe in Chapter 8, does not lose its contents. It is permanent or nonvolatile storage, such as the data stored on diskettes. For this reason, as we mentioned earlier, it is a good idea to save your work in progress to a secondary storage device. That is, if you are working on a document or a spreadsheet, every few minutes you should save, or store, the material.

Cache (pronounced "cash") **memory** improves processing by acting as a temporary high-speed holding area between the memory and the CPU. In a computer with a cache (not all machines have one), the computer detects which information in RAM is most frequently used. It then copies that information into the cache. When needed, the CPU can quickly access the information from the cache.

Flash memory chips can retain data even if power is disrupted. This type of RAM is the most expensive and used

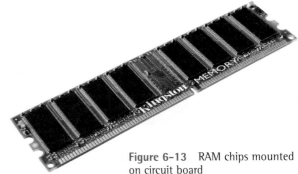

Figure 6-13   RAM chips mounted on circuit board

TV TUNER CARDS AND VIDEO CLIPS

Want to watch your favorite television program while you work? Perhaps you would like to include a video clip from television in a class presentation. It's easy using a TV tuner card.

Viewing   Once a TV tuner card has been installed, you can view your favorite TV shows, even while running other applications such as Excel, by taking the steps shown here.

- Click the *TV icon* on the desktop.

- Size and move the television window and control box window.

- Select the channel.

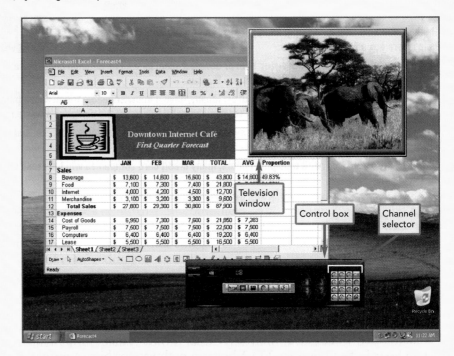

Capturing   You can capture the video playing in the TV window into a digital file by taking the steps shown here.

- Specify where to save the video clip on your computer by clicking the *Properties* button.

- Click the *Record* button to start recording.

- Click the *Stop* button to stop recording.

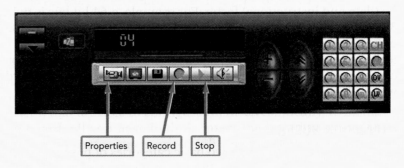

Using Once captured in a file, a video can be used in any number of ways. It can be added to a Web page, attached to an e-mail, or added to a class presentation. For example, you could include a video clip in a PowerPoint presentation by taking the steps shown here.

1 ● Insert the video clip into a page in the presentation by clicking *Insert/Movies and Sounds/Movie from File.*

2 ● Click on the image of the inserted video clip anytime during your presentation to play it.

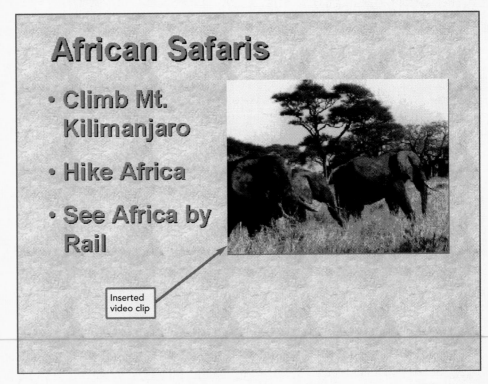

TV tuner cards are relatively inexpensive and easy to install. Some factors limiting their performance on your computer are the speed of your processor, the amount of memory, and secondary storage capacity.

TV tuner cards are continually changing, and some of the specifics presented in this Making IT Work for You may have changed. To learn about other ways to make information technology work for you, visit our Web site at www.computing2008.com and enter the keyword miw.

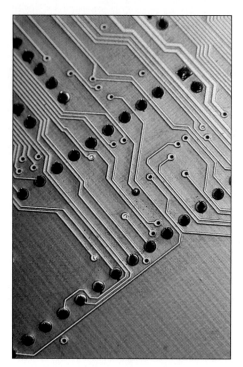

Figure 6-20 Bus is a pathway for bits

Computer systems typically have a combination of different types of expansion buses. The principal types are ISA, PCI, AGP, USB, and HPSB.

- **Industry standard architecture (ISA)** was developed for the first IBM Personal Computer. Originally, it had an 8-bit bus width. Later, it was expanded to 16 bits. Although too slow for many of today's applications, the ISA bus is still widely used.
- **Peripheral component interconnect (PCI)** was originally developed to meet the video demands of graphical user interfaces. PCI is a high-speed 32-bit or 64-bit bus that is over 20 times faster than ISA buses.
- **Accelerated graphics port (AGP)** is over twice as fast as the PCI bus. While the PCI bus is used for a variety of purposes, the AGP bus is dedicated to the acceleration of graphics performance. Widely used for graphics and 3-D animations, the AGP is replacing the PCI bus for the transfer of video data.
- **Universal serial bus (USB)** combines with a PCI bus on the system board to support several external devices without using expansion cards or slots. External USB devices are connected from one to another and then onto the USB bus. The USB bus then connects to the PCI bus on the motherboard. The first universal serial bus was called USB 1.1 and is over twice as fast as the AGP bus. Recently, a new version called USB 2.0 has been introduced that is 40 times faster than USB 1.1.
- **FireWire buses** operate much like USB buses and perform at speeds comparable to USB 2.0. FireWire and USB 2.0 buses are used for special applications that provide support for digital camcorders and video editing software.

PORTS

Figure 6-21 Ports

A **port** is a socket for external devices to connect to the system unit. (See Figure 6-21.) Some ports connect directly to the system board while others connect to cards that are inserted into slots on the system board. Some ports are standard features of most computer systems and others are more specialized.

STANDARD PORTS

Many ports, like the mouse, keyboard, and video ports, are for specific devices. Others, like those listed below, can be used for a variety of different devices.

- **Serial ports** are used for a wide variety of purposes. They are often used to connect a mouse, keyboard, modem, and many other devices to the system unit. Serial ports send data one bit at a time and are very good for sending information over a long distance.
- **Parallel ports** are used to connect external devices that need to send or receive a lot of data over a short distance. These ports typically send eight bits of data simultaneously across eight parallel wires. Parallel ports are mostly used to connect printers to the system unit.
- **Universal serial bus (USB) ports** are gradually replacing serial and parallel ports. They are faster, and one USB port can be used to connect several devices to the system unit.

- **FireWire ports** are as fast as USB 2.0 ports and provide connections to specialized FireWire devices such as camcorders.

Two of the most significant recent developments in buses and ports are **PCI Express (PCIe)** and **serial ATA (SATA).** Many of today's most powerful microcomputers include PCI Express buses and slots, which are 30 times faster than PCI. This recent development is expected to replace both PCI and AGP. SerialATA buses and ports are typically used to connect magnetic and optical disc drives to the system board with far greater speed that other buses and slots.

SPECIALIZED PORTS

In addition to standard ports, there are numerous specialty ports including MIDI and IrDA ports.

- **Musical instrument digital interface (MIDI)** ports are a special type of serial port for connecting musical instruments like an electronic keyboard to a sound card. The sound card converts the music into a series of digital instructions. These instructions can be processed immediately to reproduce the music or saved to a file for later processing.

- **Infrared Data Association (IrDA)** ports provide a wireless mechanism for transferring data between devices. Instead of cables, the IrDA ports from each device are directly aligned and infrared light waves are used to transmit data. One of the most common applications is to transfer data from either a handheld or notebook computer to a desktop computer. (See Figure 6-22.)

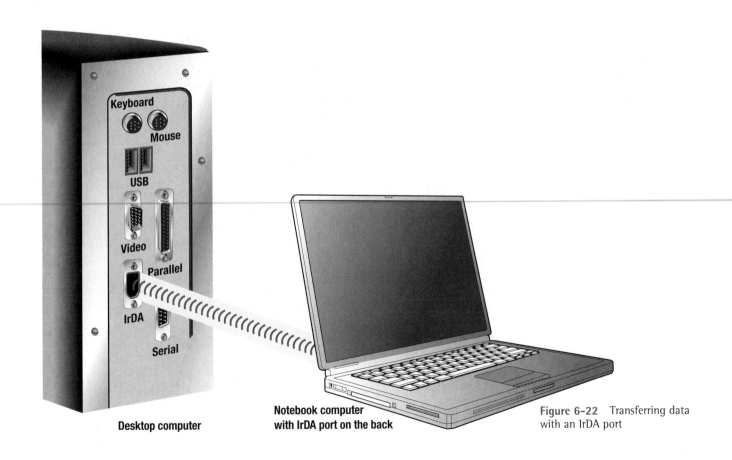

Desktop computer

Notebook computer with IrDA port on the back

Figure 6-22 Transferring data with an IrDA port

CABLES

Cables are used to connect exterior devices to the system unit via the ports. One end of the cable is attached to the device and the other end has a connector that is attached to a matching connector on the port.

POWER SUPPLY

Computers require direct current (DC) to power their electronic components and to represent data and instructions. DC power can be provided indirectly by converting alternating current (AC) from standard wall outlets or directly from batteries.

- Desktop computers have a **power supply unit** located within the system unit. (See Figure 6-23.) This unit plugs into a standard wall outlet, converts AC to DC, and provides the power to drive all of the system unit components.
- Notebook computers use **AC adapters** that are typically located outside the system unit. (See Figure 6-24.) AC adapters plug into a standard wall outlet, convert AC to DC, provide power to drive the system unit components, and can recharge batteries. Notebook computers can be operated either using an AC adapter plugged into a wall outlet or using battery power. Notebook batteries typically provide sufficient power for two to four hours before they need to be recharged.
- Like notebook computers, handheld computers use AC adapters located outside the system unit. Unlike notebook computers, however, handheld computers typically operate only using battery power. The AC adapter is used to recharge the batteries.

▼ CONCEPT CHECK

▶ What is a bus and what is its function? Describe five types.

▶ What are ports? What do they do? Describe four standard ports.

▶ What is a power supply unit? What is an AC adaptor?

Figure 6-23   Power supply unit

Figure 6-24   AC adapter

Computer technicians repair and install computer components and systems. (See Figure 6-25.) They may work on everything from personal computers and mainframe servers to printers. Some computer technicians are responsible for setting up and maintaining computer networks. Experienced computer technicians may work with computer engineers to diagnose problems and run routine maintenance on complex systems. Job growth is expected in this field as computer equipment becomes more complicated and technology expands.

Employers look for those with certification in computer repair or associate degrees from vocational schools. Employment usually begins with training, but most employers expect applicants to have prior technical experience. Computer technicians also can expect to continue their education to keep up with technological changes. Good communication skills are important in this field.

Computer technicians can expect an hourly wage of $13.00 to $22.00. Opportunities for advancement typically come in the form of work on more advanced computer systems. Some computer technicians move into customer service positions or go into sales. To learn more about other careers in information technology, visit us at www.computing2008.com and enter the keyword careers.

Figure 6-25   Computer technician

A Look to the Future

As You Walk out the Door, Don't Forget Your Computer

Wouldn't it be nice if you could conveniently access the Internet wirelessly at any time during the day? What if you could send and receive e-mail from your waist-mounted computer? What if you could maintain your personal schedule book, making new appointments with others on the fly? What if you could play interactive games and surf the Web from anywhere?

Of course, you can do all this and more using wireless technology and PDAs. Many people currently use this technology when they are away from their home or office. What if these users could accomplish these tasks with an even smaller, more portable, and less intrusive system? Will people be wearing computers rather than carrying them? What if your computer featured a head-mounted display?

Xybernaut Corporation is currently marketing personal wearable computers. These devices are composed of a computer that is worn inside a jacket or in a belt and a head-mounted display. The display allows you to see the equivalent of a desktop moniter via a small screen that is worn in front of one eye or projected onto the inside of a regular pair of eyeglasses. Some devices include music and video players and portable versions of office software.

Devices made by Xybernaut® are currently being evaluated for use in airports by security personnel. These devices are currently being used by the U.S. Department of Defense for military applications and by the Toronto Blue Jays to end long lines at ticket windows. When coupled with face recognition technology, Xybernaut's products provide security personnel portable and instant communication with the command center. Police and security officers may someday use this technology to check IDs and verify your identity. Experts say that wearable computers will be used by surgeons in operating rooms to "view" their patients.

Will we be wearing computers soon? Some of us already are. And some experts predict the majority of us will employ a wearable computer before the end of the decade. Many computer manufacturers are currently working on wearable computers, and there is even a wearable computer fashion show that showcases the latest designs. Many people are already wearing their computers, and making use of this mobile technology to read e-mail while waiting in lines or even studying their notes for the next exam. What do you think? Will Americans someday grab their keys and their computers before they leave the house? Will your computer one day be housed in your jacket?

THE SYSTEM UNIT

SYSTEM UNIT

System unit (or **system cabinet**) contains electronic components. Four basic types are: **desktop**, **notebook, tablet PC,** and **handheld. PDA (personal digital assistant)** is the most widely used handheld computer.

Electronic Representation

Our voices create continuous **analog** signals. A conversion to **digital** signals is necessary before processing. Data and instructions can be represented electronically with a two-state or **binary system** of numbers (0 and 1). Each 0 or 1 is called a **bit.** A **byte** consists of eight bits and represents one character.

Binary Coding Schemes

Binary coding schemes convert binary data into characters. Three such schemes are

- **ASCII**—the most widely used for microcomputers.
- **EBCDIC**—developed by IBM; used primarily by large computers.
- **Unicode**—16-bit code; originally designed to support international languages like Chinese and Japanese.

SYSTEM BOARD

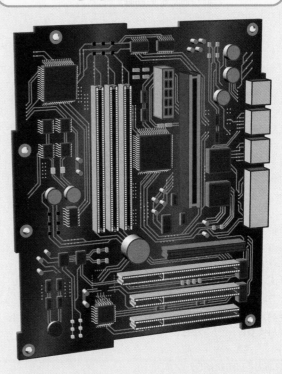

The **system board** (**motherboard**) connects all system components and allows input and output devices to communicate with the system unit. It is a flat circuit board covered with these electronic components:

- **Sockets** provide connection points for **chips (silicon chips, semiconductors, integrated circuits).** Chips are mounted on **carrier packages.**
- **Slots** provide connection points for specialized cards or circuit boards.
- **Bus lines** provide pathways to support communication.

The System Unit

To be a competent end user, you need to understand how data and programs are represented electronically. Additionally, you need to understand the functionality of the basic components in the system unit: system board, microprocessor, memory, system clock, expansion slots and cards, bus lines, and ports and cables.

MICROPROCESSOR

The **microprocessor** is a single chip that contains the **central processing unit (CPU)** or **microprocessor.** It has two basic components:

- **Control unit** tells the computer system how to carry out program instructions.
- **Arithmetic-logic unit (ALU)** performs **arithmetic** and **logical operations.**

Microprocessor Chips

A **word** is the number of bits that can be accessed by the microprocessor at one time. Older microprocessors process data and instructions in microseconds; newer ones process in nanoseconds. Supercomputers process in picoseconds.

The two most significant developments are 64-bit and **dual-core chips. Parallel processing** requires programs that allow multiple processors to work together to run large complex programs.

Specialty Processors

Specialty processors include **graphics coprocessors** (process graphic images), **smart cards** (plastic cards containing embedded chips), processors in automobiles (monitor fuel efficiency, satellite entertainment, and tracking systems), and **RFID tags** (track merchandise).

Unit	Speed
Microsecond	Millionth of a second
Nanosecond	Billionth of a second
Picosecond	Trillionth of a second

MEMORY

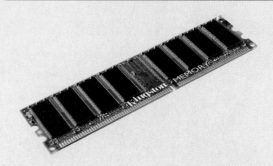

Memory holds data, instructions, and information. There are three types of memory chips: RAM, ROM, and CMOS.

RAM

RAM (random-access memory) chips are called temporary or volatile storage because their contents are lost if power is disrupted.

- **Cache memory** is a high-speed holding area for frequently used data and information.
- **Flash memory** is a special type of RAM that does not lose its contents when power is disrupted.
- **Virtual memory** divides large programs into parts that are read into RAM as needed.

ROM

ROM (read-only memory) chips are nonvolatile storage and control essential system operations.

CMOS

CMOS (complementary metal-oxide semiconductor) chips provide flexibility and expandability to computer systems.

SYSTEM CLOCK

System clock controls the speed of operations. **Clock speed** is measured in gigahertz (GHz).

EXPANSION SLOTS AND CARDS

Most computers allow users to expand their systems by providing **expansion slots** on their system boards to accept **expansion cards.**

Examples of expansion cards include **graphics cards, sound cards, modem cards, network interface cards (NIC; network adapter cards), TV tuner cards,** and **PC cards.**

Plug and Play is a set of hardware and software standards designed to assist with the installation of expansion cards.

BUS LINES

Bus lines, also known as **buses,** provide data pathways that connect various system components. **Bus width** is the number of bits that can travel simultaneously.

Expansion Buses

System buses connect CPU and memory. **Expansion buses** connect CPU and slots. Five principal expansion bus types are **ISA (industry standard architecture), PCI (peripheral component interconnect), AGP (accelerated graphics port), USB (universal serial bus),** and **FireWire bus.**

PORTS

Ports are connecting sockets on the outside of the system unit. Some ports are standard while others are more specialized.

Standard Ports

Four standard ports are

- **Serial**—send data one bit at a time.
- **Parallel**—send eight bits simultaneously.
- **USB (universal serial bus)**—faster; one port can connect several devices to system unit.
- **FireWire**—as fast as USB 2.0 ports; provide connections for specialized FireWire devices.

The two most significant recent developments in ports and buses are **PCI Express (PCIe)** and **serial ATA (SATA).**

Specialized Ports

Two specialty ports are

- **MIDI (Musical instrument digital interface)**—special port for musical instruments such as electronic keyboards.
- **IrDA (Infrared Data Association) ports**—provide wireless connections.

Cables

Cables are used to connect external devices to the system unit via ports.

POWER SUPPLY

Power supply units convert AC to DC; they are located within the desktop computer's system unit. **AC adapters** power notebook computers and tablet PCs and recharge batteries.

CAREERS IN IT

Computer technicians repair and install computer components and systems. Certification in computer repair or associate degrees from vocational schools required. Hourly wage $13.00 to $22.00.

KEY TERMS

www.computing2008.com

AC adapter   (166)
accelerated graphics port
    (AGP)   (164)
analog   (152)
arithmetic-logic unit (ALU)
    (155)
arithmetic operation   (155)
ASCII   (152)
binary coding scheme   (152)
binary system   (152)
bit   (152)
bus   (161)
bus line   (155, 161)
bus width   (161)
byte   (152)
cable   (166)
cache memory   (157)
carrier package   (154)
central processing unit
    (CPU)   (155)
chip   (154)
clock speed   (159)
complementary metal-oxide
    semiconductor (CMOS)
    (158)
computer technician   (167)
control unit   (155)
coprocessor   (156)
desktop system unit   (150)
digital   (152)
dual-core chips   (156)
EBCDIC   (152)
expansion bus   (161)
expansion card   (159)

expansion slot   (159)
FireWire bus   (164)
FireWire port   (165)
flash memory   (157)
graphics card   (160)
graphics coprocessor   (156)
handheld computer system
    unit   (151)
industry standard
    architecture (ISA)   (164)
Infrared Data Association
    (IrDA)   (165)
integrated circuit   (154)
laptop computer   (150)
logical operation   (156)
memory   (157)
microprocessor   (155)
modem card   (160)
motherboard   (153)
musical instrument digital
    interface (MIDI)   (165)
network adapter card   (160)
network interface card (NIC)
    (160)
notebook system unit   (150)
parallel port   (164)
parallel processing   (156)
PC card   (161)
PCI Express (PCIe)   (165)
peripheral component
    interconnect (PCI)   (164)
personal digital assistant
    (PDA)   (151)
Plug and Play   (160)

port   (164)
power supply unit   (166)
processor   (155)
random-access memory
    (RAM)   (157)
read-only memory (ROM)
    (158)
RFID tag   (157)
semiconductor   (154)
serial ATA (SATA)   (165)
serial port   (164)
silicon chip   (154)
slot   (154)
smart card   (156)
socket   (154)
sound card   (160)
system board   (153)
system bus   (161)
system cabinet   (150)
system clock   (159)
system unit   (150)
tablet PC   (150)
tablet PC system unit   (150)
TV tuner card   (160)
Unicode   (152)
universal serial bus (USB)
    (164)
universal serial bus (USB)
    port   (164)
virtual memory   (158)
word   (156)

To test your knowledge of these key terms with animated flash cards, visit our Web site at
www.computing2008.com and enter the keyword terms6.

CROSSWORD PUZZLE

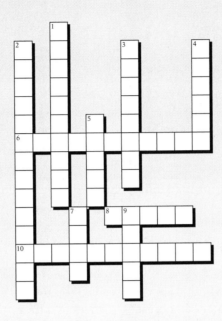

Across

6 Assists with the installation of expansion cards.

8 Memory which improves processing by acting as a temporary high-speed holding area between memory and the CPU.

10 Controls the speed of operations.

Down

1 Part of a microcomputer that contains the CPU.

2 Controls and manipulates data to produce information.

3 The number of bits traveling simultaneously down a bus

4 Holding area for data, instructions, and information.

5 Used to connect external devices to system unit via ports.

7 Unit consisting of eight bits.

9 Most widely used microprocessor binary coding scheme.

MULTIPLE CHOICE

Circle the letter or fill in the correct answer.

1. The container that houses most of the electronic components that make up a computer system is known as the
   a. arithmetic-logic unit   c. primary storage unit
   b. central processing unit   d. system unit

2. The smallest unit in a digital system is a
   a. byte   c. word
   b. bit   d. character

3. The communications medium for the entire computer system is the
   a. arithmetic-logic unit   c. motherboard
   b. semiconductor   d. coprocessor

4. These provide expansion capability for a computer system.
   a. sockets   c. ports
   b. slots   d. bays

5. The ____ tells the rest of the computer how to carry out a program's instructions.
   a. ALU   c. system unit
   b. control unit   d. motherboard

6. A 32-bit word computer can access ____ bytes at a time.
   a. 4   c. 16
   b. 8   d. 32

7. These chips are specifically designed to handle the processing requirements related to displaying and manipulating 3-D images.
   a. graphics coprocessors   c. control unit processors
   b. arithmetic-logic unit processors d. CISC chips

8. This type of memory improves processing by acting as a temporary high-speed holding area between the memory and the CPU.
   a. RAM   c. cache memory
   b. ROM   d. flash memory

9. ____ is a set of hardware and software standards.
   a. CPU   c. cache
   b. Plug and Play   d. ALU

10. ____ ports connect special types of music instruments to sound cards.
    a. BUS   c. USB
    b. CPU   d. MIDI

For an interactive version of these multiple-choice questions, visit our Web site at www.computing2008.com and enter the keyword multiple6.

MATCHING

Match each numbered item with the most closely related lettered item. Write your answers in the spaces provided.

a. bus width
b. cables
c. control unit
d. expansion card
e. PC card
f. port
g. RAM
h. smart card
i. system clock
j. system unit

1. Houses most of the electronic components in a computer system. ____
2. The number of bits that can travel down a bus at the same time. ____
3. Tells the computer system how to carry out a program's instructions. ____
4. A credit card–sized piece of plastic with an embedded chip. ____
5. Volatile storage that holds the program and data the CPU is currently processing. ____
6. Produces precisely timed electrical beats as a timing mechanism. ____
7. Plugs into slots on the system board. ____
8. Credit card-sized expansion boards used by portable computers. ____
9. Connecting socket on the outside of the system unit. ____
10. Connects input and output devices to the system unit via the ports. ____

For an interactive version of this matching exercise, visit our Web site at www.computing2008.com and enter the keyword **matching6**.

OPEN-ENDED

On a separate sheet of paper, respond to each question or statement.

1. Describe the four basic types of system units.
2. Describe the two basic components of the CPU.
3. What are the differences and similarities between the three types of memory?
4. Identify five expansion cards and describe the function of each.
5. Identify and describe four standard ports and two specialized ports.

APPLYING TECHNOLOGY

The following questions are designed to demonstrate ways that you can effectively use technology today. The first question relates directly to this chapter's Making IT Work for You feature.

1   TV Tuner Cards and Video Clips

Want to watch your favorite television program while you work? Perhaps you would like to include a video clip in a class presentation. It's easy using a video TV card. To learn more about this technology, review Making IT Work for You: TV Tuner Cards and Video Clips on pages 162 and 163. Then visit our Web site at www.computing2008.com and enter the keyword tuner. Play the video and answer the following: (a) Describe the two windows that open when the TV icon is selected. (b) What are the basic functions of the control box? (c) What is the command sequence to insert a video clip into a PowerPoint presentation?

2   Desktop and Notebook Computers

Are you thinking about purchasing a new computer? Visit our Web site at www.computing2008.com and enter the keyword computer to link to a site that presents information about the newest desktop and notebook computers. Check out different desktop and notebook models and then answer the following questions: (a) If you were to purchase a desktop computer, which one would you select? Describe how it would fit your needs and print out its specifications. (b) If you were to purchase a notebook computer, which one would you select? Describe how it would fit your needs and print out its specifications. (c) If you had to choose between the desktop and notebook, which one would you choose? Why?

3   Custom System Units

When it is time for you to purchase your next computer, you might consider shopping online. A big advantage to choosing a computer online instead of in a store is that many computer manufacturers allow you to customize your new computer and build it to order. Connect to the Dell Web site and use their online tools to customize and price a computer that meets your current needs. Then answer the following questions: (a) Which of the three types of system units did you configure? (b) What microprocessor did you choose? (c) How much and what type of memory option did you choose? (d) Would you purchase the computer you customized? Why or why not?

EXPANDING YOUR KNOWLEDGE

The following questions are designed to add depth and detail to your understanding of specific topics presented within this chapter. The questions direct you to sources other than the textbook to obtain this knowledge.

How TV Tuner Cards Work

1

The advent of digital TV and the success of digital video recorders has made TV tuner cards a popular addition to many computers. TV tuner cards allow you to watch and record TV shows on your computer, even while running other applications. To learn more about how TV tuner cards work, visit our Web site at www.computing2008.com and enter the keyword tv. Then answer the following questions: (a) What are some examples of inputs to a TV tuner card? (b) What is the function of a TV tuner card? (c) Where can the TV tuner card send the video signal once it is converted?

How Virtual Memory Works

2

Typically before a program can be executed, it must be read into RAM. Many programs, however, are too large to fit into many computer systems' RAM. One option is to increase the RAM in the system. Another way is to use virtual memory. To learn more about how virtual memory works, visit our Web site at www.computing2008.com and enter the keyword memory. Then answer the following: (a) What is virtual memory? (b) Define page file, page, and paging. (c) What is thrashing?

Binary Numbers

3

Binary numbers are the most basic unit that computers use to perform tasks. To learn more about how binary numbers work, visit our Web site at www.computing2008.com and enter the keyword binary. Then answer the following questions: (a) What character is represented by the binary number 01000011 in ASCII code? (b) What is the binary result of 1011 + 0010? What is the decimal equivalent to this number? (c) How many numbers can be represented with 1 bit (one binary "place")? How many by 2 bits? How many by 3 bits?

WRITING ABOUT TECHNOLOGY

The ability to think critically and to write effectively is essential to nearly every profession. The following questions are designed to help you develop these skills by posing thought-provoking questions about computer privacy, security, and/or ethics.

1   Processor Serial Numbers

When one of the earlier versions of the Intel Pentium microprocessor was released, each unit originally contained a unique Processor Serial Number, or PSN. This PSN could be used by online e-commerce sites to identify and track individuals by the computer they used. This tracking would be similar to keeping track of car owners by their license plate numbers. Write a one-page paper that addresses the following items: (a) What are the benefits of a PSN for a computer user? For society? Explain your answers. (b) What privacy issues does a PSN raise for a computer user? (c) Describe how a PSN could be misused.

2   Smart Cards

There have been numerous proposals in recent years to use smart card technology for personal identification, such as driver's licenses or a national ID card. Advocates claim that this would reduce identity fraud, because the cards would contain biometric information such as a fingerprint scan. Research smart card technology on the Web and then answer the following questions in a one-page paper: (a) What are the benefits of using smart cards for identification? List several examples. (b) What privacy concerns exist? Be specific. (c) Would you be in favor of using smart cards for personal identification? Why or why not?

NOTES

CHAPTER

7

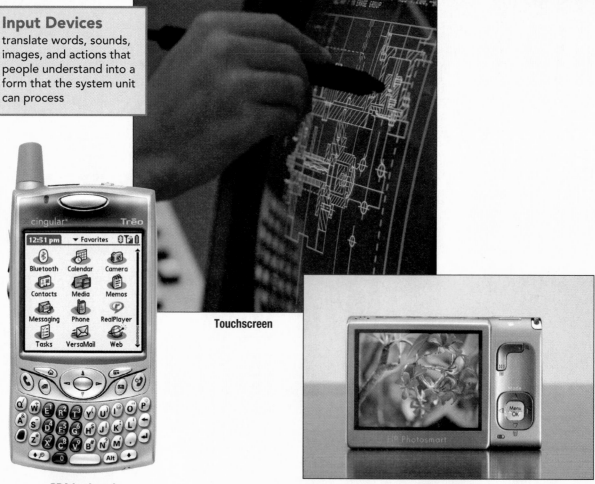

Input Devices
translate words, sounds, images, and actions that people understand into a form that the system unit can process

Touchscreen

PDA keyboard

Digital camera

Introduction

How do you get data to the CPU? How do you get information out? Here we describe one of the most important places where the computer interfaces with people. We input text, music, and even speech, but we probably never think about the relationship between what we enter and what the computer processes. People understand language, which is constructed of letters, numbers, and punctuation marks. However, computers can understand only the binary machine language of 0s and 1s. Input devices are essentially translators. Input devices translate numbers, letters, and actions that people understand into a form that computers can process.

Have you ever wondered how information processed by the system unit is converted into a form that you can use? That is the role of output devices.

While input devices convert what we understand into what the system unit can process, output devices convert what the system unit has processed into a form that we can understand. Output devices translate machine language into letters, numbers, sounds, and images that people can understand.

Competent end users need to know about the most commonly used input devices, including keyboards, mice, scanners, digital cameras, digitizing tablets, voice recognition, and MIDI devices. Additionally, they need to know about the most commonly used output devices, including monitors, printers, and audio output devices. And end users need to be aware of combination input and output devices such as fax machines, multifunctional devices, Internet telephones, and terminals.

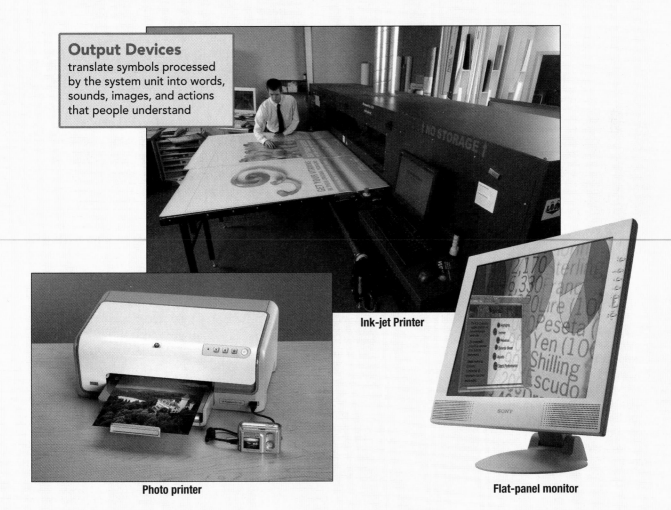

Output Devices translate symbols processed by the system unit into words, sounds, images, and actions that people understand

Ink-jet Printer

Photo printer

Flat-panel monitor

WHAT IS INPUT?

Input is any data or instructions that are used by a computer. They can come directly from you or from other sources. You provide input whenever you use system or application programs. For example, when using a word processing program, you enter data in the form of numbers and letters and issue commands such as to save and to print documents. You also can enter data and issue commands by pointing to items, or using your voice. Other sources of input include scanned or photographed images.

Input devices are hardware used to translate words, sounds, images, and actions that people understand into a form that the system unit can process. For example, when using a word processor, you typically use a keyboard to enter text and a mouse to issue commands. In addition to keyboards and mice, there are a wide variety of other input devices. These include pointing, scanning, image capturing, and audio-input devices.

KEYBOARD ENTRY

One of the most common ways to input data is by **keyboard.** As mentioned in Chapter 6, keyboards convert numbers, letters, and special characters that people understand into electrical signals. These signals are sent to, and processed by, the system unit. Most keyboards use an arrangement of keys given the name QWERTY. This name reflects the keyboard layout by taking the letters of the first six alphabetic characters found on the fourth row of keys.

KEYBOARDS

There are a wide variety of different keyboard designs. They range from the full-sized to miniature and from rigid to flexible. The most common types are

- **Traditional keyboards**—full-sized, rigid, rectangular keyboards that include function, navigational, and numeric keys.
- **Flexible keyboards**—fold or roll up for easy packing or storage. They are designed to provide mobile users with a full-sized keyboard with minimal storage requirements. (See Figure 7-1.)
- **Ergonomic keyboards**—similar to traditional keyboards. The keyboard arrangement, however, is not rectangular and a palm rest is provided. They are designed specifically to alleviate wrist strain associated with the repetitive movements of typing. (See Figure 7-2.)

Figure 7-1 Flexible keyboard

Figure 7-2 Ergonomic keyboard

- **Wireless keyboards**—transmit input to the system unit through the air. By eliminating connecting wires to the system unit, these keyboards provide greater flexibility and convenience.
- **PDA keyboards**—miniature keyboards for PDAs used to send e-mail, create documents, and more. (See Figure 7-3.)

FEATURES

A computer keyboard combines a typewriter keyboard with a **numeric keypad,** used to enter numbers and arithmetic symbols. It also has many special-purpose keys. Some keys, such as the CAPS LOCK key, are **toggle keys.** These keys turn a feature on or off. Others, such as the CTRL key, are **combination keys,** which perform an action when held down in combination with another key. To learn more about keyboard features, see Figure 7-4.

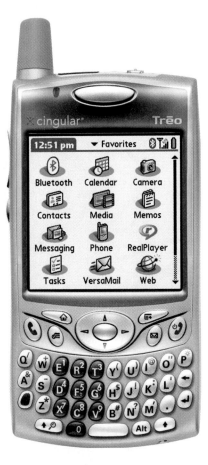

Figure 7-3　PDA keyboard

> ## ▼ CONCEPT CHECK
>
> ▶ What is input? What are input devices?
>
> ▶ Discuss the five common types of keyboard designs.
>
> ▶ What are some common keyboard features?

Escape Key
typically cancels a selection or a procedure.

Function Keys
shortcut for specific tasks. F1, for example, typically displays online Help.

Numeric Keypad
enters numbers and arithmetic symbols and controls cursor or insertion point.

Windows Key
displays the Start menu.

Spacebar
enters blank spaces between characters.

Navigation Keys
control the cursor or insertion point on the screen.

Figure 7-4　Traditional keyboard

Pointing, of course, is one of the most natural of all human gestures. Pointing devices provide a comfortable interface with the system unit by accepting pointing gestures and converting them into machine-readable input. There are a wide variety of different pointing devices, including the mouse, joystick, touch screen, light pen, and stylus.

MICE

A **mouse** controls a pointer that is displayed on the monitor. The **mouse pointer** usually appears in the shape of an arrow. It frequently changes shape, however, depending on the application. A mouse can have one, two, or more buttons, which are used to select command options and to control the mouse pointer on the monitor. Some mice have a **wheel button** that can be rotated to scroll through information that is displayed on the monitor. Although there are several different mouse types, there are three basic designs:

- **Mechanical mouse** is generally considered the traditional type and is currently the most widely used. It has a ball on the bottom and is attached with a cord to the system unit. As you move the mouse across a smooth surface, the roller rotates and controls the pointer on the screen.

- **Optical mouse** has no moving parts. It emits and senses light to detect mouse movement. This newer

Figure 7-5   Optical mouse

Figure 7-6   Trackball

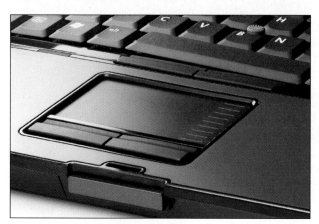

Figure 7-7   Touch pad

Figure 7-8   Pointing stick

type of mouse has some advantages compared to the mechanical mouse: it can be used on any surface, is more precise, and does not require periodic cleaning. (See Figure 7-5.)

- **Cordless** or **wireless mouse** is a battery-powered device that typically uses radio waves or infrared light waves to communicate with the system unit. These devices eliminate the mouse cord and free up desk space.

Three devices similar to a mouse are trackballs, touch pads, and pointing sticks. You can use the **trackball,** also known as the **roller ball,** to control the pointer by rotating a ball with your thumb. (See Figure 7-6.) You can use **touch pads,** to control the pointer by moving and tapping your finger on the surface of a pad. (See Figure 7-7.) You can use a **pointing stick,** located in the middle of the keyboard, to control the pointer by directing the stick with your finger. (See Figure 7-8.)

Figure 7-9 A joystick: a computer game application

JOYSTICKS

A **joystick** is the most popular input device for computer games. You control game actions by varying the pressure, speed, and direction of the joystick. Additional controls, such as buttons and triggers, are used to specify commands or initiate specific actions. (See Figure 7-9.)

TOUCH SCREENS

A **touch screen** is a particular kind of monitor with a clear plastic outer layer. Behind this layer are crisscrossed invisible beams of infrared light. This arrangement enables someone to select actions or commands by touching the screen with a finger. Touch screens are easy to use, especially when people need information quickly. They are commonly used at restaurants, automated teller machines (ATMs), and information centers. (See Figure 7-10.)

LIGHT PENS

A **light pen** is a light-sensitive penlike device. The light pen is placed against the monitor. This closes a photoelectric circuit and identifies the spot for entering or modifying data. For example, light pens are used to edit digital images and drawings. (See Figure 7-11.)

Figure 7-10 A touch screen: a consumer application

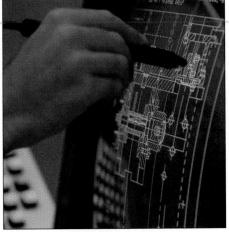

Figure 7-11 A light pen: an engineering application

STYLUS

A **stylus** is a penlike device commonly used with tablet PCs and PDAs. (See Figure 7-12.) A stylus uses pressure to draw images on a screen. A stylus interacts with the computer through handwriting recognition software. **Handwriting recognition software** translates handwritten notes into a form that the system unit can process.

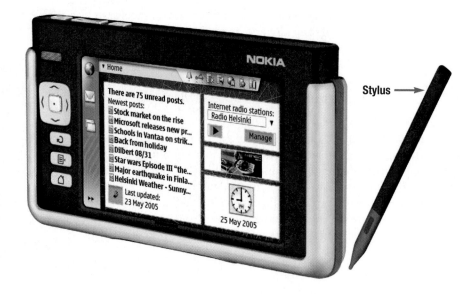

Stylus →

Figure 7-12   Stylus

▼ **CONCEPT CHECK**

▶ What is a pointing device? Describe five pointing devices.

▶ Describe three basic mouse designs.

▶ Describe trackballs, touch pads, and pointing sticks.

SCANNING DEVICES

Scanners move across text and images. Scanning devices convert scanned text and images into a form that the system unit can process. There are three types of scanning devices: optical scanners, bar code readers, and character and mark recognition devices.

OPTICAL SCANNERS

An **optical scanner,** also known simply as a scanner, accepts documents consisting of text and/or images and converts them to machine-readable form. These devices do not recognize individual letters or images. Rather, they recognize light, dark, and colored areas that make up individual letters or images. Typically, scanned documents are saved in files that can be further processed, displayed, printed, or stored for later use. There are two basic types of optical scanners: flatbed and portable. (See Figure 7-13.)

• **Flatbed scanner** is much like a copy machine. The image to be scanned is placed on a glass surface and the scanner records the image from below.

• **Portable scanner** is typically a handheld device that slides across the image, making direct contact.

Optical scanners are powerful tools for a wide variety of end users, including graphics and advertising professionals who scan images and combine them with text. Lawyers and students use portable scanners as a valuable research tool to record information.

Flatbed scanner

Portable scanner

Figure 7-13 Two types of scanners

CARD READERS

Nearly everyone uses a credit card, debit card, access (parking or building) card, and/or some type of identification card. These cards typically have the user's name, some type of identification number, and signature embossed on the card. Additionally, encoded information is often stored on the card as well. Card readers interpret this encoded information. There are two basic types:

- By far the most common is the **magnetic card reader.** The encoded information is stored on a thin magnetic strip located on the back of the card. When the card is swiped through the magnetic card reader, the information is read.

- **Radio frequency card readers** are not as common but more convenient because they do not require the card to actually make contact with the reader. The card has a small **RFID (radio frequency identification)** microchip that contains the user's encoded information. Whenever the card is passed within a few inches of the card reader, the user's information is read. (See Figure 7-14.)

Figure 7-14 Radio frequency card reader

BAR CODE READERS

You are probably familiar with **bar code readers** or **scanners** from grocery stores. (See Figure 7-15.) These devices are either handheld **wand readers** or **platform scanners.** They contain photoelectric cells that scan or read **bar codes,** or the vertical zebra-striped marks printed on product containers.

Almost all supermarkets use electronic cash registers and a bar code system called the **Universal Product Code (UPC).** At the checkout counter,

Figure 7-15 A bar code reader is used to record product codes

electronic cash registers use a bar code reader to scan each product's UPC code. The codes are sent to the supermarket's computer, which has a description, the latest price, and an inventory level for each product. The computer processes this input to update the inventory level and to provide the electronic cash register with the description and price for each product. These devices are so easy to use that many supermarkets are offering customers self-checkout stations.

CHARACTER AND MARK RECOGNITION DEVICES

Character and mark recognition devices are scanners that are able to recognize special characters and marks. They are specialty devices that are essential tools for certain applications. Three types are

- **Magnetic-ink character recognition (MICR)**—used by banks to automatically read those unusual numbers on the bottom of checks and deposit slips. A special-purpose machine known as a reader/sorter reads these numbers and provides input that allows banks to efficiently maintain customer account balances.

- **Optical-character recognition (OCR)**—uses special preprinted characters that can be read by a light source and changed into machine-readable code. A common OCR device is the handheld wand reader. (See Figure 7-16.) These are used in department stores to read retail price tags by reflecting light on the printed characters.

- **Optical-mark recognition (OMR)**—senses the presence or absence of a mark, such as a pencil mark. OMR is often used to score multiple-choice tests such as the College Board's Scholastic Aptitude Test (SAT) and the Graduate Record Examination (GRE).

Figure 7-16 A wand reader is used to record product codes

▼ CONCEPT CHECK

▶ How are pointing and scanning devices different?

▶ Describe three types of scanners.

▶ Describe three common character and mark recognition devices.

IMAGE CAPTURING DEVICES

Optical scanners, like traditional copy machines, can make a copy from an original. For example, an optical scanner can make a digital copy of a photograph. Image capturing devices, on the other hand, create or capture original images. These devices include digital cameras and digital video cameras.

DIGITAL CAMERAS

Digital cameras are similar to traditional cameras except that images are recorded digitally on a disk or in the camera's memory rather than on film and

Figure 7-17 A digital camera

then downloaded, or transferred, to your computer. (See Figure 7-17.) You can take a picture, view it immediately, and even place it on your own Web page, within minutes.

To learn more about how digital photography works, visit us on the Web at www.computing2008.com and enter the keyword photo. Digital photographs can be shared easily with others over the Internet.

DIGITAL VIDEO CAMERAS

Unlike traditional video cameras, **digital video cameras** record motion digitally on a disk or in the camera's memory. Most have the capability to take still images as well. **WebCams** are specialized digital video cameras that capture images and send them to a computer for broadcast over the Internet. (See Figure 7-18.) To learn more about WebCams, visit our Web site at www.computing2008.com and enter the keyword webcam. To learn how you can videoconference, see Making IT Work for You: WebCams and Instant Messaging on pages 190 and 191.

Figure 7-18 A WebCam

TIPS

Are you having trouble getting the kind of photos you want with a digital camera? Would you like to make the most of digital technology in your photos? Here are some tips to help you get started:

1 **Buttons and Knobs.** Get to know the functions of your camera before you begin. Most cameras have an automatic mode, but be sure you know how to turn on the flash, zoom the lens, and set the image resolution.

2 **Photography Basics.** Many digital cameras have an LCD screen on the back. You can use it to help frame your shots more accurately. Just be aware that using the LCD screen uses more battery power.

3 **Red-Eye Reduction.** Many digital cameras have a red-eye reduction feature. When photographing people in low light, you can use this setting to eliminate glassy red eyes in photos. Consult your owner's manual to learn more about this feature.

To see additional tips, visit our Web site at www.computing2008.com and enter the keyword tips.

AUDIO-INPUT DEVICES

Audio-input devices convert sounds into a form that can be processed by the system unit. By far the most widely used audio-input device is the microphone. Audio input can take many forms, including the human voice and music.

WEBCAMS AND INSTANT MESSAGING

Do you enjoy chatting with your friends? Are you working on a project and need to collaborate with others in your group? What if you could see and hear your group online? Perhaps instant messaging is just what you're looking for. It's easy and free with an Internet connection and the right software.

Sending Messages and Transferring Files   After installing free instant messaging software, you can exchange messages and files with friends. Your friends are added to a list of contacts that shows you when your friends are online and available to chat. For example, you could use Windows Messenger as follows:

1 ● Add contacts by clicking *Add a Contact* and following the onscreen instructions.

● Double-click the name of a friend who appears in the *Online* section.

● Enter your message in the window that appears.

● Click the *Send* button.

Your message appears on your friend's screen instantly. Your friend can then continue the conversation by following the steps above.

2 ● Click *Send a File or Photo* in the *I want to . . .* menu in the sidebar.

● Browse for the file you would like to share, and click *Open.*

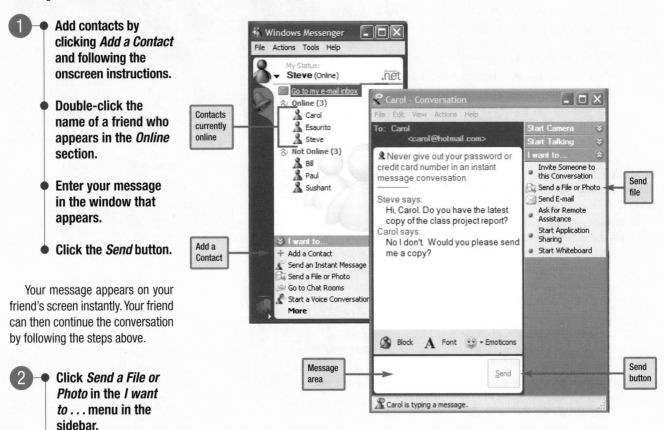

Your friend is given an option to accept the file. Once your friend accepts, you can continue your conversation without interruption while the file is transferred.

Using a WebCam In addition to typing text messages, some instant messaging software allows you to have voice or video conversations over the Internet so you can see and hear the person you are collaborating with. To do this, both users must have a microphone and speakers, as well as Web cameras for video conferencing. You could hold a video conference using Windows Messenger by following these steps.

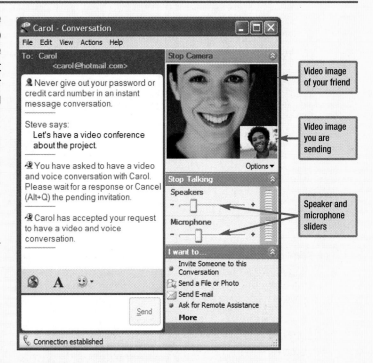

● **Start a conversation with a contact as shown in the Sending Messages and Transferring Files section.**

● **Click *Start Camera* in the sidebar.**

Your friend is given the option to accept the video conference. Once he or she accepts, the video conference begins.

● **As you speak, adjust the *Speakers* and *Microphone* sliders to comfortable levels.**

Sharing an Application Sharing applications is another way to collaborate using instant messaging software. Sharing applications allows you to surf the Web or edit a document over the Internet while working with a friend. For example, you could collaborate with a friend on a Microsoft Word document by following the steps below:

● **Start a conversation with a contact as shown in the Sending Messages and Transferring Files section.**

● **Click *Start Application Sharing* in the sidebar.**

Your friend is given the option to accept the application sharing session. Once he or she accepts, the application sharing session begins.

● **Select the application you want to share in the Share Programs list and click the *Share* button.**

● **Click the *Allow Control* button to allow your friends to control the shared application.**

● **Click the *Close* button.**

Your application can be controlled by you and your friend simultaneously.

The Web is continually changing, and some of the specifics presented in this Making IT Work for You may have changed. To learn about other ways to make information technology work for you, visit our Web site at www.computing2008.com and enter the keyword miw.

VOICE RECOGNITION SYSTEMS

Voice recognition systems use a microphone, a sound card, and special software. These systems allow users to operate computers and to create documents using voice commands. Portable voice recognition systems are widely used by doctors, lawyers, and others to record dictation. (See Figure 7-19.) These devices are able to record for several hours before connecting to a computer system to edit, store, and print the dictated information. Some systems are even able to translate dictation from one language to another, such as from English to Japanese.

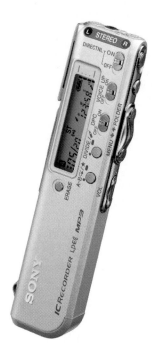

Figure 7-19 A portable voice recognition system

<table>
<tr><td>▼ CONCEPT CHECK</td></tr>
<tr><td>▶ How are digital cameras different from traditional cameras?</td></tr>
<tr><td>▶ What is a WebCam?</td></tr>
<tr><td>▶ Describe voice recognition systems.</td></tr>
</table>

WHAT IS OUTPUT?

Output is processed data or information. Output typically takes the form of text, graphics, photos, audio, and/or video. For example, when you create a presentation using a presentation graphics program, you typically input text and graphics. You also could include photographs and even add voice narration. The output would be the completed presentation.

Output devices are any hardware used to provide or to create output. They translate information that has been processed by the system unit into a form that humans can understand. There are a wide range of output devices. The most widely used are monitors, printers, and audio-output devices.

MONITORS

Pixel

Figure 7-20 Monitor resolution

The most frequently used output device is the **monitor.** Also known as **display screens,** monitors present visual images of text and graphics. The output is often referred to as soft copy. Monitors vary in size, shape, and cost. Almost all, however, have some basic distinguishing features.

FEATURES

The most important characteristic of a monitor is its clarity. **Clarity** refers to the quality and sharpness of the displayed images. It is a function of several monitor features, including resolution, dot pitch, refresh rate, and size.

• **Resolution** is one of the most important features. Images are formed on a monitor by a series of dots or **pixels (picture elements).** (See Figure 7-20.) Resolution is expressed as a matrix of these dots or pixels. For example, many monitors today have a resolution of 1,600 pixel columns by 1,200 pixel rows for a total of 1,920,000 pixels. The higher a monitor's resolution (the more pixels), the clearer the image produced. See Figure 7-21 for the most common monitor resolutions.

- **Dot (pixel) pitch** is the distance between each pixel. Most newer monitors have a dot pitch of .31 mm (31/100th of a millimeter) or less. The lower the dot pitch (the shorter the distance between pixels), the clearer the images produced.

- **Refresh rate** indicates how often a displayed image is updated or redrawn on the monitor. Most monitors operate at a rate of 75 hertz, which means that the monitor is redrawn 75 times each second. Images displayed on monitors with refresh rates lower than 75 hertz appear to flicker and can cause eye strain. The faster the refresh rate (the more frequently images are redrawn), the better the quality of images displayed.

- Size is measured by the diagonal length of a monitor's viewing area. Common sizes are 15, 17, 19, and 21 inches. The smaller the monitor size, the better the quality of images displayed.

Standard	Pixels
SVGA	800 × 600
XGA	1,024 × 768
SXGA	1,280 × 1,024
UXGA	1,600 × 1,200
QXGA	2,048 × 1,536

Figure 7-21 Resolution standards

CATHODE-RAY TUBES

Until recently, the most common type of monitor for the office and the home was the **cathode-ray tube (CRT).** (See Figure 7-22.) These monitors are typically placed directly on the system unit or on the desktop. CRTs are similar in size and technology to televisions. Compared to other types of monitors, their primary advantages are low cost and excellent resolution. Their primary disadvantage is that they are bulky and occupy a considerable amount of space on the desktop.

FLAT-PANEL MONITORS

Because CRTs are too bulky to be transported easily, portable monitors, known as **flat-panel monitors,** were developed. Flat-panel monitors are much thinner and require less power to operate than CRTs. As a result, flat-panel monitors are rapidly replacing CRTs. (See Figure 7-23.)

Almost all of today's flat-panel monitors are **LCD (liquid crystal display).** There are two basic types: passive-matrix and active-matrix. **Passive-matrix** or **dual-scan monitors** create images by scanning the entire screen. This type requires very little power, but the clarity of the images is not as sharp. **Active-matrix** or **thin film transistor (TFT) monitors** do not scan down the screen; instead, each pixel is independently activated. They can display more colors with better clarity. Active-matrix monitors are more expensive and require more power.

Figure 7-22 CRT monitor

OTHER MONITORS

There are several other types of monitors. These monitors are used for more specialized applications, such as reading books, making presentations, and watching television. Three of these specialized devices are e-books, data projectors, and high-definition television.

- **E-books** are handheld, book-sized devices that display text and graphics. Using content downloaded from the Web or from special cartridges, these devices are used to read newspapers, magazines, and entire books. (See Figure 7-24.)

Figure 7-23   A flat-panel monitor

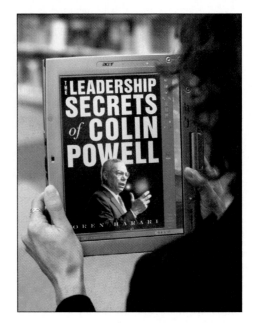

Figure 7-24   E-book

- **Data projectors** are specialized devices similar to slide projectors. These devices, however, connect to microcomputers and project computer output just as it would appear on a monitor. Data projectors are commonly used for presentations almost anywhere from the classroom to the boardroom.
- **High-definition television (HDTV)** delivers a much clearer and more detailed wide-screen picture than regular television. Because the output is digital, users can readily freeze video sequences to create high-quality still images. The video and still images can then be digitized, edited, and stored on disk for later use. This technology is very useful to graphic artists, designers, and publishers.

On the Web Explorations

HDTV is expected to be the standard in television broadcasting by 2006. To learn more about HDTV, visit our Web site at www.cmputing2008.com and enter the keyword hdtv.

▼ CONCEPT CHECK

▶ What is output? What are output devices?

▶ Define these monitor features: resolution, dot pitch, refresh rate, and size.

▶ Describe CRT, flat-panel, and other more specialized monitors.

PRINTERS

You probably use a printer with some frequency to print homework assignments, photographs, and Web pages. **Printers** translate information that has been processed by the system unit and present the information on paper. Printer output is often called hard copy.

FEATURES

There are many different types of printers. Almost all, however, have some basic distinguishing features, including resolution, color capability, speed, and memory.

- **Resolution** for a printer is similar to monitor resolution. It is a measure of the clarity of images produced. Printer resolution, however, is measured in **dpi (dots per inch).** (See Figure 7-25.) Most printers designed for personal use average 1,200 dpi. The higher the dpi, the better the quality of images produced.

300 dpi

1200 dpi

Figure 7-25   Dpi comparison

- Color capability is provided by most printers today. Users typically have the option to print either with just black ink or with color. Because it is more expensive to print in color, most users select black ink for letters, drafts, and homework. Color is used more selectively for final reports containing graphics and for photographs.

- Speed is measured in the number of pages printed per minute. Typically, printers for personal use average 15 to 19 pages per minute for single-color (black) output and 13 to 15 pages per minute for color output.

- Memory within a printer is used to store printing instructions and documents waiting to be printed. The more memory in a printer, the faster it will be able to create large documents.

INK-JET PRINTERS

Ink-jet printers spray ink at high speed onto the surface of paper. This process not only produces a letter-quality image but also permits printing to be done in a variety of colors, making them ideal for select special applications. (See Figure 7-26.) Ink-jet printers are the most widely used printers. They are reliable, quiet, and relatively inexpensive. The most costly aspect of ink-jet printers is replacing the ink cartridges. For this reason, most users specify black ink for the majority of print jobs and use the more expensive color printing for select applications. Typical ink-jet printers produce 17 to 19 pages per minute of black-only output and 13 to 15 pages of color output.

Figure 7-26   A special-application ink-jet printer

LASER PRINTERS

The **laser printer** uses a technology similar to that used in a photocopying machine. Laser printers use a laser light beam to produce images with

Input and Output

Figure 7-27 A laser printer

excellent letter and graphics quality. More expensive than ink-jet printers, laser printers are faster and are used in applications requiring high-quality output. (See Figure 7-27.)

TIPS Do you find extra pages in the printer when you try to print from the Web? Would you like to print your favorite articles without all the ads and hyperlinks? There are several ways to get what you want in a printout. Here are a few suggestions you can use with Internet Explorer:

1. **Preview.** To see what will be printed, choose *Print Preview* from the *File* menu. You can scroll through the pages and make sure the items you want will be printed.

2. **Choose Printer Friendly.** Many Web pages have a Printer Friendly button that removes all the ads and sidebars. Look for the button at the conclusion of most Web articles.

3. **Print Selection.** You can highlight and print only the text you would like to print. Highlight the text and graphics you would like to print and choose *File/Print* and check the *Selection* option under the *Page range* box.

To see other tips, visit our Web site at www.computing2008.com and enter the keyword tips.

There are two categories of laser printers. **Personal laser printers** typically do not support color, are less expensive, and are used by many single users. They typically can print 15 to 17 pages a minute. **Shared laser printers** typically support color, are more expensive, and are used (shared) by a group of users. Shared laser printers typically print over 50 pages a minute.

THERMAL PRINTERS

A **thermal printer** uses heat elements to produce images on heat-sensitive paper. Originally these printers were only used in scientific labs to record data. More recently, color thermal printers have been widely used to produce very high-quality color artwork and text.

Color thermal printers are not as popular because of their cost and the requirement of specially treated paper. They are special-use printers that produce near-photographic output. They are widely used in professional art and design work where very high-quality color is essential.

OTHER PRINTERS

There are several other types of printers. These printers include dot-matrix printers, plotters, photo printers, and portable printers:

* **Dot-matrix printers** form characters and images using a series of small pins on a print head. Once a widely used microcomputer printer, they are inexpensive and reliable but quite noisy. In general, they are used for tasks where high-quality output is not required.

* **Plotters** are special-purpose printers for producing a wide range of specialized output. Using output from graphics tablets and other graphical input devices, plotters can create maps, images, and architectural and engineering drawings. Plotters are widely used by graphic artists, engineers, and architects to print out designs, sketches, and drawings.

* **Photo printers** are special-purpose printers designed to print photo-quality images from digital cameras. (See Figure 7-28.) Most photo printers print 3 × 5″ or 4 × 6″ images on glossy, photo-quality paper.

* **Portable printers** are usually small and lightweight printers designed to work with a notebook computer. Portable printers may be ink-jet or laser printers, print in black and white or color, and connect with USB or parallel port connections.

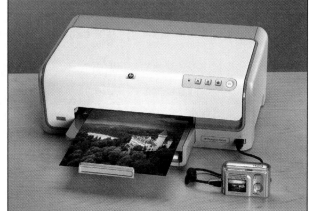

Figure 7-28   Photo printer

▼ CONCEPT CHECK

▶ Discuss these printer features: resolution, color capability, speed, and memory.

▶ What are the three printer types commonly used with microcomputers?

▶ Discuss dot-matrix, plotter, photo, and portable printers.

AUDIO-OUTPUT DEVICES

Audio-output devices translate audio information from the computer into sounds that people can understand. The most widely used audio-output devices are **speakers** and **headphones.** These devices are connected to a sound card in the system unit. The sound card is used to capture as well as play back recorded sounds. Audio-output devices are used to play music, vocalize translations from one language to another, and communicate information from the computer system to users.

Creating voice output is not anywhere near as difficult as recognizing and interpreting voice input. In fact, voice output is quite common. It is used with many soft-drink machines, telephones, and cars. It is used as a reinforcement

Figure 7-29 Digital music player

tool for learning, such as to help students study a foreign language. It also is used in many supermarkets at the checkout counter to confirm purchases. One of its most powerful capabilities is to assist the physically challenged.

Digital music players, also known as **digital media players,** are specialized devices for storing, transferring, and playing audio files. Older players are only able to play music saved in a special compressed audio file format known as MP3. Today, most players are able to use a wide variety of audio files. Many are capable of displaying video files as well. Two of the best-known audio and video players are iPod and iRiver. (See Figure 7-29.)

TIPS Has your iPod stopped responding? First check that your battery is charged and that the Hold button is off. If your iPod is still not working, follow the steps below to restart your iPod.

1 **Connect.** Connect your iPod to an electrical outlet using the charging cable.

2 **Turn off.** Slide the Hold switch to the hold position and return it to the off position.

3 **Restart.** Press and hold the Play/Pause and Menu buttons for several seconds. The iPod logo should appear on the screen and you are ready to go.

To see additional tips, visit our Web site at www.computing2008.com and enter the keyword tips.

COMBINATION INPUT AND OUTPUT DEVICES

Many devices combine input and output capabilities. Sometimes this is done to save space. Other times it is done for very specialized applications. Common combination devices include fax machines, multifunctional devices, Internet telephones, and terminals.

FAX MACHINES

A **fax machine** is a standard tool in nearly every office. At one time, all fax machines were separate stand-alone devices for sending and receiving images over telephone lines. Now, most computer systems have that capability with the simple addition of a fax/modem board. To send a fax, these devices scan the image of a document converting the light and dark areas into a format that can be sent electronically over standard telephone lines. To receive a fax, these devices reverse the process and print the document (or display the document on your monitor) using signals received from the telephone line.

MULTIFUNCTIONAL DEVICES

Multifunctional devices (MFD) typically combine the capabilities of a scanner, printer, fax, and copy machine. These multifunctional devices offer a cost and space advantage. They cost about the same as a good printer or copy machine but require much less space than the single-function devices they replace. Their disadvantage is that the quality and functionality are not quite as good as those of the separate single-purpose devices. Even so, multifunctional devices are widely used in home and small business offices.

INTERNET TELEPHONES

Internet telephones are specialized input and output devices for receiving and sending voice communication. (See Figure 7-30.) Typically, these devices connect to the system unit through a USB port and operate much like a traditional telephone.

Telephony is the transmission of telephone calls over computer networks. Also known as **Internet telephony, IP telephony,** and **Voice over IP (VoIP),** telephony uses the Internet rather than traditional communication lines to support voice communication. To place telephone calls using telephony requires a high-speed Internet connection and special software and/or hardware. The three most popular approaches are

- **Computer-to-computer** communications allow individuals to place free long-distance calls. This application requires that both parties have a computer and that their computers are on and connected to the Internet when a call is placed. The required software is available from a variety of sources for free or at very low cost. MSN Explorer is one of the most widely used.

- **Computer-to-traditional telephone** communications allow a user to call almost any traditional telephone from his or her computer. Only the person making the call needs to have a computer connected to the Internet. The calling party subscribes to a special Internet phone service provider that supplies the required software and charges a small monthly and/or per-minute fee. To see how this works, visit our Web site at www.computing2008.com and enter the keyword phone.

- **Traditional telephone-to-traditional telephone** communications do not require a computer. The calling party subscribes to a special Internet phone service provider that supplies a special hardware adapter that connects a traditional telephone to the Internet. The cost for this service is similar to the computer-to-traditional telephone approach.

Compared to traditional telephone calls, Internet-supported calls may have a lower sound quality. However, most users report that this difference is not significant. Telephony promises to dramatically impact the telecommunications industry and to reduce our costs for telephone communications.

Figure 7-30   Internet telephone

TERMINALS

A **terminal** is an input and output device that connects you to a mainframe or other type of computer. There are three kinds of terminals:

- A **dumb terminal** can be used to input and receive data, but it cannot process data independently. It is used to gain access and to send information to a computer. Such a terminal is often used by airline reservation clerks to access a mainframe computer for flight information.

- Essentially, an **intelligent terminal** is a microcomputer with communications software and a telephone hookup (modem) or other communications link. These connect the terminal to the larger computer or to the Internet.

- A **network terminal,** also known as a **thin client,** is a low-cost alternative to an intelligent terminal. Most network terminals do not have a hard-disk drive and must rely on a host computer or server for application and system software. These devices are becoming increasingly popular in many organizations.

▼ CONCEPT CHECK

► What are the two most widely used audio-output devices?

► Describe the three most popular Internet telephony approaches.

► Describe the following combination devices: fax machine, MFD, Internet telephone, and terminal.

CAREERS IN IT

Technical writers prepare instruction manuals, technical reports, and other scientific or technical documents. (See Figure 7-31.) Most technical writers work for computer software firms, government agencies, or research institutions. They translate technical information into easily understandable instructions or summaries. As new technology continues to develop and expand, the need for technical writers who can communicate technical expertise to others is expected to increase.

Technical writing positions typically require a college degree in communications, journalism, or English and a specialization in, or familiarity with, a technical field. However, individuals with strong writing skills sometimes transfer from jobs in the sciences to positions in technical writing.

Technical writers can expect to earn an annual salary in the range of $41,000 to $69,000. Advancement opportunities can be limited within a firm or company, but there are additional opportunities in consulting. To learn about other careers in information technology, visit us at www.computing2008.com and enter the keyword careers.

Figure 7-31   Technical writer

Crashing Through the Foreign Language Barrier

Have you ever wished you could speak more than one language fluently? What if you could speak hundreds of languages instantly? Would you like to have your own personal interpreter to accompany you whenever you traveled to a foreign country? What if you could take a picture of a foreign road sign or restaurant menu and have it immediately translated for you? Technology called *electronic interpretation* may soon exist to do all of these things. The military and private sector are funding a variety of research projects on electronic interpreters, and the commercial opportunities are enormous. The worldwide translation services market is already a $5 billion a year industry and is expected to grow to $7.6 billion by 2006.

Prototype portable handheld electronic interpreters are currently in a testing phase at the U.S. Office of Naval Research. In fact, it is expected that these devices will be widely used within the next year. The company SpeechGear has developed a machine called Interact that takes verbal statements in one language, converts the statements to text, translates that text to another language, and then vocalizes the translated text. And it does all this in two seconds! The military is particularly interested in electronic interpreters as they focus on peacekeeping objectives. More than ever before, U.S. soldiers find themselves needing to communicate with non-English-speaking civilians to settle disputes and maintain order.

Despite the achievements of Interact and other translation hardware, several challenges remain that plague all translation hardware. Current translation techniques are labor intensive; they require linguists and programmers to create large lists of words and their corresponding meanings. Unfortunately, computers have a difficult time understanding idioms, such as "It is raining cats and dogs." They may also have difficulty correctly identifying words by their context. For example, the sentences "The refrigerator is cool" and "The Fonz is cool" use the same word, *cool,* but it has a very different meaning in each sentence. Entrepreneurs in New York City may have a solution to these problems with the EliMT project. Instead of translating from word to word, EliMT compares books that have been translated in different languages, looking for sentence fragment patterns. By comparing sentence fragments, it is hoped that translation programs will be able to identify word groupings and translate them into another language's comparable word grouping, essentially translating concepts instead of individual words.

What are the uses for such a device? Will the average person want or need an electronic translator? What type of professions and professionals will use them? What industries would benefit most from electronic translators? How could you use this technology?

INPUT AND OUTPUT

INPUT

Input is any data or instructions used by a computer. Input devices translate words, images, and actions into a form a computer can process.

Keyboards

Keyboards are the most common way to input data. The most common types are

- **Traditional**—full-sized, rigid, rectangular.
- **Flexible**—roll up for easy packing.
- **Ergonomic**—designed to minimize wrist strain.
- **Wireless**—no wire provides greater flexibility.
- **PDA**—miniature keyboards for PDAs.

Features include **numeric keypads, toggle keys,** and **combination keys.**

Pointing Devices

Pointing devices accept pointing gestures and convert them to machine-readable input.

- **Mouse** controls a **mouse pointer. A wheel button** rotates to scroll through information. Three basic mouse designs are **mechanical, optical,** and **cordless (wireless).** Similar devices include t**rackball (roller ball), touch pad,** and **pointing stick.**
- **Joysticks** are popular for computer games. Operations are controlled by varying pressure, speed, and direction.

INPUT

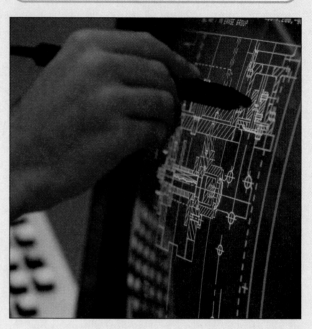

- **Touch screens** have a clear plastic layer over crisscrossed invisible beams. Operations are controlled by finger touching the screen.
- **Light pens** are light-sensitive penlike devices. Operations are controlled by placing light pen against monitor.
- **Stylus** is a penlike device used with tablet PCs and PDAs. **Handwriting recognition software** translates handwritten notes.

Scanners

Scanners move across text and graphics. Scanning devices convert scanned text and images into a form that can be processed by the system unit.

- **Optical scanners** record light, dark, and colored areas of scanned text or images. There are two types: **flatbed** and **portable.**
- Card readers interpret encoded information. Two types: **magnetic** (reads **magnetic strip**) and **radio frequency** (reads **RFID** microchip) card readers.

To be a competent end user, you need to be aware of the most commonly used input and output devices. These devices are translators for information into and out of the system unit. Input devices translate words, sounds, and actions into symbols the system unit can process. Output devices translate symbols from the system unit into words, images, and sounds that people can understand.

INPUT

- **Bar code readers** are used with electronic cash registers in supermarkets. **Wand readers** or **platform scanners** read **UPC** codes that are used to determine product descriptions and prices and to update inventory levels.

- Character and mark recognition devices recognize special characters and marks. Three types: **MICR** (read by readers/ sorters), **OCR,** and **OMR.**

Image Capturing Devices

Image capturing devices create or capture original images. These devices include **digital cameras** (images downloaded to system unit for further processing and/or printing) and **digital video cameras** (**Webcams** capture and send images over the Internet).

Audio-Input Devices

Audio-input devices convert sounds into a form that can be processed by the system unit. Audio input takes many forms including the human voice and music. **Voice recognition systems** use a combination of a microphone, a sound card, and special software.

OUTPUT

Output is data or information processed by a computer. Output devices translate processed text, graphics, audio, and video into a form humans can understand.

Monitors

Monitors (**display screens**) present visual images of text and graphics. Monitor output is described as soft copy.

   Clarity is a function of several monitor features including **resolution** (expressed as matrix of **pixels** or **picture elements**), **dot (pixel) pitch, refresh rate,** and size.

- **Cathode-ray tubes (CRTs)** use technology similar to a television. Low cost with excellent resolution. However, bulky and occupy considerable space on the desktop.

- **Flat-panel monitors** compared to CRTs are thinner and require less power. Most are **LCD (liquid crystal display.** Two types are **passive-matrix (dual-scan)** and **active-matrix (thin film transistor, TFT).**

Three specialized types of monitors are **e-books, data projectors,** and **high-definition television (HDTV).**

OUTPUT

Printers

Printers translate information processed by system unit and present the information on paper. Output from printers is described as hard copy. Some distinguishing features of printers include **resolution** (measured in **dpi** or **dots per inch**), color capability, speed, and memory.

- **Ink-jet printers** spray ink to produce high-quality output. These printers are inexpensive and the most widely used type of printer.
- **Laser printers** use technology similar to photocopying machines. Two categories are **personal** and **shared.**
- **Thermal printers** use heat elements and heat-sensitive paper. Used to record data and to provide very high-quality artwork and text.

Other printers include **dot-matrix printers, plotters, photo printers,** and **portable printers.**

Audio-Output Devices

Audio-output devices translate audio information from the computer into sounds that people can understand. **Speakers** and **headphones** are the most widely used audio-output devices.

Digital music players (digital media players) store, transfer, and play audio files. Older players only use MP3 files. Many players also display video files.

COMBINATION DEVICES

Combination devices combine input and output capabilities. Common types include

Fax Machines

Fax machines send and receive images via standard telephone lines.

Multifunctional Devices

Multifunctional devices (MFD) typically combine the capabilities of a scanner, printer, fax, and copy machine.

Internet Telephone

Internet telephones receive and send voice communication. **Telephony (Internet telephony, IP telephony,** and **Voice over IP, VoIP)** uses networks (Internet) to place long-distance calls. Three approaches are computer-to-computer, computer-to-traditional telephone, and traditional telephone-to-traditional telephone.

Terminals

Terminals are input and output devices that connect to a mainframe or other type of computer. There are three kinds: **dumb** (no processing), **intelligent** (microcomputer with communication software and communication link), and **network** (low-cost alternative, also known as **thin client.**

CAREERS IN IT

Technical writers prepare instruction manuals, technical reports, and other documents. Bachelor's degree in communication, journalism, or English and a specialization in, or familiarity with, a technical field required. Salary range $41,000 to $69,000.

KEY TERMS

active-matrix monitor   (193)
bar code   (187)
bar code reader   (187)
bar code scanner   (187)
cathode-ray tube (CRT)
   monitor   (193)
clarity   (192)
combination key   (183)
cordless mouse   (185)
data projector   (194)
digital camera   (188)
digital media player   (198)
digital music player   (198)
digital video camera   (189)
display screen   (192)
dot-matrix printer   (197)
dot pitch   (193)
dots-per-inch (dpi)   (195)
dual-scan monitor   (193)
dumb terminal   (199)
e-book   (193)
ergonomic keyboard   (182)
fax machine   (198)
flat-panel monitor   (193)
flatbed scanner   (186)
flexible keyboard   (182)
handwriting recognition
   software   (185)
headphones   (197)
high-definition television
   (HDTV)   (194)
ink-jet printer   (195)
intelligent terminal   (199)
Internet telephone   (199)
Internet telephony   (199)

IP telephony   (199)
joystick   (185)
keyboard   (182)
laser printer   (195)
light pen   (185)
liquid crystal display (LCD)
   (193)
magnetic card reader   (187)
magnetic-ink character
   recognition (MICR)   (188)
mechanical mouse   (184)
monitor   (192)
mouse   (184)
mouse pointer   (184)
multifunctional device
   (MFD)   (198)
network terminal   (199)
numeric keypad   (183)
optical-character recognition
   (OCR)   (188)
optical-mark recognition
   (OMR)   (188)
optical mouse   (184)
optical scanner   (186)
passive-matrix monitor   (193)
PDA keyboard   (183)
personal laser printer   (196)
photo printer   (197)
picture elements   (192)
pixel   (192)
pixel pitch   (193)
platform scanner   (187)
plotter   (197)
pointing stick   (185)
portable printer   (197)

portable scanner   (186)
printer   (194)
radio frequency card reader
   (187)
radio frequency identification
   (RFID)   (187)
refresh rate   (193)
resolution   (192, 195)
roller ball   (185)
shared laser printer   (196)
speakers   (197)
stylus   (185)
technical writer   (200)
telephony   (199)
terminal   (199)
thermal printer   (196)
thin client   (199)
thin film transistor (TFT)
   monitor   (193)
toggle key   (183)
touch pad   (185)
touch screen   (185)
trackball   (185)
traditional keyboard   (182)
Universal Product Code
   (UPC)   (187)
Voice over IP (VoIP)   (199)
voice recognition system
   (192)
wand reader   (187)
WebCam   (189)
wheel button   (184)
wireless keyboard   (183)
wireless mouse   (185)

FEATURES

Animations

Careers in IT

DVD Direct

Expansions

Making IT Work for You

On the Web Explorations

TechTV

Tips

CHAPTER REVIEW

Applying Technology

Crossword Puzzle

Expanding Your Knowledge

Key Terms

Matching

Multiple Choice

Open-Ended

Writing About Technology

To test your knowledge of these key terms with animated flash cards, visit our Web site at www.computing2008.com and enter the keyword terms7.

CROSSWORD PUZZLE

www.computing2008.com

Across

6 Used to grade multiple choice exams.

9 Specialized digital camera that broadcasts images over the Internet.

10 Records images digitally on a disk.

13 Most popular input device used for computer games.

14 Delivers much clearer picture than regular TV.

16 Resolution is expressed as a matrix of these dots.

17 Keyboard that rolls up for storage and transport.

Down

1 The distance between each pixel.

2 Most commonly used way to input data.

3 Button rotated to scroll through information displayed on the monitor.

4 Most widely used type of mouse.

5 Type of terminal that does no processing.

7 Number of times a screen is redrawn each second.

8 Measure of resolution.

11 Keys that turn features on and off.

12 Translates processed information into hard copy.

15 Bar code system used in supermarkets.

For an interactive version of this crossword, visit our Web site at www.computing2008.com and enter the keyword crossword7.

MULTIPLE CHOICE

Circle the letter or fill in the correct answer.

1. Hardware used to translate words, sounds, images, and actions that people understand into a form that the system unit can process is known as

    a. input devices

    b. output devices

    c. device readers

    d. device drivers

2. This type of keyboard provides the greatest amount of flexibility and convenience by eliminating cables connected to the system unit.

    a. ergonomic keyboard

    b. wireless keyboard

    c. traditional keyboard

    d. flexible keyboard

3. The mouse _____ usually appears in the shape of an arrow.

    a. pointer

    b. marker

    c. indicator

    d. meter

4. This type of pointing device is located in the middle of the keyboard.

    a. joystick

    b. pointing stick

    c. wireless

    d. light pen

5. This type of pointing device has crisscrossed invisible beams of infrared light that are protected with a clear plastic outer layer.

    a. optical mouse

    b. light pen

    c. pointing stick

    d. touch screen

6. A Universal Product Code is read by what type of scanner?

    a. bar code

    b. flatbed

    c. OCR

    d. MICR

7. _____ input devices convert sounds into a form that can be processed by the system unit.

    a. Electrolyzing

    b. Plotting

    c. WebCam

    d. Audio

8. The most important characteristic of a monitor is its

    a. dot pitch

    b. resolution

    c. clarity

    d. viewable size

9. Which of the following printer types requires special paper?

    a. chain

    b. laser

    c. ink-jet

    d. thermal

10. _____ is a specialized input and output device for receiving and sending voice communication.

    a. Fax machine

    b. Internet telephone

    c. Network terminal

    d. PDA

For an interactive version of these multiple-choice questions, visit our Web site at www.computing2008.com and enter the keyword **multiple7**.

MATCHING

Match each numbered item with the most closely related lettered item. Write your answers in the spaces provided.

a. clarity

b. CRT

c. dpi

d. HDTV

e. joystick

f. stylus

g. TFT

h. thermal

i. toggle

j. UPC

1. These keys turn a feature on or off. ____
2. A pointing device widely used for computer games. ____
3. Penlike device commonly used with tablet PCs and PDAs. ____
4. Type of bar code used in supermarkets. ____
5. Refers to quality and sharpness of displayed images. ____
6. Type of monitor similar to a traditional television set. ____
7. Monitors that have independently activated pixels. ____
8. Delivers a much clearer wide-screen picture than regular television. ____
9. Measurement used to determine a printer's resolution. ____
10. Printer that uses heat to produce images on heat-sensitive paper. ____

For an interactive version of this matching exercise, visit our Web site at www.computing2008.com and enter the keyword **matching7**.

OPEN-ENDED

On a separate sheet of paper, respond to each question or statement.

1. Define input and output devices.
2. Describe the different types of pointing, scanning, image capturing, and audio-input devices.
3. Describe the three categories of output devices.
4. Define output and output devices.
5. What are combination input and output devices? Describe four such devices.

APPLYING TECHNOLOGY

The following questions are designed to demonstrate ways that you can effectively use technology today. The first question relates directly to this chapter's Making IT Work for You feature.

WebCams and Instant Messaging

1

Do you enjoy chatting with friends? Are you working on a project and need to collaborate with others in your group? What if you could see and hear your group online? Perhaps instant messaging and WebCams are just what you're looking for. It's easy and free with an Internet connection and the right software. To learn more about WebCams and instant messaging, review Making IT Work for You: WebCams and Instant Messaging on pages 190 and 191. Then answer the following questions: (a) How do you add a new friend to Windows Messenger? (b) What hardware is necessary to video conference with Windows Messenger? (c) When sharing an application, how do you give control of the application to a friend?

Internet Telephones

2

Do you need a cheaper way to stay in touch with friends and family? Did you know you can use your computer and the Internet to make long-distance calls to regular phones? All you need is some software and an Internet connection to get started. To learn more about this technology, visit our Web site at www.computing2008.com and enter the keyword phone. Then answer the following questions: (a) Which Internet phone service provider is featured in the examples? (b) What are the sliders used for in the Setup Wizard? (c) Which button is clicked to end a call?

Voice Recognition

3

Through voice recognition technology you can control your computer or dictate a term paper. Connect to our Web site at www.computing2008.com and enter the keyword voice to link to a leader in voice recognition software. Once there, read about the product's features and then answer the following: (a) Describe the features offered by the voice recognition software. (b) What input devices are required to use this software? (c) Do you think voice recognition software will replace keyboards and mice as primary input devices? Justify your answer.

Input and Output

EXPANDING YOUR KNOWLEDGE

The following questions are designed to add depth and detail to your understanding of specific topics presented within this chapter. The questions direct you to sources other than the textbook to obtain this knowledge.

1 How Digital Cameras Work

While traditional cameras capture images on film, digital cameras capture images, then convert them into a digital form. These images can be viewed immediately and saved to a disk or into the camera's memory. To learn more about how digital cameras work, visit our Web site at www.computing2008. com and enter the keyword photo. Then answer the following questions: (a) What is a CCD and what is its function? (b) What is an ADC and what is its function? (c) How are images transported from a digital camera to a computer?

2 How Internet Telephones Works

Internet telephones offer a low-cost alternative to making long-distance calls. Using the Internet telephone (or other appropriate audio-input and audio-output devices), the Internet, a special service provider, a sound card, and special software, you can place long-distance calls to almost anywhere in the world. To learn more about how Internet telephony works, visit our Web site at www. computing2008.com and enter the keyword phone. Then answer the following questions: (a) What input and output devices are used? (b) What advantages and disadvantages would these devices have compared to an Internet telephone? (c) If Chris were to place a call to Steve, would she incur traditional long-distance charges? Why or why not? (d) Create a drawing similar to the animation that would represent computer-to-computer telephony. Be sure to include and number the appropriate steps.

3 Handwriting Recognition

Handwriting recognition is a developing technology for direct input. Conduct a Web search with the keywords "handwriting recognition" to learn more about this technology. Then answer the following questions: (a) What types of devices and applications use handwriting recognition now? (b) What are some applications where handwriting recognition is the best choice for input? Why is this the case? (c) What are current limitations of handwriting recognition?

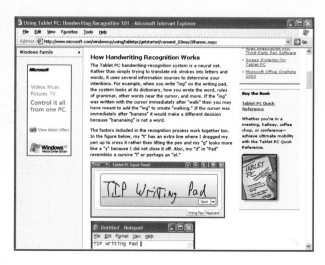

WRITING ABOUT TECHNOLOGY

The ability to think critically and to write effectively is essential to nearly every profession. The following questions are designed to help you develop these skills by posing thought-provoking questions about computer privacy, security, and/or ethics.

WebCams

1

Many WebCams broadcast live views of public places, such as university campuses, football stadiums, and city centers. Anyone with a WebCam and the right software can set up a WebCam broadcast. Visit our Web site at www.computing2008.com and enter the keyword broadcast to

link to a directory of public WebCams. Once connected, browse a few WebCam broadcasts and write a one-page paper that answers the following questions: (a) What WebCam broadcasts did you view? Describe the experience. (b) How does a user list his or her WebCam on the directory site? (c) Do you think WebCams can be used to enhance security? Justify your answer. (d) Do you think WebCams can be a violation of personal privacy? Justify your answer.

Electronic Security

2

Electronic monitoring equipment is becoming more widely used in stores, in the workplace, and in public. Consider the following questions and discuss your answers. Write a one-page summary of your analysis that answers the following questions: (a) What common applications of electronic monitoring or surveillance equipment have you noticed recently? (b) Does knowing that an electronic security device is in place make you feel more secure? (c) Have you ever felt that electronic surveillance equipment was an invasion of your privacy? (d) Consider the trade-off between security and privacy. In what cases is one more important than the other? Are these cases the same for everyone? Explain your answer.

CHAPTER

8

Floppy Disks
use magnetic charges to record data and are inexpensive, removable storage media

Optical Discs
use reflected light to record data and have very large storage capacities

Hard Disks
use magnetic charges to record data, have large storage capacities and fast retrieval times

SECONDARY STORAGE

Introduction

Secondary storage devices are used to save, to back up, and even to transport files consisting of data or programs from one location or computer to another. Not long ago, almost all files contained only numbers and letters. The demands for saving these files were easily met with low-capacity floppy disk drives and hard-disk drives.

Data storage has expanded from text and numeric files to include digital music files, photographic files, video files, and much more. These new types of files require secondary storage devices that have much greater capacity.

Secondary storage devices have always been an indispensable element in any computer system. They have similarities to output and input devices. Like output devices, secondary storage devices receive information from the system unit in the form of the machine language of 0s and 1s. Rather than translating the information, however, secondary storage devices save the information in machine language for later use. Like input devices, secondary storage devices send information to the system unit for processing. However, the information, since it is already in machine form, does not need to be translated. It is sent directly to memory (RAM), where it can be accessed and processed by the CPU.

Competent end users need to be aware of the different types of secondary storage. They need to know the capabilities, limitations, and uses of floppy disks, hard disks, optical discs, and other types of secondary storage. Additionally, they need to be aware of specialty storage devices for portable computers and to be knowledgeable about how large organizations manage their extensive data resources.

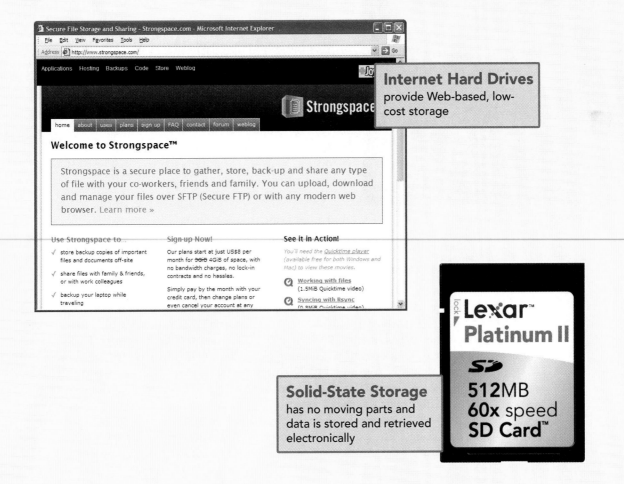

Internet Hard Drives provide Web-based, low-cost storage

Solid-State Storage has no moving parts and data is stored and retrieved electronically

An essential feature of every computer is the ability to save, or store, information. As discussed in Chapter 6, random-access memory (RAM) holds or stores data and programs that the CPU is presently processing. Before data can be processed or a program can be run, it must be in RAM. For this reason, RAM is sometimes referred to as **primary storage.**

Unfortunately, most RAM provides only temporary or volatile storage. That is, it loses all of its contents as soon as the computer is turned off. Its contents also are lost if there is a power failure that disrupts the electric current going into the system unit. This volatility results in a need for more permanent or nonvolatile storage for data and programs. We also need external storage because users need much more storage capacity than is typically available in a computer's primary or RAM memory.

Secondary storage provides permanent or nonvolatile storage. Using **secondary storage devices** such as a floppy disk drive, data and programs can be retained after the computer has been shut off. This is accomplished by *writing* files to and *reading* files from secondary storage devices. Writing is the process of saving information *to* the secondary storage device. Reading is the process of accessing information *from* secondary storage. This chapter focuses on secondary storage devices.

Some important characteristics of secondary storage include

- **Media** are the actual physical material that holds the data and programs. (See Figure 8-1.)
- **Capacity** measures how much a particular storage medium can hold.
- **Storage devices** are hardware that reads data and programs from storage media. Most also write to storage media.
- **Access speed** measures the amount of time required by the storage device to retrieve data and programs.

Most desktop microcomputer systems have floppy, hard, and optical disk drives.

Figure 8-1   Secondary storage media

FLOPPY DISKS

Floppy disks are portable or removable storage media. They are typically used to store and transport relatively small word processing, spreadsheet, and other types of files. They use flexible flat circular pieces of Mylar plastic that have been coated with a magnetic material. **Floppy disk drives (FDD)** store data and programs by altering the electromagnetic charges on the disk's surface to represent 1s and 0s. Floppy disk drives retrieve data and programs by reading these charges from the magnetic disk. Characters are represented by positive ($+$) and negative ($-$) charges using the ASCII, EBCDIC, or Unicode binary codes. For example, the number 3 would require a series of 8 charges. (See Figure 8-2.)

TRADITIONAL FLOPPY DISK

The traditional floppy disk is the 1.44 MB 2HD 3½-inch disk; 2HD means two-sided, high-density. Two-sided indicates that data can be stored on both sides of the disk. **Density** refers to how tightly the bits (electromagnetic charges) can be packed next to one another. These disks have a capacity of 1.44 megabytes—the equivalent of over 350 typewritten pages.

Floppy disks have a thin exterior jacket made of hard plastic to protect the flexible disk inside. (See Figure 8-3.) A **shutter** on the disk slides to the side to expose the recording surface. **Labels** provide users with an area to write or document the contents of the disk. The **write-protection notch** has a slide that opens and closes. In either position, files can be read from the floppy disk. When the notch is closed, files can be saved to the disk. In the open position, files cannot be saved to the floppy disk.

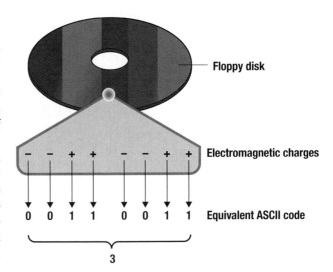

Figure 8-2 How charges on a disk surface store the number 3

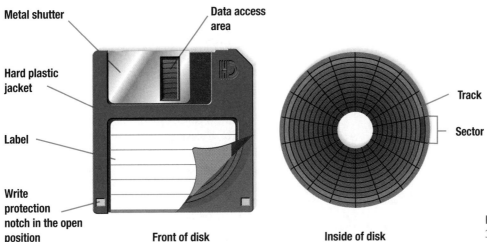

Figure 8-3 The parts of a 3½-inch floppy disk

As we discussed in Chapter 5, files are stored and organized on the flexible disk according to tracks and sectors. **Tracks** are rings of concentric circles without visible grooves. Each track is divided into invisible wedge-shaped sections called **sectors.** Each track's sector can store up to 512 bytes or characters.

To see how a floppy disk drive works, visit our Web site at www.computing2008.com and enter the keyword disk.

HIGH-CAPACITY FLOPPY DISKS

High-capacity disks are also known as **floppy disk cartridges.** Like the traditional floppy, the high-capacity disks are 3½ inches in diameter. However, they are able to store more information, are thicker, and require special disk drives. The most widely used high-capacity disk is the Zip disk produced by Iomega. These disks typically have a 100 MB, 250 MB, or 750 MB capacity—over 500 times as much as today's standard floppy disk. Zip disks are typically used to store multimedia, database, large text, and spreadsheet files. (See Figure 8-4.)

Figure 8-4 Zip disk and drive

At one time, floppy disks were adequate to handle most storage requirements and floppy disk drives were a standard feature of most system units. Floppy disks, however, do not have the capacity to store most of today's video and music files. As a result, floppy disks and floppy disk drives are not as widely used.

▼ CONCEPT CHECK

▶ Discuss four important characteristics of secondary storage.

▶ What is the traditional floppy disk? What is a high-capacity floppy disk?

▶ What is density? What are tracks and shutters?

HARD DISKS

Like floppy disks, hard disks save files by altering the magnetic charges of the disk's surface. While a floppy disk uses a thin flexible plastic disk, a **hard disk** uses thicker, rigid metallic platters that are stacked one on top of another. Hard disks store and organize files using tracks, sectors, and cylinders. A **cylinder** runs through each track of a stack of platters. Although not needed by floppy disks that have a single platter, cylinders are necessary to differentiate files stored on the same track and sector of different platters. When a hard disk is formatted, tracks, sectors, and cylinders are assigned.

Compared to floppy disks, hard disks are able to store and retrieve information much faster and have a greater capacity. They are, however, sensitive instruments. Their read/write heads ride on a cushion of air about 0.000001 inch thick. It is so thin that a smoke particle, fingerprint, dust, or human hair could cause what is known as a head crash. (See Figure 8-5.)

A **head crash** occurs when a read/write head makes contact with the hard disk's surface or with particles on its surface. A head crash is a disaster for a hard disk. The disk surface is scratched and some or all of the data is destroyed. At one time, head crashes were commonplace. Now, fortunately, they are rare.

There are three types of hard disks: internal hard disk, hard-disk cartridge, and hard-disk pack.

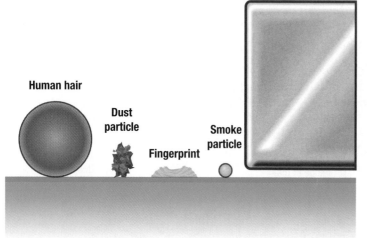

Figure 8-5 Materials that can cause a head crash

INTERNAL HARD DISK

An **internal hard disk** is located inside the system unit. For most microcomputer systems, the internal hard disk drive is designated as the C drive. It is used to store programs and large data files. For example, nearly every microcomputer uses its internal hard disk to store its operating system and major applications such as Word and Excel.

Internal hard disks have two advantages over floppy disks: capacity and access speed. A 700-gigabyte internal hard disk, for instance, can hold almost as much information as 490,000 standard floppy disks. Because hard disks rotate faster and their read/write heads are closer to the recording surface, the time required to find and retrieve information (access speed) is much faster than for floppy disks. For these reasons, almost all of today's powerful applications are designed to be stored on and run from an internal hard disk. To see how a hard disk works, visit our Web site at www.computing2008.com and enter the keyword disk.

www.computing2008.com

To ensure adequate performance of your internal hard disk, you should perform routine maintenance and periodically make backup copies of all important files. For hard-disk maintenance and backup procedures, refer to Chapter 5's coverage of the Windows utilities Backup, Disk Cleanup, and Disk Defragmenter.

HARD-DISK CARTRIDGES

While internal hard disks provide fast access, they have a fixed amount of storage and cannot be easily removed from the system cabinet. **Hard-disk cartridges** are as easy to remove as a cassette from a videocassette recorder. The amount of storage available to a computer system is limited only by the number of cartridges.

Hard-disk cartridges are used primarily to complement an internal hard disk. Because the cartridges are easily removed, they are particularly useful to protect or secure sensitive information. Other uses for hard-disk cartridges include backing up the contents of the internal hard disk and providing additional hard-disk capacity.

> **TIPS**
>
> Does your internal hard-disk drive run a lot and seem slow? Are you having problems with lost or corrupted files? The problem could be with fragmented files—files that when saved were broken into pieces (fragments) and stored in different locations on your hard disk. To clean up the disk and speed up access, consider defragging. If you are using Windows 98, 2000, or XP:
>
> **1** **Start Disk Defragmenter.** As discussed in Chapter 5, use Start/All Programs/Accessories/System Tools/Disk Defragmenter to start defragmenting your disk. Defragging rearranges the file parts so that they are stored in adjacent locations.
>
> **2** **Keep working.** You can continue running other applications while your disk is being defragmented. Unfortunately, your computer operates more slowly, and Disk Defragmenter takes longer to finish.
>
> **3** **Automate.** Use Start/All Programs/Accessories/System Tools/Scheduled Tasks to schedule this task to be done automatically for you in the future.
>
> To see additional tips, visit our Web site at www.computing2008.com and enter the keyword tips.

Hard-disk cartridges for desktop computers have typical capacities of 20 to 100 GB (gigabytes). One of the most widely used hard-disk cartridges is the Removable Hard Disk from Iomega. (See Figure 8-6.) Credit card–size hard-disk cartridges called **PC Card hard disks** are available for notebook computers with typical capacities up to 5 gigabytes. Two well-known PC Card hard disks are IBM's Microdrive and Toshiba's MK5002. (See Figure 8-7.)

Figure 8-6 Removable hard disk and drive

Figure 8-7 PC Card hard disk

HARD-DISK PACKS

Hard-disk packs are removable storage devices used to store massive amounts of information. (See Figure 8-8.) Their capacity far exceeds the other types of hard disks. Although you may never have seen one, it is almost certain that you have used them. Microcomputers that have access to the Internet, minicomputers, or mainframes often have access to external hard-disk packs through communication lines. Banks and credit card companies use them to record financial information.

Like internal hard disks, hard-disk packs have multiple recording platters aligned one above the other. Hard-disk packs, however, use much larger platters, use more platters, and are not enclosed in a special container. Hard-disk packs are stored in a hard plastic cover that is removed when the pack is mounted onto special drives. The drive rotates the pack and access arms move in and out between the rotating platters. Each access arm has two read/write heads. One reads the disk surface above it; the other reads the disk surface below it. All the access arms move in and out together. However, only one of the read/write heads is activated at a given moment. A disk pack with 11 disks provides 20 recording surfaces. This is because the top and bottom outside surfaces of the pack are not used. (See Figure 8-9.)

For a summary of the different types of hard disks, see Figure 8-10.

Figure 8-8 Hard-disk pack enclosed in a plastic cover

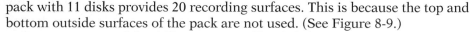

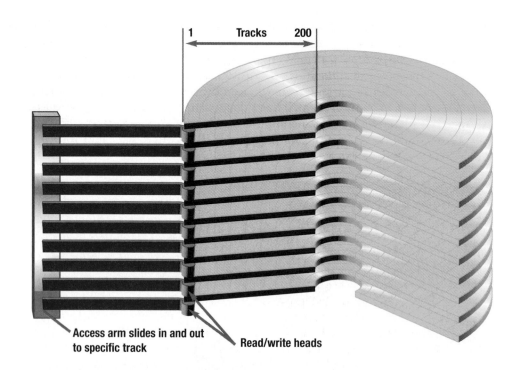

Access arm slides in and out to specific track

Read/write heads

Figure 8-9 Hard-disk pack

Type	Description
Internal	Fast access to applications, fixed
Cartridge	Complement to internal hard disk, removable
Disk pack	Massive storage capacity, removable

Figure 8-10 Types of hard disks

PERFORMANCE ENHANCEMENTS

Three ways to improve the performance of hard disks are disk caching, redundant arrays of inexpensive disks, and file compression/decompression.

Disk caching improves hard-disk performance by anticipating data needs. It performs a function similar to cache memory discussed in Chapter 6. While cache memory improves processing by acting as a temporary high-speed holding area between memory and the CPU, disk caching improves processing by acting as a temporary high-speed holding area between a secondary storage device and the CPU. Disk caching requires a combination of hardware and software. During idle processing time, frequently used data is read from the hard disk into memory (cache). When needed, the data is then accessed directly from memory. The transfer rate from memory is much faster than from the hard disk. As a result, overall system performance is often increased by as much as 30 percent.

Figure 8-11   RAID storage device

Redundant arrays of inexpensive disks (RAID) improve performance by expanding external storage, improving access speed, and providing reliable storage. Several inexpensive hard-disk drives are connected to one another. These connections can be by a network or within specialized RAID devices. (See Figure 8-11.) The connected hard-disk drives are related or grouped together, and the computer system interacts with the RAID system as though it were a single large-capacity hard-disk drive. The result is expanded storage capability, fast access speed, and high reliability. For these reasons, RAID is often used by Internet servers and large organizations.

File compression and **file decompression** increase storage capacity by reducing the amount of space required to store data and programs. File compression is not limited to hard-disk systems. It is frequently used to compress files on floppy disks as well. File compression also helps to speed up transmission of files from one computer system to another. Sending and receiving compressed files across the Internet is a common activity.

TIPS

Are you running short of hard-disk storage space? Want to send a large file or several files at once over the Internet? You can save both space and valuable connection time by compressing the files first. Compression/decompression utility programs are available in Windows XP. If you don't have Windows XP, consider using WinZip, a popular compression program:

1 **Start.** Start the WinZip program.

2 **Create file.** Click the *New* button on the toolbar to create and name a zip file.

3 **Select.** Locate and select the file(s) you want to compress.

4 **Compress.** Click the *Add* button to compress and add the selected file(s) to the zip file.

You can now replace the selected file(s) with the much smaller zip file. To access the original files at any time, start the WinZip program, select the file(s) to decompress, and click the WinZip *Extract* button.

To see additional tips, visit our Web site at www.computing2008.com and enter the keyword tips.

File compression programs scan files for ways to reduce the amount of required storage. One way is to search for repeating patterns. The repeating patterns are replaced with a token, leaving enough tokens so that the original can be rebuilt or decompressed. These programs often shrink files to a quarter of their original size. To learn more about file compression, visit our Web site at www.computing2008.com and enter the keyword compression.

You can compress and decompress files using specialized utilities such as WinZip from Nico Mak Computing and PKZip from PKWare. Or, if these specialized utilities are not available, you can use utility programs in Windows XP. For a summary of performance enhancement techniques, see Figure 8-12.

Technique	Description
Disk caching	Uses cache and anticipates data needs
RAID	Linked, inexpensive hard-disk drives
File compression	Reduces file size
File decompression	Expands compressed files

Figure 8-12   Performance enhancement techniques

▼ **CONCEPT CHECK**

▶ Compare floppy and hard disks. What is a head crash?

▶ What are the three types of hard disks? Briefly describe each.

▶ List and describe three ways to improve the performance of hard disks.

OPTICAL DISCS

Today's **optical discs** can hold over 50 gigabytes of data. (See Figure 8-13.) That is the equivalent of millions of typewritten pages or a medium-sized library all on a single disc. Optical discs are having a great impact on storage today, but we are probably only beginning to see their effects.

In optical-disc technology, a laser beam alters the surface of a plastic or metallic disc to represent data. Unlike floppy and hard disks, which use magnetic charges to represent 1s and 0s, optical discs use reflected light. The 1s and 0s are represented by flat areas called **lands** and bumpy areas called **pits** on the disc surface. The disc is read by an **optical disc drive** using a laser that projects a tiny beam of light on these areas. The amount of reflected light determines whether the area represents a 1 or a 0. To see how an optical disc drive works, visit our Web site at www.computing2008.com and enter the keyword optical.

Like floppy and hard disks, optical discs use tracks and sectors to organize and store files. Unlike the concentric tracks and wedge-shaped sectors used for floppy and hard disks, however, optical discs typically use a single track that spirals toward the center of the disc. This single track is divided into equally sized sectors.

Figure 8-13   Optical disc

COMPACT DISC

Compact disc, or as it is better known, **CD,** is one of the most widely used optical formats. CD drives are standard on many microcomputer systems. Typically, CD drives can store from 650 MB (megabytes) to 1 GB (gigabyte) of data on one side of a CD.

There are three basic types of CDs: read only, write once, and rewritable:

- **Read only—CD-ROM,** which stands for **compact disc–read-only memory,** is similar to a commercial music CD. *Read only* means it cannot be written on or erased by the user. Thus, you as a user have access only to the data imprinted by the publisher. CD-ROMs are used to distribute large databases and references. They also are used to distribute large software application packages.

- **Write once—CD-R,** which stands for **CD-recordable,** can be written to once. After that they can be read many times without deterioration but cannot be written on or erased. CD-R drives often are used to archive data and to record music downloaded from the Internet. To learn about how music is downloaded from the Internet, visit our Web site at www.computing2008.com and enter the keyword music.

- **Rewriteable—CD-RW** stands for **compact disc rewritable.** Also known as **erasable optical discs,** these discs are very similar to CD-Rs except that the disc surface is not permanently altered when data is recorded. Because they can be changed, CD-RWs are often used to create and edit multimedia presentations.

DIGITAL VERSATILE DISC

DVD stands for **digital versatile disc** or **digital video disc.** This is a newer format that has replaced CDs as the standard optical disc. DVDs are very similar to CDs except that more data can be packed into the same amount of space. (See Figure 8-14.) DVD discs can store 4.7 GB to 17 GB on a single DVD disc—17 times the capacity of CDs. There are three basic types of DVDs, similar to CDs: read only, write once, and rewriteable.

Figure 8-14 DVD disc drive

- **Read only—DVD-ROM** stands for **digital versatile disc–read-only memory.** DVD-ROM drives are also known as **DVD players.** DVD-ROMs are having a major impact on the video market. While CD-ROMs are effective for distributing music, they can only contain just over an hour of fair-quality video. DVD-ROMs can provide over two hours of high-quality video and sound comparable to that found in motion picture theaters. The motion picture industry has rapidly shifted video distribution from video cassettes to DVD-ROMs.

- **Write once—DVD+R** and **DVD−R** are two competing write-once formats. Both stand for **DVD recordable.** Each has a slightly different way in which it formats its discs. Fortunately, most new DVD players can use either format. These drives are typically used to create permanent archives for large amounts of data and to record videos. DVD recordable drives are rapidly replacing CD-R drives due to their massive capacity.

- **Rewriteable—DVD+RW, DVD−RW,** and **DVD-RAM** are the three most widely used formats. DVD+RW and DVD−RW stand for **DVD rewriteable. DVD-RAM** stands for **DVD random-access memory.** Each format has a unique way of storing data. Unfortunately, older DVD players typically can read only one type of format. Newer DVD players, however, are able to read and use any of the formats. Rewriteable DVD disc drives have rapidly replaced CD rewriteable drives. Applications range from recording video from camcorders to developing multimedia presentations that include extensive graphics and video.

HIGH-DEFINITION DISCS

While CDs and DVDs are the most widely used optical discs today, the future belongs to discs of even greater capacity. While DVD discs have sufficient capacity to record standard-definition movies and music, they are insufficient for recording high-definition video, which requires about four times as much storage. This next generation of optical disc is called **hi def (high definition),** with a far greater capacity than DVDs. Like CDs and DVDs, hi def has three basic types: read only, write once, and rewriteable.

Two different hi-def formats are competing to become the next optical disc standard. These versions are HD DVD and Blue-Ray:

- **HD DVD** stands for **high-definition DVD.** This format is very similar to DVD except that its storage capacity is much greater. HD DVD discs have a capacity of 15 to 45 gigabytes, or enough to store eight hours of high-definition video or enough to save an entire standard definition television series. One advantage of this standard is that current manufacturing plants producing standard DVD discs can be easily converted to mass produce HD DVD discs.
- **Blu-Ray** is a very different format than either the DVD or the HD DVD format. These discs, also known as **BDs,** have a capacity of 25 to 50 gigabytes, exceeding HD DVD disc capacity. Unlike HD DVD discs, however, Blue-Ray discs cannot be easily manufactured in existing DVD disc manufacturing plants. As a result, the widespread introduction of HD DVD discs will precede the widespread introduction of Blu-Ray discs.

Unfortunately, the HD DVD and Blu-Ray formats are not compatible with one another. This means that disk drives designed for HD DVD discs will not be able to read and write to Blu-Ray discs and vice versa. As a result, only one format is likely to become the next optical standard. Which one will it be? The Blue-Ray format has the endorsement of six major motion picture studios including Sony, Twentieth Century Fox, and Disney. The HD DVD format, however, uses less expensive discs and disc drives. Fortunately, disc drives able to use both formats are expected to become available in the near future.

For a summary of the different types of optical discs, see Figure 8-15.

Format	Typical Capacity	Description
CD	650 MB to 1 GB	Once the standard optical disc
DVD	4.7 GB to 17 GB	Current standard
HD DVD	15 GB to 45 GB	Hi-def format, similar to DVD
Blu-Ray	25 GB to 50 GB	Hi-def format, large capacity

Figure 8-15 Types of optical discs

▼ CONCEPT CHECK

► How is data represented on optical discs?

► Compare CD and DVD formats. Why did DVDs replace CDs?

► What is hi def? Compare HD DVD to Blu-Ray.

OTHER TYPES OF SECONDARY STORAGE

For the typical microcomputer user, the three basic storage options— floppy disk, hard disk, and optical disc—are complementary, not competing. Almost all microcomputers today have at least one floppy-disk drive, one hard-disk drive, and one optical drive. For many users, these secondary storage devices are further complemented with more specialized storage such as solid-state storage, Internet hard drives, and magnetic tape.

SOLID-STATE STORAGE

Each of the secondary storage devices discussed thus far has moving parts. For example, hard disks rotate and read/write heads move in and out. Unlike these devices, **solid-state storage** devices have no moving parts. Data and information are stored and retrieved electronically directly from these devices much as they would be from conventional computer memory. While this type of storage is more expensive than the others, it is more reliable and requires less power. For these reasons, this technology is becoming widely used for specialized secondary storage.

Figure 8-16   Flash memory card

Flash memory cards are credit card–sized solid-state storage devices widely used in notebook computers. (See Figure 8-16.) Flash memory also is used in a variety of specialized input devices to capture and transfer data to desktop computers. For example, flash memory is used to store images captured from digital cameras and then to transfer the images to desktop and other computers. Flash memory is used in digital media players like the iPod to store and play music and video files. To learn more about digital video players, see Making IT Work for You: iPods and Music from the Internet on pages 224 and 225.

Did you know that you can use your iPod as an external storage device to store and transfer files? It's easy and often convenient. Just follow the steps below.

TIPS

1 **Attach.** Connect your iPod to your computer.

2 **Start.** If the iTunes program is not active, start the program.

3 **Select.** Select Preference from the Edit menu then select the iPod tab.

4 **Enable.** Select Enable disk use.

5 **Store/transfer.** Your computer now recognizes your iPod as a secondary storage device and you can move files between your iPod and your computer.

To see additional tips, visit our Web site at www.computing2008.com and enter the keyword tips.

IPODs AND MUSIC FROM THE INTERNET

Did you know you can use the Internet to locate and play music? You can even create your own compact discs, or transfer music to a digital media player. All you need is the right software, hardware, and a connection to the Internet.

Finding Music There are many services on the Internet for finding music. The first step is to download software that connects with a music service. You can use this software to search for songs, create a playlist of songs you will listen to frequently, and play them. For example, to create a playlist using Apple iTunes:

1 ● Connect to *www.apple.com* and follow the on-screen instructions for downloading and installing the iTunes software.

2 ● Select *Music Store* from the Source List and follow the on-screen instructions to locate and purchase music files.

● Click the *Create a Playlist* button and enter a name for your playlist.

● Click *Library* in the Source list to view your songs.

● Drag songs you would like to hear to your playlist.

● Select your playlist and click the *Play* button to hear your music.

Creating a Custom CD   If your computer is equipped with a CD-R or CD-RW drive, creating a custom CD is one way to take your favorite tunes with you. To create a CD using iTunes:

①
● **Create a playlist as shown in the previous step.**

● **Select your playlist from the Source list.**

● **Click the _Burn Disc_ button.**

● **Insert a blank CD into your CD drive.**

● **Click the _Burn Disc_ button once more to create the CD.**

Uploading to a Digital Media Player   Another popular way to take your favorite tunes with you is to upload them to a digital media player. These players are lightweight digital storage devices that do not require cassettes or disks but that store music files internally. For example, you could transfer music to an iPod using iTunes software by following the steps below:

①
● **Connect your iPod to your computer. iTunes starts automatically and synchronizes with the songs in the iTunes library.**

● **To transfer individual music files, select them from the Library and drag them to _iPod_ in the source list.**

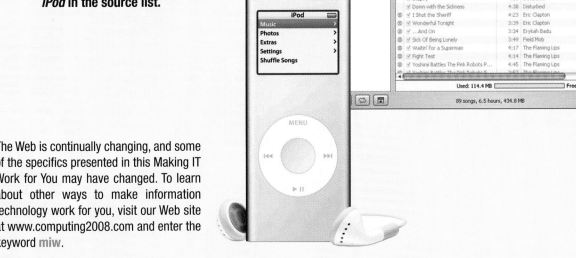

The Web is continually changing, and some of the specifics presented in this Making IT Work for You may have changed. To learn about other ways to make information technology work for you, visit our Web site at www.computing2008.com and enter the keyword miw.

Figure 8-17 USB drives

USB drives are so compact that they can be transported on a key ring or a necklace. (See Figure 8-17.) These drives conveniently connect directly to a computer's USB port to transfer files and have typical capacities of 2 GB. Due to their convenient size and large capacities, some predict that key chain hard drive devices may replace the floppy disk for transporting data and information between computers and a variety of specialty devices.

INTERNET HARD DRIVES

Special service sites on the Web provide users with storage. This storage is called an **Internet hard drive.** (See Figure 8-18.)

Advantages of Internet hard drives compared to other types of secondary storage include low cost and the flexibility to access information from any location using the Internet. Because all information must travel across the Internet, however, access speed is slower. Another consideration is that users are dependent on the availability and security procedures of the service site. Because of these limitations, Internet hard drives are typically used as a specialized secondary storage device and not for storing highly personalized or sensitive information.

Typically, Internet hard drive sites focus on supplying their services either to businesses or to individuals. The business-oriented sites provide faster access and greater security for a fee. The individual-focused sites provide limited storage for much lower cost and some sites are free. (See Figure 8-19.)

MAGNETIC TAPE

To find a particular song on an audiotape, you may have to play several inches of tape. Finding a song on an audio compact disc, in contrast, can be much faster. You select the track, and the disc player moves directly to it. That, in brief, represents the two different approaches to external storage. The two approaches are called **sequential access** and **direct access.**

Disks provide fast direct access. Tapes provide slower sequential access. With tape, information is stored in sequence, such as alphabetically. For example, all the grades of students at your school could be recorded on tape arranged alphabetically by their last names. To find the grades for one student, say Chris Reed, the search would begin at the start of the tape and search alphabetically past all the

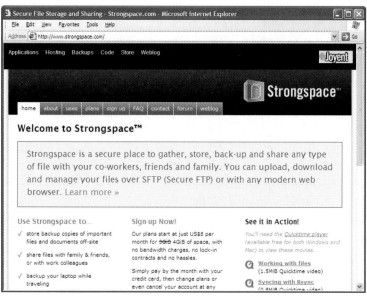

Figure 8-18 An Internet hard drive site

Focus	Company	Location
Individual	iBackup	www.ibackup.com
Individual	xDrive	www.xdrive.com
Business	Amerivault	www.amerivault.com
Business	Iron Mountain Digital	www.ironmountain.com

Figure 8-19 Internet hard drive sites

last names beginning with A to Q before ultimately reaching Reed. This may involve searching several inches or feet, which takes time.

Like floppy and hard disks, **magnetic tape** stores data and programs by altering the electromagnetic charges on a recording surface. Although slower to access specific information, magnetic tape is an effective and commonly used tool for backing up data. At one time, mainframe computers used **magnetic tape reels** exclusively. This type of tape is typically ½ inch wide and 1½ miles long and provides massive storage capacity. Now, most mainframes as well as microcomputers use **tape cartridges** or **magnetic tape streamers** to back up data. (See Figure 8-20.)

Figure 8-20 Magnetic tape cartridge

CONCEPT CHECK

▶ What is solid-state storage? What are USB drives?

▶ What are Internet hard drives? What are they used for?

▶ Discuss magnetic tape reels and tape cartridges.

MASS STORAGE DEVICES

It is natural to think of secondary storage media and devices as they relate to us as individuals. It may not be as obvious how important these matters are to organizations. **Mass storage** refers to the tremendous amount of secondary storage required by large organizations. **Mass storage devices** are specialized high-capacity secondary storage devices designed to meet organizational demands for data.

Most large organizations have established a strategy called an **enterprise storage system** to promote efficient and safe use of data across the networks within their organizations. (See Figure 8-21.) Some of the mass storage devices

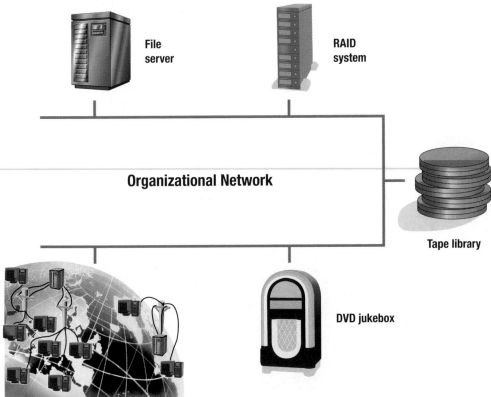

File server

RAID system

Organizational Network

Tape library

DVD jukebox

Internet backup

Figure 8-21 Enterprise storage system

that support this strategy are

- **File servers**—dedicated computers with very large storage capacities that provide users access to fast storage and retrieval of data.
- **RAID systems**—larger versions of the specialized devices discussed earlier in this chapter that enhance organizational security by constantly making backup copies of files moving across the organization's networks.
- **Tape library**—device that provides automatic access to data archived on a large collection or library of tapes.
- **DVD-ROM** and **CD-ROM jukeboxes**—provide automatic access to a large collection or library of optical discs.
- **Organizational Internet storage**—high-speed Internet connection to a dedicated remote organizational Internet drive site.

The availability, security, and organization of data are essential to the efficient operations of any organization.

▼ CONCEPT CHECK

▶ Define mass storage and mass storage devices.

▶ What is an enterprise storage system?

▶ List and describe five mass storage devices.

CAREERS IN IT

Software engineers analyze users' needs and create application software. (See Figure 8-22.) Software engineers typically have experience in programming but focus on the design and development of programs using the principles of mathematics and engineering. They rarely write code themselves.

A bachelor's degree in computer science or information systems and an extensive knowledge of computers and technology are required by most employers. Internships may provide students with the kinds of experience employers look for in a software engineer. Those with specific experience with networking, the Internet, and Web applications may have an advantage over other applicants. Employers typically look for software engineers with good communication and analytical skills.

Software engineers can expect to earn an annual salary in the range of $53,000 to $88,000. Advancement opportunities are usually tied to experience. Experienced software engineers may be promoted to project manager or have opportunities in systems design. To learn about other careers in information technology, visit us at www.computing2008.com and enter the keyword careers.

Figure 8-22 Software engineer

Your Entire Life Recorded on a Single Disk

Imagine if you could store every conversation you ever had on a single disk. What if you could capture your entire life on video stored on just a few disks? What if you could hold in your pocket the contents of the Library of Congress? Innovations in secondary storage capacity using molecular storage promise all of this and more.

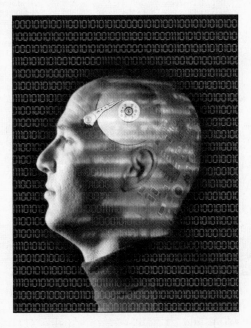

Currently, information is stored on magnetic or optical discs. In the future, the electron state of atoms in a molecule will hold information at a much greater density. Currently, experiments have yielded densities of 100 gigabytes per square inch. If successfully brought to market, such a product would yield a terabyte on one disc, enough to hold every conversation a person has throughout his or her entire lifetime. Experiments with three dimensional storing (where information is stored in height as well as area) and optical holography (where information is stored by light photons on specially treated crystals) promise to yield even greater storage in smaller packages.

The capability to store vast amounts of data offers a future both tantalizing and problematic. Although having a video of your life would be a wonderful memory tool, how could you sort and use so much information? Imagine having to search through hours of video just to verify the time of a lunch date or to remember where you parked your car. Fortunately, computer scientists are developing computer programs that can rapidly sort through and understand audio and visual material. Great strides have been made in creating programs that can scan photos and videos searching for a particular person's face. This technology is currently being used in airports to identify suspected terrorists. In the future, you may use this technology to search for photos of a loved one or video of the family vacation.

Is there a downside to recording every event in a person's life? Could your personal video log be used to incriminate you in a court of law? Could someone else's video log be an invasion of your right to privacy? The technology will soon be here. Are you ready for it? Would you use it to record your every move?

SECONDARY STORAGE

STORAGE

RAM is **primary storage.** Most RAM is volatile, meaning that it loses its contents whenever power is disrupted. **Secondary storage** provides nonvolatile storage. Secondary storage retains data and information after the computer system is turned off.

Writing is the process of saving information to **secondary storage devices.** Reading is the process of accessing information from secondary storage devices.

Important characteristics of secondary storage include

- **Media**—actual physical material that retains data and programs.
- **Capacity**—how much a particular storage medium can hold.
- **Storage devices**—hardware that reads and writes to storage media.
- **Access speed**—time required to retrieve data from a secondary storage device.

FLOPPY DISKS

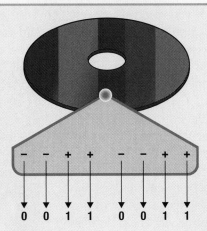

Floppy disks are flexible flat circular pieces of Mylar plastic coated with a magnetic material. **Floppy disk drives (FDD)** store data and programs by charging the disk surface.

Traditional Floppy Disk

The traditional floppy disk is the 2HD 1.44 MB 3½-inch disk. 2HD indicates two-sided high-**density** disk. Disks have **shutters** that open to provide access to the recording surface, **labels** to record disk content, and **write-protection notches** to allow or prohibit writing to the disk.

Files are stored and organized according to **tracks** (concentric circles) and **sectors** (wedge shapes).

High-Capacity Floppy Disks

High-capacity disks (floppy disk cartridges) have greater capacity than the traditional floppy disk. The most widely used are Zip disks, with typical capacities of 100 MB, 250 MB, and 750 MB.

Due to their limited storage capacity, floppy disks and floppy disk drives are no longer widely used.

To be a competent end user, you need to be aware of the different types of secondary storage. You need to know their capabilities, limitations, and uses. There are four widely used storage media: floppy disk, hard disk, optical disc, and other types of secondary storage.

HARD DISKS

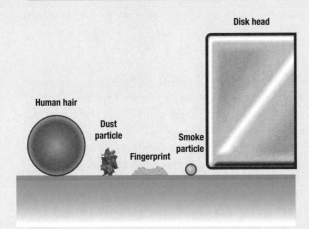

Compared to floppy disks, **hard disks** use rigid metallic platters that provide much greater capacity. Files are organized according to **tracks, sectors,** and **cylinders.**

A **head crash** occurs when the hard disk makes contact with the drive's read/write heads.

Three types of hard disks are internal hard disks, hard-disk cartridges, and hard-disk packs.

Internal Hard Disk
Internal hard disks are located within the system unit and typically identified as the C drive.

Hard-Disk Cartridge
Unlike internal hard disks, **hard-disk cartridges** are removable and their capacity is limited only by the number of cartridges. **PC Card hard disks** are for notebook computers.

HARD DISKS

Hard-Disk Packs
Hard-disk packs are removable and have several platters and extensive capacity. A disk pack typically has 11 platters with 20 recording surfaces.

Performance Enhancements
Three ways to improve hard disk performance are disk caching, RAID, and file compression and decompression.

- **Disk caching**—provides a temporary high-speed holding area between a secondary storage device and the CPU; improves performance by anticipating data needs and reducing time to access data from secondary storage.

- **RAID (redundant array of inexpensive disks)**—several inexpensive hard-disk drives are connected together; improves performance by providing expanded storage, fast access, and high reliability.

- **File compression** and **decompression**—files compressed before storing and then decompressed before being used again; improves performance through efficient storage.

OPTICAL DISCS

Optical discs use laser technology. 1s and 0s are represented by **pits** and **lands. Optical disc drives** project light and measure the reflected light.

Compact Disc
Compact discs (CDs) have typical capacity of 650 MB to 1 GB. Three types are **CD-ROM (compact disc–read-only memory), CD-R (CD-recordable** (CD-R drives are also known as CD burners)), and **CD-RW (compact disc rewritable, erasable optical discs).**

Digital Versatile Disc
DVDs (digital versatile discs, digital video discs) have far greater capacity than CDs (4.7 GB to 17 GB). Three types are **DVD-ROM (digital versatile disc–read-only memory; DVD players** are drives), write once **(DVD+R, DVD−R),** and rewriteable **(DVD+RW, DVD−RW, DVD-RAM).**

High-Definition Disc
Hi-def (high-definition) discs are the next standard optical disc. Two competing standards:

- **HD DVD (high-definition DVD)**—similar to DVD with greater storage (15 GB to 45 GB).
- **Blu-Ray discs (BDs)**—very different from DVD; greater capacity than HD DVD (25 GB to 50 GB).

OTHER TYPES

The three basic storage options (floppy, hard, and optical) are complementary and not competitive. Many users complement with more specialized devices including

- **Solid-state storage**—no moving parts. **Flash memory cards** are solid-state storage devices. **USB drives** provide very compact storage.
- **Internet hard drives**—Web-based, low-cost storage. Accessible from any Internet connection, these drives are often slow and security is an issue.
- **Magnetic tape—sequential access** (disks provide **direct access**) used primarily for backing up data. **Magnetic tape reels** were widely used with mainframes. Now **tape cartridges (magnetic tape streamers)** are most widely used for mainframes and microcomputers.

MASS STORAGE

Mass storage refers to the tremendous amount of secondary storage required by large organizations. **Mass storage devices** are specialized high-capacity secondary storage devices designed to meet organizational demands for data.

Most large organizations have established a strategy called an **enterprise storage system** to promote efficient and safe use of data across the networks within their organizations.

Mass storage devices that support this strategy are **file servers, RAID systems, tape libraries, DVD-ROM** and **CD-ROM jukeboxes,** and **organizational Internet storage.**

CAREERS IN IT

Software engineers analyze users' needs and create application software. Bachelor's degree in computer science or information systems and extensive knowledge of computers and technology required. Salary range $53,000 to $88,000.

KEY TERMS

www.computing2008.com

access speed   (214)
Blu-Ray (BD)   (222)
capacity   (214)
CD (compact disc)   (220)
CD-R (CD-recordable)   (220)
CD-ROM (compact disc–read-only
   memory)   (220)
CD-ROM jukebox   (228)
CD-RW (compact disc rewritable)   (221)
cylinder   (216)
density   (215)
direct access   (226)
disk caching   (219)
DVD (digital versatile disc or digital video
   disc)   (221)
DVD player   (221)
DVD−R (DVD recordable)   (221)
DVD+R (DVD recordable)   (221)
DVD-RAM (DVD random-access memory)
   (221)
DVD-ROM (DVD–read-only memory)   (221)
DVD-ROM jukebox   (228)
DVD−RW (DVD rewritable)   (221)
DVD+RW (DVD rewritable)   (221)
enterprise storage system   (227)
erasable optical disc   (221)
file compression   (219)
file decompression   (219)
file server   (228)
flash memory card   (223)
floppy disk   (214)
floppy disk cartridge   (214, 215)
floppy disk drive (FDD)   (214)
hard disk   (216)
hard-disk cartridge   (217)
hard-disk pack   (218)

HD DVD (high-definition DVD)   (222)
head crash   (216)
hi def (high definition)   (222)
high-capacity disk   (215)
internal hard disk   (216)
Internet hard drive   (226)
label   (215)
land   (220)
magnetic tape   (226)
magnetic tape reel   (227)
magnetic tape streamer   (227)
mass storage   (227)
mass storage devices   (227)
media   (214)
optical disc   (220)
optical disc drive   (220)
organizational Internet storage   (228)
PC Card hard disk   (217)
pit   (220)
primary storage   (214)
RAID system   (228)
redundant array of inexpensive disks (RAID)
   (219)
secondary storage   (214)
secondary storage device   (214)
sector   (215)
sequential access   (226)
shutter   (215)
software engineer   (228)
solid-state storage   (223)
storage device   (214)
tape cartridge   (227)
tape library   (228)
track   (215)
USB drive   (226)
write-protection notch   (215)

To test your knowledge of these key terms with animated flash cards, visit our Web site at
www.computing2008.com and enter the keyword **terms8**.

CROSSWORD PUZZLE

www.computing2008.com

FEATURES

Animations

Careers in IT

DVD Direct

Expansions

Making IT Work for You

On the Web Explorations

TechTV

Tips

CHAPTER REVIEW

Applying Technology

Crossword Puzzle

Expanding Your Knowledge

Key Terms

Matching

Multiple Choice

Open-Ended

Writing About Technology

Across

5 Improves hard disk performance by anticipating data needs.

6 Web-based storage.

7 Invisible wedge-shaped division of a track.

8 Portable and removable storage device.

10 Runs through each track of a stack of platters.

11 How tightly the bits can be packed next to each other.

Down

1 Ring of concentric circles without visible grooves.

2 Grouped disk drives treated as one hard disk by the computer system.

3 Measures the amount of time required to retrieve data.

4 Represent 1s and 0s.

9 Disk with 500 times the storage as a standard floppy.

For an interactive version of this crossword, visit our Web site at www.computing2008.com and enter the keyword **crossword8**.

MULTIPLE CHOICE

Circle the letter or fill in the correct answer.

1. Primary storage is referred to as ____ storage.
   - a. volatile
   - b. sequential
   - c. direct
   - d. nonvolatile

2. The amount of time required by a storage device to retrieve data and programs is its
   - a. access speed
   - b. capacity
   - c. memory
   - d. storage

3. How tightly the bits can be packed next to one another on a disk is referred to as
   - a. tracks
   - b. sectors
   - c. density
   - d. configuration

4. Thick, rigid metal platters that are capable of storing and retrieving information at a high rate of speed are known as
   - a. hard disks
   - b. soft disks
   - c. cartridges
   - d. packs

5. The data on an optical disc is represented by flat areas called ____ on the disc surface.
   - a. surfaces
   - b. flats
   - c. lands
   - d. pits

6. A CD-ROM disc
   - a. cannot be erased and rewritten
   - b. has more storage capacity than a CD-R
   - c. holds less data than a floppy disk
   - d. can be written to only once

7. DVD stands for
   - a. digital video data
   - b. direct video disc
   - c. digital versatile disc
   - d. direct versatile disc

8. This type of storage device has no moving parts.
   - a. hard disks
   - b. floppy disks
   - c. optical discs
   - d. solid state

9. Tape is described as using this type of access.
   - a. magneto-optical
   - b. DVD
   - c. direct
   - d. sequential

10. Specialized high-capacity secondary storage device designed to meet organizational demands for data.
    - a. Blue-Ray
    - b. hi def
    - c. mass storage
    - d. Zip disk

For an interactive version of these multiple-choice questions, visit our Web site at www.computing2008.com and enter the keyword multiple8.

MATCHING

Match each numbered item with the most closely related lettered item. Write your answers in the spaces provided.

a. access speed
b. file compression
c. flash memory card
d. hard-disk pack
e. hi def
f. Internet hard drive
g. RAM
h. solid-state storage
i. track
j. Zip disk

1. A type of storage that is volatile. ____
2. Time required to retrieve data and programs. ____
3. A high-capacity floppy disk. ____
4. Closed concentric ring on a disk on which data is recorded. ____
5. Several platters aligned one above the other, allowing greater storage capacity. ____
6. Increases storage capacity by reducing the amount of space required to store data and programs. ____
7. Stores data electronically and has no moving parts. ____
8. Solid-state storage device used in portable computers. ____
9. Free or low-cost storage available at special service Web sites. ____
10. The next generation of optical discs. ____

For an interactive version of this matching exercise, visit our Web site at www.computing2008.com and enter the keyword **matching8**.

OPEN-ENDED

On a separate sheet of paper, respond to each question or statement.

1. Discuss the traditional and high-capacity floppy disks.
2. What are the three types of hard disks? Describe three ways to improve hard disk performance.
3. What are the two most common optical disc formats? What is hi def? Describe the basic types for each format.
4. Discuss solid-state storage, Internet hard drives, and magnetic tape. What are the advantages and disadvantages of each?
5. Discuss mass storage, enterprise storage systems, and mass storage devices.

APPLYING TECHNOLOGY

The following questions are designed to demonstrate ways that you can effectively use technology today. The first question relates directly to this chapter's Making IT Work for You feature.

iPods and Music from the Internet

Did you know that you could use the Internet to locate music, download it to your computer, and create your own compact discs? All it takes is the right software, hardware, and a connection to the Internet. To learn more about creating your own CDs, review Making IT Work for You: iPods and Music from the Internet on pages 224 and 225. Then answer the following questions: (a) In iTunes, what is the difference between the library and the playlist? (b) What button do you press to have iTunes burn a playlist to a CD? (c) How do you transfer individual music files from the iTunes library to a portable music player?

iPod

Apple's iPod is a personal portable music player that stores a large number of digital music files. Connect to our Web site at www.computing2008.com and enter the keyword ipod to link to the iPod Web site. Once connected, read about the features and capabilities of iPod, and then answer the following questions: (a) How are music files transferred to iPod? (b) What type of secondary storage does iPod use? (c) What is iPod's storage capacity?

USB Storage Devices

Do you need to carry more data than will fit on a single floppy disk or CD? A USB storage device might be for you. These devices store large amounts of data in a package small enough to travel with your car keys. Connect to our Web site at www.computing2008.com and enter the keyword keychain to link to a site that features USB storage devices. Explore the site and then answer the following questions: (a) What type of secondary storage do USB storage devices use? (b) How is data transferred to and from computer systems? (c) What system software are the USB storage devices compatible with? (d) What are typical capacities of the USB storage devices?

EXPANDING YOUR KNOWLEDGE

The following questions are designed to add depth and detail to your understanding of specific topics presented within this chapter. The questions direct you to sources other than the textbook to obtain this knowledge.

1 How Music Is Downloaded from the Internet

One of the most popular activities on the Internet is to locate and download music files. Using a CD-R drive, the files are saved onto an optical disc. These discs can then be played in a variety of different types of devices. To learn more about how music is downloaded, visit our Web site at www.compuitng2008.com and enter the keyword music. Then answer the following questions: (a) Go to the Web and find a Web site where you can download music from the Internet. What Web site did you find? How much do they charge to download music? (b) When you download music from the Internet, where is it stored on your computer? (c) Name three ways you can play music from the Internet.

2 File Compression

A common problem for computer users is that they run out of hard disk space. File compression software can open up space on a full hard drive, improve system performance, and make files easier to find and organize. To learn more about file compression, visit our Web site at www.computing2008.com and enter the keyword compression. Then answer the following questions: (a) What are the two types of file compression? How do they differ? (b) What type of file compression is used for home movies? Why? (c) What type of file compression is used for a resume? Why? (d) Research a compression/decompression utility on the Web. What types of files does your utility create? Is this a lossy or lossyless file compression?

3 Internet Hard Drives

Internet hard drives offer remote file storage or backup. Research an Internet hard drive service on the Web and then answer the following questions: (a) What Internet hard drive did you research? (b) What is the cost for using the Internet hard drive, and what services do you get for that price? (c) How are files accessed from and uploaded to the Internet hard drive? (d) What

assurances does the Internet hard drive service provider offer concerning availability of your data? What about security?

WRITING ABOUT TECHNOLOGY

The ability to think critically and to write effectively is essential to nearly every profession. The following questions are designed to help you develop these skills by posing thought-provoking questions about computer privacy, security, and/or ethics.

CD-R and Music Files

1

Creating a custom CD of your favorite music is a popular use of secondary storage. Many sites on the Web offer free music that you can download. However, not all music files that are available on the Internet are freely distributable. Consider the following questions and write a one-page paper addressing them: (a) Is it fair to make a copy on your computer of a CD you have purchased? (b) Would it be fair to give a burned copy of a CD to a friend? What if the friend would not have otherwise purchased that CD? (c) People have been making illegal copies of music cassette tapes for some time. Why is using the Internet to make and distribute copies of music receiving so much attention?

Storage Trade-offs

2

As you have seen in this chapter, there are many different types of secondary storage. No one type is best for all situations or purposes, and any choice in selecting secondary storage involves certain trade-offs. Write a one-page paper titled "Secondary Storage Trade-offs" that addresses the following: (a) Summarize the following types of secondary storage: hard disks, optical discs, floppy disks, and solid state. Rank each type of storage based on the following considerations: capacity, access time, and cost. *Hint: You may wish to organize this in a table.* (b) Based on your summary, describe some situations for each type of secondary storage where that type is a good choice. (c) What relationships do you see between capacity and access time, cost and access time, and cost and capacity?

CHAPTER

9

COMPETENCIES

After you have read this chapter, you should be able to:

1 Discuss connectivity, the wireless revolution, and communication systems.

2 Describe physical and wireless communications channels.

3 Discuss connection devices, including modems, T1, DSL, cable modem, satellite, and cellular connections.

4 Describe data transmission factors, including bandwidths and protocols.

5 Discuss networks and key network terminologies.

6 Describe different types of networks, including local area, metropolitan area, and wide area networks.

7 Describe network architectures, including configurations and strategies.

8 Describe organizational uses of Internet technologies, including intranets, extranets, and firewalls.

Connectivity
provides incredible power to you while at and away from your desk

Communication Channels
transmit data via telephone lines, coaxial cables, microwave, and satellite

Connection Devices
convert analog and digital signals; modems, DSL, cable, satellites, and cellular provide connections

Introduction

The mobile telephone and other wireless technologies are revolutionizing how we use computers today. You can connect your microcomputer to other people's microcomputers, to the Internet, and to other, larger computers located throughout the world. As we've mentioned earlier, this connectivity puts incredible power on your desk. The result is increased productivity—for you as an individual and for the groups and organizations of which you are a member. Connectivity has become particularly important in business, where individuals now find themselves connected in networks to other individuals and departments.

Communication systems are the electronic systems that transmit data over communications lines from one location to another. You might work for an organization whose computer system is spread throughout a building, or even throughout the country or world. Or you might use telecommunications lines—telephone lines—to tap into information located in an outside data bank. You could then transmit it to your microcomputer for your own reworking and analysis.

You can even set up a network in your home or apartment using existing telephone lines. Or you can set up a wireless network. Then you can share files, use one Internet connection, and play interactive games with others in your home.

Competent end users need to understand the concept of connectivity, the impact of the wireless revolution, and the elements of a communication system. Additionally, they need to understand the basics of communication channels, connection devices, data transmission, networks, network types, network architectures, and organizational networks.

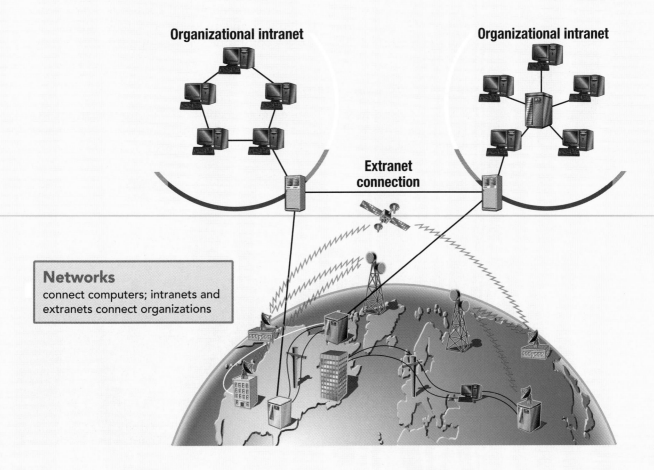

Organizational intranet

Organizational intranet

Extranet connection

Networks
connect computers; intranets and extranets connect organizations

Computer communications is the process of sharing data, programs, and information between two or more computers. We have discussed numerous applications that depend on communication systems, including

- **E-mail**—provides a fast, efficient alternative to traditional mail by sending and receiving electronic documents.
- **Instant messaging**—supports direct, "live" electronic communication between two or more friends or buddies.
- **Internet telephone**—provides a very low-cost alternative to long-distance telephone calls using electronic voice delivery.
- **Electronic commerce**—buying and selling goods electronically.

In this chapter, we will focus on the communication systems that support these and many other applications. Connectivity, the wireless revolution, and communication systems are key concepts and technologies for the 21st century.

CONNECTIVITY

Connectivity is a concept related to using computer networks to link people and resources. For example, connectivity means that you can connect your microcomputer by telephone or other telecommunications links to other computers and information sources almost anywhere. With this connection, you are linked to the world of larger computers and the Internet. This includes minicomputers and mainframes and their extensive information resources. Thus, becoming computer competent and knowledgeable becomes a matter of knowing not only about connectivity through networks to microcomputers, but also about larger computer systems and their information resources.

THE WIRELESS REVOLUTION

The single most dramatic change in connectivity and communications in the past five years has been the widespread use of mobile or wireless telephones. Students, parents, teachers, businesspeople, and others routinely talk and

Figure 9-1 Connectivity options

communicate with these devices. It is estimated that over 600 million mobile telephones are in use worldwide. This wireless technology allows individuals to stay connected with one another from almost anywhere at any time.

So what's the revolution? While this wireless technology was originally intended for voice communication, it is now becoming widely used to support all kinds of communication, especially computer communication. In addition, wireless technology promises to allow a wide variety of nearby devices to communicate with one another without any physical connection. You can share a high-speed printer, share data files, and collaborate on working documents with a nearby co-worker without having your computers connected by cables or telephone—wireless communication. Other wireless technology allows individuals to connect to the Internet and share information from almost anywhere in the world. (See Figure 9-1.) But is it a revolution? Most experts say yes and that the revolution is just beginning.

COMMUNICATION SYSTEMS

Communication systems are electronic systems that transmit data from one location to another. Whether wired or wireless, every communication system has four basic elements (see Figure 9-2.)

- **Sending and receiving devices.** These are often a computer or specialized communication device. They originate (send) as well as accept (receive) messages in the form of data, information, and/or instructions.
- **Communication channel.** This is the actual connecting or transmission medium that carries the message. This medium can be a physical wire or cable, or it can be wireless.
- **Connection devices.** These devices act as an interface between the sending and receiving devices and the communication channel. They convert outgoing messages into packets that can travel across the communication channel. They also reverse the process for incoming messages.
- **Data transmission specifications.** These are rules and procedures that coordinate the sending and receiving devices by precisely defining how the message will be sent across the communication channel.

For example, if you wanted to send an e-mail to a friend, you could create and send the message using your computer, the *sending device*. Your modem, a *connection device*, would modify and format the message so that it could travel efficiently across *communication channels*, such as telephone

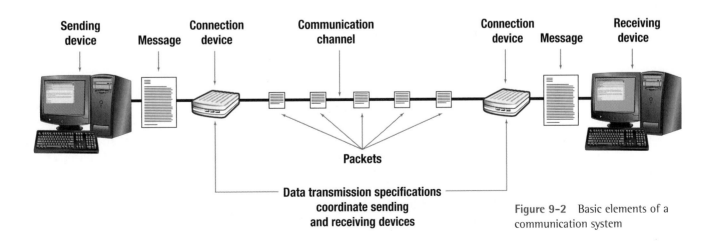

Figure 9-2 Basic elements of a communication system

lines. The specifics describing how the message is modified, reformatted, and sent would be described in the *data transmission specifications*. After your message traveled across the channel, the receiver's modem, a connection device, would reform it so that it could be displayed on your friend's computer, the *receiving device*. (Note: This example presents the basic communication system elements involved in sending e-mail. It does not and is not intended to demonstrate all the specific steps and equipment involved in an e-mail delivery system.)

▼ CONCEPT CHECK

▶ Define communications and connectivity.

▶ What is the wireless revolution?

▶ Describe the four elements of every communication system.

COMMUNICATION CHANNELS

Communication channels are an essential element of every communication system. These channels actually carry the data from one computer to another. There are two categories of communication channels. One category connects sending and receiving devices by providing a physical connection, such as a wire or cable. The other category is wireless.

PHYSICAL CONNECTIONS

Physical connections use a solid medium to connect sending and receiving devices. These connections include telephone lines (twisted pair), coaxial cable, and fiber-optic cable.

Figure 9-3   Twisted-pair cable

Figure 9-4   Coaxial cable

Figure 9-5   Fiber-optic cable

- **Telephone lines** you see strung on poles consist of twisted-pair cable, which is made up of hundreds of copper wires. A single twisted pair culminates in a wall jack into which you can plug your phone and computer. (See Figure 9-3.) Telephone lines have been the standard transmission medium for years for both voice and data. However, they are now being phased out by more technically advanced and reliable media.

- **Coaxial cable,** a high-frequency transmission cable, replaces the multiple wires of telephone lines with a single solid-copper core. (See Figure 9-4.) In terms of the number of telephone connections, a coaxial cable has over 80 times the transmission capacity of twisted pair. Coaxial cable is used to deliver television signals as well as to connect computers in a network.

- **Fiber-optic cable** transmits data as pulses of light through tiny tubes of glass. (See Figure 9-5.) In terms of the number of telephone connections, fiber-optic cable has over 26,000 times the transmission capacity of twisted-pair cable. Compared to coaxial cable, they are lighter and more reliable at transmitting data. They transmit information using beams of light at light speeds instead of pulses of electricity, making them far faster than copper cable. Fiber-optic cable is rapidly replacing twisted-pair cable telephone lines.

WIRELESS CONNECTIONS

Wireless connections do not use a solid substance to connect sending and receiving devices. Rather, they use the air itself. Primary technologies used for wireless connections are infrared, broadcast radio, microwave, and satellite.

Figure 9-6   Microwave dish

- **Infrared** uses infrared light waves to communicate over short distances. It is sometimes referred to as line-of-sight communication because the light waves can only travel in a straight line. This requires that sending and receiving devices must be in clear view of one another without any obstructions blocking that view. One of the most common applications is to transfer data and information from a portable device such as a notebook computer or PDA to a desktop computer.

- **Broadcast radio** uses radio signals to communicate with wireless devices. For example, cellular telephones and many Web-enabled devices use broadcast radio to place telephone calls and/or to connect to the Internet. Some end users connect their notebook or handheld computers to a cellular telephone to access the Web from remote locations. Most of these Web-enabled devices follow a standard known as **Wi-FI (wireless fidelity).** This wireless standard is widely used to connect computers to each other and to the Internet.

- **Microwave** communication uses high-frequency radio waves. Like infrared, microwave communication provides line-of-sight communication because microwaves travel in a straight line. Because the waves cannot bend with the curvature of the earth, they can be transmitted only over relatively short distances. Thus, microwave is a good medium for sending data between buildings in a city or on a large college campus. For longer distances, the waves must be relayed by means of microwave stations with microwave dishes or antennas. (See Figure 9-6.) These stations can be installed on towers, high buildings, and mountaintops.

  Bluetooth is a short-range wireless communication standard that uses microwaves to transmit data over short distances of up to approximately 33 feet. Unlike traditional microwaves, Bluetooth does not require line-of-sight communication. Rather, it uses radio waves that can pass through nearby walls and other nonmetal barriers. It is anticipated that within the next few years, this technology will be widely used to connect a variety of different communication devices.

Figure 9-7   Satellite

- **Satellite** communication uses satellites orbiting about 22,000 miles above the earth as microwave relay stations. (See Figure 9-7.) Many of these are offered by Intelsat, the International Telecommunications Satellite Consortium, which is owned by 114 governments and forms a worldwide communication system. Satellites rotate at a precise point and speed above the earth. They can amplify and relay microwave signals from one transmitter on the ground to another. Satellites can be used to send and receive large volumes of data. Uplink is a term relating to sending data to a satellite. Downlink refers to receiving data from a satellite. The major drawback to satellite communication is that bad weather can sometimes interrupt the flow of data.

  One of the most interesting applications of satellite communications is for global positioning. A network of 24 satellites owned and managed by the Defense Department continuously sends location information to earth. **Global positioning system (GPS)** devices use that information to uniquely determine the geographical location of the device. Available in some automobiles to provide navigational support, these systems are often mounted into the dash with a monitor to display maps and speakers to provide spoken directions. (See Figure 9-8.)

Figure 9-8 GPS navigation

Channel	Description
Twisted pair	Copper wire, standard voice telephone line
Coaxial cable	Solid copper core, more than 80 times the capacity of twisted pair
Fiber-optic cable	Light carries data, more than 26,000 times the capacity of twisted pair
Infrared	Infrared light travels in a straight line
Broadcast radio	Radio waves used by cellular telephones and other wireless devices
Microwave	High-frequency radio waves, travels in straight line through the air
Satellite	Microwave relay station in the sky, used by GPS devices

Figure 9-9 Types of communication channels

For a summary of communication channels, see Figure 9-9.

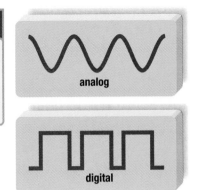

Figure 9-10 Analog versus digital signals

CONNECTION DEVICES

A great deal of computer communication takes place over telephone lines. However, because the telephone was originally designed for voice transmission, telephones typically send and receive **analog signals,** which are continuous electronic waves. Computers, in contrast, send and receive **digital signals.** (See Figure 9-10.) These represent the presence or absence of an electronic pulse—the on/off binary signals we mentioned in Chapter 6. To convert the digital signals to analog signals and vice versa, you need a modem.

MODEMS

The word **modem** is short for *modulator-demodulator.* **Modulation** is the name of the process of converting from digital to analog. **Demodulation** is the process of converting from analog to digital. The modem enables digital microcomputers to communicate across analog telephone lines. This communication includes both voice and data communications.

The speed with which modems transmit data varies. This speed, called **transfer rate,** is typically measured in **bits per second (bps).** (See Figure 9-11.) The higher the speed, the faster you can send and receive information. For example, transferring an image like Figure 9-10 might take 75 seconds with a 33.6 kbps modem and only 45 seconds with a 56 kbps modem.

There are four basic types of modems: external, internal, PC Card, and wireless. (See Figure 9-12.)

Unit	Speed
bps	bits per second
kbps	thousand bits per second
mbps	million bits per second
gbps	billion bits per second

Figure 9-11 Transfer speeds

- The **external modem** stands apart from the computer and typically is connected by a cable to the computer's serial port. Another cable connects the modem to the telephone wall jack.

- The **internal modem** consists of a plug-in circuit board inside the system unit. A telephone cable connects the modem to the telephone wall jack.

- The **PC Card modem** is a credit card–size expansion board that is inserted into portable computers. A telephone cable connects the modem to the telephone wall jack.

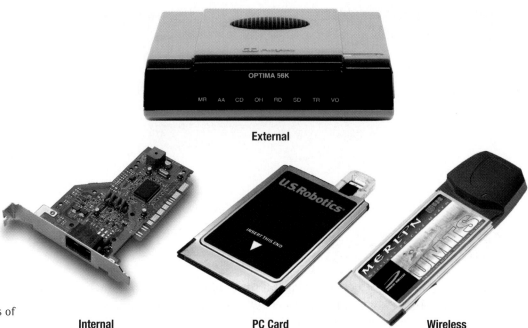

Figure 9-12 Basic types of modems

External

Internal

PC Card

Wireless

- A **wireless modem** may be internal, external, or a PC Card. Unlike the other modems, it does not use cables. Instead, wireless modems send and receive through the air.

CONNECTION SERVICE

Standard telephone lines and conventional modems provide what is called a **dial-up service.** Although still the most popular type of connection service, dial-up service is quite slow, and many users find it inadequate to meet their communication needs.

For years, large corporations have been leasing special high-speed lines from telephone companies. These lines—known as **T1, T2, T3,** and **T4 lines**—support all digital communications, do not require conventional modems, and provide very high capacity. Unfortunately, this type of connection is very expensive. For example, T1 lines provide a speed of 1.5 mbps (over 26 times as fast as a conventional modem) and cost several thousand dollars.

While the special high-speed lines are too costly for most individuals, there are affordable connections that provide significantly higher capacity than standard dial-up service. These include DSL, cable modems, satellite, and cellular. For a comparison of typical user connection costs and speeds, see Figure 9-13.

- **Digital subscriber line (DSL)** uses existing telephone lines to provide high-speed connections. **ADSL (asymmetric digital subscriber line)** is one of the most widely used types of DSL. This technology is widely available in most areas.

- **Cable modems** use existing television cables to provide high-speed connections as fast as a T1 or DSL connection, at a lower cost. Although cable connections reach 90 percent of the homes in America, all cable companies do not support cable modems. Industry observers, however, predict 100 percent availability within the next few years.

Type	Monthly Fee	Speed	Seconds to Receive Image
Dial-up	$10	56 kbps	45.0 seconds
DSL	30	30 mbps	0.85 second
Cable modem	40	40 mbps	0.65 second
Satellite	75	900 kbps	2.8 seconds
Cellular	55	550/50 kbps	4.6/51.0 seconds

Figure 9-13 Typical user connection costs and speeds

- **Satellite/air connection services** use satellites and the air to download (downlink) or send data to users at a rate seven times faster than dial-up connections. While older satellite services could not upload (uplink) or send data to satellites and had to rely on slow dial-up connections, newer two-way satellite connections are now available. While slower than DSL and cable modems, satellite/air connections are available almost anywhere that a satellite-receiving disk can be aimed at the southern skies.

- **Cellular services** offer an alternative for mobile devices and laptops. Using **3G cellular networks**, devices such as cell phones and appropriately equipped laptop computers can download data from the Internet at 400 to 700 kbps. Uploading data, however, is a much slower 50 kbps. At present, the availability of this service is limited to specific metropolitan areas. In the future, however, this service is expected to be more widespread and to operate at speeds comparable to DSL.

▼ CONCEPT CHECK

▶ What is the function of a modem?

▶ Compare the four types of modems.

▶ Describe the high-speed Internet connection options affordable to most users.

DATA TRANSMISSION

Several factors affect how data is transmitted. These factors include bandwidth and protocols.

BANDWIDTH

Bandwidth is a measurement of the width or capacity of the communication channel. Effectively, it means how much information can move across the communication channel in a given amount of time. For example, to transmit text documents, a slow bandwidth would be acceptable. However, to effectively transmit video and audio, a wider bandwidth is required. There are three categories of bandwidth.

- **Voiceband,** also known as **low bandwidth,** is used for standard telephone communication. Microcomputers with standard modems and dial-up service use this bandwidth. While effective for transmitting text documents, it is too slow for many types of transmission, including high-quality audio and video. Typical speeds are 56 to 96 kbps.

- **Medium band** is the bandwidth used in special leased lines to connect minicomputers and mainframes as well as to transmit data over long distances. Unlike voiceband and broadband, medium band is not typically used by individuals.

- **Broadband** is the bandwidth used for high-capacity transmissions. Microcomputers with DSL, cable, and satellite connections as well as other more specialized high-speed devices use this bandwidth. It is capable of effectively meeting most of today's communication needs, including transmitting high-quality audio and video. Speeds are typically 1.5 mbps, although much higher speeds are possible.

PROTOCOLS

For data transmission to be successful, sending and receiving devices must follow a set of communication rules for the exchange of information. These rules for exchanging data between computers are known as **protocols.**

The standard protocol for the Internet is **TCP/IP (transmission control protocol/Internet protocol).** The essential features of this protocol involve (1) identifying sending and receiving devices and (2) reformatting information for transmission across the Internet.

- **Identification:** Every computer on the Internet has a unique numeric address called an **IP address (Internet protocol address).** Similar to the way a postal service uses addresses to deliver mail, the Internet uses IP addresses to deliver e-mail and to locate Web sites. Because these numeric addresses are difficult for people to remember and use, a system was developed to automatically convert text-based addresses to numeric IP addresses. This system uses a **domain name server (DNS)** that converts text-based addresses to IP addresses. For example, whenever you enter a URL, say www.computing2008.com, a DNS converts this to an IP address before a connection can be made. (See Figure 9-14.)

- **Reformatting:** Information sent or transmitted across the Internet usually travels through numerous interconnected networks. Before the message is sent, it is reformatted or broken down into small parts called **packets.** Each packet is then sent separately over the Internet, possibly traveling different routes to one common destination. At the receiving end, the packets are reassembled into the correct order.

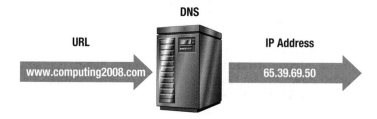

Figure 9-14 DNS converts text-based addresses to numeric IP addresses

▼ CONCEPT CHECK

▶ What is bandwidth? Describe the three categories.

▶ What are protocols? What is TCP/IP? What is DNS? What are packets?

NETWORKS

A **computer network** is a communication system that connects two or more computers so that they can exchange information and share resources. Networks can be set up in different arrangements to suit users' needs. (See Figure 9-15.)

TERMS

There are a number of specialized terms that describe computer networks. These terms include

- **Node**—any device that is connected to a network. It could be a computer, printer, or data storage device.

- **Client**—a node that requests and uses resources available from other nodes. Typically, a client is a user's microcomputer.

- **Server**—a node that shares resources with other nodes. Dedicated servers specialize in performing specific tasks. Depending on the specific task, they may be called an application server, communication server, database server, file server, printer server, or Web server.

- **Hub**—the center or central node for other nodes. This device can be a server or simply a connection point for cables from other nodes.

- **Network interface cards (NIC)**—as discussed in Chapter 6, these are expansion cards located within the system unit that connect the computer to a network. Sometimes referred to as a LAN adapter.

- **Network operating systems (NOS)**—control and coordinate the activities of all computers and other devices on a network. These activities include electronic communication and the sharing of information and resources.

- **Distributed processing**—a system in which computing power is located and shared at different locations. This type of system is common in decentralized organizations where divisional offices have their own computer systems. The computer systems in the divisional offices are networked to the organization's main or centralized computer.

- **Host computer**—a large centralized computer, usually a minicomputer or a mainframe.

- **Network administrator**—a computer specialist responsible for efficient network operations and implementation of new networks.

A network may consist only of microcomputers, or it may integrate microcomputers or other devices with larger computers. Networks can be controlled by all nodes working together equally or by specialized nodes coordinating and supplying all resources. Networks may be simple or complex, self-contained or dispersed over a large geographical area.

▼ CONCEPT CHECK

▶ What is a computer network? What are nodes, clients, servers, hubs, and host computers?

▶ What is the function of an NIC and an NOS?

▶ What is distributed processing and what is a network administrator?

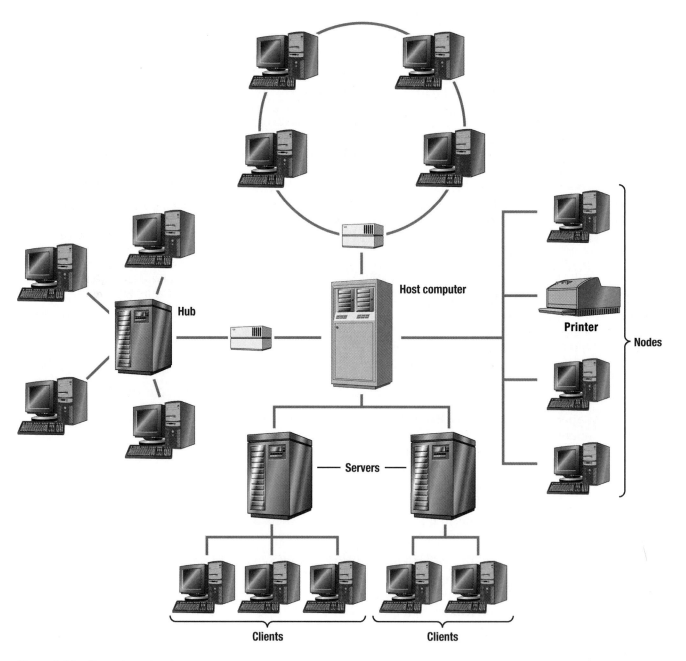

Figure 9-15   Computer network

Clearly, different types of channels—cable or air—allow different kinds of networks to be formed. Telephone lines, for instance, may connect communications equipment within the same building or within a home. Networks also may be citywide and even international, using both cable and air connections. Local area, metropolitan area, and wide area networks are distinguished by the geographical area they serve.

LOCAL AREA NETWORKS

Networks with nodes that are in close physical proximity—within the same building, for instance—are called **local area networks (LANs).** Typically, LANs span distances less than a mile and are owned and operated by individual organizations. LANs are widely used by colleges, universities, and other types of organizations to link microcomputers and to share printers and other resources. For a simple LAN, see Figure 9-16.

The LAN represented in Figure 9-16 is a typical arrangement and provides two benefits: economy and flexibility. People can share costly equipment. For instance, the four microcomputers share the laser printer and the file server, which are expensive pieces of hardware. Other equipment or nodes also may be added to the LAN—for instance, more microcomputers, a mainframe computer, or optical-disc storage devices. Additionally, the **network gateway** is a device that allows one LAN to be linked to other LANs or to larger networks. For example, the LAN of one office group may be connected to the LAN of another office group.

There are a variety of different standards or ways in which nodes can be connected to one another and ways in which their communications are controlled in a LAN. The most common standard is known as **Ethernet.** LANs using this standard are sometimes referred to as Ethernet LANs.

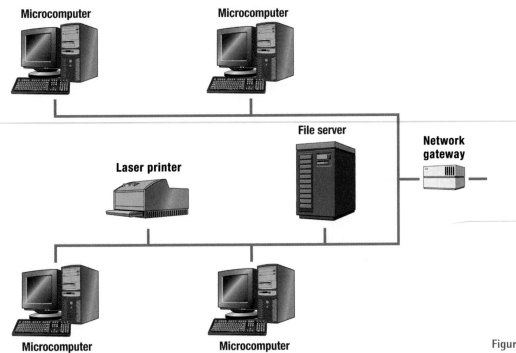

Figure 9-16   Local area network

HOME NETWORKS

While LANs have been widely used within organizations for years, they are now being commonly used by individuals in their homes and apartments. These LANs, called **home networks,** allow different computers to share resources, including a common Internet connection. Computers can be connected in a variety of ways, including electrical wiring, telephone wiring, and special cables. One of the simplest ways, however, is without cables, or wireless.

A wireless local area network is typically referred to as a **wireless LAN (WLAN).** It uses radio frequencies to connect computers and other devices. All communications pass through the network's centrally located **wireless receiver** or **base station.** This receiver interprets incoming radio frequencies and routes communications to the appropriate devices. To see how home networks work, visit our Web site at www.computing2008.com and enter the keyword network.

To learn more about how to set up and use a wireless home network, see Making IT Work for You: Home Networking on page 256 and 257.

METROPOLITAN AREA NETWORKS

The next step up from the LAN is the **MAN**—the **metropolitan area network.** MANs span distances up to 100 miles. These networks are frequently used as links between office buildings that are located throughout a city.

Unlike a LAN, a MAN is typically not owned by a single organization. Rather, it is either owned by a group of organizations who jointly own and operate the network or by a single network service provider who provides network services for a fee.

WIDE AREA NETWORKS

Wide area networks (WANs) are countrywide and worldwide networks. These networks provide access to regional service (MAN) providers and typically span distances greater than 100 miles. They use microwave relays and satellites to reach users over long distances—for example, from Los Angeles to Paris. Of course, the widest of all WANs is the Internet, which spans the entire globe.

The primary difference between a LAN, MAN, and WAN is the geographical range. Each may have various combinations of hardware, such as microcomputers, minicomputers, mainframes, and various peripheral devices.

For a summary of network types see Figure 9-17.

Type	Description
LAN	Local area network; located within close proximity
Home	Local area network for home and apartment use; typically wireless
MAN	Metropolitan area network; typically spans cities with coveraage up to 100 miles
WAN	Wide area network for countrywide or worldwide coverage; the Internet is the largest WAN

Figure 9–17   Types of networks

▼ **CONCEPT CHECK**

▶ What are the four types of networks? What is their primary difference?

▶ What is a home network?

▶ What is a WLAN? What is a wireless receiver?

NETWORK ARCHITECTURE

Network architecture describes how a network is arranged and how resources are coordinated and shared. It encompasses a variety of different network specifics, including network configurations and strategies. Network configurations describe the physical arrangement of the network. Network strategies define how information and resources are shared.

CONFIGURATIONS

A network can be arranged or configured in several different ways. This arrangement is called the network's **topology.** The four principal network topologies are star, bus, ring, and hierarchical.

In a **star network,** a number of small computers or peripheral devices are linked to a central unit. (See Figure 9-18.) The central unit is the **network hub** and is typically a host computer or file server.

All communications pass through this central unit. Control is maintained by **polling.** That is, each connecting device is asked ("polled") whether it has a message to send. Each device is then in turn allowed to send its message.

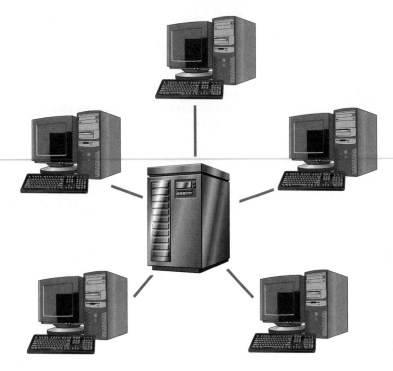

Figure 9-18   Star network

HOME NETWORKING

Computer networks are not just for corporations and schools anymore. If you have more than one computer, you can use a home network to share files and printers, to allow multiple users access to the Internet at the same time, and to play multiplayer computer games.

Installing the Network   Each computer on a wireless network requires a wireless network card. Cards are often available in kits that also include a base station. Once the cards are installed in each computer, the base station must be configured for sharing the Internet. Then, each computer can be configured to share files and printers. For example, to set up a wireless network using Agere System's Residential Gateway and Windows XP:

1 ● Install a compatible wireless card in each computer. In most cases, simply plugging the card in is all that is required.

● Run the included software to set up the base station for accessing and sharing the Internet.

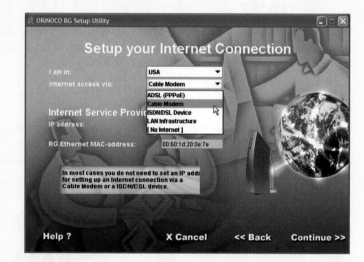

2 ● Click *Start/My Network Places* and click *Set up a home or small office network.*

● Follow the instructions in the wizard to set up your computer for file and printer sharing and to access the Internet through the residential gateway.

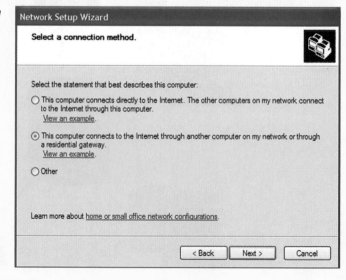

Using the Network   Now your computers are ready to share their resources. The four most common uses of a home network are to share files, printers, and Internet access and to run multiplayer computer games.

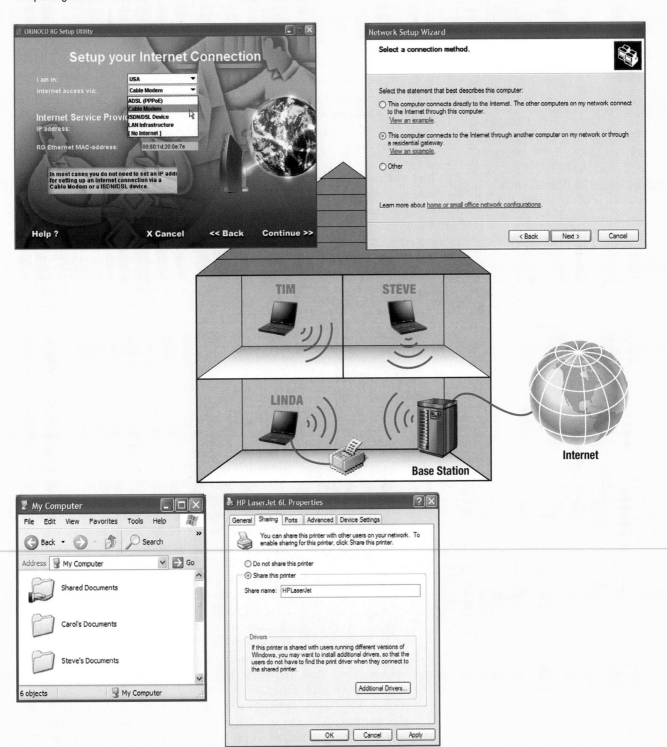

Home networks are continually changing, and some of the specifics presented in this Making IT Work for You may have changed. To learn about other ways to make information technology work for you, visit our Web site at www.computing2008.com and enter the keyword miw.

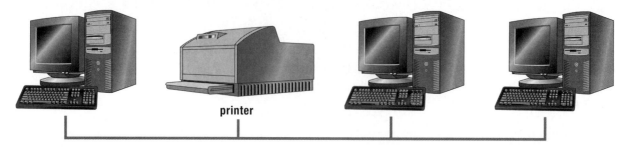

Figure 9-19   Bus network

One particular advantage of the star topology is that it can be used to support a **time-sharing system.** That is, several users can share resources (time) on a central computer. The star is a common topology for linking microcomputers to a mainframe that allows access to an organization's database.

In a **bus network** each device in the network handles its own communications control. There is no host computer. All communications travel along a common connecting cable called a **bus** or **backbone.** (See Figure 9-19.) As the information passes along the bus, it is examined by each device to see if the information is intended for it.

The bus network is typically used when only a few microcomputers are to be linked together. This arrangement is common for sharing data stored on different microcomputers. Because a star network typically provides a more direct path to shared resources, it is more efficient than a bus network for sharing these resources. However, a bus network is easy to install and is less expensive.

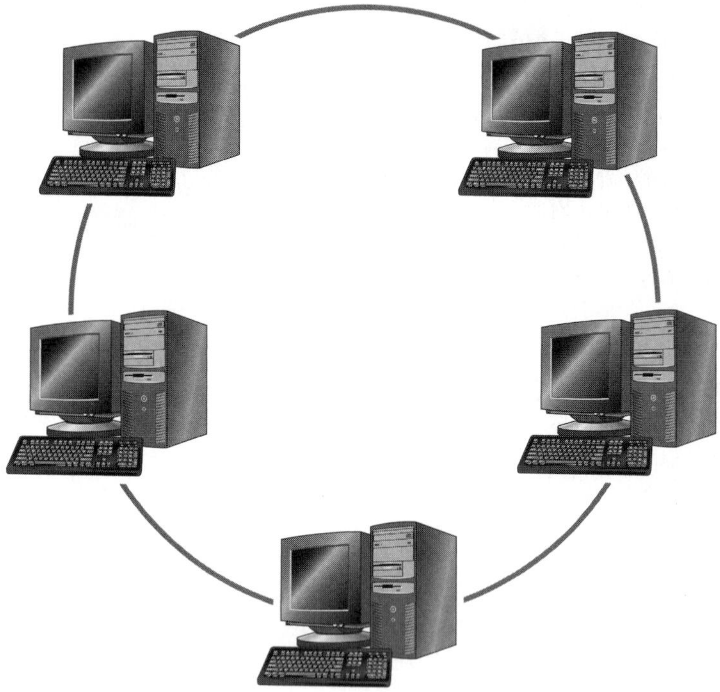

In a **ring network,** each device is connected to two other devices, forming a ring. (See Figure 9-20.) There is no central file server or computer. Messages are passed around the ring until they reach the correct destination. With microcomputers, the ring arrangement is the least frequently used of the four networks. However, it often is used to link mainframes, especially over wide geographical areas. These mainframes tend to operate fairly autonomously. They perform most or all of their own processing and only occasionally share data and programs with other mainframes.

A ring network is useful in a decentralized organization because it makes possible a **distributed data processing system.** That is, computers can perform processing tasks at their own dispersed locations. However, they also can share programs, data, and other resources with each other.

Figure 9-20   Ring network

The **hierarchical network** consists of several computers linked to a central host computer, just like a star network. However, these other computers are also hosts to other, smaller computers or to peripheral devices. (See Figure 9-21.)

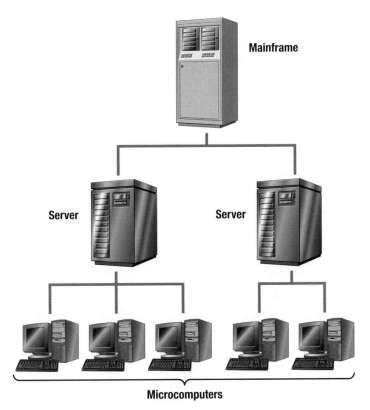

Figure 9-21 Hierarchical network

Thus, the host at the top of the hierarchy could be a mainframe. The computers below the mainframe could be minicomputers, and those below, microcomputers. The hierarchical network allows various computers to share databases, processing power, and different output devices.

A hierarchical network is useful in centralized organizations. For example, different departments within an organization may have individual microcomputers connected to departmental minicomputers. The minicomputers in turn may be connected to the corporation's mainframe, which contains data and programs accessible to all.

For a summary of the network configurations, see Figure 9-22.

Topology	Description
Star	Several computers connected to a central server or host; all communications travel through central server; good for sharing common resources
Bus	Computers connected by a common line; communication travels along this common line; less expensive than star
Ring	Each computer connected to two others, forming a ring; communications travel around ring; often used to link mainframe computers in decentralized organizations
Hierarchical	One top-level host computer connected to next-level computers, which are connected to third-level computers; often used in centralized organizations

Figure 9-22 Principal network configurations

▼ CONCEPT CHECK

▶ What is a network topology? What are the four principal network topologies?

▶ What is a time-sharing system? What is a distributed data processing system?

STRATEGIES

Every network has a **strategy,** or way of coordinating the sharing of information and resources. The most common network strategies are terminal, client/server, and peer-to-peer.

In a **terminal network,** processing power is centralized in one large computer, usually a mainframe. The nodes connected to this host computer are either terminals with little or no processing capabilities or microcomputers running special software that allows them to act as terminals. (See Figure 9-23.) The star and hierarchical networks are typical configurations with UNIX as the operating system.

Many airline reservation systems are terminal networks. A large central computer maintains all the airline schedules, rates, seat availability, and so on. Travel agents use terminals to connect to the central computer and to schedule reservations. Although the tickets may be printed along with travel itineraries at the agent's desk, nearly all processing is done at the central computer.

One advantage of terminal networks is the centralized location and control of technical personnel, software, and data. One disadvantage is the lack of control and flexibility for the end user. Another disadvantage is that terminal networks do not use the full processing power available with microcomputers. Though the terminal strategy was once very popular, most new systems do not use it.

Client/server networks use one computer to coordinate and supply services to other nodes on the network. The server provides access to resources such as Web pages, databases, application software, and hardware. (See Figure 9-24.) This strategy is based on specialization. Server nodes coordinate and supply specialized services, and client nodes request the services. Commonly used network operating systems are Novell's NetWare, Microsoft's Windows NT, IBM's LAN Server, and Banyan Vines.

Client/server networks are widely used on the Internet. For example, Napster (the once popular music service) originally employed a version of this strategy. Music enthusiasts used the Internet to connect to Napster servers. The Napster

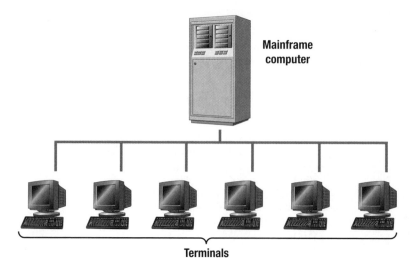

Figure 9-23 Terminal network

servers provided lists of music files (some of which were copyrighted) that were available to be copied from participating Napster users. The music enthusiasts were clients requesting services (information regarding the location of others willing to share music files) from Napster servers.

To learn more about the original Napster network, visit our Web site at www.computing2008.com and enter the keyword **napster**.

One advantage of the client/server network strategy is the ability to handle very large networks efficiently. Another advantage is the availability of powerful network management software to monitor and control network activities. The major disadvantages are the cost of installation and maintenance.

In a **peer-to-peer network,** nodes have equal authority and can act as both clients and servers. For example, one microcomputer can obtain files located on another microcomputer and also can provide files to other microcomputers. (See Figure 9-25.) A typical configuration for a peer-to-peer system is the bus network. Commonly used network operating systems are Novell's NetWare Lite, Microsoft's Windows NT, and Apple's Macintosh Peer-to-Peer LANs.

Many current popular music-sharing services use this network strategy. In fact, the Napster approach was actually a hybrid network in which the Napster server worked in a client/server environment providing a service to clients. Once a Napster user had the location of requested music files, he or she could sign off the network and then connect directly to the source, forming a very simple peer-to-peer network. Each node could act as a server by providing access to music files and as a client by receiving copies of music files. Today, Gnutella is a widely used peer-to-peer network system for sharing all kinds of files, including music files. Unlike the Napster approach, Gnutella networks directly connect users without a central server acting as the focal point for operations. There are various different versions of Gnutella. To learn more about one of the most popular versions, visit our Web site at www.computing2008.com and enter the keyword **gnutella**.

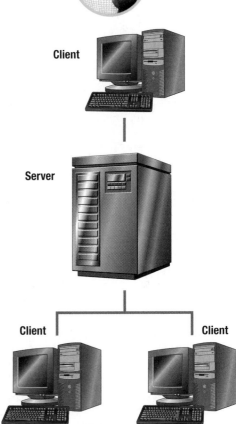

Figure 9-24 Client/server network

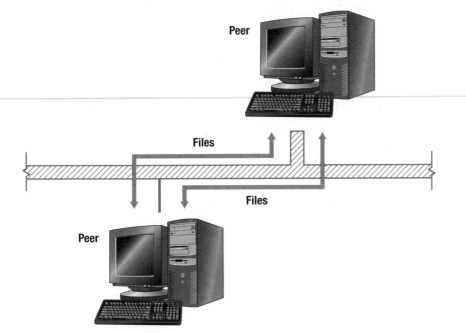

Figure 9-25 Peer-to-peer network

There are several advantages to the peer-to-peer network strategy. The networks are inexpensive and easy to install, and they usually work well for smaller systems with fewer than 10 nodes. Unlike the client/server network strategy, network operations are not dependent upon a single central node. As the number of nodes increases, however, the performance of the network declines. Another disadvantage is the lack of powerful management software to effectively monitor a large network's activities. For these reasons, peer-to-peer networks are typically used by smaller networks within organizations and for sharing files on the Internet.

For a summary of network strategies, see Figure 9-26.

Strategy	Description
Terminal	One large computer provides nearly all processing; strong central control; limited flexibility and control for users
Client/server	Several clients or computers depend upon one server or computer to coordinate and supply services
Peer-to-peer	Computers act as both servers and clients; inexpensive and easy to install; works well in small networks and for sharing files on the Internet.

Figure 9-26   Networks strategies

▼ CONCEPT CHECK

▶ What is a network strategy? Discuss the three most common network strategies.

▶ Compare the network strategies employed by Napster and Gnutella.

ORGANIZATIONAL INTERNETS

Computer networks in organizations have evolved over time. Most large organizations have a complex and wide range of different network configurations, operating systems, and strategies. Integrating or connecting all of these networks has been a very challenging task. One way is to apply Internet technologies to support communication within and between organizations using intranets and extranets.

INTRANETS

An **intranet** is a *private* network within an organization that resembles the Internet. Like the *public* Internet, intranets use browsers, Web sites, and Web pages. Intranets typically provide e-mail, mailing lists, newsgroups, and FTP services accessible only to those within the organization.

Organizations use intranets to provide information to their employees. Typical applications include electronic telephone directories, e-mail addresses, employee benefit information, internal job openings, and much more. Employees find surfing their organizational intranets to be as easy and as intuitive as surfing the Internet.

EXTRANETS

An **extranet** is a *private* network that connects *more than one* organization. Many organizations use Internet technologies to allow suppliers and others limited access to their networks. The purpose is to increase efficiency and reduce costs. For example, General Motors has thousands of suppliers for the parts that go into making an automobile. By having access to the production schedules, suppliers can schedule and deliver parts as they are needed at the General Motors assembly plants. In this way, General Motors can be assured of having adequate parts without maintaining large inventories.

FIREWALLS

Organizations have to be very careful to protect their information systems. A **firewall** is a security system designed to protect an organization's network against external threats. It consists of hardware and software that control access to a company's intranet or other internal networks.

Typically organizational firewalls include a special computer called a **proxy server.** This computer is a gatekeeper. All communications between the company's internal networks and the outside world must pass through it. By evaluating the source and the content of each communication, the proxy server decides whether it is safe to let a particular message or file pass into or out of the organization's network. (See Figure 9-27.)

Of course, end users have security issues as well. We are subject to many of the same types of security concerns that face organizations. Additionally, we need to be concerned about the privacy of our personal information. In the next chapter, we will discuss personal firewalls and other ways to protect personal privacy and security.

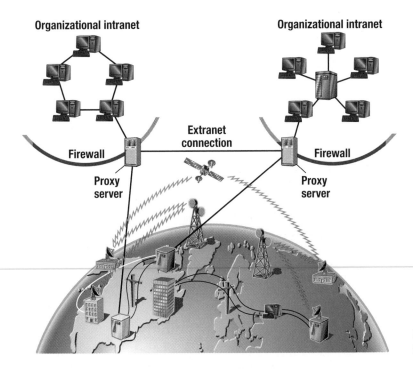

Figure 9-27 Intranets, extranets, firewalls, and proxy servers

▼ CONCEPT CHECK

▶ What are intranets? Compare intranets to the Internet.

▶ What are extranets? Compare intranets and extranets.

▶ What are firewalls? What is a proxy server?

Network administrators manage a company's LAN and WAN networks. (See Figure 9-28.) They may be responsible for design, implementation, and maintenance of networks. Responsibilities usually include maintenance of both hardware and software related to a company's intranet and Internet networks. Network administrators are typically responsible for diagnosing and repairing problems with these networks. Some network administrators are responsible for planning and implementations of network security as well.

Employers typically look for candidates with a bachelor's degree in computer science or information systems and practical networking experience. Experience with network security and maintenance is preferred. Technical certification also may be helpful in obtaining this position. Because network administrators are involved directly with people in many departments, good communication skills are essential.

Network administrators can expect to earn an annual salary of $43,000 to $68,000. Opportunities for advancement typically include upper management positions. This position is expected to be among the fastest-growing jobs in the near future. To learn about other careers in information technology, visit us at www.computing2008.com and enter the keyword careers.

Figure 9-28   Network administrator

A Look to the Future

Cars That Monitor and Respond to Your Moods, Watch Out for Pedestrians, and Communicate with Other Cars

Have you ever found yourself driving around an unfamiliar city, wishing you could connect to the Internet and download driving directions? Have you ever longed for access to your favorite Internet radio station while you drive around? What if you could send and receive e-mail while you wait in traffic?

Wouldn't it be convenient if your car would just send an e-mail whenever it needed maintenance? Toyota and Sony are collaborating on a car called "Pod" that does all this and more.

Pod stands for personalization on demand. Toyota hopes this new car will predict and respond to your moods, likes, and dislikes. It features lighting that may display red if you drive erratically or orange if you seem happy. It features voice recognition technology and responds to verbal commands. Pod is designed to learn and adapt to your driving habits and needs. Some say it is the car equivalent of the Sony AIBO robotic pet.

The Pod connects wirelessly to a portable terminal called the Mini Pod to share data and serve the user's needs. For example, Pod might use the information stored in the PDA-like Mini Pod to download music from the Internet it thinks you might like. The Pod also uses GPS information and the Internet to make recommendations concerning local restaurants as you drive around.

Pod uses technology developed by Suzuki Motors to notify the owner by telephone if the car is broken into or needs mechanical attention. Pod can even communicate with other cars by using a horn messaging system. It also locates pedestrians and warns the driver to correct speed or course to avoid them. Pod also can phone ahead to your destination to advise those waiting if it detects you will be delayed. It may even alert you when you drive by restaurants that it thinks you may like.

Many new cars come equipped with wireless technology and GPS devices. Some car enthusiasts look forward to a car that senses your mood and downloads songs to match it. For now Pod is a concept vehicle, but many of the features it includes may soon be found in your next car. What do you think? Would you buy a car that communicates with other cars, the Internet, and you?

COMMUNICATIONS AND NETWORKS

COMMUNICATIONS

Communications is the process of sharing data, programs, and information between two or more computers. Applications include e-mail, instant messaging, Internet telephones, and electronic commerce.

Connectivity
Connectivity is a concept related to using computer networks to link people and resources. You can link or connect to large computers and the Internet providing access to extensive information resources.

The Wireless Revolution
Mobile or wireless telephones have brought dramatic changes in connectivity and communications. These wireless devices are becoming widely used for computer communication.

Communication Systems
Communication systems transmit data from one location to another. Four basic elements are

- Sending and receiving devices
- Communication channel (transmission medium)
- Connection (communication) devices
- Data transmission specifications

COMMUNICATION CHANNELS

Communication channels carry data from one computer to another.

Physical Connections
Physical connections use a solid medium to connect sending and receiving devices. These connections include **telephone lines** (twisted pair), **coaxial cable,** and **fiber-optic cable.**

Wireless Connections
Wireless connections use air rather than solid substance to connect devices.

- **Infrared**—uses light waves over a short distance; line-of-sight communication.
- **Broadcast radio**—uses radio signals; **Wi-FI (wireless fidelity)** is widely used standard.
- **Microwave**—uses high-frequency radio waves; line-of-sight communication; uses microwave stations and dishes; **Bluetooth** is a widely used short-range standard.
- **Satellite**—microwave relay station in the sky to uplink and downlink data; **GPS (global positioning system)** tracks geographical locations.

To be a competent end user you need to understand the concepts of connectivity, the wireless revolution, and communication systems. Additionally, you need to know the essential parts of communication technology, including channels, connection devices, data transmission, networks, network architectures, and network types.

CONNECTION DEVICES

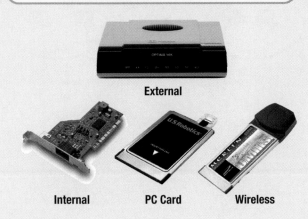

External

Internal   **PC Card**   **Wireless**

Many communication systems use standard telephone lines and **analog signals.** Computers use **digital signals.**

Modems

Modems modulate (convert digital signals to analog) and **demodulate. Transfer rate** is measured in **bits per second.** Four types of conventional modems are **external, internal, PC Card modem,** and **wireless.**

Connections Service

Dial-up services use standard telephone lines and conventional modems. **T1, T2, T3,** and **T4** support very high-speed, all-digital transmission. More affordable technologies include **DSL (digital subscriber line, ADSL** widely used), **cable modems, satellite/air,** and **cellular services (3G cellular networks).**

DATA TRANSMISSION

Bandwidth is a measure of a communication channel's width or capacity. Three bandwidths are **voiceband (low bandwidth), medium band** (uses special leased lines), and **broadband** (high-capacity transmissions). **Protocols** are rules for exchanging data. **TCP/IP** is standard Internet protocol. **IP addresses** are unique numeric Internet addresses. **DNS** converts text-based addresses to numeric IP addresses. **Packets** are small parts of messages.

NETWORKS

Computer networks connect two or more computers. Some specialized network terms include

- **Node**—any device connected to a network.
- **Client**—node requesting resources.
- **Server**—node providing resources; specialized servers such as application, communication, database, file, printer, and Web servers are called dedicated servers.
- **Hub**—center or central node.
- **NIC (network interface cards)**—LAN adapter card for connecting to a network.
- **NOS (network operating system)**—controls and coordinates network operations.
- **Distributed processing**—system where processing is located and shared at different locations.
- **Host computer**—large centralized computer.
- **Network administrator**—network specialist responsible for network operations.

NETWORK TYPES

Networks can be citywide or even international, using both cable and air connections.

- **Local area networks (LANs)** connect nearby devices. **Network gateways** connect networks to one another. **Ethernet** is a LAN standard. These LANs are called Ethernet LANs.
- **Home networks** are LANs used in homes. **Wireless LANs (WLANs)** use a **wireless receiver (base station)** as a hub.
- **Metropolitan area networks (MANs)** link office buildings within a city, spanning up to 100 miles.
- **Wide area networks** or **WANs** are the largest type. They span states and countries or form worldwide networks. The Internet is the largest wide area network in the world.

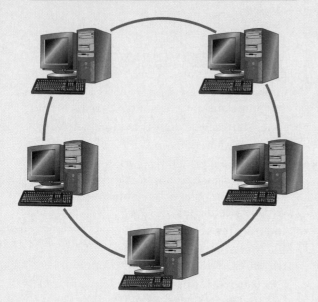

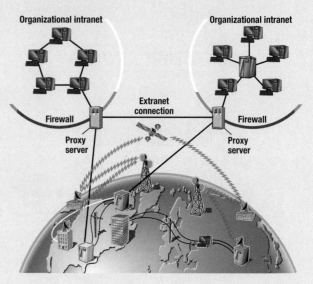

Network architecture describes how a computer network is configured and what strategies are employed.

Configurations

A network's configuration is called its **topology.** Principal topologies are **star network** (each device is linked to the **network hub;** control maintained by **polling**) often used for **time-sharing systems), bus network** (nodes connect by cable called a **bus** or **backbone**), **ring network** (often used in **distributed data processing systems**), and **hierarchical network.**

Strategies

Every network has a **strategy,** or way of sharing information and resources. Common strategies include

- **Terminal network**—a centralized computer distributes power to several terminals.
- **Client/server network**—client computers request resources from a server computer; Napster servers operated with client/server strategy.
- **Peer-to-peer network**—each computer acts as both a server and a client. Gnutella supports peer-to-peer file sharing.

Many organizations use Internet technologies to support communication within and between organizations using intranets and extranets.

Intranets

Intranets are *private* networks within an organization that resemble the Internet. Like the Internet, they use browsers, Web sites, and Web pages. Unlike the Internet, intranets are available only to those within the organization.

Extranets

Extranets are similar to intranets, except that extranets connect more than one organization. Extranets are often used to connect suppliers and producers to increase efficiency.

Firewalls

A **firewall** is a security system to protect against external threats. It consists of both hardware and software. All communications into and out of an organization pass through a special security computer called a **proxy server.**

Network administrators manage a company's LAN and WAN networks. Bachelor's degree in computer science or information systems and practical networking experience required. Salary range $43,000 to $68,000.

KEY TERMS

3G cellular network   (249)
analog signal   (247)
asymmetric digital subscriber
   line (ADSL)   (248)
backbone   (258)
bandwidth   (249)
base station   (254)
bits per second (bps)   (247)
Bluetooth   (245)
broadband   (250)
broadcast radio   (245)
bus   (258)
bus network   (258)
cable modem   (249)
cellular service   (249)
client   (251)
client/server network   (260)
coaxial cable   (244)
communication
   channel   (244)
communication
   system   (243)
computer network   (251)
connectivity   (242)
demodulation   (247)
dial-up service   (248)
digital signal   (247)
digital subscriber line
   (DSL)   (248)
distributed data processing
   system   (258)
distributed processing   (251)
domain name server
   (DNS)   (250)

Ethernet   (253)
external modem   (247)
extranet   (262)
fiber-optic cable   (244)
firewall   (263)
global positioning system
   (GPS)   (245)
hierarchical network   (258)
home network   (254)
host computer   (251)
hub   (251)
infrared   (245)
internal modem   (248)
intranet   (262)
IP address (Internet protocol
   address)   (250)
local area network
   (LAN)   (253)
low bandwidth   (250)
medium band   (250)
metropolitan area network
   (MAN)   (254)
microwave   (245)
modem   (247)
modulation   (247)
network administrator
   (251, 264)
network architecture   (255)
network gateway   (253)
network hub   (255)
network interface card
   (NIC)   (251)
network operating system
   (NOS)   (251)

node   (251)
packet   (250)
PC Card modem   (248)
peer-to-peer network   (261)
polling   (255)
protocol   (250)
proxy server   (263)
ring network   (258)
satellite   (245)
satellite/air connection
   service   (249)
server   (251)
star network   (255)
strategy   (260)
T1, T2, T3, T4 lines   (248)
telephone line   (244)
terminal network   (260)
time-sharing system   (258)
topology   (255)
transfer rate   (247)
transmission control
   protocol/Internet protocol
   (TCP/IP)   (250)
voiceband   (250)
wide area network
   (WAN)   (254)
Wi-FI (wireless
   fidelity)   (245)
wireless LAN (WLAN)
   (254)
wireless modem   (248)
wireless receiver   (254)

FEATURES

Animations

Careers in IT

DVD Direct

Expansions

Making IT Work for You

On the Web Explorations

TechTV

Tips

CHAPTER REVIEW

Applying Technology

Crossword Puzzle

Expanding Your Knowledge

Key Terms

Matching

Multiple Choice

Open-Ended

Writing About Technology

To test your knowledge of these key terms with animated flash cards, visit our Web site at
www.computing2008.com and enter the keyword terms9.

CROSSWORD PUZZLE

Across

5 Interprets and routs incoming radio frequencies.

7 Continuous electronic waves.

9 Configuration of a network.

10 Network Interface Card.

11 Transfer speed or transfer rate.

12 Short-range wireless communication standard.

14 Measurement of the width of the communication channel.

Down

1 Node that requests and uses resources available from other nodes.

2 Each device in the network handles its own communications.

3 Device that allows links between LANs.

4 Process that converts digital to analog.

6 Pieces of a message sent over the Internet.

8 Global Positioning System.

13 Any device that is connected to a network.

15 Uses existing telephone lines to provide high-speed connections.

16 Central node for other nodes.

For an interactive version of this crossword, visit our Web site at www.computing2008.com and enter the keyword **crossword9**.

MULTIPLE CHOICE

Circle the letter or fill in the correct answer.

1. Connectivity is a concept related to
   a. transmitting information, either by computer or by phone
   b. the interconnections within a computer
   c. using computer networks to link people and resources
   d. being in an active session with your computer

2. The transmission medium that carries the message is referred to as the
   a. send and receive device
   b. communication channel
   c. protocol
   d. gateways

3. Bluetooth is a type of radio wave information transmission system that is good for about
   a. 30 feet
   b. 30 yards
   c. 30 miles
   d. 300 miles

4. Special high-speed lines used by large corporations to support digital communications are known as
   a. satellite/air connection service lines
   b. cable modems
   c. digital subscriber lines
   d. T1, T2, T3, and T4 lines

5. The rules for exchanging data between computers are called
   a. interconnections
   b. synchronous packages
   c. protocols
   d. data transmission synchronization

6. Two or more computers connected so that they can communicate with each other and share information are called a
   a. satellite
   b. protocol
   c. broadcast
   d. network

7. A device, connected to a network, that shares resources with other nodes is called a
   a. client
   b. server
   c. host
   d. NOS

8. The arrangement of the computers in a network is called the
   a. NOS
   b. topology
   c. node layout
   d. protocol

9. A way of coordinating the sharing of information and resources is called a network ____.
   a. topology
   b. strategy
   c. protocol
   d. architecture

10. A(n) ____ protects an organization's network from outside attack.
    a. fortress
    b. extranet
    c. proxy
    d. firewall

For an interactive version of these multiple-choice questions, visit our Web site at www.computing2008.com and enter the keyword **multiple9**.

MATCHING

Match each numbered item with the most closely related lettered item. Write your answers in the spaces provided.

a. bandwidth
b. Bluetooth
c. client
d. distributed processing
e. DNS
f. firewall
g. infrared
h. packets
i. TCP/IP
j. topology

1. Wireless connection that uses light waves over short distances. ____
2. Uses microwaves to transmit data over short distances up to 33 feet. ____
3. Measurement of the width of a communication channel. ____
4. Standard protocol for the Internet. ____
5. Broken-down parts of a message sent over the Internet. ____
6. Converts text-based addresses to IP addresses. ____
7. A node that requests resources from other nodes. ____
8. The configuration of a network. ____
9. System in which computing power is located and shared at different locations. ____
10. Protects network from external threats. ____

For an interactive version of this matching exercise, visit our Web site at www. computing2008.com and enter the keyword **matching9**.

OPEN-ENDED

On a separate sheet of paper, respond to each question or statement.

1. Define and discuss connectivity, the wireless revolution, and communications.
2. Identify and describe the various physical and wireless communication channels.
3. Identify the standard Internet protocol and discuss its essential features.
4. Define and discuss the four principal network topologies.
5. Define and discuss the three most common network strategies.

APPLYING TECHNOLOGY

The following questions are designed to demonstrate ways that you can effectively use technology today. The first question relates directly to this chapter's Making IT Work for You feature.

Home Networking   1

Computer networks are not just for corporations and schools anymore. If you have more than one computer, you can use a home network to share files and printers, to allow multiple users access to the Internet at the same time, and to play multiplayer computer games. To learn more about this technology, review Making IT Work for You: Home Networking on pages 256 and 257. Then answer the following: (a) Describe the window shown for the setup of the wireless base station. (b) What are the four most common uses of a home network? (c) What are the names of the folders displayed in the My Computer window?

Distributed Computing   2

When networked computers are not in use, their processing power can be combined with other networked computers to perform a common task. In some cases, the problems that can be solved by many individual computers are far too large to be solved by any single computer. Connect to our site at www.computing2008.com and enter the keyword distributed for a link to a site that features distributed computing. Explore the site and answer the following questions: (a) What type of problem does this site solve with distributed computing? (b) How do users donate unused computer time to this project? (c) Would you donate your extra computer time to a distributed computing project? Why or why not?

Palm   3

Palm is a leader in personal digital assistants, or PDAs. Recent advances in technology allow PDAs to communicate on the go. Visit our Web site at www.computing2008.com and enter the keyword palm to link to Palm's Web site. Once connected, review the latest PDA products and then answer the following questions: (a) What support for Internet connection is available? (b) What is required to connect PDAs to the Internet? (c) What type of Internet information is accessible? Is there any type that is not accessible? (d) Would you use an Internet-connected PDA? Why or why not?

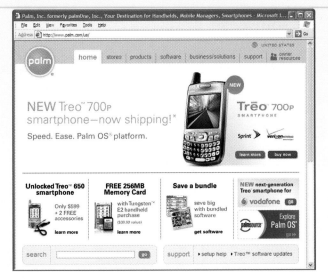

EXPANDING YOUR KNOWLEDGE

The following questions are designed to add depth and detail to your understanding of specific topics presented within this chapter. The questions direct you to sources other than the textbook to obtain this knowledge.

1 How Wireless Home Networks Work

Wireless home networks are becoming very popular. These LANs are easy to set up and use. They allow different computers to share resources including a common Internet connection and printer. To learn how home networks work, visit our Web site at www.computing2008.com and enter the keyword network. Then answer the following questions. (a) What is a node? (b) What is a base station and what is its function? (c) What is a wireless card and what is its function? (d) If one or more requests to print a document are made at exactly the same time, what node determines which document is printed first? (e) Can the nodes TIM, LINDA, and STEVE access and use the Internet at the same time? If yes, how can this be done with a single Internet connection?

2 How Napster and Gnutella Work

Many popular file-sharing services use different strategies to allow users to share files. To learn how Napster and Gnutella work, visit our Web site at www.computing2008.com and enter the keywords napster and gnutella. Then answer the following: (a) Describe how Napster used a client/server network system. (b) Describe how Gnutella uses a peer-to-peer network. (c) Both network systems connect users willing to share files. Which system do you think would be more efficient? Defend your answer. (d) Discuss the advantages and disadvantages of each strategy.

3 Hotspots

Hotspots are areas set up to provide public access to wireless Internet service. Find them in coffee shops, airports, or hotels. Connect to our Web site at www. computing2008.com and enter the keyword hotspots to link to a directory of hotspots. Locate one near you. Where is the hotspot? What equipment is necessary to use the hotspot? What does it cost to use the hotspot?

WRITING ABOUT TECHNOLOGY

The ability to think critically and to write effectively is essential to nearly every profession. The following questions are designed to help you develop these skills by posing thought-provoking questions about computer privacy, security, and/or ethics.

Electronic Monitoring

1

Programs known as "sniffers" are sometimes used to monitor communications on corporate networks. Recently, the FBI unveiled a technology known as Carnivore that can monitor an individual's Internet activity and eavesdrop on e-mail messages. Write a one-page paper that answers the following questions: (a) Is it a violation of an employee's privacy for an organization or corporation to use sniffer programs to monitor communications on their network? (b) Is it a violation of privacy for a government agency such as the FBI to use programs like Carnivore to monitor communications on the Internet? (c) Under what conditions are the types of monitoring discussed in parts (a) and (b) acceptable and ethical? (d) How can these conditions be enforced?

Digital Rights Management

2

In response to the issue of sharing copyrighted material over computer networks discussed in this chapter, many different forms of digital rights management, or DRM, have been proposed. However, DRM is controversial and hotly debated by industry groups and consumer advocates. Use the Web to research DRM, and then write a one-page paper titled "Digital Rights Management" that addresses the following topics: (a) Define "digital rights management." (b) What systems have been proposed for DRM? (c) Why are some consumers opposed to these systems? (d) Do you think DRM is a fair solution to online piracy? Justify your answer.

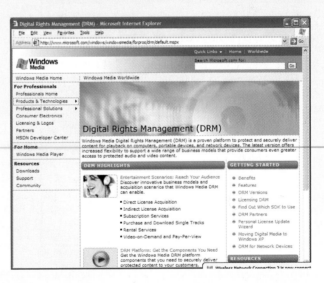

FEATURES

Animations

Careers in IT

DVD Direct

Expansions

Making IT Work for You

On the Web Explorations

TechTV

Tips

CHAPTER REVIEW

Applying Technology

Crossword Puzzle

Expanding Your Knowledge

Key Terms

Matching

Multiple Choice

Open-Ended

Writing About Technology

CHAPTER

10

COMPETENCIES

After you have read this chapter, you should be able to:

1 Discuss the privacy issues related to the presence of large databases, private networks, the Internet, and the Web.

2 Describe and control cookies, Web bugs, and spyware.

3 Describe the security threats posed by computer criminals, computer crime, and other hazards.

4 Discuss ways that individuals and organizations protect their security.

5 Describe the common types of physical and mental risks associated with computer use and ways to protect yourself against these risks.

6 Discuss what the computer industry is doing, and what you can do, to protect the environment.

Privacy
concerns collection and use of data

Security
helps to keep private information safe from criminals, natural hazards, and civil unrest

PRIVACY AND SECURITY

Introduction

The tools and products of the information age do not exist in a world by themselves. As we said in Chapter 1, a computer system consists not only of software, hardware, data, and procedures, but also of people. Because of people, computer systems may be used for both good and bad purposes.

There are more than 300 million microcomputers in use today. What are the consequences of the widespread presence of this technology? Does technology make it easy for others to invade our personal privacy? When we apply for a loan or for a driver's license, or when we check out at the supermarket, is that information about us being distributed and used without our permission? When we use the Web, is information about us being collected and shared with others?

Does technology make it easy for others to invade the security of business organizations like our banks or our employers? What about health risks to people who use computers? What about the environment? Do computers pose a threat to our ecology?

This technology prompts lots of questions—very important questions. Perhaps these are some of the most important questions for the 21st century. Competent end users need to be aware of the potential impact of technology on people and how to protect themselves on the Web. They need to be sensitive to and knowledgeable about personal privacy, organizational security, ergonomics, and the environmental impact of technology.

Ergonomics is the study of human factors related to the devices people use

Environmental Protection discovering ways to discourage waste in the microcomputer industry

As we have discussed, information systems consist of people, procedures, software, hardware, and data. This chapter focuses on people. (See Figure 10-1.) While most everyone agrees that technology has had a very positive impact on people, it is important to recognize the negative, or potentially negative, impacts as well.

Effective implementation of computer technology involves maximizing its positive effects while minimizing its negative effects. The most significant concerns are

- **Privacy:** What are the threats to personal privacy and how can we protect ourselves?
- **Security:** How can access to sensitive information be controlled and how can we secure hardware and software?
- **Ergonomics:** What are the physical and mental risks to technology and how can these risks be eliminated or controlled?
- **Environmental protection:** What can individuals and organizations do to minimize the impact of technology on our environment?

Figure 10-1 People are part of an information system

Let us begin by examining privacy.

PRIVACY

What do you suppose controls how computers can be used? You probably think first of laws. Of course that is right, but technology is moving so fast that it is very difficult for our legal system to keep up. The essential element that controls how computers are used today is *ethics*.

Ethics, as you may know, are standards of moral conduct. **Computer ethics** are guidelines for the morally acceptable use of computers in our society. There are four primary computer ethics issues:

- **Privacy** concerns the collection and use of data about individuals.
- **Accuracy** relates to the responsibility of those who collect data to ensure that the data is correct.
- **Property** relates to who owns data and rights to software.
- **Access** relates to the responsibility of those who have data to control who is able to use that data.

We are all entitled to ethical treatment. This includes the right to keep personal information, such as credit ratings and medical histories, from getting into unauthorized hands. Many people worry that this right is severely threatened. Let us examine some of the concerns.

LARGE DATABASES

Large organizations are constantly compiling information about us. The federal government alone has over 2,000 databases. Every day, data is gathered about us and stored in large databases. For example, telephone companies compile lists of the calls we make, the numbers called, and so on. A special telephone directory (called a **reverse directory**) lists telephone numbers sequentially. (See Figure 10-2.) Using it, government authorities and others can easily get the names, addresses, and other details about the persons we call.

Credit card companies keep similar records. Supermarket scanners in grocery checkout counters record what we buy, when we buy it, how much we buy, and the price. Financial institutions, including banks and credit unions, record how much money we have, what we use it for, and how much we owe. Publishers of magazines, newspapers, and mail-order catalogues have our names, addresses, phone numbers, and what we order.

A vast industry of data gatherers known as **information resellers** or **information brokers** now exists that collects and sells such personal data. Using publicly available databases and in many cases nonpublic databases, information resellers create **electronic profiles** or highly detailed and personalized descriptions of individuals. Very likely, you have an electronic profile that includes your name, address, telephone number, Social Security number, driver's license number, bank account numbers, credit card numbers, telephone records, and shopping and purchasing patterns. Information resellers sell these electronic profiles to direct marketers, fundraisers, and others. Many provide these services on the Web for free or for a nominal cost. (See Figure 10-3.)

Your personal information, including preferences, habits, and financial data, has become a marketable commodity. This raises many issues, including

- **Spreading information without personal consent:** How would you feel if an employer were using your medical records to make decisions about hiring, placement, promotion, and firing? A University of Illinois survey found that half the Fortune 500 companies were using medical records for just these purposes.

  How would you feel if someone obtained a driver's license and credit cards in your name? What if that person then assumed your identity to buy clothes, cars, and a house? It happens every day. Every year, well over 10 million people are victimized in this way. It is called **identify theft.** Identity theft is the illegal assumption of someone's identity for the purposes of economic gain. It is one of the fastest-growing crimes in the country. To learn more about identity theft and how to minimize your risk, visit our Web site at www.computing2008.com and enter the keyword theft.

- **Spreading inaccurate information:** How would you like to be turned down for a home loan because of an error in your credit history? This is much more common than you might expect. What if you could not find a job or were fired from a job because of an error giving you a serious criminal history? This can and has happened due to simple clerical errors. In one case, an arresting officer while

Figure 10-2 Reverse directory Web site

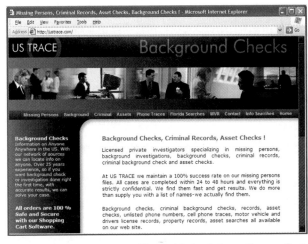

Figure 10-3 Information reseller's Web site

TIPS
Identity theft is a growing problem, and can be financially devastating if you are a victim. Here are some steps to help protect your identity.

1. Never give personal information on the Internet or in response to e-mail. One common scam known as *phishing* involves e-mail that has been forged to appear to come from your bank or school.

2. Only do business on the Internet with companies you know to be legitimate, or large companies with a solid reputation.

3. When selling a computer, be sure to completely remove all personal information from the hard drive. Many programs are available to ensure data is completely removed.

4. Check your credit reports from the three major credit bureaus for unusual activity or inaccuracy at least once a year.

To see more tips, visit our Web site at www.computing2008.com and enter the keyword tips.

completing an arrest warrant incorrectly recorded the Social Security number of a criminal. From that time forward, this arrest and the subsequent conviction became part of another person's electronic profile. This is an example of **mistaken identity** in which the electronic profile of one person is switched with another.

It's important to know that you have some recourse. The law allows you to gain access to those records about you that are held by credit bureaus. Under the **Freedom of Information Act,** you are also entitled to look at your records held by government agencies. (Portions may be deleted for national security reasons.)

To learn more about mistaken identity, visit our Web site at www. computing2008.com and enter the keyword id.

▼ CONCEPT CHECK

▶ What are four primary computer ethics issues?

▶ What is identity theft? What is mistaken identity? How are they different?

▶ What is the Freedom of Information Act?

PRIVATE NETWORKS

Suppose you use your company's electronic mail system to send a co-worker an unflattering message about your supervisor or to send a highly personal message to a friend. Later you find the boss has been spying on your exchange. This is legal and a recent survey revealed that nearly 75 percent of all businesses search employees' electronic mail and computer files using so-called **snoopware.** (See Figure 10-4.) These programs record virtually everything you do on your computer. One proposed law would not prohibit this type of electronic monitoring but would require employers to provide prior written notice. Employers also would have to alert employees during the monitoring with some sort of audible or visual signal.

Figure 10–4 Snoopware

THE INTERNET AND THE WEB

When you send e-mail on the Internet or browse the Web, do you have any concerns about privacy? Most people do not. They think that as long as they are using their own computer and are selective about disclosing their names or other personal information, then little can be done to invade their personal privacy. Experts call this the **illusion of anonymity** that the Internet brings.

Did you know that when you browse the Web, your activity is monitored? Whenever you visit a Web site, your browser stores critical information onto your hard disk, typically without your explicit permission or knowledge. For example, your browser creates a **history file** that includes the locations of sites visited by your computer system. This history file can be displayed by your browser. To view the history file using Internet Explorer version 6.0, follow the steps in Figure 10-5.

Another way your Web activity is monitored is by **cookies** or specialized programs that are deposited on your hard disk from Web sites you have visited. Typically, these programs are deposited without your explicit knowledge

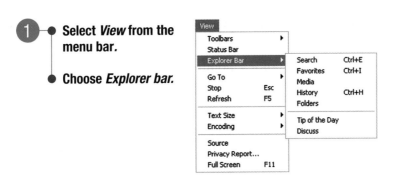

① ● Select *View* from the menu bar.

● Choose *Explorer bar.*

② ● Select *History.*

Figure 10-5   Viewing history files

① ● Select *Tools* from the *menu bar.*

● Choose *Internet Options.*

② ● Select *Settings* in the *General* tab.

● Click *View files.*

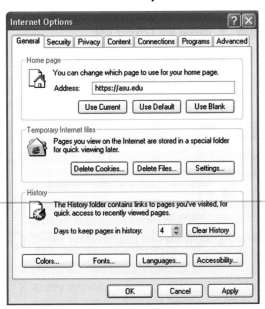

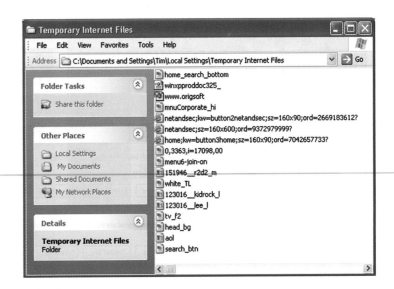

Figure 10-6   Viewing cookies

or consent. They record what sites you visit, what you do at the sites, and other information you provide, such as passwords and credit card numbers. To view the cookies on a hard drive using Internet Explorer version 6.0, follow the steps in Figure 10-6.

Figure 10–13 Crashes can result in lost data

- **Technological failures:** Hardware and software don't always do what they are supposed to do. For instance, too little electricity, caused by a brownout or blackout, may cause the loss of data in primary storage. Too much electricity, as when lightning or some other electrical disturbance affects a power line, may cause a **voltage surge,** or **spike.** This excess of electricity may destroy chips or other electronic components of a computer.

  Microcomputer users should use a **surge protector,** a device that separates the computer from the power source of the wall outlet. When a voltage surge occurs, it activates a circuit breaker in the surge protector, protecting the computer system.

  Another technological catastrophe occurs when a hard-disk drive suddenly crashes, or fails (as discussed in Chapter 8), perhaps because it has been bumped inadvertently. If the user has forgotten to make backup copies of data on the hard disk, data may be lost. (See Figure 10-13.)

- **Human errors:** Human mistakes are inevitable. Data-entry errors are probably the most commonplace and, as we have discussed, can lead to mistaken identity. Programmer errors also occur frequently. Some mistakes may result from faulty design, as when a software manufacturer makes a deletion command closely resembling another command. Some errors may be the result of sloppy procedures. One such example occurs when office workers save important documents under file names that are not descriptive and not recognizable by others.

▼ **CONCEPT CHECK**

▶ Describe malware, including viruses, worms, and Trojan horses.

▶ Compare a worm to a denial of service attack. How are they similar? How are they different?

▶ Describe the five most common types of Internet scams.

MEASURES TO PROTECT COMPUTER SECURITY

Security is concerned with protecting information, hardware, and software from unauthorized use as well as from damage from intrusions, sabotage, and natural disasters. Considering the numerous ways in which computer systems and data can be compromised, we can see why security is a growing field. Some of the principal measures to protect computer security are encryption, restricting access, anticipating disasters, and backing up data.

Encrypting Messages

Whenever information is sent over a network, the possibility of unauthorized access exists. The longer the distance the message has to travel, the higher the security risk is. For example, an e-mail message on a LAN meets a limited number of users operating in controlled environments such as offices. An e-mail message traveling across the country on the Internet affords greater opportunities for the message to be intercepted.

Businesses have been **encrypting,** or coding, messages for years. They have become so good at it that some law enforcement agencies are unable to wiretap messages from suspected criminals. Some federal agencies have suggested that a standard encryption procedure be used so that law enforcement agencies can monitor suspected criminal communications. Individuals also are using encryption programs to safeguard their private communications. One of the most widely used personal encryption programs is Pretty Good Privacy. (See Figure 10-14.)

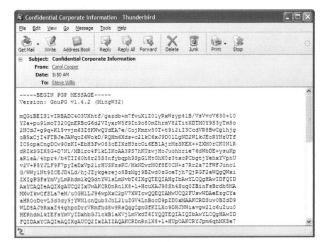

Figure 10-14   Encrypted e-mail

Restricting Access

Security experts are constantly devising ways to protect computer systems from access by unauthorized persons. Sometimes security is a matter of putting guards on company computer rooms and checking the identification of everyone admitted. Other times it is using **biometric scanning** devices such as fingerprint and iris (eye) scanners. (See Figure 10-15.)

Oftentimes it is a matter of being careful about assigning passwords to people and of changing the passwords when people leave a company. **Passwords** are secret words or numbers that must be keyed into a computer

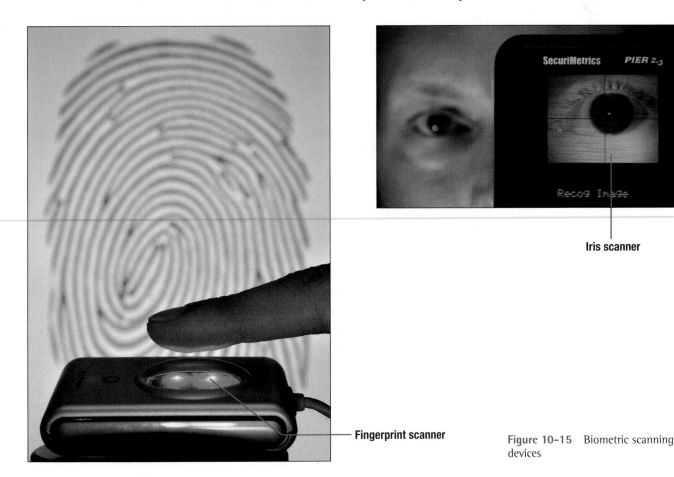

Fingerprint scanner

Iris scanner

Figure 10-15   Biometric scanning devices

Privacy and Security

system to gain access. In some dial-back computer systems, the user telephones the computer, punches in the correct password, and then hangs up. If the password is verified by the computer system, it then calls the user back at a certain preauthorized telephone number. For many applications on the Web, users assign their own passwords.

As mentioned in previous chapters, most major corporations today use special hardware and software called firewalls to control access to their internal computer networks. **Firewalls** act as a security buffer between the corporation's private network and all external networks, including the Internet. All electronic communications coming into and leaving the corporation must be evaluated by the firewall. Security is maintained by denying access to unauthorized communications. To learn how to use Windows XP's built-in firewall, visit our Web site at www.computing2008.com and enter the keyword firewall.

On the Web Explorations

Encryption is the only thing between criminals and private information on the Internet, such as bank accounts, passwords, and even tax returns. To learn more about one encryption company, visit our Web site at www.computing2008.com and enter the keyword encryption.

Anticipating Disasters

Companies (and even individuals) should prepare themselves for disasters. **Physical security** is concerned with protecting hardware from possible human and natural disasters. **Data security** is concerned with protecting software and data from unauthorized tampering or damage. Most large organizations have a **disaster recovery plan** describing ways to continue operating until normal computer operations can be restored.

Backing Up Data

Equipment can always be replaced. A company's *data,* however, may be irreplaceable. Most companies have ways of trying to keep software and data from being tampered with in the first place. They include careful screening of job applicants, guarding of passwords, and auditing of data and programs from time to time. An essential procedure, however, is to make frequent backups of data and to store them in safe remote locations.

See Figure 10-16 for a summary of the different measures to protect computer security.

▼ CONCEPT CHECK

► What is encryption? What is Pretty Good Privacy?

► Discuss biometric scanning, passwords, and firewalls.

► Define physical security, data security, and disaster recovery plans.

Measure	Description
Encrypting	Code all messages sent over a network
Restricting	Limit access to authorized persons using such measures as passwords, dial-back systems, and firewalls
Anticipating	Prepare for disasters by ensuring physical security and data security through a disaster recovery plan
Backing up	Routinely copy data and store it at a remote location

Figure 10-16 Measures to protect computer security

ERGONOMICS

Computers have become a common business tool because they increase productivity. Unfortunately, there are certain ways in which computers may actually make people less productive. Many of those affected are in positions that involve intensive data entry, such as clerks and word processor operators. However, anyone whose job involves heavy use of the computer may be affected. As a result, there has been great interest in a field known as ergonomics.

Ergonomics (pronounced "er-guh-nom-ix") is defined as the study of human factors related to things people use. It is concerned with fitting the job to the worker rather than forcing the worker to contort to fit the job. As computer use has increased, so has interest in ergonomics. People are devising ways that computers can be designed and used to increase productivity and avoid health risks.

PHYSICAL HEALTH

Sitting in front of a screen in awkward positions for long periods may lead to physical problems such as eyestrain, headaches, and back pain. Computer users can alleviate these problems by taking frequent rest breaks and by using well-designed computer furniture. Some recommendations by ergonomics experts for the ideal microcomputer setup are illustrated in Figure 10-17.

The physical health matters related to computers that have received the most attention recently are the following:

- **Eyestrain and headache:** Our eyes were made for most efficient seeing at a distance. However, monitors require using the eyes at closer range for a long time, which can create eyestrain, headaches, and double vision.

    To make the computer easier on the eyes, take a 15-minute break every hour or two. Avoid computer screens that flicker. Keep computer screens

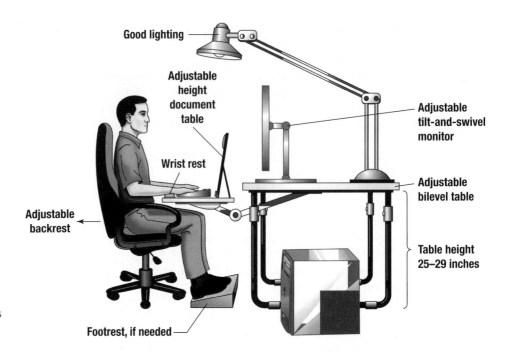

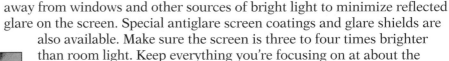

Good lighting

Adjustable height document table

Adjustable tilt-and-swivel monitor

Wrist rest

Adjustable bilevel table

Adjustable backrest

Table height 25–29 inches

Footrest, if needed

Figure 10-17 Recommendations for the ideal microcomputer work environment

Figure 10-18 Back and neck pain

away from windows and other sources of bright light to minimize reflected glare on the screen. Special antiglare screen coatings and glare shields are also available. Make sure the screen is three to four times brighter than room light. Keep everything you're focusing on at about the same distance. For example, the computer screen, keyboard, and a document holder containing your work might be positioned about 20 inches away. Clean the screen of dust from time to time.

- **Back and neck pain:** Many people work at monitors and keyboards that are in improper positions. The result can be pains in the back and neck. (See Figure 10-18.) To avoid such problems, make sure equipment is adjustable. You should be able to adjust your chair for height and angle, and the chair should have good back support. The table on which the monitor stands also should be adjustable, and the monitor itself should be of the tilt-and-swivel kind. The monitor should be at eye level or slightly below eye level. Use a footrest, if necessary, to reduce leg fatigue.

- **Repetitive strain injury:** Data-entry operators may make as many as 23,000 keystrokes a day. Some of these workers and other heavy keyboard users have fallen victim to a disorder known as repetitive strain injury.

  Repetitive strain injury (RSI)—also called **repetitive motion injury** and **cumulative trauma disorder**—is the name given to a number of injuries. These result from fast, repetitive work that can cause neck, wrist, hand, and arm pain. RSI is by far the greatest cause of workplace illnesses in private industry. It accounts for billions of dollars in compensation claims and lost productivity every year. Some RSI sufferers are slaughterhouse, textile, and automobile workers, who have long been susceptible to the disorder. One particular type of RSI, **carpal tunnel syndrome,** found among heavy computer users, consists of damage to nerves and tendons in the hands. (See Figure 10-19.) Some victims report the pain is so intense that they cannot open doors or shake hands and that they require corrective surgery.

Ergonomically correct keyboards have recently been developed to help prevent injury from heavy computer use. (See Figure 10-20.) In addition to using ergonomic keyboards, you should take frequent short rest breaks and gently massage your hands.

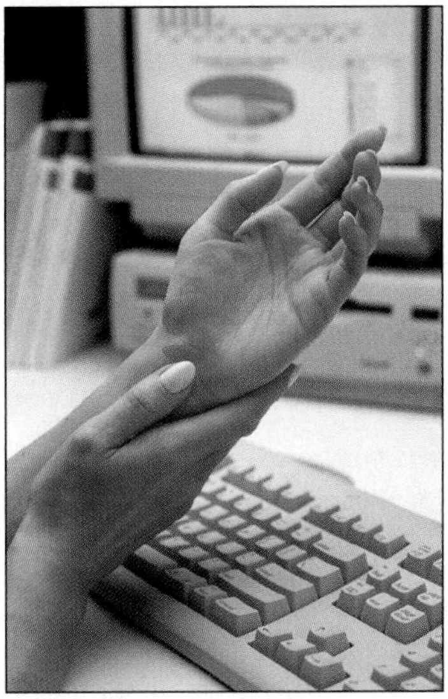

MENTAL HEALTH

Computer technology offers many ways of improving productivity, but it also creates some irritants that may be counterproductive.

Figure 10-19 Carpal tunnel syndrome

Figure 10-20 Ergonomic keyboard

- **Noise:** Computing can be quite noisy. Voice input and output can be distracting for co-workers. Working next to some types of printers can leave one with ringing ears. Also, users may develop headaches and tension from continual exposure to the high-frequency, barely audible squeal produced by cooling fans and vibrating parts inside the system unit.

   Head-mounted microphones and earphones greatly reduce the effect of voice input and output. Acoustical tile and sound-muffling covers are available for reducing the noise from co-workers and impact printers. Tightening loose system unit components will reduce high-frequency noise.

- **Electronic monitoring:** Research shows that workers whose performance is monitored electronically suffer more health problems than do those watched by human supervisors. For instance, a computer may monitor the number of keystrokes a data-entry clerk completes in a day. It might tally the time a customer-service person takes to handle a call. The company might then decide to shorten the time allowed and to continue **electronic monitoring** to ensure compliance. By so doing, it may force a pace leading to physical problems, such as RSI, and mental health difficulties. One study found that electronically monitored employees reported more tension, extreme anxiety, depression, anger, and severe fatigue than those who were not electronically monitored.

   Recently it has been shown that electronic monitoring actually is not necessary. For instance, both Federal Express and Bell Canada replaced electronic monitoring with occasional monitoring by human managers, and they found that employee productivity stayed up and even increased.

A new word—*technostress*—has been proposed to describe the stress associated with computer use that is harmful to people. **Technostress** is the tension that arises when we have to adapt unnaturally to computers rather than having computers adapt to us.

DESIGN

Electronic products from microcomputers to microwave ovens to VCRs offer the promise of more efficiency and speed. Often, however, the products are so overloaded with features that users cannot figure them out. Because a microprocessor chip handles not just one operation but several, some

Problem	Remedy
Eyestrain and headache	Take frequent breaks, avoid screen glare, place object at fixed focal distance
Back and neck pain	Use adjustable equipment
Repetitive strain injury	Use ergonomically correct keyboards, take frequent breaks
Noise	Use head-mounted microphones and earphones, install acoustical tile and sound-muffling covers, tighten system unit components
Stress from excessive monitoring	Remove electronic monitoring

Figure 10-21 Summary of ergonomic concerns

manufacturers feel obliged to pile on the bells and whistles. Thus, many home and office products, while being fancy technology platforms, are difficult for humans to use.

A recent trend among manufacturers is to deliberately strip down the features offered, rather than to constantly do all that is possible. In appliances, this restraint is shown among certain types of high-end audio equipment, which comes with fewer buttons and lights. In computers, there are similar trends. Surveys show that consumers want plug-and-play equipment—machines that they can simply turn on and with which they can quickly start working. Thus, computers are being made easier to use, with more menus, windows, icons, and pictures.

For a summary of ergonomic concerns, see Figure 10-21.

▼ CONCEPT CHECK

▶ What is ergonomics and why is it important?

▶ Discuss some of the most significant physical concerns created by frequent computer use and how they can be avoided.

▶ Discuss some of the most significant mental concerns created by frequent computer use and how they can be avoided.

ENVIRONMENTAL PROTECTION

What do you suppose uses the greatest amount of electricity in the workplace? Microcomputers do. They account for 5 percent of the electricity used. Increased power production translates to increased air pollution, depletion of nonrenewable resources, and other environmental hazards.

The Environmental Protection Agency (EPA) has created the **Energy Star** program to discourage waste in the microcomputer industry. Along with over 50 manufacturers, the EPA has established a goal of reducing power requirements for system units, monitors, and printers. The industry has responded with the concept of the **Green PC.** (See Figure 10-22.)

THE GREEN PC

The basic elements of the Green PC are

• **System unit:** Using existing technology from portable computers, the system unit (1) uses an energy-saving microprocessor that requires a minimal amount of power, (2) employs microprocessor and hard-disk drives that shift to an energy-saving or sleep mode when not in operation, (3) replaces

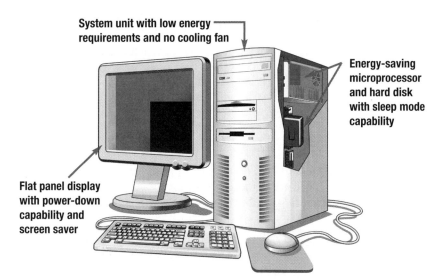

System unit with low energy requirements and no cooling fan

Energy-saving microprocessor and hard disk with sleep mode capability

Flat panel display with power-down capability and screen saver

Figure 10-22 The Green PC

the conventional power supply unit with an adapter that requires less electricity, and (4) eliminates the cooling fan.

- **Display:** Displays have been made more energy efficient by using (1) flat panels that require less energy than the traditional monitors, (2) special power-down monitors that automatically reduce power consumption when not in use, and (3) screen-saver software that clears the display whenever it is not in use.

- **Manufacturing:** Computer manufacturers such as Intel, Apple, Compaq, and others are using fewer harmful chemicals in production. Particular attention is given to **chlorofluorocarbons (CFCs)** in solvents and cleaning agents. (CFCs can travel into the atmosphere and are suspected by some in the scientific community of depleting the earth's ozone layer.) Toxic nickel and other heavy metals are being eliminated or reduced in the manufacturing processes.

Of course, not all of these technologies and manufacturing processes are used for all microcomputers. But more and more of them are.

PERSONAL RESPONSIBILITY

Some of the things that you, as a computer user, can do to help protect the environment are the following:

- **Conserve:** The EPA estimates that 30 to 40 percent of computer users leave their machines running days, nights, and weekends. When finished working for the day, turn off all computers and other energy-consuming devices. The EPA also estimates that 80 percent of the time a monitor is on, no one is looking at it. Use screen-saver programs that blank the computer screen after three to five minutes of inactivity.

- **Recycle:** U.S. businesses use an enormous amount of paper each year—a pile 48,900 miles high. Much of that, as well as the paper we throw out at home, can be recycled. Other recyclable items include computer boxes, packaging material, printer cartridges, and floppy disks. Last year over 24 million computers were thrown away. (See Figure 10-23.) Only 14 percent were recycled. Recycle discarded computers by contacting any one of the groups listed in Figure 10-24.

Figure 10-23 Discarded computer components

Privacy and Security

Organization	Web Site
Computers for Schools	www.pcsforschools.org
National Cristina Foundation	www.cristina.org
Retire-IT	www.retire-it.com
Share Technology	www.sharetechnology.org

Figure 10-24   Computer recycling groups

- **Educate:** Be aware of and learn more about ecological dangers of all types. Make your concerns known to manufacturers and retail agencies. Support ecologically sound products.

▼ CONCEPT CHECK

▶ What is the Energy Star program?

▶ What is a Green PC? What are the basic elements of the Green PC?

▶ What actions can you take to help protect the environment?

CAREERS IN IT

Figure 10-25   Cryptographer

Cryptography is the science of disguising and revealing encrypted information, in terms of information technology, cryptography usually refers to keeping any intercepted information private. For example, such information may be financial data, like banking and credit card information used in online shopping, or private e-mail and correspondence. **Cryptographers** design systems, break systems, and do research on encryption. (See Figure 10-25.) Responsibilities typically do not include building and maintaining the computer networks that use cryptography; these are the duties of security engineers and network administrators. In general, cryptographers are mathematicians who specialize in making and breaking codes.

Many cryptographers work as consultants or professors of cryptography, yet there are full-time positions available at some large corporations or for the government. A PhD in cryptography is usually an essential prerequisite for a position as a cryptographer. However, all cryptographers must have broad experience in both mathematics and computer science or information systems.

Cryptographers can expect to earn an annual salary of $60,000 to $101,000. Opportunities for advancement typically depend on experience; the most competitive field will be research positions at universities. Those with experience in computer science and information technology should be among the most employable mathematicians and increasingly in demand. To learn more about becoming a cryptographer, visit us at www.computing2008.com and enter the keyword careers.

Presence Technology Will Keep Track of You, Your Friends, and Everyone Else

How would you like the devices you use to alert others when you are using them? What if you sat down to watch television and a message popped up alerting you that a friend wants to chat? What if you could instantly know what is the best way to get in touch with someone you know? Presence technology is designed to meet all of these needs, and many more.

Many people are currently exposed to presence technology through their instant messaging software. When a user signs on to a system, friends are alerted to his or her presence. Many manufacturers of personal computing devices and cellular phones are currently developing presence technology. Analysts expect presence technology to become a feature of everything from your computer to your car. Some even anticipate that your friends will be able to tell where you are and which device (PDA, television, telephone) is the best way to contact you. While there are many advantages to such a system, the potential loss of privacy is of concern to many. They argue the potential abuse by advertisers and others makes presence technology a threat to privacy. Supporters of this technology suggest that the user would have control over when and where they are "seen."

What do you think? Would you like to know that you are always available to those who need to get in touch with you? What are the potential advantages of this type of technology? Some experts suggest presence technology will become a standard feature of new cars, phones, and appliances. What do you think? Would you buy a television that lets everyone know you are watching TV instead of working on homework or studying for exams?

PRIVACY AND SECURITY

PRIVACY

PRIVACY

Computer ethics are guidelines for moral computer use. Four computer ethics issues are **privacy, accuracy, property,** and **access.**

Large Databases

Large organizations are constantly compiling information about us. **Reverse directories** list telephone numbers followed by subscriber names. **Information resellers (information brokers)** collect and sell personal data. **Electronic profiles** are compiled from databases to provide highly detailed and personalized descriptions of individuals.

Identity theft is the illegal assumption of someone's identity for the purposes of economic gain. **Mistaken identity** occurs when an electronic profile of one person is switched with another. The **Freedom of Information Act** entitles individuals access to governmental records relating to them.

Private Networks

Many organizations monitor employee e-mail and computer files using special software called **snoopware.**

Internet and the Web

Many people believe that, while using the Web, as long as they are selective about disclosing their name and other personal information, little can be done to invade their privacy. This is called the **illusion of anonymity.**

History files record locations of sites visited by a computer system. **Cookies** record sites visited, activity at sites, and other information. Two basic types are **traditional cookies** and **ad network cookies (adware cookies).**

The term **spyware** describes a wide range of programs designed to secretly record and report an individual's activities on the Internet. Ad network cookies are one type of spyware. Two other types are **Web bugs** and **computer monitoring (keystroke loggers). Anti-spyware (spy removal programs)** detects Web bugs and monitoring software.

Program	Web Site
Ad-adware	www.lavasoft.com
CounterSpy	www.counterspy.com
Spy Doctor	www.spydoctor.com
Spy Sweeper	www.spysweeper.com

Major Laws on Privacy

There are numerous federal laws governing privacy matters. **Financial Modernization Act** protects personal financial information. Privacy remains primarily an ethical issue.

To be a competent end user, you need to be aware of the potential impact of technology on people. You need to be sensitive to and knowledgeable about personal privacy, organizational security, ergonomics, and the environmental impact of technology.

Computer Criminals

Computer criminals include employees, outside users, hackers and crackers (**hackers** gain access for the fun and challenge while **crackers** do it for malicious purposes; **bomb** is a destructive program), organized crime, and terrorists.

Computer Crime

Computer crime is an illegal action involving special knowledge of computer technology.

- Malicious programs, or **malware,** include **viruses** (**Computer Abuse Amendments Act** makes spreading a virus a federal offense), **worms** (self-replicate to slow or stop a computer's operations), and **Trojan horses** (enter a computer system disguised as something else). Antivirus programs alert users when certain viruses and worms enter their systems.

- **Denial of service attack (DoS)** is an attempt to shut down or stop a computer system or network. It floods a computer or network with requests for information and data. Servers under attack are unable to respond to legitimate users.

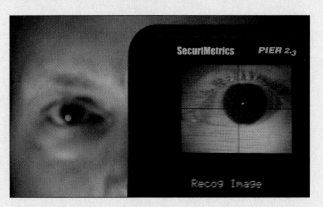

- **Scams** are fraudulent or deceptive acts or operations designed to trick individuals into spending their time and money with little or no return. Common **Internet scams** include identity theft, chain letters, auction fraud, vacation prizes, and advance fee loans.

- Theft takes many forms including stealing hardware, software, data, and computer time. Unauthorized copying of programs is called **software piracy** and protected by the **Software Copyright Act.**

- Data manipulation involves changing data or leaving prank messages. The **Computer Fraud and Abuse Act** helps protect against data manipulation.

- Other hazards include natural disasters, civil strife, terrorism, technological failures (**surge protectors** protect against **voltage surges** or **spikes**), and human error.

Measures to Protect Computer Security

Security is concerned with keeping hardware, software, data, and programs safe from unauthorized personnel. Some measures are **encrypting,** restricting access by using **biometric scanning** devices, **passwords,** and **firewalls;** anticipating disasters (**physical** and **data security, disaster recovery plans**), and backing up data.

ERGONOMICS

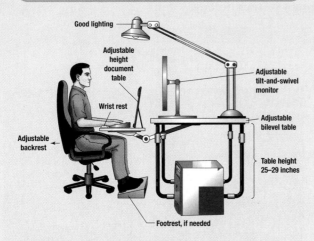

Good lighting

Adjustable height document table

Adjustable tilt-and-swivel monitor

Wrist rest

Adjustable bilevel table

Adjustable backrest

Table height 25–29 inches

Footrest, if needed

Ergonomics is the study of human factors related to things people use, including computers.

Physical Health
Physical health problems and their solutions include

- Eyestrain and headache—take frequent breaks; avoid glare on the monitor.
- Back and neck pains—use adjustable chairs, tables, monitor stands, footrests.
- **Repetitive strain injury (RSI, repetitive motion injury, cumulative trama disorder)** includes **carpal tunnel syndrome**—take frequent breaks; use good posture; adopt healthy lifestyle; use ergonomic keyboards.

Mental Health
Counterproductive mental irritations include

- Noise from clattering printers and high-frequency squeals from computers.
- Stress from electronic monitoring.

Unnatural adaptation to computers can cause **technostress.**

Design
Computers are being designed for easier and healthier use. There is a trend toward simplifying features offered on new models.

ENVIRONMENTAL PROTECTION

Organization	Web Site
Computers for Schools	www.pcsforschools.org
National Cristina Foundation	www.cristina.org
Retire-IT	www.retire-it.com
Share Technology	www.sharetechnology.org

The EPA has established the **Energy Star** program to promote energy-efficient computer use. The computer industry has responded with the concept of the **Green PC.**

The Green PC
The basic elements of the Green PC include

- System units with energy-saving processors, sleep-mode capability, efficient adapters, and no cooling fans.
- Flat panels with power-down monitors and screen-saver software.
- Elimination or reduction of harmful chemicals in manufacturing (**chlorofluorocarbons** or **CFCs,** nickel, and other heavy metals).

Personal Responsibility
As a responsible computer user, you can help protect the environment by

- Conserving energy by turning off computer systems at night and using screen savers.
- Recycling paper, computer boxes, packaging materials, printer cartridges, and floppy disks.
- Educating yourself and others about ecological dangers and using ecologically sound products.

CAREERS IN IT

Cryptographers design systems, break systems, and do research on encryption. PhD in cryptography and broad experience in mathematics and computer science or information systems is required. Salary range $60,000 to $101,000.

KEY TERMS

access   (278)
accuracy   (278)
ad network cookie   (282)
adware cookie   (282)
anti-spyware   (283)
biometric scanning   (291)
bomb   (286)
carpal tunnel syndrome   (294)
chlorofluorocarbons (CFCs)   (297)
Computer Abuse Amendments Act   (287)
computer crime   (286)
computer ethics   (278)
Computer Fraud and Abuse Act   (289)
computer monitoring software   (283)
cookies   (280)
cracker   (286)
cryptographer   (298)
cumulative trauma disorder   (294)
data security   (292)
denial of service (DoS) attack   (288)
disaster recovery plan   (292)
electronic monitoring   (295)
electronic profile   (279)
encrypting   (291)
Energy Star   (296)
environmental protection   (278)
ergonomics   (278, 293)
ethics   (278)
Financial Modernization Act   (286)
firewall   (292)
Freedom of Information Act   (280)
Green PC   (296)
hacker   (286)

history file   (280)
identity theft   (279)
illusion of anonymity   (280)
information broker   (279)
information reseller   (279)
Internet scam   (288)
keystroke logger   (283)
malware   (287)
mistaken identity   (280)
password   (291)
physical security   (292)
privacy   (278)
property   (278)
repetitive motion injury   (294)
repetitive strain injury (RSI)   (294)
reverse directory   (278)
scam   (288)
security   (278, 290)
snoopware   (280)
Software Copyright Act   (289)
software piracy   (289)
spike   (290)
spy removal program   (283)
spyware   (282)
surge protector   (290)
technostress   (295)
traditional cookies   (282)
Trojan horse   (288)
virus   (287)
voltage surge   (290)
Web bug   (282)
worm   (287)

FEATURES
Animations
Careers in IT
DVD Direct
Expansions
Making IT Work for You
On the Web Explorations
TechTV
Tips

CHAPTER REVIEW
Applying Technology
Crossword Puzzle
Expanding Your Knowledge
Key Terms
Matching
Multiple Choice
Open-Ended
Writing About Technology

To test your knowledge of these key terms with animated flash cards, visit us at www.computing2008.com and enter the keyword **terms10**.

CROSSWORD PUZZLE

Across

3 Malicious software.

6 Program that records keystrokes and activities.

7 Used to record virtually everything done on a computer.

8 Those who gain access to systems for the fun and challenge.

9 Includes the locations of sites visited by your browser.

Down

1 Programs that record information on Web site visitors.

2 Device that separates the computer from the power source.

4 Study of human factors related to the things people use.

5 Those who gain access to systems for malicious purposes.

For an interactive version of this crossword, visit us at www.computing2008.com and enter the keyword **crossword10**.

MULTIPLE CHOICE

Circle the letter or fill in the correct answer.

1. The standards of moral conduct that control how computers are used are called
   - **a.** ethics
   - **b.** laws
   - **c.** security requirements
   - **d.** business demands

2. The ethical issue that involves who is able to read and use data is
   - **a.** access
   - **b.** property
   - **c.** accuracy
   - **d.** privacy

3. Two types of cookies are _____.
   - **a.** advanced and remedial
   - **b.** traditional and natural
   - **c.** natural and ad network
   - **d.** ad network and traditional

4. People who gain unauthorized access to computers for the fun of it, but do not intentionally do damage, are _____.
   - **a.** employees
   - **b.** hackers
   - **c.** crackers
   - **d.** members of organized crime

5. A program that migrates through networks and operating systems by attaching itself to different programs and databases is a _____.
   - **a.** virus
   - **b.** worm
   - **c.** denial-of-service attack
   - **d.** Web bug

6. An attempt to slow down or stop a computer system or network by flooding the system with requests for information is called a
   - **a.** virus
   - **b.** worm
   - **c.** denial-of-service attack
   - **d.** Trojan horse

7. Secret words or numbers used to gain access to a computer system are called
   - **a.** encryption
   - **b.** codes
   - **c.** crackers
   - **d.** passwords

8. One of the more common types of technological failures is when your computer experiences too much electricity. This is known as _____.
   - **a.** a protector
   - **b.** a brownout
   - **c.** a voltage surge
   - **d.** energizing

9. _____ is the study of human factors relating to things people use.
   - **a.** EPA
   - **b.** ergonomics
   - **c.** encryption
   - **d.** privacy

10. The computer industry response to the Energy Star program is the
    - **a.** CFC Association
    - **b.** Encryption Act
    - **c.** Freedom of Information Act
    - **d.** Green PC

For an interactive version of these multiple-choice questions, visit us at www.computing2008.com and enter the keyword multiple10.

MATCHING

www.computing2008.com

Match each numbered item with the most closely related lettered item. Write your answers in the spaces provided.

a. ad network cookies

b. computer crime

c. cracker

d. DoS

e. firewall

f. illusion of anonymity

g. property

h. snoopware

i. virus checkers

j. worm

1. Relates to who owns data and rights to software. ____
2. Programs that record virtually every activity on a computer system. ____
3. Belief that there is little threat to personal privacy via the Internet. ____
4. Monitor Web activity and send reports to marketing groups. ____
5. Illegal action involving special knowledge of computer technology. ____
6. Gains unauthorized access to a system for malicious purposes. ____
7. Fills a computer system with self-replicating information. ____
8. An attack that overwhelms Web sites with data, making them inaccessible. ____
9. Programs that alert users when certain viruses enter a system. ____
10. Security hardware and software that controls access to internal computer networks. ____

For an interactive version of this matching exercise, visit our Web site at www.computing2008.com and enter the keyword **matching10**.

OPEN-ENDED

On a separate sheet of paper, respond to each question or statement.

1. Discuss the impact of large databases, private networks, the Internet, and the Web on privacy.
2. Discuss the various kinds of computer criminals.
3. What are the principal measures used to protect computer security? What is encryption? How is it used by corporations and individuals?
4. What is ergonomics? How does computer use impact mental health? Physical health?
5. Describe the basic elements of the Green PC and what you can do to protect the environment.

APPLYING TECHNOLOGY

The following questions are designed to demonstrate ways that you can effectively use technology today. The first question relates directly to this chapter's Making IT Work for You feature.

Spyware

1

Have you installed any free software from the Internet? Did you know that seemingly harmless software might actually be spying on you, even sending personal information to advertisers or worse? Fortunately, spyware removal programs can help. After reviewing Making IT Work for You: Spyware Removal on pages 284 and 285, answer the following: (a) Define spyware and discuss how it works. (b) Describe the process for downloading and installing Lavasoft's Ad-aware. (c) Describe the capabilities of Ad-aware. (d) Do you think that spyware might be on your computer? If yes, how do you suppose the spyware was deposited onto your system? If no, why are you so confident?

Personal Firewalls

2

At one time, firewalls were used only for large servers. Today firewalls are available for almost any device that connects to the Internet and are essential to ensure security. Connect to our Web site at www.computing2008.com and enter the keyword security to link to a personal firewall product for home users. Once connected, read about the firewall and then answer the following: (a) Is this firewall a hardware or software solution? (b) Describe the procedure for installing the firewall. (c) What types of security risks does this firewall protect against? (d) Are there any security risks the firewall does not cover? If so, how can those risks be reduced?

Ergonomic Workstations

3

As public awareness and understanding of repetitive motion workplace injuries have grown, more ergonomic products have become available. Visit our Web site at www.computing2008.com and enter the keyword workstation to link to a site that educates the public on correct ergonomics for safety and comfort. Once connected, explore the site, and briefly answer the following: (a) What office equipment or furniture is covered? (b) Summarize the recommendations for each component. (c) What additional resources are available from the site to assist in creating an ergonomic workplace?

EXPANDING YOUR KNOWLEDGE

The following questions are designed to add depth and detail to your understanding of specific topics presented within this chapter. The questions direct you to sources other than the textbook to obtain this knowledge.

1 How Web Bugs Work

The Internet is popular because it is fast, cheap, and open to everyone. These qualities also make it an ideal tool for criminals. Unscrupulous people can use programs called Web bugs to spy on you when you use the Internet. To learn more about how Web bugs work, visit our Web site at www.computing2008.com and enter the keyword **bugs**. Then answer the following questions: (a) How can a Web bug infect your computer? (b) When a Web bug is delivered by e-mail, it typically sends a copy of that e-mail back to the server. What is the significance or purpose of this activity? (c) Do you think Web bugs are really a privacy concern? Do you think your computer may have one? How could you find out?

2 Mistaken Identity

A simple typo can result in mistaken identity. Such mistakes can have a tremendous impact on a person's career, family, and future. To learn more about mistaken identity, visit our Web site at www.computing2008.com and enter the keyword **id**. Then answer the following questions: (a) Have you been a victim of mistaken identity? If so, please discuss. (b) If your response was "yes," how would you verify that mistaken identity has occurred? (c) Perhaps you have been a victim without knowing it. List the questions that should be considered.

3 Air Travel Database

- To curb possible terrorist threats, the government has implemented a controversial database, known as the Computer Assisted Passenger Pre-screening System (CAPPS), to perform background checks on travelers before allowing them on aircraft. This database determines a "possible threat score" for each individual to determine whether he or she can fly. This system relies on airlines to share information on passengers that once was considered confidential. Research CAPPS on the Internet and then answer the following questions: (a) How does CAPPS determine who is a security risk? (b) What personal information is gathered by CAPPS? (c) How might CAPPS infringe on personal privacy? (d) Would you prefer to travel with or without the CAPPS system in place? Justify your answer.

WRITING ABOUT TECHNOLOGY

The ability to think critically and to write effectively is essential to nearly every profession. The following questions are designed to help you develop these skills by posing thought-provoking questions about computer privacy, security, and/or ethics.

Facial Recognition

1

As new technologies emerge that promise to enhance our security, our privacy may be at stake. A recent example is the introduction of facial recognition systems in public places for use by police officers. Such systems have recently caught the attention of privacy advocates, as well as the ACLU. Research facial recognition systems on the Web and then write a one-page paper titled "Facial Recognition" that addresses the following topics: (a)

Describe how facial recognition technology works. (b) How can facial recognition technology enhance security? (c) In what ways might facial recognition technology compromise privacy? (Hint: Consider security cameras in department or grocery stores.) (d) Do you approve of facial recognition technology? Explain your answer.

Plagiarism

2

Suspicious of cheating, a professor at the University of Virginia developed a program to compare the term papers of his current and past students. Alarmingly, he found that 122 students' work suggested plagiarizing. Consider the implications of this case and then write a one-page paper titled "Plagiarism" that addresses the following questions: (a) With more and more academic submissions being stored in an electronic format, how is it easier to copy another's work? (b) For the same reason, how is detecting an unoriginal work easier? (c) Have you ever copied and pasted text from a Web site or other electronic document and passed it off as your own? (d) How does "borrowing" work in this way affect other students? What about the original author? Explain.

FEATURES

Animations

Careers in IT

DVD Direct

Expansions

Making IT Work for You

On the Web Explorations

TechTV

Tips

CHAPTER REVIEW

Applying Technology

Crossword Puzzle

Expanding Your Knowledge

Key Terms

Matching

Multiple Choice

Open-Ended

Writing About Technology

CHAPTER

11

COMPETENCIES

After you have read this chapter, you should be able to:

1 Explain why it's important to have an individual strategy to be a "winner" in the information age.

2 Describe how technology is changing the nature of competition.

3 Discuss four ways people may react to new technology.

4 Describe how you can stay current with your career.

5 Describe different careers in information technology.

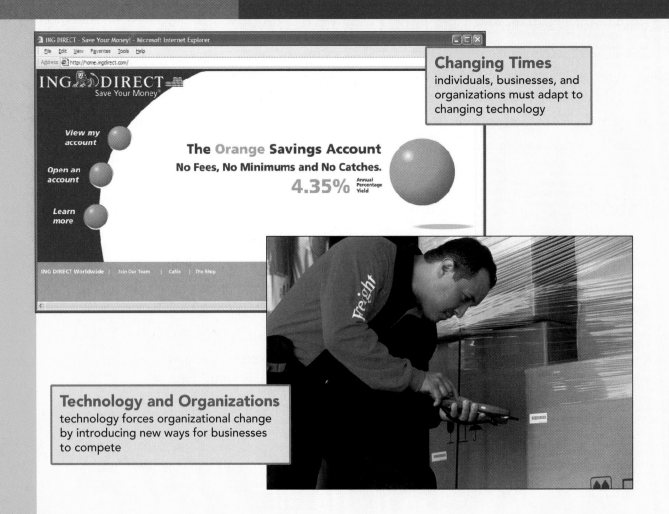

Changing Times
individuals, businesses, and organizations must adapt to changing technology

Technology and Organizations
technology forces organizational change by introducing new ways for businesses to compete

YOUR FUTURE AND INFORMATION TECHNOLOGY

Introduction

Throughout this book, we have emphasized practical subjects that are useful to you now or will be very soon. Accordingly, this final chapter is not about the far future, say, 10 years from now. Rather, it is about today and the near future—about developments whose outlines we can already see. It is about how organizations adapt to technological change. It is also about what you as an individual can do to keep your computer competency up to date.

Are the times changing any faster now than they ever have? It's hard to say. People who were alive when radios, cars, and airplanes were being introduced certainly lived through some dramatic changes.

Has technology made our own times even more dynamic? Whatever the answer, it is clear we live in a fast-paced age. The challenge for you as an individual is to devise ways to stay current and to use technology to your advantage. For example, you can use the Web to locate job opportunities.

To stay competent, end users need to recognize the impact of technological change on organizations and people. They need to know how to use change to their advantage and how to be winners. Although end users do not need to be specialists in information technology, they should be aware of career opportunities in the area.

Be a Winner
stay current, develop specialties, and be alert to organizational changes and opportunities for innovation

Technology and People
some people react negatively to technological change by being cynical, naive, or frustrated, but the most positive reaction to technological change is to be proactive

Almost all businesses have become aware that they must adapt to changing technology or be left behind. Most organizations are now making formal plans to keep track of technology and implement it in their competitive strategies. For example, banks have found that automated teller machines (ATMs) are vital to retail banking. (See Figure 11-1.) Not only do they require fewer human tellers, but also they are available 24 hours a day. More and more banks also are trying to go electronic, doing away with paper transactions wherever possible. ATM cards are used to buy almost anything from gas to groceries.

What's next for the banking industry? Almost all banks also are trying to popularize home banking so that customers can use microcomputers for certain financial tasks. Some banks, known as Internet banks, have even done away with physical bank buildings and conduct all business over the Web. (See Figure 11-2.) In addition, banks are exploring the use of some very sophisticated application programs. These programs will accept cursive writing (the handwriting on checks) directly as input, verify check signatures, and process the check without human intervention.

Clearly, such changes do away with some jobs—those of many bank tellers and cashiers, for example. However, they create opportunities for other people. New technology requires people who are truly capable of working with it. These are not the people who think every piece of equipment is so simple they can just turn it on and use it. Nor are they those who think each new machine is a potential disaster. In other words, new technology needs people who are not afraid to learn about it and are able to manage it. The real issue, then, is not how to make technology better. Rather, it is how to integrate the technology with people.

You are in a very favorable position compared with many other people in industry today. After reading the previous chapters, you have learned more than just the basics of hardware, software, connectivity, and the Internet. You have learned about the most current technology. You are therefore able to use these tools to your advantage—to be a winner.

How do you become and stay a winner? In brief, the answer is: You must form your own individual strategy for dealing with change. First let us look at how businesses are handling technological change. Then let's look at how people are reacting to these changes. Finally, we will offer a few suggestions that will enable you to keep up with and profit from the information revolution.

Figure 11-1 Automated teller machines are examples of technology used in business strategy

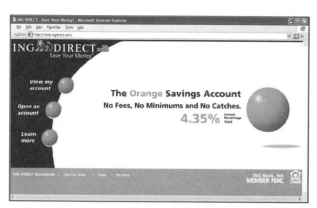

Figure 11-2 Internet banks conduct business over the Web

TECHNOLOGY AND ORGANIZATIONS

Technology can introduce new ways for businesses to compete with each other. Some of the principal changes are as follows.

NEW PRODUCTS

Technology creates products that operate faster, are priced cheaper, are often of better quality, or are wholly new. Indeed, new products can be individually tailored to a particular customer's needs. For example, financial services companies such as Merrill Lynch have taken advantage of technology to launch cash management accounts. (See Figure 11-3.) These accounts combine information on a person's checking, savings, credit card, and securities accounts into a single monthly statement. It automatically sets aside "idle" funds into interest-bearing money market funds. Customers can access their accounts on the Web and get a complete picture of their financial condition at any time. However, even if they don't pay much attention to their statements, their surplus funds are invested automatically.

NEW ENTERPRISES

Information technology can build entirely new businesses. Two examples are Internet service providers and Web site development companies.

- Just a few years ago, the only computer connectivity options available to individuals were through online service providers like America Online and through colleges and universities. Now, hundreds of national service providers and thousands of local service providers are available.

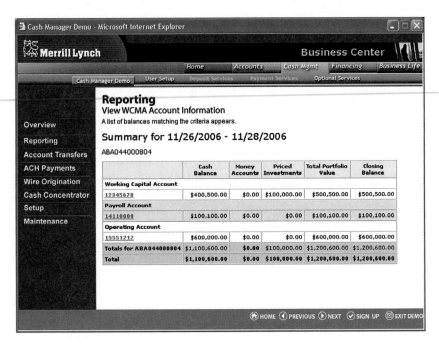

Figure 11-3 Merrill Lynch's cash management account

Figure 11-4 New technology helps FedEx maintain customer loyalty

- Thousands of small companies specializing in Web site development have sprung up in the past three years. These companies help small- to medium-sized organizations by providing assistance in evaluating, creating, and maintaining Web sites.

NEW CUSTOMER AND SUPPLIER RELATIONSHIPS

Businesses that make their information systems easily available may make their customers less likely to take their business elsewhere. For instance, Federal Express, the overnight package delivery service, does everything possible to make its customers dependent on it. Upon request, customers receive airbills with their name, address, and account number preprinted on them, making shipping and billing easier. Package numbers are scanned into the company's information system so that they can be tracked from pickup point to destination. (See Figure 11-4.) Thus, apprehensive customers can be informed very quickly of the exact location of their package as it travels toward its destination.

▼ CONCEPT CHECK

▶ What is the role of technology in creating new products?

▶ Describe two new enterprises built by information technology.

▶ Discuss how technology can create new customers and affect supplier relationships.

TECHNOLOGY AND PEOPLE

Clearly, recent technological changes, and those sure to come in the near future, will produce significant changes and opportunities in the years ahead. How should we be prepared for them?

People have different coping styles when it comes to technology. It has been suggested, for instance, that people react to changing technology in one of four ways: cynicism, naivete, frustration, and proactivity.

CYNICISM

The **cynic** feels that, for a manager at least, the idea of using a microcomputer is overrated. (See Figure 11-5.) Learning and using it take too much time, time that could be delegated to someone else. Doing spreadsheets and word processing, according to the cynic, are tasks that managers should understand. However, the cynic feels that such tasks take time away from a manager's real job of developing plans and setting goals for the people being supervised.

Cynics may express their doubts openly, especially if they are top managers. Or they may only pretend to be interested in microcomputers, when actually they are not interested at all.

Figure 11-5 The cynic: "These gadgets are overrated."

Figure 11-6 The frustrated person: "This stuff doesn't make sense half the time."

NAIVETE

Many **naive** people are unfamiliar with computers. They may think computers are magic boxes capable of solving all kinds of problems that computers really can't handle. On the other hand, some naive persons are actually quite familiar with computers but underestimate the difficulty of changing computer systems or of generating certain information.

FRUSTRATION

The **frustrated** person may already be quite busy and may hate having to take time to learn about microcomputers. Such a person feels it is an imposition to have to learn something new or is too impatient to try to understand the manuals explaining what hardware and software are supposed to do. The result is continual frustration. (See Figure 11-6.) Some people are frustrated because they try to do too much. Or they're frustrated because they find manuals difficult to understand. In some cases poorly written manuals are at fault.

PROACTIVITY

Webster's Collegiate Dictionary defines **proactive,** in part, as "acting in anticipation of future problems, needs, or changes." A proactive person looks at technology in a positive realistic way. (See Figure 11-7.) They are not cynics,

Figure 11-7 The proactive person: "How can I use this new tool?"

underestimating the likely impact of technology on their lives. They are not naive, overestimating the ability of technology to solve the world's or their problems. They do not become frustrated easily and give up using technology. Proactive people are positive in their outlook and look at new technology as providing new tools that, when correctly applied, can positively impact their lives.

Most of us fall into one of the four categories. Cynicism, naivete, frustration, and proactivity are common human responses to change. Do you see yourself or others around you responding to technology in any of these ways? For those who respond negatively, just being aware of their reaction can help them become more positive and proactive to tomorrow's exciting new changes in technology.

> ### ▼ CONCEPT CHECK
>
> ▶ Describe three negative ways people cope with technological changes in the workplace.
>
> ▶ Describe one positive way people cope with technological change in the workplace.
>
> ▶ Define proactive.

HOW YOU CAN BE A WINNER

Making IT work for you

So far we have described how progressive organizations are using technology in the information age. Now let's concentrate on you as an individual. (See Making IT Work for You: Locating Job Opportunities Online on pages 318 and 319.) How can you stay ahead? Here are some ideas.

STAY CURRENT

Whatever their particular line of work, successful professionals keep up both with their own fields and with the times. We don't mean you should try to become a computer expert and read a lot of technical magazines. Rather, you should concentrate on your profession and learn how computer technology is being used within it.

Every field has trade journals, whether the field is interior design, personnel management, or advertising. Most such journals regularly present articles about the uses of computers. It's important that you also belong to a trade or industry association and go to its meetings. Many associations sponsor seminars and conferences that describe the latest information and techniques.

Another way to stay current is by participating electronically with special-interest newsgroups on the Internet.

MAINTAIN YOUR COMPUTER COMPETENCY

Actually, you should try to stay ahead of the technology. Books, journals, and trade associations are the best sources of information about new technology that apply to your field. The general business press—*BusinessWeek, Fortune, Inc.,*

The Wall Street Journal, and the business section of your local newspaper—also carries computer-related articles.

However, if you wish, you can subscribe to a magazine that covers microcomputers and information more specifically. Examples are *InfoWorld, PC World,* and *MacWorld.* You also may find it useful to look at newspapers and magazines that cover the computer industry as a whole. An example of such a periodical is *ComputerWorld.* Most of these magazines also have online versions available on the Web. (See Figure 11-8.)

Figure 11-8 *PC World* on the Web

DEVELOP PROFESSIONAL CONTACTS

Besides being members of professional associations, successful people make it a point to maintain contact with others in their field. They stay in touch by telephone, e-mail, and newsgroups and go to lunch with others in their line of work. Doing this lets them learn what other people are doing in their jobs. It tells them what other firms are doing and what tasks are being automated. Developing professional contacts can keep you abreast not only of new information but also of new job possibilities. (See Figure 11-9.) It also offers social benefits. An example of a professional organization found in many areas is the local association of realtors.

DEVELOP SPECIALTIES

Develop specific as well as general skills. You want to be well-rounded *within* your field, but certainly not a "jack of all trades, master of none." Master a trade or two within your profession. At the same time, don't become identified with a specific technological skill that might very well become obsolete.

Figure 11-9 Professional organizations and contacts help you keep up in your field

LOCATING JOB OPPORTUNITIES ONLINE

Did you know that you can use the Internet to find a job? You can locate and browse through job listings. You can even electronically post your resume for prospective employers to review.

Browsing Job Listings Three well-known job search sites on the Web are hotjobs.com, Yahoo!jobs, and monster.com. You can connect to these sites and browse through job opportunities. For example, after connecting to monster.com, you can search for a job by following steps similar to those shown below.

1 • Connect to *www.monster.com.*

• Click the *Search Jobs* link.

2 • Select a location to search.

• Select a category to search.

• Optionally, enter any keywords to search.

• Click *Search Jobs.*

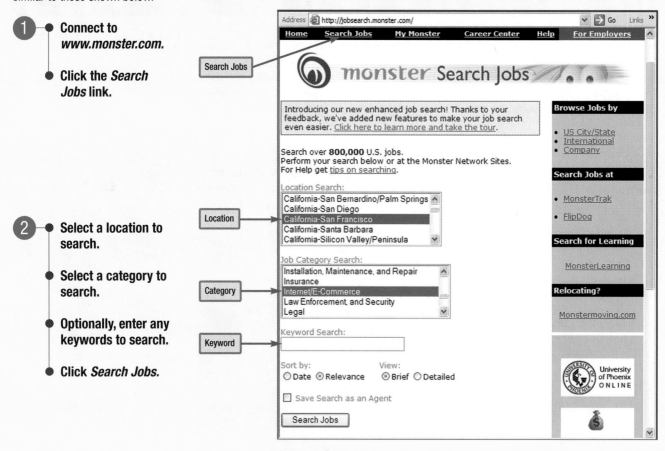

3 ● Select a job title to learn more about a job posting.

Jobs 1 to 40 of 40			Show Jobs Posted: Last 60 days ⌄
Sort: Date | **Relevance**			View: **Brief** | Detailed
Date	**Location**	**Job Title**	**Company**
Jul 10	US-CA-San Francisco	WIN32 Developer	TRS
Jul 10	US-CA-San Francisco	Senior Software Sales Executive	Management Recruiters Intntl
Jul 9	US-CA-San Francisco	★ Software Developers Wanted!	CFH Enterprises, Inc.
Jul 9	US-CA-San Francisco	★ ASSOCIATE WEB EDITOR	CFH Enterprises, Inc.
Jul 8	US-CA-San Francisco	Director of Public Relations	Management Recruiters Intntl
Jul 8	US-CA-San Francisco	QUALITY ASSURANCE ANALYST 3	Wells Fargo

A detailed job posting, including description, company information, and contact information, is displayed.

CFH Enterprises, Inc.

US-CA-San Francisco-ASSOCIATE WEB EDITOR

Will write, edit, proofread and copy edit various in house documents. Plans out and prepares articles on online newsletters. This position is part-time. A Bachelor's degree in a related field required. At least 2 years previous experience working for an Internet based company.

Please visit http://www.careersfromhome.com/internal.asp to apply.

Posting Your Resume   To make your qualifications known to prospective employers, you can post your resume at the job search site.

1 ● Select *My Monster*.

● Select the *Create your new My Monster account* link.

● Follow the on-screen instructions to create an account.

2 ● Log onto your new account.

● Select the *Create a New Resume* link.

● Complete the on-screen resume form.

● Click *Submit Resume*.

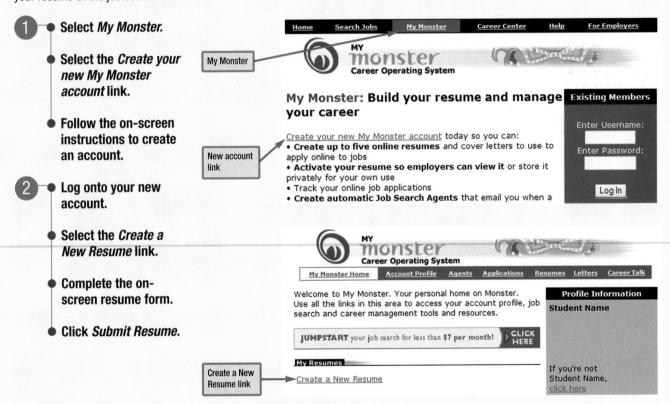

My Monster

New account link

Create a New Resume link

Your agent will search new job listings and alert you to new opportunities by e-mail.

The Web is continually changing, and some of the specifics presented in this Making IT Work for You may have changed. To learn about other ways to make information technology work for you, visit our Web site at www.computing2008.com and enter the keyword miw.

Figure 11-10 Desktop publishing: A good specialty to develop for certain careers

The best advice is to specialize to some extent. However, don't make your specialty so tied to technology that you'll be in trouble if the technology shifts. For example, if your career is in marketing or graphics design, it makes sense to learn about desktop publishing and Web page design. (See Figure 11-10.) In this way, you can learn to make high-quality, inexpensive graphics layouts. It would not make as much sense for you to become an expert on, say, the various types of monitors used to display the graphics layouts, because such monitors are continually changing.

Expect to take classes during your working life to keep up with developments in your field. Some professions require more keeping up than others—a computer specialist, for example, compared to a human resources manager. Whatever the training required, always look for ways to adapt and improve your skills to become more productive and marketable. There may be times when you are tempted to start all over again and learn completely new skills. However, a better course of action may be to use emerging technology to improve your present base of skills. This way you can build on your current strong points and then branch out to other fields from a position of strength.

BE ALERT FOR ORGANIZATIONAL CHANGE

Every organization has formal lines of communication—for example, supervisor to middle manager to top manager. However, there is also the *grapevine*—informal lines of communication. (See Figure 11-11.) Some service departments

Figure 11-11 Informal communication can alert you to important organizational changes

will serve many layers of management and be abreast of the news on all levels. For instance, the art director for advertising may be aware of several aspects of a companywide marketing campaign. Secretaries and administrative assistants know what is going on in more than one area.

Being part of the office grapevine can alert you to important changes—for instance, new job openings—that can benefit you. However, you always have to assess the validity of what you hear on the grapevine. Moreover, it's not advisable to be a contributor to office gossip. Behind-the-back criticisms of other people have a way of getting back to the person criticized.

Be especially alert for new trends within the organization—future hiring, layoffs, automation, mergers with other companies, and the like. Notice which areas are receiving the greatest attention from top management. One tip-off is to see what kind of outside consultants are being brought in. Independent consultants are usually invited in because a company believes it needs advice in an area with which it has insufficient experience.

LOOK FOR INNOVATIVE OPPORTUNITIES

You may understand your job better than anyone—even if you've only been there a few months. Look for ways to make it more efficient. How can present procedures be automated? How can new technology make your tasks easier? Discuss your ideas with your supervisor, the training director, or the head of the information systems department. Or discuss them with someone else who can see that you get the recognition you deserve. (Co-workers may or may not be receptive and may or may not try to take credit themselves.)

A good approach is to present your ideas in terms of saving money rather than "improving information." Managers are generally more impressed with ideas that can save dollars than with ideas that seem like potential breakthroughs in the quality of decisions.

In general, it's best to concentrate on the business and organizational problems that need solving. Then look for a technological way of solving them. That is, avoid becoming too enthusiastic about a particular technology and then trying to make it fit the work situation.

▼ CONCEPT CHECK

▶ Outline the strategies you can use to stay ahead and be successful in your career.

▶ Discuss the advantages and disadvantages of specialization.

▶ Describe how you would stay alert for organizational changes.

Being a winner does not necessarily mean having a career in information systems. There are, however, several jobs within information technology that you might like to consider. We have discussed many of these careers in the preceding chapters. (See Figure 11-12.)

To learn more about these careers, visit our Web site at www.computing2008.com and enter the keyword careers.

Career	Responsibilities
Computer support specialist	Provides technical support to customers and other users
Computer technician	Repairs and installs computer components and systems
Computer trainer	Instructs users on the latest software or hardware
Cryptographer	Designs, tests, and researches encryption procedures
Data entry worker	Inputs customer information, lists, and other types of data
Database administrator	Uses database management software to determine the most efficient ways to organize and access data
Desktop publisher	Creates and formats publication-ready material
Information systems manager	Oversees the work of programmers, computer specialists, systems analysts, and other computer professionals
Network administrator	Creates and maintains networks
Programmer	Creates, tests, and troubleshoots computer programs
Software engineer	Analyzes users' needs and creates application software
Systems analyst	Plans and designs information systems
Technical writer	Prepares instruction manuals, technical reports, and other scientific or technical documents
Webmaster	Develops and maintains Web sites and Web resources

Figure 11-12 Careers in information systems

Maintaining Computer Competency and Becoming Proactive

This is not the end; it is the beginning. Being a skilled computer end user and having computer competency are not a matter of thinking, "Someday I'll have to learn all about that." They are a matter of living in the present and keeping an eye on the future. Computer competency also demands the discipline to keep up with emerging technology. Yet it is important not to focus on the "what ifs" of technology. Computer competency demands concentration on your goals and dedication to learning how the computer can aid you in obtaining these goals. Being an end user, in short, is not about trying to avoid failure. Rather, it is about always moving toward success—about taking control of the exciting new tools available to you.

YOUR FUTURE AND INFORMATION TECHNOLOGY

CHANGING TIMES

Individuals, businesses, and organizations must adapt to changing technology or be left behind.

Banking Industry

The banking industry uses automated teller machines (ATMs) to provide 24-hour service without incurring additional employee costs. Internet banks conduct all business over the Web.

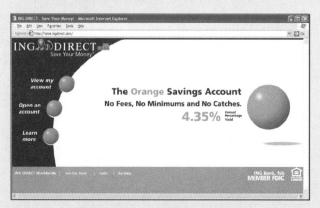

Many changes do away with jobs. Technology, however, creates opportunities. New technology requires people who are truly capable of working with it. To become and stay a winner, you must form your own individual strategy for dealing with changes.

TECHNOLOGY AND ORGANIZATIONS

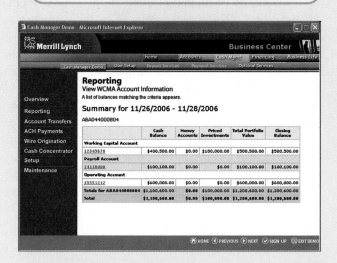

Technology can introduce new ways for businesses to compete with each other. They can compete by *creating new products, establishing new enterprises,* and *developing new customer and supplier relationships.*

New Products

Technology creates products that operate faster, are priced more cheaply, are often better quality, or are wholly new. New products can be individually tailored to a particular customer's needs.

New Enterprises

Technology can build entirely new businesses. Two examples:

- Internet service providers—just a few years ago, only a few Internet service providers were available. Now, thousands of national and local providers are available.
- Web site development companies—thousands of small companies specializing in developing Web sites have sprung up in just the past three years.

New Customer and Supplier Relationships

Businesses that make their information systems easily available may make their customers less likely to take their business elsewhere (e.g., overnight delivery services closely track packages and bills).

To stay competent, you need to recognize the impact of technological change on organizations and people. You need to know how to use change to your advantage and how to become a winner. Although you do not need to be a specialist in information technology, you should be aware of career opportunities in the area.

TECHNOLOGY AND PEOPLE

People have different coping styles when it comes to technology. Four common reactions to new technology are cynicism, naivete, frustration, and proactivity.

Cynicism
The **cynics** feel that new technology is overrated and too troublesome to learn. Some cynics openly express their doubts. Others pretend to be interested.

Naivete
Naive people may be unfamiliar or quite familiar with computers. People who are unfamiliar tend to think of computers as magic boxes. Even those familiar with technology often underestimate the time and difficulty of using technology to generate information.

Frustration
Frustrated users are impatient and irritated about taking time to learn new technology. Often these people have too much to do, find manuals difficult to understand, and/or feel stupid.

Proactivity
A **proactive** person looks at technology in a positive and realistic way. He or she is not cynical, naive, or frustrated regarding new technology. Proactive people are positive and look at new technology as providing new tools that can positively impact their lives.

HOW YOU CAN BE A WINNER

There are six ongoing activities that can help you be successful.

Stay Current
Read trade journals and the general business press, join professional associations, and participate in interest groups on the Internet.

Maintain Your Computer Competency
Stay current by reading computer-related articles in the general press and trade journals.

Develop Professional Contacts
Stay active in your profession and meet people in your field. This provides information about other people, firms, job opportunities, and social contacts.

Develop Specialties
Develop specific as well as general skills. Expect to take classes periodically to stay current with your field and technology.

Be Alert for Organizational Change
Use formal and informal lines of communication. Be alert for new trends within the organization.

Look for Innovative Opportunities
Look for ways to increase efficiency. Present ideas in terms of saving money rather than "improving information."

Your Future and Information Technology

Computer Support Specialist
Computer support specialists provide technical support to customers and other users.

Computer Technician
Computer technicians repair and install computer components and systems.

Computer Trainer
Computer trainers instruct users on the latest software or hardware.

Cryptographer
Cryptographers design, test, and research encryption procedures.

Data Entry Worker
Data entry workers input customer information, lists, and other types of data.

Database Administrator
Database administrators use database management software to determine the most efficient ways to organize and access data.

Desktop Publisher
Desktop publishers create and format publication-ready material.

Information Systems Manager
Information systems managers oversee the work of programmers, computer specialists, systems analysts, and other computer professionals.

Network Administrator
Network administrators create and maintain networks.

Programmer
Programmers create, test, and troubleshoot computer programs.

Software Engineer
Software engineers analyze users' needs and create application software.

Systems Analyst
Systems analysts plan and design information systems.

Technical Writer
Technical writers prepare instruction manuals, technical reports, and other scientific or technical documents.

Webmaster
Webmasters develop and maintain Web sites and Web resources.

KEY TERMS

computer support specialist   (322)
computer technician   (322)
computer trainer   (322)
cryptographer   (322)
cynic   (314)
data entry worker   (322)
database administrator (DBA)   (322)
desktop publisher   (322)
frustrated   (315)

information systems manager   (322)
naive   (315)
network administrator   (322)
proactive   (315)
programmer   (322)
software engineer   (322)
systems analyst   (322)
technical writer   (322)
Webmaster   (322)

FEATURES
Animations

Careers in IT

DVD Direct

Expansions

Making IT Work for You

On the Web Explorations

TechTV

Tips

CHAPTER REVIEW
Applying Technology

Crossword Puzzle

Expanding Your Knowledge

Key Terms

Matching

Multiple Choice

Open-Ended

Writing About Technology

To test your knowledge of these key terms with animated flash cards; visit our Web site at www.computing2008.com and enter the keyword terms15.

CROSSWORD PUZZLE

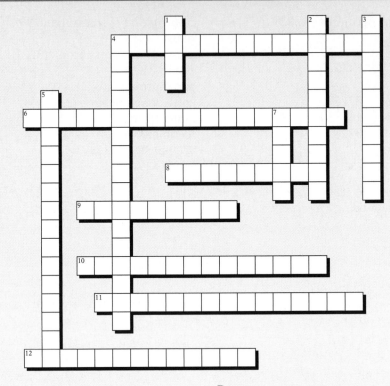

Across

4 Inputs customer information and other data.

6 Repairs and installs computer components and systems.

8 Acting in anticipation of future problems, needs, or changes.

9 Develops and maintains Web sites.

10 Plans and designs information systems.

11 Prepares instruction manuals and technical reports.

12 Designs, tests, and researches encryption procedures.

Down

1 Person that is unfamiliar with computers.

2 Creates, tests, and troubleshoots computer programs.

3 Person that feels learning about computers is an imposition.

4 Creates and formats publication-ready material.

5 Instructs users on the latest software and hardware.

7 Person that feels the idea of using a microcomputer is overrated.

For an interactive version of this crossword, visit our Web site at www.computing2008.com and enter the keyword **crossword15**.

MULTIPLE CHOICE

Circle the letter or fill in the correct answer.

1. Changes in technology require people who
   a. think every piece of equipment is so simple they can just turn it on and use it
   b. know just the basics about the technology
   c. think each new machine is a potential disaster
   d. are not afraid to learn and manage new technology

2. One of the advantages of the changes in information technology is
   a. people are put out of work
   b. new businesses are created
   c. data can be lost and/or stolen
   d. new skills are constantly in demand

3. The _____ user believes that learning and using computers take time away from his or her real job.
   a. cynical
   b. proactive
   c. frustrated
   d. naive

4. Generally, a proactive person
   a. feels that the idea of using a microcomputer is overrated
   b. is unfamiliar with computers
   c. hates to take time to learn about microcomputers
   d. looks at technology in a positive, realistic way

5. To maintain your computer competence, you should try to stay ahead of technology by
   a. learning a new trade
   b. reviewing the systems life cycle
   c. reading books, journals, newspapers, and magazines
   d. quiting your current job and going back to school

6. Successful people make it a point to
   a. develop nonspecific skills
   b. avoid contact with others
   c. get their education and relax
   d. maintain contact with others in their field

7. These individuals design, test, and research encryption procedures.
   a. database administrator
   b. technical writer
   c. cryptographer
   d. computer trainer

8. _____ oversee the work of programmers, computer specialists, and other computer professionals.
   a. Systems analysts
   b. Database administrators
   c. Information systems managers
   d. Network managers

9. These individuals are responsible for creating, testing, and troubleshooting computer programs.
   a. systems analysts
   b. database administrators
   c. network managers
   d. programmers

10. _____ develop and maintain Web sites and Web resources.
    a. Systems analysts
    b. Webmasters
    c. Network managers
    d. Programmers

For an interactive version of these multiple-choice questions, visit our Web site at www.computing2008.com and enter the keyword **multiple15**.

MATCHING

www.computing2008.com

Match each numbered item with the most closely related lettered item. Write your answers in the spaces provided.

a. database administrator
b. computer technician
c. computer trainer
d. cynic
e. software engineer
f. technical writer
g. network administrator
h. programmer
i. systems analyst
j. Webmaster

1. Computer user who feels the idea of using microcomputers is overrated. _____
2. A computer specialist employed to evaluate, create, and maintain Web sites. _____
3. Computer professional who creates, tests, and troubleshoots computer programs. _____
4. Computer specialist who uses database management software to determine the most efficient ways to organize and access data. _____
5. Computer professional who analyzes users' needs and creates application software. _____
6. Computer professional who plans and designs information systems. _____
7. Computer professional who repairs and installs computer components and systems. _____
8. Computer professional who creates and maintains networks. _____
9. Computer professional who instructs users on the latest software or hardware. _____
10. Computer professional who prepares instruction manuals, technical reports, and other scientific or technical documents. _____

For an interactive version of this matching exercise, visit our Web site at www.computing2008.com and enter the keyword **matching15**.

OPEN-ENDED

On a separate sheet of paper, respond to each question or statement.

1. Why is strategy important to individual success in the information age? What is your strategy?
2. Describe how technology changes the nature of competition.
3. How can your computer competencies and knowledge help you get ahead in today's market?
4. What does proactive mean? What is a proactive computer user? What advantages does this type of user have over the other types?
5. Discuss several different careers in information technology. Which are of interest to you?

APPLYING TECHNOLOGY

The following questions are designed to demonstrate ways that you can effectively use technology today. The first question relates directly to this chapter's Making IT Work for You feature.

Jobs Online
1

Did you know that you can use the Internet to find a job? You can browse through job listings, post resumes for prospective employers, and even use special agents to continually search for that job that's just right for you. To learn more about online job searches, review Making IT Work for You: Locating Job Opportunities Online on pages 318 and 319. Then visit our Web site at www.computing2008.com and enter the keyword jobs. Once at that site, play the video and answer the following: (a) What locations and categories were selected for the job search? (b) Describe the process for posting a resume. (c) What search criteria were used to set up the job search agent?

Maintain Computer Competence
2

There are several sources of information to help keep you up to date on current computing trends. Visit our Web site at www.computing2008.com and enter the keyword competence to link to a few computing sites. Explore the site and then answer the following: (a) List the sites you visited and describe the focus of each. (b) Which of these sites was most useful? Why? (c) Which of these sites was least useful? Why? (d) What are other ways you can stay in step with current computing issues?

EXPANDING YOUR KNOWLEDGE

The following questions are designed to add depth and detail to your understanding of specific topics presented within this chapter. The questions direct you to sources other than the textbook to obtain this knowledge.

1 Your Career

Have you thought about what your career might be? Perhaps it is in marketing, education, or information technology. If you have a career in mind, conduct a Web search to learn more about your chosen career. If you don't have a career in mind, select one of the information systems careers presented in this chapter and conduct a Web search to learn more about that career. After reviewing at least five sites, answer the following: (a) Describe your career of choice. (b) Why did you choose that career? (c) How is information technology used in this career? (d) How will changing technology impact your chosen career?

2 Resume Advice

There are several excellent resources available online to help you write a winning resume. Conduct a Web search using the keywords "resume help" to learn more. Review at least five sites and then compose a sample resume for yourself, applying the information from the sites.

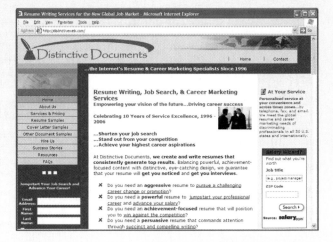

WRITING ABOUT TECHNOLOGY

The ability to think critically and to write effectively is essential to nearly every profession. The following questions are designed to help you develop these skills by posing thought-provoking questions about computer privacy, security, and/or ethics.

Writing About Privacy and Ethics   1

Regardless of your career path, critical thinking, analysis, and writing are essential skills. In each of the preceding chapters, the Writing About Technology feature presented questions about privacy and ethics. These questions are designed to help you develop critical thinking, analysis, and writing skills. Select the five questions you feel are most important to privacy or ethics from the Writing About Technology questions in the preceding chapters. Write a two-page paper that addresses the questions you chose and describe why they are of interest to you.

Writing About Security   2

The importance of computer security is often overshadowed by the functions and features of new technology. The Writing About Technology feature presented many questions about security in the

preceding chapters. These questions are designed to increase your awareness of important computer security topics and further develop your writing skills. Select the five questions you feel are most important to security from the Writing About Technology questions in the preceding chapters. Write a two-page paper that addresses the questions you chose and describe why they are of interest to you.

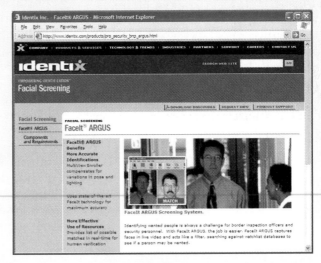

THE EVOLUTION OF THE COMPUTER AGE

Many of you probably can't remember a world without computers, but for some of us, computers were virtually unknown when we were born and have rapidly come of age during our lifetime.

Although there are many predecessors to what we think of as the modern computer—reaching as far back as the 18th century, when Joseph Marie Jacquard created a loom programmed to weave cloth and Charles Babbage created the first fully modern computer design (which he could never get to work)—the computer age did not really begin until the first computer was made available to the public in 1951.

The modern age of computers thus spans slightly more than 50 years (so far), which is typically broken down into five generations. Each generation has been marked by a significant advance in technology.

- **First Generation (1951–57):** During the first generation, computers were built with vacuum tubes—electronic tubes that were made of glass and were about the size of light bulbs.

- **Second Generation (1958–63):** This generation began with the first computers built with transistors—small devices that transfer electronic signals across a resistor. Because transistors are much smaller, use less power, and create less heat than vacuum tubes, the new computers were faster, smaller, and more reliable than the first-generation machines.

- **Third Generation (1964–69):** In 1964, computer manufacturers began replacing transistors with integrated circuits. An integrated circuit (IC) is a complete electronic circuit on a small chip made of silicon (one of the most abundant elements in the earth's crust). These computers were more reliable and compact than computers made with transistors, and they cost less to manufacture.

- **Fourth Generation (1970–90):** Many key advances were made during this generation, the most significant being the microprocessor—a specialized chip developed for computer memory and logic. Use of a single chip to create a smaller "personal" computer (as well as digital watches, pocket calculators, copy machines, and so on) revolutionized the computer industry.

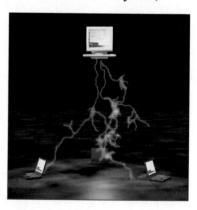

- **Fifth Generation (1991–2008 and beyond):** Our current generation has been referred to as the "Connected Generation" because of the industry's massive effort to increase the connectivity of computers. The rapidly expanding Internet, World Wide Web, and intranets have created an information superhighway that has enabled both computer professionals and home computer users to communicate with others across the globe.

This appendix provides you with a timeline that describes in more detail some of the most significant events in each generation of the computer age.

First Generation
The Vacuum Tube Age

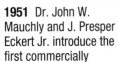

1951 Dr. John W. Mauchly and J. Presper Eckert Jr. introduce the first commercially available electronic digital computer—the UNIVAC—built with vacuum tubes. This computer was based on their earlier ENIAC (Electronic Numerical Integrator and Computer) design completed in 1946.

1951–53 IBM adds computers to its business equipment products and sells over 1,000 IBM 650 systems.

1951 1952 1953 1954 1955 1956 1957

1957 Introduction of first high-level programming language—FORTRAN (FORmula TRANslator).

1952 Development team led by Dr. Grace Hopper, former U.S. Navy programmer, introduces the A6 Compiler—the first example of software that converts high-level language symbols into instructions that a computer can execute.

The Evolution of the Computer Age

Second Generation
The Transistor Age

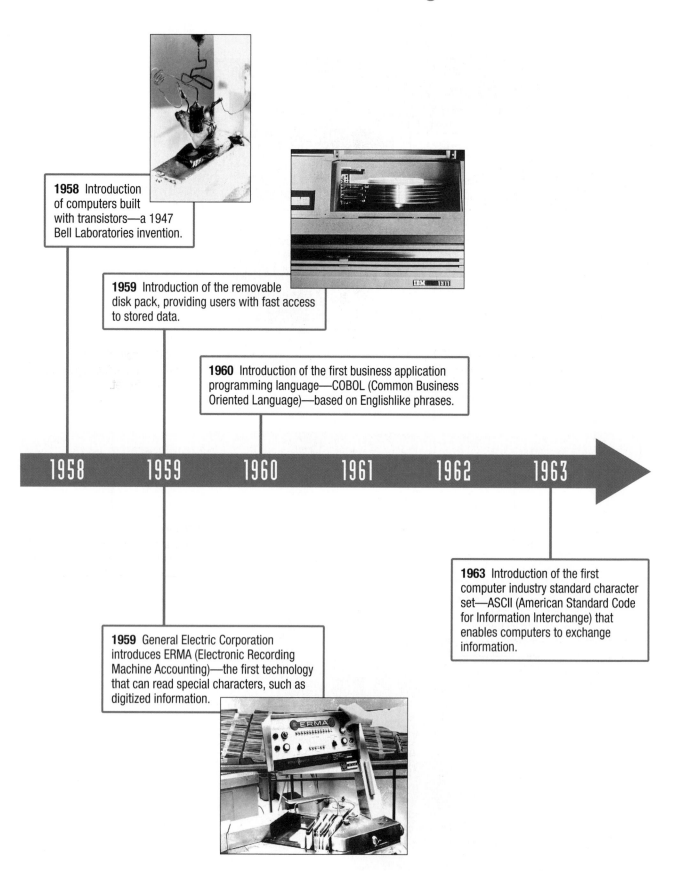

1958 Introduction of computers built with transistors—a 1947 Bell Laboratories invention.

1959 Introduction of the removable disk pack, providing users with fast access to stored data.

1960 Introduction of the first business application programming language—COBOL (Common Business Oriented Language)—based on Englishlike phrases.

1958 1959 1960 1961 1962 1963

1963 Introduction of the first computer industry standard character set—ASCII (American Standard Code for Information Interchange) that enables computers to exchange information.

1959 General Electric Corporation introduces ERMA (Electronic Recording Machine Accounting)—the first technology that can read special characters, such as digitized information.

Third Generation
The Integrated Circuit Age

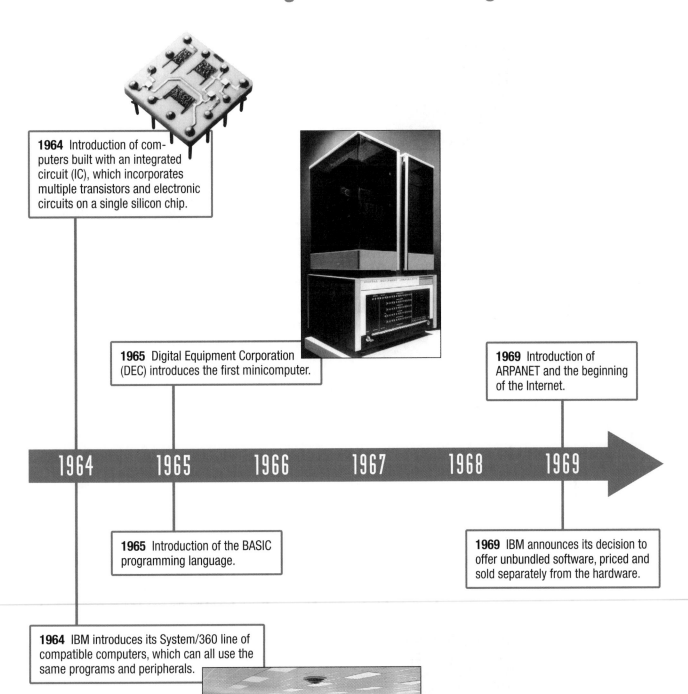

1964 Introduction of computers built with an integrated circuit (IC), which incorporates multiple transistors and electronic circuits on a single silicon chip.

1965 Digital Equipment Corporation (DEC) introduces the first minicomputer.

1969 Introduction of ARPANET and the beginning of the Internet.

1964   1965   1966   1967   1968   1969

1965 Introduction of the BASIC programming language.

1969 IBM announces its decision to offer unbundled software, priced and sold separately from the hardware.

1964 IBM introduces its System/360 line of compatible computers, which can all use the same programs and peripherals.

Fifth Generation
The Age of Connectivity

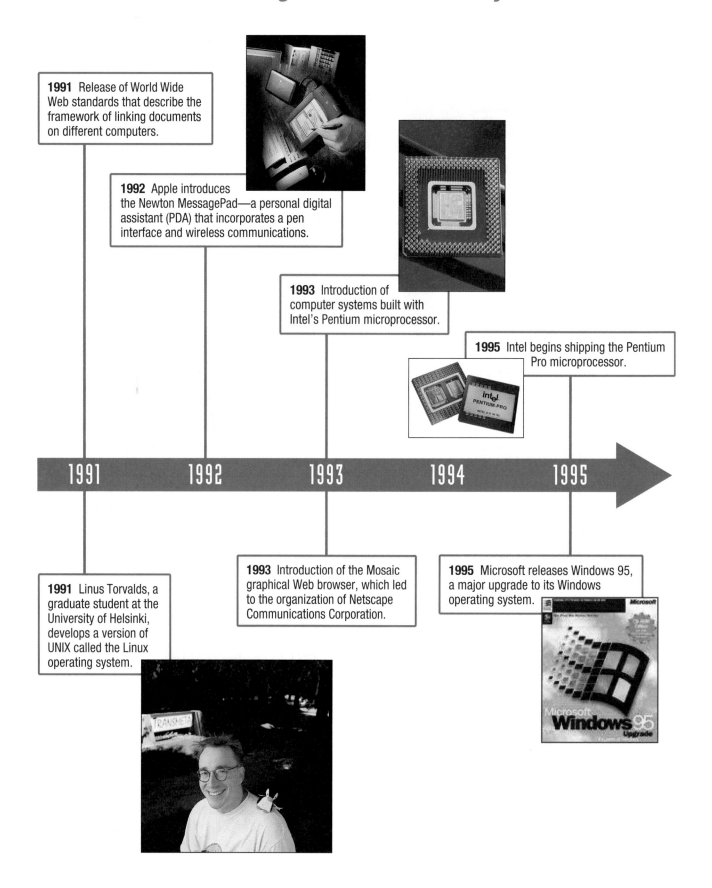

1991 Release of World Wide Web standards that describe the framework of linking documents on different computers.

1992 Apple introduces the Newton MessagePad—a personal digital assistant (PDA) that incorporates a pen interface and wireless communications.

1993 Introduction of computer systems built with Intel's Pentium microprocessor.

1995 Intel begins shipping the Pentium Pro microprocessor.

1991 1992 1993 1994 1995

1991 Linus Torvalds, a graduate student at the University of Helsinki, develops a version of UNIX called the Linux operating system.

1993 Introduction of the Mosaic graphical Web browser, which led to the organization of Netscape Communications Corporation.

1995 Microsoft releases Windows 95, a major upgrade to its Windows operating system.

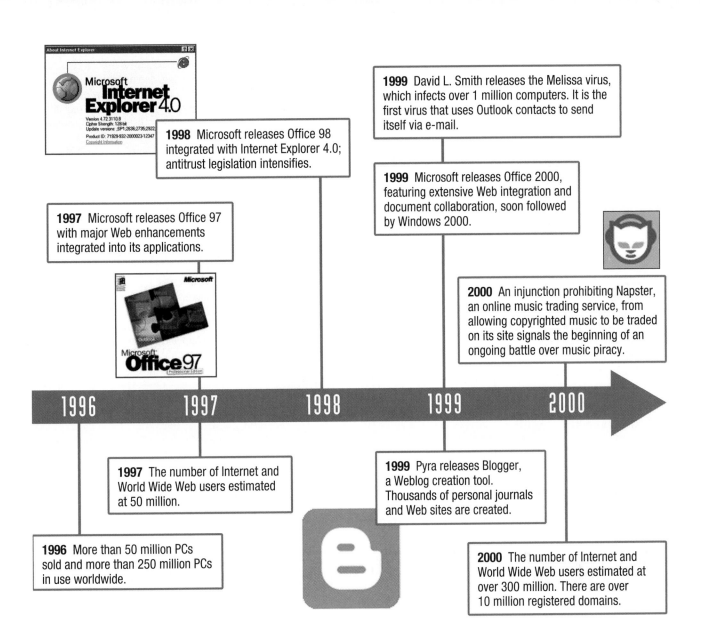

1999 David L. Smith releases the Melissa virus, which infects over 1 million computers. It is the first virus that uses Outlook contacts to send itself via e-mail.

1998 Microsoft releases Office 98 integrated with Internet Explorer 4.0; antitrust legislation intensifies.

1999 Microsoft releases Office 2000, featuring extensive Web integration and document collaboration, soon followed by Windows 2000.

1997 Microsoft releases Office 97 with major Web enhancements integrated into its applications.

2000 An injunction prohibiting Napster, an online music trading service, from allowing copyrighted music to be traded on its site signals the beginning of an ongoing battle over music piracy.

1996 1997 1998 1999 2000

1997 The number of Internet and World Wide Web users estimated at 50 million.

1999 Pyra releases Blogger, a Weblog creation tool. Thousands of personal journals and Web sites are created.

1996 More than 50 million PCs sold and more than 250 million PCs in use worldwide.

2000 The number of Internet and World Wide Web users estimated at over 300 million. There are over 10 million registered domains.

The Evolution of the Computer Age

2002 Amazon.com, the largest online retailer, announces its first profitable quarter nearly 10 years after the company was founded.

2004 CAN-SPAM Act enacted, requiring unsolicited e-mail to be labeled and making it illegal to use deceptive headers and anonymous return addresses. The law also requires unsolicited e-mail to allow recipients to opt out and authorizes the FTC to create a "do-not-e-mail" registry.

2002 Microsoft initiates its .NET platform that allows users to create a profile for use across platforms and allows developers to create Web services quickly.

2005 Wireless connections (WiFi) to the Internet, called hot spots, allow the public to access the Internet at airports, hotels, and many cafes. Many expect WiFi connections to be available almost everywhere in the next few years—from doctors' offices to airplanes. By 2007 it is expected that nearly 20 million people will use WiFi to access the Web.

2003 Apple opens the iTunes music store with a catalog of over 700,000 songs. Users can buy and then download songs for 99¢.

2001 Microsoft releases Windows XP and Office XP with enhanced user interfaces, better integration and collaboration tools, and increased stability.

2001 | **2002** | **2003** | **2004** | **2005**

2002 Internet2, with over 200 university affiliates, regularly broadcasts live theater and HDTV transmissions.

2004 Google releases invitations to test Gmail, its e-mail service that includes a search function and 1 GB of storage.

2001 Apple releases Mac OS X with a UNIX backbone and new interface.

Gmail™
by Google   BETA

Mac OS
X

THE BUYER'S GUIDE
How to Buy Your Own Microcomputer System

FOUR STEPS IN BUYING A MICROCOMPUTER SYSTEM

The following is not intended to make buying a microcomputer an exhausting experience. Rather, it is to help you clarify your thinking about what you need and can afford.

The four steps in buying a microcomputer system are presented on the following pages. We divide each step into two parts based on the assumptions that both your needs and the money you have to spend on a microcomputer may change.

STEP 1
What Needs Do I Want a Computer to Serve?

The trick is to distinguish between your needs and your wants. Sure, you *want* a cutting-edge system powerful enough to run every conceivable program you'll ever need. And you want a system fast enough to process them all at the speed of light. But do you *need* this? Your main concern is to address the following two questions:

- What do I need a computer system to do for me today?
- What will I need it to do for me in another year or two?

The questionnaire at the end of this guide will help you determine the answers to both questions.

Suggestions

Consider the type of computer most available on campus. Some schools favor Apple computers; others favor Windows-based computers. If you own a system that's incompatible with most computers on campus, you may be stuck if your computer breaks down.

Look ahead and determine whether your major requires a computer. Business and engineering students may find one a necessity; physical education and drama majors may not. Your major also may determine the kind of computer that's best. A journalism major may want a Windows-based notebook. An architecture major may want a powerful desktop Macintosh with a laser printer that can produce elaborate drawings. Ask your academic advisor for some recommendations.

Example

Suppose you are a college student beginning your sophomore year, with no major declared. Looking at the courses you will likely take this year, you decide you will probably need a computer mainly for word processing. That is, you need a system that will help you write short (10- to 20-page) papers for a variety of courses.

By this time next year, however, you may be an accounting major. Having talked to some juniors and seniors, you find that courses in this major, such as financial accounting, will require you to use elaborate spreadsheets. Or maybe you will be a fine arts or architecture major. Then you may be required to submit projects for which drawing and painting desktop publishing software would be helpful.

STEP 2
How Much Money Do I Have to Spend on a Computer System?

When you buy your first computer, you are not necessarily buying your last. Thus, you can think about spending just the bare-bones amount for a system that meets your needs while in college. Then you might plan to get another system later on.

You know the amount of money you have to spend. Your main concern is to answer the following two questions:

- How much am I prepared to spend on a computer system today?
- How much am I prepared to spend in another year or two?

The questionnaire at the end of this guide asks you this.

Suggestions

You can probably buy a good used computer of some sort for under $300 and a printer for under $50. On the other hand, you might spend $1,000 to $2,500 on a new state-of-the-art system. When upgraded, this computer could meet your needs for the next five years.

There is nothing wrong with getting a used system if you have a way of checking it out. For a reasonable fee, a computer-repair shop can examine it prior to your purchase. Look at newspaper ads and notices on campus bulletin boards for good buys on used equipment. Also try the Internet. If you stay with recognized brands, such as Apple, IBM, Compaq, or Dell, you probably won't have any difficulties.

If you're buying new equipment, be sure to look for student discounts. Most college bookstores, for instance, offer special prices to students. Also check the Web. There are numerous sites specializing in discounted computer systems.

Example

Perhaps you have access to a microcomputer at the campus student computing center, the library, or the dormitory. Or you can borrow a friend's. However, this computer isn't always available when it's convenient for you. Moreover, you're not only going to college, but you're also working, so both time and money are tight. Having your own computer would enable you to write papers when it's convenient for you. Spending more than $350 might cause real hardship, so a new microcomputer system may be out of the question. You'll need to shop the newspaper classified ads or the campus bulletin boards to find a used but workable computer system.

Or maybe you can afford to spend more now—say, between $1,000 and $2,000—but probably only $500 next year. By this time next year, however, you'll know your major and how your computer needs have changed.

STEP 3

What Kind of Software Will Best Serve My Needs?

Most computer experts urge that you determine what software you need before you buy the hardware. The reasoning here is that some hardware simply won't run the software that is important to you. This is certainly true once you get into *sophisticated* software. Examples include specialized programs available for certain professions (such as certain agricultural or retail-management programs). However, if all you are interested in today are the basic software tools—word processing, spreadsheet, and communications programs—these are available for nearly all microcomputers. The main caution is that some more recent versions of application software won't run on older hardware. Still, if someone offers you a free computer, don't say no because you feel you have to decide what software you need first. You will no doubt find it sufficient for many general purposes, especially during your early years in college.

That said, you are better served if you follow step 3 after step 2—namely, finding the answers to the following two questions:

- What kind of software will best serve my needs today?

- What kind will best serve my needs in another year or two?

The questionnaire at the end of this guide will help you determine your answers.

Suggestions

No doubt some kinds of application software are more available on your campus—and in certain departments on your campus—than others. Are freshman and sophomore students mainly writing their term papers in Word, WordPerfect, or Word Pro? Which spreadsheet is most often used by business students: Excel, Lotus 1-2-3, or Quattro Pro? Which desktop publishing program is most favored by graphic arts majors: PageMaker, Quark Express, or MS Publisher? Do engineering and architecture majors use their own machines for CAD/CAM applications? Start by asking other students and your academic advisor.

If you're looking to buy state-of-the-art software, you'll find plenty of advice in various computer magazines. Several of them rate the quality of newly issued programs. Such periodicals include *PC World* and *MacWorld*.

Example

Suppose you determine that all you need is software to help you write short papers. In that case, nearly any kind of word processing program would do. But will this software be sufficient a year or two from now? Looking ahead, you guess that you'll major in theater arts and minor in screenwriting, which you may pursue as a career. At that point, a simple word processing program might not do. You learn from juniors and seniors in that department that screenplays are written using special screenwriting programs. This is software that's not available for some computers. Or, as an advertising and marketing major, you're expected to turn word-processed promotional pieces into brochures. For this, you need desktop publishing software. Or, as a physics major, you discover you will need to write reports on a word processor that can handle equations. In short, you need to look at your software needs not just for today but also for the near future. You especially want to consider what programs will be useful to you in building your career.

STEP 4

What Kind of Hardware Will Best Serve My Needs?

A bare-bones hardware system might include a three-year-old desktop or notebook computer with a CD-ROM disc drive and a hard-disk drive. It also should include a monitor and a printer. On the one hand, as a student—unless you're involved in some very specialized activities—it's doubtful you'll really need such things as voice-input devices, touch screens, scanners, and the like. On the other hand, you will probably need speakers and a DVD-ROM drive. The choices of equipment are vast.

As with the other steps, the main task is to find the answers to the following two questions:

- What kind of hardware will best serve my needs today?
- What kind will best serve my needs in another year or two?

There are several questions on the questionnaire at the end of this guide to help you determine answers to these concerns.

Suggestions

Clearly, you should let the software be your guide in determining your choice of hardware. Perhaps you've found that the most popular software in your department runs on an Apple computer rather than a Windows-based computer. If so, that would seem to determine your general brand of hardware.

Whether you buy IBM or Macintosh, a desktop or a notebook, we suggest you get a hard-disk drive with at least 10 gigabytes of storage, a DVD drive, at least 512 megabytes of memory, and an ink-jet printer.

As with software, several computer magazines not only describe new hardware but also issue ratings. See *PC World* and *MacWorld*, for example.

Example

Right now, let's say, you're mainly interested in using a computer to write papers, so almost anything would do. But you need to look ahead.

Suppose you find that Word seems to be the software of choice around your campus. You find that Word 2000 will run well on a Pentium machine with 8 megabytes of memory and a 1-gigabyte hard disk. Although this equipment is now outdated, you find from looking at classified ads that there are many such used machines around. Plus, they cost very little—well under $500 for a complete system.

Your choice then becomes: Should I buy an inexpensive system now that can't be upgraded, then sell it later and buy a better one? Or should I buy at least some of the components of a good system now and upgrade it over the next year or so?

As an advertising major, you see the value of learning desktop publishing. This will be a useful if not essential skill once you embark on a career. In exploring the software, you learn that Word includes some desktop publishing capabilities. However, the hardware you previously considered simply isn't sufficient. Moreover, you learn from reading about software and talking to people in your major that there are better desktop publishing programs. Specialized desktop publishing programs like Ventura Publisher are considered more versatile than Word. Probably the best software arrangement, in fact, is to have Word as a word processing program and Ventura Publisher for a desktop publishing program.

To be sure, the campus has computers that will run this software available to students. If you can afford it, however, you're better off having your own. Now, however, we're talking about a major expense. A computer running a Pentium 4 microprocessor, with 1 gigabyte of memory, a rewriteable DVD disc drive, and a 200-gigabyte hard disk, plus a modem, color monitor, and laser printer, could cost in excess of $1,500.

DEVELOPING A PHILOSOPHY ABOUT COMPUTER PURCHASING

It's important not to develop a case of "computer envy." Even if you buy the latest, most expensive microcomputer system, in a matter of months something better will come along. Computer technology is still in a very dynamic state, with more powerful, versatile, and compact systems constantly hitting the marketplace. So what if your friends have the hottest new piece of software or hardware? The main question is: Do you need it to solve the tasks required of you or to keep up in your field? Or can you get along with something simpler but equally serviceable?

VISUAL SUMMARY
The Buyer's Guide:
How to Buy Your Own Microcomputer System

NEEDS

What do I need a computer system to do for me today? In another year or two?

I WISH TO USE THE COMPUTER FOR:

	Today	1–2 years
Word processing—writing papers, letters, memos, or reports	❏	❏
Business or financial applications—balance sheets, sales projections, expense budgets, or accounting problems	❏	❏
Record keeping and sorting—research bibliographies, scientific data, or address files	❏	❏
Graphic presentations of business, scientific, or social science data	❏	❏
Online information retrieval to campus networks, service providers, or the Internet	❏	❏
Publications, design, or drawing for printed newsletters, architectural drawing, or graphic arts	❏	❏
Multimedia for video games, viewing, creating, presenting, or research	❏	❏
Other (specify): _____	❏	❏

BUDGET

How much am I prepared to spend on a system today? In another year or two?

I CAN SPEND:

	Today	1–2 years
Under $500	❏	❏
Up to $1,000	❏	❏
Up to $1,500	❏	❏
Up to $2,000	❏	❏
Up to $2,500	❏	❏
Over $3,000 (specify): _____	❏	❏

Buying a Microcomputer System	
Step	**Questions**
1	*My needs:* What do I need a computer system to do for me today? In another year or two?
2	*My budget:* How much am I prepared to spend on a system today? In another year or two?
3	*My software:* What kind of software will best serve my needs today? In another year or two?
4	*My hardware:* What kind of hardware will best serve my needs today? In another year or two?

To help clarify your thinking about buying a microcomputer system, complete the questionnaire by checking the appropriate boxes.

SOFTWARE

What kinds of software will best serve my needs today? In another year or two?

The application software I need includes:

	Today	1–2 years
Word processing—Word, WordPerfect, or other (specify): _____	❏	❏
Spreadsheet—Excel, Lotus 1-2-3, or other (specify): _____	❏	❏
Database—Access, Paradox, or other (specify): _____	❏	❏
Presentation graphics—PowerPoint, Freelance, CorelPresentations, or other (specify): _____	❏	❏
Browsers—Netscape Navigator, Microsoft Internet Explorer, or other (specify): _____	❏	❏
Other—integrated packages, software suites, graphics, multimedia, Web authoring, CAD/CAM, other (specify): _____	❏	❏

The system software I need:

	Today	1–2 years
Windows 98	❏	❏
Windows 2000	❏	❏
Windows XP	❏	❏
Mac OS	❏	❏
UNIX	❏	❏
Other (specify): _____	❏	❏

HARDWARE

What kinds of hardware will best serve my needs today? In another year or two?

The hardware I need includes:

	Today	1–2 years
Microprocessor—Pentium 4, Pentium III, Apple G4, other (specify): _____	❏	❏
Memory—(specify amount): _____	❏	❏
Monitor—size (specify): _____	❏	❏
Floppy disk drives—3½" and/or Zip (specify): _____	❏	❏
Optical disc drive—CD-ROM, DVD-ROM (specify type, speed, and capacity): _____	❏	❏
Hard-disk drive—(specify capacity): _____	❏	❏
Portable computer—laptop, notebook, subnotebook, personal digital assistant (specify): _____	❏	❏
Printer—ink-jet, laser, color (specify): _____	❏	❏
Other—modem, network card, speakers, fax, surge protector (specify): _____	❏	❏

THE UPGRADER'S GUIDE
How to Upgrade Your Microcomputer System

If you own a microcomputer, chances are that your machine is not the latest and greatest. Microcomputers are always getting better—more powerful and faster. While that is a good thing, it can be frustrating trying to keep up.

What can you do? If you have lots of money, you can simply buy a new one. Another alternative is to upgrade or add new components to increase the power and speed of your current microcomputer. You probably can increase your system's performance at a fraction of the cost of a new one.

THREE STEPS IN UPGRADING A MICROCOMPUTER SYSTEM

The following is not intended to detail specific hardware upgrades. Rather, it is intended to help you clarify your thinking about what you need and can afford.

The three steps in upgrading a microcomputer system are presented on the following pages. Each step begins by asking a key question and then provides some suggestions or factors to consider when responding to the question.

STEP 1

Is It Time to Upgrade?

Almost any upgrade you make will provide some benefit; the trick is determining if it is worth the monetary investment. It is rarely practical to rebuild an older computer system into a newer model piece by piece. The cost of a complete upgrade typically far exceeds the purchase price of a new system. But if your system is just a piece or two away from meeting your needs, an upgrade may be in order.

Clearly defining what you hope to gain with an upgrade of some of your system's hardware will enable you to make the most relevant and cost-effective selections. Before deciding what to buy, decide what goal you hope to accomplish. Do you want to speed up your computer's performance? Do you need more space to save your files? Do you want to add a new component such as a DVD-RW drive?

Suggestions

A good place to start is to look at the documentation on the packaging of any software you use or plan to use. Software manufacturers clearly label the minimum requirements to use their products. These requirements are usually broken down into categories that relate to specific pieces of hardware. For instance, how much RAM (random access memory) does a new program require? How much hard disk space is needed? Keep in mind these ratings are typically the bare minimum. If your system comes very close to the baseline in any particular category, you should still consider an upgrade.

Another thing to investigate is whether there is a software solution that will better serve your needs. For instance, if you are looking to enhance performance or make more room on your hard disk, there are diagnostic and disk optimization utility programs that may solve your problem. In Chapter 5, we discuss a variety of utility programs, such as Norton SystemWorks, that monitor, evaluate, and enhance system performance and storage capacity.

Typical objectives of an upgrade are to improve system performance, increase storage capacity, or add new technology.

STEP 2

What Should I Upgrade?

Once you have clearly defined your objectives, the focus shifts to identifying specific components to meet those objectives.

Suggestions

If your objective is to improve performance, three components to consider are RAM, the microprocessor, and expansion cards. If your objective is to increase storage capacity, two components to consider are hard-disk drive and optical disc drive. If you are adding new technology, consider the capability of your current system to support new devices.

Performance

If you want to increase the speed of your computer, consider increasing the amount of RAM. In most cases, this upgrade is relatively inexpensive and will yield the highest performance result per dollar invested. How much your system's performance will increase depends on how much RAM you start with, the size of programs you run, and how often you run large programs.

Another way to increase speed is to replace your system's microprocessor. Processor speed is measured in gigahertz (GHz). This rating is not a direct measurement of how fast the processor works, but rather it gives you a general idea of how it compares to other processors. (Computing magazines such as *PC World* often publish articles comparing the relative effectiveness of different processors.) The concept behind a microprocessor upgrade is simple: A faster processor will process faster. This is often an expensive upgrade and not as cost-effective as increasing RAM.

If you are looking at upgrading for a specific type of application, perhaps an expansion card is your answer. Expansion cards connect to slots on the system board, provide specialized support, and often free up resources and increase overall system performance. For example, if you run graphics-intensive programs, such as a drafting program or a video game, a video-card upgrade may be a good buy. An upgraded video card can be used to support higher resolution displays, handle all video data, and speed up overall system performance.

Storage Capacity

It's not hard to know when it's time to upgrade your storage capacity. If you frequently have to delete old files to make way for new ones, then it is probably time for more space. A larger or an additional hard drive is usually the solution. Two things to consider when comparing new hard drives are (1) size, which is usually rated in gigabytes (GB) of data the drive can hold, and (2) seek time, which is a rating of the average time it takes the drive to access any particular piece of data.

If you are storing a lot of data that you no longer use, such as old term papers, you might consider adding a high-capacity floppy disk drive. This is usually cheaper and is a good way to archive and transport data. Access time is slower than from a hard drive, so this is an option best suited for infrequently used data or for backing up data.

New Technology

Perhaps you are not looking to modify existing hardware, but would like to add a new device. Examples include large high-resolution monitors, DVD-RW drives, and high-speed printers.

The key consideration is whether the new device will work with your existing hardware. The requirements for these devices are typically printed on the outside packaging or available at the product's Web site. If not, then refer to the product's operating manuals. Obviously, if your current system cannot support the new technology, you need to evaluate the cost of the new device plus the necessary additional hardware upgrades.

STEP 3

Who Should Do the Upgrade?

Once you've decided that the cost of the upgrade is justified and you know what you want to upgrade, the final decision is who is going to do it. Basically, there are two choices. You can either do it yourself or pay for professional installation.

Suggestions

The easiest way, and many times the best way, is to have a professional perform the upgrade. If you select this option, be sure to include the cost of installation in your analysis. If you have had some prior hardware experience or are a bit adventurous, you may want to save some money and do it yourself.

Visit a few computer stores that carry the upgrades you have selected. Most stores that provide the parts will install them as well. Talk with their technical people, describe your system (better yet, bring your system unit to the store), and determine the cost of professional installation. If you are thinking of doing it yourself, ask for their advice. Ask if they will provide assistance if you need it.

If you decide to have the components professionally installed, get the total price in writing and inquire about any guarantees that might exist. Before leaving your system, be sure that it is carefully tagged with your name and address. After the service has been completed, pay by credit card and thoroughly test the upgrade. If it does not perform satisfactorily, contact the store and ask for assistance. If the store's service is not satisfactory, you may be able to have your credit card company help to mediate any disputes.

VISUAL SUMMARY
The Upgrader's Guide: How to Upgrade Your Microcomputer System

Upgrading a Microcomputer System	
Step	**Questions**
1	*Needs:* Is it time to upgrade? What do I need that my current system is unable to deliver?
2	*Analysis:* What should I upgrade? Will the upgrade meet my needs and will it be cost-effective?
3	*Action:* Who should do the upgrade? Should I pay a professional or do it myself?

NEEDS

Is it time to upgrade? What do I need that my current system is unable to deliver?

I am considering an upgrade to:
- ❑ **Improve performance because**
  - ❑ My programs run too slowly
  - ❑ I cannot run some programs I need
- ❑ **Increase storage capacity because**
  - ❑ I don't have enough space to store all my files
  - ❑ I don't have enough space to install new programs
  - ❑ I need a secure place to back up important files
  - ❑ I'd like to download large files from the Internet
- ❑ **Add new technology**
  - ❑ Zip drive
  - ❑ DVD-RW
  - ❑ High-performance monitor
  - ❑ Printer
  - ❑ TV tuner card
  - ❑ Enhanced video card
  - ❑ Enhanced sound card
  - ❑ Other _____

ANALYSIS

What should I upgrade? Will the upgrade meet my needs and will it be cost-effective?

I will improve:
- ❑ **Performance by**
  - ❑ Adding random-access memory (RAM)
    Current RAM (MB) _____
    Upgrade to _____
    Cost $ _____
    Expected improvement _____
    Other factors _____
  - ❑ Replacing the current microprocessor
    Current processor _____
    Upgrade processor _____
    Cost $ _____
    Expected improvement _____
    Other factors _____
  - ❑ Adding an expansion card
    Type _____
    Purpose _____
    Cost $ _____
    Expected improvement _____
    Other factors _____
- ❑ **Storage capacity by**
  - ❑ Adding a hard-disk drive
    Current size (GB) _____
    Upgrade size (GB) _____
    Cost $ _____
    Expected improvement _____
    Other factors _____
  - ❑ Adding a Zip disk drive
    Upgrade size (GB) _____
    Cost $ _____
    Type _____
    Expected improvement _____
    Other factors _____

❏ **Functionality by adding**
  New technology _____
  System requirements _____
  Cost $ _____

Expected improvement _____
Other factors _____

To help clarify your thinking about upgrading a microcomputer system, complete the questionnaire by checking the appropriate boxes.

ACTION

Who should do the upgrade? Should I do it myself or should I pay a professional?

The two choices are:

❏ **Professional installation**

The easiest way, and many times the best way, is to have a professional perform the upgrade. If you select this option, be sure to include the cost of installation in your analysis. Pay with a credit card, and make sure your system is tagged with your name and address before you part with it.

❏ **Do-it-yourself installation**

If you have had some prior hardware experience or are a bit adventurous, you may want to save some money and do it yourself. Avoid touching sensitive electronic parts and be sure to ground yourself by touching an unpainted metal surface in your computer.

Glossary

3G Cellular Network: A network that allows devices such as cell phones and properly equipped laptop computers to download data from the Internet.

3GLs (third-generation languages): High-level procedural language. *See* Procedural language.

4GLs (fourth-generation languages): Very high-level or problem-oriented languages. *See* Problem-oriented language.

5GLs (fifth-generation languages): *See* Fifth-generation language.

802.11: *See* Wi-Fi (wireless fidelity).

A

AC adapter: Notebook computers use AC adapters that are typically outside the system unit. They plug into a standard wall outlet, convert AC to DC, provide power to drive the system components, and can recharge batteries.

Accelerated graphics port (AGP): A type of bus line that is dedicated to the acceleration of graphics performance.

Access: Refers to the responsibility of those who have data to control who is able to use that data.

Access speed: Measures the amount of time required by the storage device to retrieve data and programs.

Accounting: The organizational department that records all financial activity from billing customers to paying employees.

Accounts payable: The activity that shows the money a company owes to its suppliers for the materials and services it has received.

Accounts receivable: The activity that shows what money has been received or is owed by customers.

Accuracy: Relates to the responsibility of those who collect data to ensure that the data is correct.

Active-matrix monitor: Type of flat-panel monitor in which each pixel is independently activated. Displays more colors with better clarity; also known as thin film transistor (TFT) monitors.

Ad network cookies: Cookies that monitor your activities across all sites you visit and are continually active in collecting information on your Web activities.

Add Printer Wizard: A Windows wizard that provides step-by-step guidance for selecting and installing an appropriate printer driver for a new printer.

Address: Located in the header of an e-mail message; the e-mail address of the persons sending, receiving, and, optionally, anyone else who is to receive copies.

Advanced Research Project Agency Network (ARPANET): A national computer network from which the Internet developed.

Adware cookie: *See* Ad network cookies.

Analog signal: Signals that represent a range of frequencies, such as the human voice. They are a continuous electronic wave signal as opposed to a digital signal that is either on or off. To convert the digital signals of your computer to analog and vice versa, you need a modem. Another cable connects the modem to the telephone wall jack.

Analytical graphs or charts: Form of graphics used to put numeric data into objects that are easier to analyze, such as bar charts, line graphs, and pie charts.

Animation: Feature involving special visual and sound effects like moving pictures, audio, and video clips that play automatically when selected.

Antispyware: *See* spy removal program.

Antivirus program: A utility program that guards a computer system from viruses or other damaging programs.

Applets: Web pages contain links to programs called applets, which are written in a programming language called Java. These programs are used to add interest to a Web site by presenting animation, displaying graphics, providing interactive games, and so forth.

Application generation subsystem: Provides tools to create data entry forms and specialized programming languages that interface or work with common languages, such as COBOL.

Application generator: Also called program coder; provides modules of prewritten code to accomplish various tasks, such as calculation of overtime pay.

Application software: Software that can perform useful work, such as word processing, cost estimating, or accounting tasks. The user primarily interacts with application software.

Arithmetic-logic unit (ALU): The part of the CPU that performs arithmetic and logical operations.

Arithmetic operation: Fundamental math operations: addition, subtraction, multiplication, and division.

Artificial intelligence (AI): A field of computer science that attempts to develop computer systems that can mimic or simulate human thought processes and actions.

Artificial reality: *See* Virtual reality.

ASCII (American Standard Code for Information Interchange): Binary coding scheme widely used on all computers, including microcomputers. Eight bits form each byte, and each byte represents one character.

Assembly language: A step up from machine language, using names instead of numbers. These languages use abbreviations or mnemonics, such as ADD, that are automatically converted to the appropriate sequence of 1s and 0s.

Asymmetric digital subscriber line (ADSL): One of the most widely used types of telephone high-speed connections (DSL).

Attachment: A file, such as a document or worksheet, that is attached to an e-mail message.

Attribute: A data field represents an attribute (description or characteristic) of some entity (person, place, thing, or object). For example, an employee is an entity with many attributes, including his or her last name, address, phone, etc.

Auction house sites: Web sites that operate like a traditional auction to sell merchandise to bidders.

Audio editing software: Allows you to create and edit audio clips like filtering out pops and scratches in an old recording.

AutoContent wizard: This Microsoft wizard steps you through the process of creating a PowerPoint presentation.

Automated design tool: Software package that evaluates hardware and software alternatives according to requirements given by the systems analyst. Also called computer-aided software engineering (CASE) tools.

B

Backbone: *See* Bus.

Backup: A Windows utility program. *See* Backup program.

Backup program: A utility program that helps protect you from the effects of a disk failure by making a copy of selected or all files that have been saved onto a disk.

Balance sheet: Lists the overall financial condition of an organization.

Bandwidth: Bandwidth determines how much information can be transmitted at one time. It is a measurement of the communication channel's capacity. There are three bandwidths: voiceband, medium band, and broadband.

Bar code: Code consisting of vertical zebra-striped marks printed on product containers, read with a bar code reader.

Bar code reader: Photoelectric scanner that reads bar codes for processing.

Bar code scanner: *See* Bar code reader.

Base station: *See* Wireless receiver.

Basic application: Applications used for doing common tasks, such as browsers and word processors, spreadsheets, databases, management systems, and presentation graphics. Also known as productivity applications.

Batch processing: Processing performed all at once on data that has been collected over time.

BD (Blue-Ray discs): A type of high-definition disc with a capacity of 25 to 50 gigabytes.

Beta testing: Testing by a select group of potential users in the final stage of testing a program.

Binary coding schemes: The representation of characters as 0s and 1s, or "off" and "on" electrical states, in a computer. Two of the most popular binary coding

schemes use eight bits to form each byte as in the ASCII and EBCDIC codes.

Binary system: Numbering system in which all numbers consist of only two digits: 0 and 1.

Biometric scanning: Devices that check fingerprints or retinal scans.

Bit (binary digit): Each 1 or 0 is a bit; short for binary digit.

Bitmap image: Graphic file in which an image is made up of thousands of dots (pixels).

Bits per second (bps): Speed at which data is transferred.

Blog: *See* Web log.

Bluetooth: A recent wireless technology that allows nearby devices to communicate without the connection of cables or telephone systems.

Bomb: A destructive computer program.

Boot camp: Feature of Leopard, the new version of Mac OS, that allows appropriately equipped Apple computers to run both Mac OS and Windows XP.

Booting: Starting or restarting your computer.

Broadband: Bandwidth that includes microwave, satellite, coaxial cable, and fiber-optic channels. It is used for very high-speed computers.

Broadcast radio: Communication using transceivers to send and receive signals from wireless devices.

Browser: Special Internet software connecting you to remote computers; opens and transfers files, displays text and images, and provides an uncomplicated interface to the Internet and Web documents. Examples of browsers are Internet Explorer and Netscape Navigator.

Bulleted list: The sequence of topics arranged on a page and organized by bullets.

Bus: All communication travels along a common connecting cable called a bus or a backbone. As information passes along the bus, it is examined by each device on the system board to see if the information is intended for that device. *See* Bus line and Ethernet.

Bus line: Electronic data roadway, along which bits travel, connects the parts of the CPU to each other and links the CPU with other important hardware. The common connecting cable in a bus network.

Bus network: Also known as Ethernet. Network in which all communications travel along a common connecting cable called a bus. Each device in the network handles its own communications control. There is no host computer or file server.

Bus width: The number of bits traveling simultaneously down a bus is the bus width.

Business suite: *See* Productivity suites.

Business-to-business (B2B): A type of electronic commerce that involves the sale of a product or service from one business to another. This is typically a manufacturer–supplier relationship.

Business-to-consumer (B2C): A type of electronic commerce that involves the sale of a product or service to the general public or end users.

Button: A special area you can click to make links that "navigate" through a presentation.

Byte: Unit consisting of eight bits. There are 256 possible bit combinations in a byte and each byte represents one character.

C

Cable: Cords used to connect input and output devices to the system unit.

Cable modem: Allows all digital communication, which is a speed of 27 million bps.

Cache memory: Area of random-access memory (RAM) set aside to store the most frequently accessed information. Cache memory improves processing by acting as a temporary high-speed holding area between memory and the CPU, allowing the computer to detect which information in RAM is most frequently used.

Capacity: Capacity is how much data a particular storage medium can hold and another characteristic of secondary storage.

Carder: Criminal who steals credit cards over the Internet.

Carpal tunnel syndrome: Disorder found among frequent computer users, consisting of damage to nerves and tendons in the hands. *See also* Repetitive strain injury.

Carrier package: The material that chips are mounted on which then plugs into sockets on the system board.

Cathode-ray tube (CRT) monitor: Desktop-type monitor built in the same way as a television set. The most common type of monitor for office and home use. These monitors are typically placed directly on the system unit or on top of a desk.

CD: *See* Compact disc.

CD-R: Stands for CD-recordable. This optical disc can be written to only once. After that it can be read many times without deterioration but cannot be written on or erased. Used to create custom music CDs and to archive data.

CD-ROM (compact disc–read only memory): Optical disc that allows data to be read but not recorded. Used to distribute large databases, references, and software application packages.

CD-ROM jukebox: Provides automatic access to a large collection or library of optical discs.

CD-RW (compact disc rewriteable): A reusable, optical disc that is not permanently altered when data is recorded. Used to create and edit large multimedia presentations.

Cell: The space created by the intersection of a vertical column and a horizontal row within a worksheet in a program like Microsoft Excel. A cell can contain text or numeric entries.

Cellular service: Links car phones and portable phones.

Center for European Nuclear Research (CERN): In Switzerland, where the Web was introduced in 1992.

Central processing unit (CPU): The part of the computer that holds data and program instructions for processing the data. The CPU consists of the control unit and the arithmetic-logic unit. In a microcomputer, the CPU is on a single electronic component called a microprocessor chip.

Character: A single letter, number, or special character, such as a punctuation mark or $.

Character effect: Change appearance of font characters by using bold, italic, shadow, and colors.

Chart: Displaying numerical data in a worksheet as a pie chart or a bar chart, making it easier to understand.

Checklist: In analyzing data, a list of questions helps guide the systems analyst and end user through key issues for the present system.

Child node: A node one level below the node being considered in a hierarchical database or network. *See* Parent node.

Chip: A tiny circuit board etched on a small square of sandlike material called silicon. A chip is also called a silicon chip, semiconductor, or integrated circuit.

Chlorofluorocarbons (CFCs): Toxic chemicals found in solvents and cleaning agents. CFCs can travel into the atmosphere and deplete the earth's ozone layer.

Clarity: Indicated by the resolution, or number of pixels, on a monitor. The greater the resolution, the better the clarity.

Class: In an object-oriented database, classes are similar objects grouped together.

Client: A node that requests and uses resources available from other nodes. Typically, a client is a user's microcomputer.

Client/server network: Network in which one powerful computer coordinates and supplies services to all other nodes on the network. Server nodes coordinate and supply specialized services, and client nodes request the services.

Clip art: Graphic illustrations representing a wide variety of topics.

Clock speed: Also called clock rate. It is measured in gigahertz, or billions of beats per second. The faster the clock speed, the faster the computer can process information and execute instructions.

Coaxial cable: High-frequency transmission cable that replaces the multiple wires of telephone lines with a single solid-copper core. It is used to deliver television signals as well as to connect computers in a network.

Code: Writing a program using the appropriate computer language.

Coding: Actual writing of a computer program, using a programming language.

Cold boot: Starting the computer after it has been turned off.

Column: Using Microsoft Excel, for example, a vertical block of cells one cell wide all the way down the worksheet.

Combination key: Keys such as the Ctrl key that perform an action when held down in combination with another key.

Common data item: In a relational database, all related tables must have a common data item or key field.

Common operational database: Contains details about the operations of the company, such as inventory, production, and sales.

Common user database: Company database that contains selected information from both the common operational database and outside (proprietary) databases.

Communication channel: The actual connecting medium that carries the message between sending and receiving devices. This medium can be a physical wire, cable, or wireless connection.

Communication device: Computer systems that communicate with other computer systems using modems. For example, it modifies computer output into a form that can be transmitted across standard telephone lines.

Communication system: Electronic system that transmits data over communications lines from one location to another.

Compact disc (CD): Widely used optical disc format. It holds 650 MB (megabytes) to 1 GB (gigabyte) of data on one side of the CD.

Compact disc–read only memory: *See* CD-ROM.

Compact disc rewritable: *See* CD-RW.

Company database: Also called shared databases. Stored on a mainframe, users throughout the company have access to the database through their microcomputers linked by a network.

Compiler: Software that converts the programmer's procedural-language program (source code) into machine language (object code). This object code can then be saved and run later.

Complementary metal-oxide semiconductor (CMOS): A CMOS chip provides flexibility and expandability for a computer system. Unlike RAM, it does not lose its contents if power is turned off, and unlike ROM, its contents can be changed.

Computer Abuse Amendments Act: Outlaws transmittal of viruses and other harmful computer code.

Computer-aided design/computer-aided manufacturing (CAD/CAM) system: Knowledge work systems that run programs to integrate the design and manufacturing activities. CAD/CAM is widely used in manufacturing automobiles.

Computer-aided software engineering (CASE) tool: A type of software development tool that helps provide some automation and assistance in program design, coding, and testing. *See* Automated design tool.

Computer competency: Becoming proficient in computer-related skills.

Computer crime: Illegal action in which a perpetrator uses special knowledge of computer technology. Criminals may be employees, outside users, hackers and crackers, and organized crime members.

Computer ethics: Guidelines for the morally acceptable use of computers in our society.

Computer Fraud and Abuse Act: Law allowing prosecution of unauthorized access to computers and databases.

Computer monitoring software: The most invasive and dangerous type of spyware. These programs record every activity made on your computer, including credit card numbers, bank account numbers, and e-mail messages.

Computer network: Communications system connecting two or more computers and their peripheral devices to exchange information and share resources.

Computer support specialist: Specialists include technical writers, computer trainers, computer technicians, and help-desk specialists who provide technical support to customers and other users.

Computer technician: Specialist who installs hardware and software and troubleshoots problems for users.

Computer trainer: Computer professional who provides classes to instruct users.

Computer virus: Destructive programs that can come in e-mail attachments and spam.

Connectivity: Capability of the microcomputer to use information from the world beyond one's desk. Data and information can be sent over telephone or cable lines and through the air so that computers can talk to each other and share information.

Consumer-to-consumer (C2C): A type of electronic commerce that involves individuals selling to individuals.

Contextual tabs: New feature of Microsoft Office 2003 that appears automatically when needed.

Control unit: Section of the CPU that tells the rest of the computer how to carry out program instructions.

Conversion: Also known as systems implementation; four approaches to conversion: direct, parallel, pilot, and phased. *See* Systems implementation.

Cookies: Programs that record information on Web site visitors.

Coprocessor: Specialized processing chip designed to improve specific computer operations, such as the graphics coprocessor.

Cordless mouse: A battery-powered mouse that typically uses radio waves or infrared light waves to communicate with the system unit. Also known as wireless mouse.

Cracker: One who gains unauthorized access to a computer system for malicious purposes.

Cryptographer: Designs, tests, and researches encryption procedures.

Cumulative trauma disorder: *See* Repetitive strain injury.

Cybercash: *See* Electronic cash.

Cylinder: Hard disks store and organize files using tracks, sectors, and cylinders. A cylinder runs through each track of a stack of platters. Cylinders differentiate files stored on the same track and sector of different platters.

Cynic: Individual who feels that the idea of using a microcomputer is overrated and too troublesome to learn.

D

Dashboard Widgets: A collection of specialized programs on the Mac OS X operating system that constantly updates and displays information such as stock prices and weather information.

Data: Raw, unprocessed facts that are input to a computer system that will give compiled information when the computer processes those facts. Data is also defined as facts or observations about people, places, things, and events.

Data administration subsystem: Helps manage the overall database, including maintaining security, providing disaster recovery support, and monitoring the overall performance of database operations.

Data bank: *See* Proprietary database.

Data definition subsystem: This system defines the logical structure of the database by using a data dictionary.

Data dictionary: Dictionary containing a description of the structure of data in a database.

Data entry worker: Inputs customer information, lists, and other types of data.

Data flow diagram: Diagram showing data or information flow within an information system.

Data integrity: Database characteristics relating to the consistency and accuracy of data.

Data maintenance: Maintaining data includes adding new data, deleting old data, and editing existing data.

Data manipulation subsystem: Provides tools to maintain and analyze data.

Data mining: Technique of searching data warehouses for related information and patterns.

Data model: Defines rules and standards for all data in a database. There are five data models: hierarchical, network, relational, multidimensional, and object-oriented. For example, Access uses the relational data model.

Data processing system (DPS): Transaction processing system that keeps track of routine operations and records these events in a database. Also called transaction processing system (TPS).

Data projector: Specialized device, similar to slide projector, that connects to microcomputers and projects computer output.

Data redundancy: A common database problem in which data is duplicated and stored in different files.

Data security: Protection of software and data from unauthorized tampering or damage.

Data warehouse: Data collected from a variety of internal and external databases and stored in a database called a data warehouse. Data mining is then used to search these databases.

Data worker: Person involved with the distribution and communication of information, such as secretaries and clerks.

Database: A collection of related information, like employee names, addresses, and phone numbers. It is organized so that a computer program can quickly select the desired pieces of information and display them for you.

Database administrator (DBA): Uses database management software to determine the most efficient way to organize and access data.

Database file: File containing highly structured and organized data created by database management programs.

Database management system (DBMS): To organize, manage, and retrieve data. DBMS programs have five subsystems: DBMS engine, data definition, data manipulation, applications generation, and data administration. An example of a database management system is Microsoft Access. *See* Database manager.

Database manager: Software package used to set up, or structure, a database such as an inventory list of supplies. It also provides tools to edit, enter, and retrieve data from the database.

DBMS engine: Provides a bridge between the logical view of data and the physical view of data.

Debugging: Programmer's word for testing and then eliminating errors in a program. Programming errors are of two types: syntax and logic errors.

Decision model: The decision model gives the decision support system its analytical capabilities. There are three types of models included in the decision model: tactical, operational, and strategic models.

Decision support system (DSS): Flexible analysis tool that helps managers make decisions about unstructured problems, such as effects of events and trends outside the organization.

Decision table: Table showing decision rules that apply when certain conditions occur and what action should take place as a result.

Demand report: A demand report is produced on request. An example is a report on the numbers and types of jobs held by women and minorities done at the request of the government.

Demodulation: Process performed by a modem in converting analog signals to digital signals.

Denial of service (DoS) attack: A variant virus in which Web sites are overwhelmed with data and users are unable to access the Web site. Unlike a worm that self-replicates, a DoS attack floods a computer or network with requests for information and data.

Density: Refers to how tightly the bits (electromagnetic charges) can be packed next to one another on a floppy disk.

Design template Provides professionally selected combinations of color schemes, slide layouts, and special effects for presentation graphics.

Desk checking: Process of checking out a computer program by studying a printout of the program line by line, looking for syntax and logic errors.

Desktop: The screen that is displayed on the monitor when the computer starts up. All items and icons on the screen are considered to be on your desktop and are used to interact with the computer.

Desktop computer: Computer small enough to fit on top of or along the side of a desk and yet too big to carry around.

Desktop operating systems: *See* Stand-alone operating system.

Desktop publisher: One who creates and formats publication-ready material.

Desktop publishing program: Program that allows you to mix text and graphics to create publications of professional quality.

Desktop system unit: A system unit that typically contains the system's electronic components and selected secondary storage devices. Input and output devices, such as the mouse, keyboard, and monitor, are located outside the system unit.

Device driver: Every device that is connected to the computer has a special program associated with it called a device driver that allows communication between the operating system and the device.

Diagnostic program: *See* Troubleshooting program.

Dialog box: Provides additional information and requests user input.

Dial-up: Method of accessing the Internet using a high-speed modem and standard telephone lines.

Digital: Computers are digital machines because they can only understand 1s and 0s. It is either on or off. For example, a digital watch states the exact time on the face, whereas an analog watch has the second hand moving in constant motion as it tells the time.

Digital camera: Similar to a traditional camera except that images are recorded digitally in the camera's memory rather than on film.

Digital cash: Currency for Internet purchases. Buyers purchase digital cash from a third party (a bank that specializes in electronic currency) by transferring funds from their banks.

Digital media player: Also known as digital music player; a specialized device for storing, transferring, and playing audio files.

Digital music palyer: Also known as digital media player; a specialized device for storing, transferring, and playing audio files.

Digital signal: Computers can only understand digital signals. Before processing can occur within the system unit, a conversion must occur from what we understand (analog) to what the system unit can electronically process (digital). *See* Analog signal.

Digital subscriber line (DSL): Provides high-speed connection using existing telephone lines.

Digital versatile disc (DVD): A type of optical disc similar to CD-ROMs except that more data can be packed into the same amount of space. *Also see* DVD digital versatile disc.

Digital video camera: Input device that records motion digitally.

Digital video disc: *See* DVD (digital versatile disc).

Direct access: A fast approach to external storage, provided by disks, where information is not in a set sequence.

Direct approach: Approach for systems implementation whereby the old system is simply abandoned for the new system.

Directory search: A search engine option that provides a directory or list of categories or topics to choose from, such as Arts & Humanities, Business & Economics, or

Computers & Internet, that help you narrow your search until a list of Web sites appears.

Disaster recovery plan: Plan used by large organizations describing ways to continue operations following a disaster until normal computer operations can be restored.

Disk: *See* Floppy disk.

Disk caching: Method of improving hard-disk performance by anticipating data needs. Frequently used data is read from the hard disk into memory (cache). When needed, data is then accessed directly from memory, which has a much faster transfer rate than from the hard disk. Increases performance by as much as 30 percent.

Disk Cleanup: A Windows troubleshooting utility that eliminates nonessential files.

Disk Defragmenter: A Windows utility that optimizes disk performance by eliminating unnecessary fragments and rearranging files.

Display screen: *See* Monitor.

Distributed data processing system: In a network, computers that perform processing tasks at their own dispersed locations while also sharing programs, data, and other resources with each other.

Distributed database: Database that can be made accessible through a variety of communications networks, which allow portions of the database to be located in different places.

Distributed processing: System in which computing power is located and shared at different locations.

DO UNTIL structure: Loop structure in programming that appears at the end of a loop. The DO UNTIL loop means that the loop statements will be executed at least once. In other words, this program tells you to DO option one UNTIL it is no longer true.

DO WHILE structure: Loop structure in programming that appears at the beginning of a loop. The DO WHILE loop will keep executing as long as there is information to be processed. For example, DO option one WHILE (or as long as) option one remains true.

Document: Any kind of text material.

Document file: File created by a word processor to save documents such as letters, research papers, and memos.

Documentation: Written descriptions and procedures about a program and how to use it. *See* Program documentation.

Domain code:

Domain name: The second part of the URL; it is the name of the server where the resource is located. For example, www.mtv.com.

Domain name server (DNS): Internet addressing method that assigns names and numbers to people and computers. Because the numeric IP addresses are difficult to remember, the DNS server was developed to automatically convert text-based addresses to numeric IP addresses.

Dot-matrix printer: A type of printer that forms characters and images using a series of small pins on a print head. Used where high-quality output is not required.

Dot pitch: Distance between each pixel. The lower the dot pitch, the shorter the distance between pixels, and the higher the clarity of images produced.

Dots-per-inch (dpi): Printer resolution is measured in dpi. The higher the dpi, the better the quality of images produced.

Downloading: Process of transferring information from a remote computer to the computer one is using.

Drawing program: Program used to help create artwork for publications. *See* Illustration program.

Driver: *See* Device driver.

DSL: *See* Digital subscriber line.

Dual-core chip: A new type of chip that provides two independent CPUs, allowing two programs to run simultaneously. *Also see* Central Processing Unit.

Dual-scan monitor: *See* Passive-matrix monitor.

Dumb terminal: Terminal that can be used to input and receive data but cannot process data independently. It is used to gain access to information. An example is the type of terminals airline reservation clerks use.

DVD (digital versatile disc or digital video disc): Similar to CD-ROMs except that more data can be packed into the same amount of space. DVD drives can store 4.7 GB to 17 GB on a single DVD disc or 17 times the capacity of CDs.

DVD player: Also known as DVD-ROM drives. *See* DVD.

DVD–R (DVD recordable): A DVD with a write-once format that differs slightly from the format of DVD+R. Typically used to create permanent archives for large amounts of data and to record videos.

DVD+R (DVD recordable): A DVD with a write-once format that differs slightly from the format of DVD–R. Typically used to create permanent archives for large amounts of data and to record videos.

DVD-RAM (DVD random-access memory): A high-capacity, maximum-performance disc that allows the user to read the information, write over it, and erase the data if necessary. Used like a floppy disk to copy, delete files, and run programs. It has up to 8 times the storage capacity of a CD and also can be used to read CD and DVD formats.

DVD-ROM (DVD–read only memory): Used to distribute full-length feature films with theater-quality video and sound. Also known as DVD players. Are read-only.

DVD-ROM jukebox: Provides automatic access to a large collection or library of optical discs.

DVD–RW (DVD rewritable): A type of reusable DVD disc that is more flexible than the DVD-RAM. DVD–RW is able to create and read CD discs along with creating and editing large-scale multimedia presentations.

DVD+RW (DVD rewritable): Another DVD format to record and erase repeatedly. Able to create and read CD discs along with creating and editing large-scale multimedia presentations.

E

EBCDIC (Extended Binary Coded Decimal Interchange Code): Binary coding schemes that are a standard for minicomputers and mainframe computers.

E-book: Handheld, book-sized devices that display text and graphics. Using content downloaded from the Web or special cartridges, these devices are used to read newspapers, magazines, and books.

E-commerce: Buying and selling goods over the Internet.

Economic feasibility: Comparing the costs of a new system to the benefits it promises.

Editing: Features that modify a document such as using a thesaurus, find and replace, or spell check.

E-learning: A Web application that allows one to take educational courses online.

Electronic commerce (e-commerce): Buying and selling goods over the Internet.

Electronic mail: Transmission of electronic messages over the Internet. Also known as e-mail.

Electronic monitoring: Monitoring workers' performance electronically rather than by human supervisors.

Electronic profile: Using publicly and privately available databases, information resellers create electronic profiles, which are highly detailed and personalized descriptions of individuals.

E-mail: Communicate with anyone in the world who has an Internet address or e-mail account with a system connected to the Internet. You can include a text message, graphics, photos, and file attachments.

Embedded operating system: An operating system that is completely stored within the ROM (read only memory) of the device that it is in; used for handheld computers and smaller devices like PDAs.

Encrypting: Coding information so that only the user can read or otherwise use it.

End user: Person who uses microcomputers or has access to larger computers.

Energy Star: Program created by the Environmental Protection Agency to discourage waste in the microcomputer industry.

Enterprise storage system: Using mass storage devices, a strategy is designed for organizations to promote efficient and safe use of data across the networks within their organizations.

Entity: In an object-oriented database, a person, place, thing, or event that is to be described.

Erasable optical disc: Optical disc on which the disk drive can write information and also erase and rewrite information. Also known as CD-RW or compact disc rewritable.

Ergonomic keyboard: Keyboard arrangement that is not rectangular with a palm rest, which is designed to alleviate wrist strain.

Ergonomics: Study of human factors related to things people use. It is concerned with fitting the job to the worker rather than forcing the worker to contort to fit the job.

Ethernet: Otherwise known as Ethernet bus or Ethernet LAN. The Ethernet bus is the pathway or arterial to which all nodes (PCs, file servers, print servers, Web servers, etc.) are connected. All of this is connected to a local area network (LAN) or a wide area network (WAN). *See* Bus network.

Ethics: Standards of moral conduct.

Exception report: Report that calls attention to unusual events.

Executive information system (EIS):   Sophisticated software that can draw together data from an organization's databases in meaningful patterns and highly summarized forms.

Executive support system (ESS):   *See* Executive information system.

Expansion bus: Connects the CPU to slots on the system board. There are different types of expansion buses such as industry standard architecture (ISA), peripheral component interconnect (PCI), accelerated graphics port (AGP), universal serial bus (USB), and FireWire buses. *See* System bus.

Expansion card: Optional device that plugs into a slot inside the system unit to expand the computers' abilities. Ports on the system board allow cables to be connected from the expansion board to devices outside the system unit.

Expansion slots: Openings on a system board. Users can insert optional devices, known as expansion cards, into these slots, allowing users to expand their systems. *See* Expansion card.

Expert system: Computer program that provides advice to decision makers who would otherwise rely on human experts. It's a type of artificial intelligence that uses a database to provide assistance to users.

External data: Data gathered from outside an organization. Examples are data provided by market research firms.

External modem: Modem that stands apart from the computer and is connected by a cable to the computer's serial port.

Extranet: Private network that connects more than one organization.

F

Fax machine: A device for sending and receiving images over telephone lines.

Fiber-optic cable: Special transmission cable made of glass tubes that are immune to electronic interference. Data is transmitted through fiber-optic cables in the form of pulses of light.

Field: Each column of information within a record is called a field. A field contains related information on a specific item like employee names within a company department.

Fifth-generation language (5GL):   Computer language that incorporates the concept of artificial intelligence to allow direct human communication. *See* Visual programming languages.

File: A collection of related records that can store data and programs. For example, the payroll file would include payroll information (records) for all of the employees (entities).

File compression: Process of reducing the storage requirements for a file.

File compression program: Utility programs that reduce the size of files so they require less storage on the

computer and can be sent more efficiently over the Internet. Examples of such programs are WinZip and Wizard.

File decompression: Process of expanding a compressed file.

File server: Dedicated computer with large storage capacity providing users access to shared folders or fast storage and retrieval of information used in that business.

File transfer protocol (FTP):   Internet service for uploading and downloading files.

Filter: (1) A filter blocks access to selected Web sites. (2) A filter will locate or display records from a table that fit a set of conditions or criteria when using programs like Excel.

Financial Modernization Act: Protects personal financial information.

Find and replace: An editing tool that finds a selected word or phrase and replaces it with another. Click *edit, find.*

Firewall: Security hardware and software. All communications into and out of an organization pass through a special security computer, called a proxy server, to protect all systems against external threats.

FireWire bus: Operates much like USB buses on the system board but at higher speeds.

FireWire port: Used to connect high-speed printers, and even video cameras, to system unit.

Flash: An interactive animation program from Adobe that is usually full screen and highly dynamic, displaying moving text or complicated interactive features.

Flash memory: RAM chips that retain data even when power is disrupted. Flash memory is an example of solid-state storage and is typically used to store digitized images and record MP3 files.

Flash memory card: A solid-state storage device widely used in notebook computers. Flash memory also is used in a variety of specialized input devices to capture and transfer data to desktop computers.

Flat-panel monitor: Or liquid crystal display (LCD) monitor. These monitors are much thinner than CRTs and can be used for desktop systems as well.

Flatbed scanner: An input device similar to a copying machine.

Flexible keyboard: Fold or rollup for easy packing or storage; designed for mobile users who want a full-size keyboard.

Floppy disk: Flat, circular piece of magnetically treated mylar plastic that rotates within a jacket. A floppy disk is $3^1/_2$ inches and holds 1.44 MB of information. It is a portable or removable secondary storage device.

Floppy-disk cartridge: *See* High-capacity disk.

Floppy disk drive (FDD):   Stores data programs by altering the electromagnetic charges on the disk's surface to represent 1s and 0s. The floppy drive retrieves the data by reading these charges from the magnetic disk.

Folder: A named area on a disk that is used to store related subfolders and files.

Font: Also known as typeface, is a set of characters with a specific design.

Font size: The height of a character measured in points, with each point being ¹⁄₇₂ inch.

Form: Electronic forms reflecting the contents of one record or table. Primarily used to enter new records or make changes to existing records.

Format: Features that change the appearance of a document like font, font sizes, character effects, alignment, and bulleted and numbered lists.

Formatting language: Also known as markup language. Uses symbols, words, and phrases that instruct a computer on how to display information to the user. For example, HTML is a formatting language used to display Web pages.

Formula: Instructions for calculations in a spreadsheet. It is an equation that performs calculations on the data contained within the cells in a worksheet or spreadsheet.

Fourth-generation language (4GL): Problem-oriented languages are designed to solve a specific problem and require little special training on the part of the end user.

Fragmented: Storage technique that breaks up large files and stores the parts wherever space is available in adjacent sectors and clusters.

Freedom of Information Act of 1970: Law giving citizens the right to examine data about them in federal government files, except for information restricted for national security reasons.

Frustrated: Person who feels it is an imposition to have to learn something new like computer technology.

Function: A built-in formula in a spreadsheet that performs calculations automatically.

Fuzzy logic: Used by expert systems to allow users to respond by using qualitative terms, such as *great* and *OK*.

G

Galleries: New feature of Microsoft Office 2003 that simplify the process of making selections from a list of alternatives by replacing dialog boxes with visual presentation of results.

General ledger: Activity that produces income statements and balance sheets based on all transactions of a company.

Generations (of programming languages): The five generations are machine languages, assembly languages, procedural languages, problem-oriented languages, and natural languages. *See* Levels.

Global positioning system (GPS): Devices use location information to determine the geographic location of your car, for example.

Grammar checker: In word processing, a tool that identifies poorly worded sentences and incorrect grammar.

Graphical map: Diagram of a Web site's overall design.

Graphical user interface (GUI): Special screen that allows software commands to be issued through the use of graphic symbols (icons) or pull-down menus.

Graphics card: They connect the system board to the computer monitor. The cards convert the internal electronic signals to video signals so they can be displayed on the monitor.

Graphics coprocessor: Designed to handle requirements related to displaying and manipulating 2-D and 3-D graphic images.

Graphics suite: Group of graphics programs offered at a lower cost than if purchased separately, like CorelDraw.

Green PC: Microcomputer industry concept of an environmentally friendly, low-power-consuming machine.

Grid chart: Chart that shows the relationship between input and output documents.

Group decision support system (GDSS): System used to support the collective work of a team addressing large problems.

H

Hacker: Person who gains unauthorized access to a computer system for the fun and challenge of it.

Handheld computer: *See* Personal digital assistant (PDA) and Palm computers.

Handheld computer system unit: Smallest type of system unit designed to fit into the palm of one hand.

Handwriting recognition software: Translates handwritten notes into a form that the system unit can process.

Hard disk: Enclosed disk drive containing one or more metallic disks. Hard disks use magnetic charges to record data and have large storage capacities and fast retrieval times.

Hard-disk cartridge: Hard disk that is easily removed. Used primarily to complement an internal hard disk.

Hard-disk pack: Several platters align one above the other, offering much greater storage capacity. They are removable storage devices with a massive amount of available storage. Used in big business companies.

Hardware: Equipment that includes a keyboard, monitor, printer, the computer itself, and other devices that are controlled by software programming.

HD DVD (High-definition DVD): A high-definition disc with a format similar to DVD with a much higher storage capacity. *Also see* DVD.

Head crash: When a read-write head makes contact with the hard disk's surface or particles on its surface, the disk surface becomes scratched and some or all data is destroyed.

Header: A typical e-mail has three elements: header, message, and signature. The header appears first and includes addresses, subject, and attachments.

Headphones: Audio-output devices connected to a sound card in the system unit. The sound card is used to capture as well as play back recorded sound.

Help: A feature in most application software providing options that typically include an index, a glossary, and a search feature to locate reference information about specific commands.

Hi def (high definition): The next generation of optical disc, which offers increased storage capacities.

Hierarchical database: Database in which fields or records are structured in nodes. Organized in the shape of a pyramid, and each node is linked directly to the nodes beneath it. Also called one-to-many relationship.

Hierarchical network: Also called a hybrid network. Consists of several computers linked to a central host computer. The computers linked to the host are themselves hosts to other computers or devices.

High-capacity disk: Also a 3½ inch floppy-disk cartridge. It is thicker than a floppy disk and requires a special drive. For example, Zip disks.

High-definition television (HDTV): All-digital television that delivers a much clearer and more detailed widescreen picture.

Higher level: Programming languages that are closer to the language humans use.

History file: Created by browser to store information on Web sites visited by your computer system.

Hits: The sites that a search engine returns after running a keyword search, ordered from most likely to least likely to contain the information requested.

Home network: LAN network for homes allowing different computers to share resources, including a common Internet connection.

Home software: *See* Integrated package.

Home suite: *See* Personal suite.

Host computer: Also called a server or provider, is a large centralized computer.

HTML: *See* Hypertext Markup Language.

HTML editor: *See* Web authoring program.

Hub: The center or central node for other nodes. This device can be a server or a connection point for cables from other nodes.

Human resources: The organizational department that focuses on the hiring, training, and promoting of people, as well as any number of human-centered activities within the organization.

Hyper cube: An extension of relational databases that is able to analyze more sides of the information. Also called multidimensional databases.

Hyperlink: Connection or link to other documents or Web pages that contain related information.

Hypertext Markup Language (HTML): Programming language that creates document files used to display Web pages.

I

Icons: Graphic objects on the desktop used to represent programs and other files.

Identity theft: The illegal assumption of someone's identity for the purpose of economic gain.

IF-THEN-ELSE structure: Logical selection structure whereby one of two paths is followed according to IF, THEN, and ELSE statements in a program. *See* Selection structure.

IFPS (interactive financial planning system): A 4GL language used for developing financial models.

Illusion of anonymity: The misconception that being selective about disclosing personal information on the Internet can prevent an invasion of personal privacy.

Illustration program: Also known as drawing programs; used to create digital illustrations and modify vector images and thus create line art, 3-D models, and virtual reality.

Image editor: An application for modifying bitmap images.

Image gallery: Libraries of electronic images.

Immersive experience: Allows the user to walk into a virtual reality room or view simulations on a virtual reality wall.

Income statement: A statement that shows a company's financial performance, income, expenses, and the difference between them for a specific time period.

Individual database: Collection of integrated records used mainly by just one person. Also called microcomputer database.

Industrial robot: Robot used in factories to perform a variety of tasks. For example, machines used in automobile plants to do painting and polishing.

Industry standard architecture (ISA): Bus-line standard developed for the IBM Personal Computer. It first consisted of an 8-bit-wide data path, then a 16-bit-wide data path. *See* Peripheral component interconnect (PCI).

Information: Data that has been processed by a computer system.

Information broker: *See* Information reseller.

Information reseller: Also known as information broker. It gathers personal data on people and sells it to direct markets, fund raisers, and others, usually for a fee.

Information system: Collection of hardware, software, people, data, and procedures that work together to provide information essential to running an organization.

Information systems manager: Oversees the work of programmers, computer specialists, systems analysts, and other computer professionals.

Information technology (IT): Computer and communication technologies, such as communication links to the Internet, that provide help and understanding to the end user.

Information utility: *See* Proprietary database.

Information worker: Employee who creates, distributes, and communicates information.

Infrared: Uses infrared light waves to communicate over short distances. Sometimes referred to as line-of-sight communication because light waves can only travel in a straight line.

Infrared Data Association (IrDA): A wireless mechanism for transferring data between devices using infrared light waves.

Ink-jet printer: Printer that sprays small droplets of ink at high speed onto the surface of the paper, producing letter-quality images, and can print in color.

Input device: Piece of equipment that translates data into a form a computer can process. The most common input devices are the keyboard and the mouse.

Instant messaging (IM): A program allowing communication and collaboration for direct, "live," connections over the Internet between two or more people.

Integrated circuit: *See* Silicon chip.

Integrated package: A single program providing functionality of a collection of programs but not as extensive as a specialized program like Microsoft Word. Popular with home users who are willing to sacrifice some advanced features for lower cost and simplicity.

Intelligent terminal: Terminal that includes a processing unit, memory, secondary storage, communications software, and a telephone hook-up or other communication links.

Interactivity: User participation in a multimedia presentation.

Internal data: Data from within an organization consisting principally of transactions from the transaction processing system.

Internal hard disk: Storage device consisting of one or more metallic platters sealed inside a container. Internal hard disks are installed inside the system cabinet of a microcomputer. It stores the operating system and major applications like Word.

Internal modem: The internal modem consists of a plug-in circuit board inside the system unit. A telephone cable connects the modem to the telephone wall jack. *See* Modem card.

Internet: A huge computer network available to everyone with a microcomputer and a means to connect to it. It is the actual physical network made up of wires, cables, and satellites as opposed to the Web, which is the multimedia interface to resources available on the Internet.

Internet hard drive: A special service site on the Web providing users with free or low-cost storage, allowing access to information from any computer that is connected to the Internet.

Internet scam: Using the Internet, a fraudulent act or operation designed to trick individuals into spending their time and money for little or no return.

Internet security suite: Collection of utility programs designed to make using the internet easier and safer.

Internet service provider (ISP): Provides access to the Internet.

Internet telephone: Low-cost alternative to long-distance telephone calls using electronic voice delivery.

Internet telephony: *See* Telephony.

Interpreter: Software that converts a procedural language one statement at a time into machine language just before the statement is executed. No object code is saved.

Intranet: Like the Internet, it typically provides e-mail, mailing lists, newsgroups, and FTP services, but it is accessible only to those within the organization. Organizations use intranets to provide information to their employees.

Inventory: Material or products that a company has in stock.

Inventory control system: A system that keeps records of the number of each kind of part or finished goods in the warehouse.

IP address (Internet Protocol address): The unique numeric address of a computer on the Internet that facilitates the delivery of e-mail.

IP telephony: *See* Telephony.

J

Java: Programming language for creating special programs like applets. *See* Applets.

Joystick: Popular input device for computer games. You control game actions by varying the pressure, speed, and direction of the joystick.

K

Key field: The common field by which tables in a database are related to each other. This field uniquely identifies the record. For example, in university databases, a key field is the Social Security number. Also known as primary field or primary key.

Keyboard: Input device that looks like a typewriter keyboard but has additional keys.

Keystroke logger: Also known as computer monitoring software and sniffer programs. They can be loaded onto your computer without your knowledge.

Keyword search: A type of search option that causes the search engine to compare your entry against its database and return with a list of sites, or hits, that contain the keyword you entered.

Knowledge base: A system that uses a database containing specific facts, rules to relate these facts, and user input to formulate recommendations and decisions.

Knowledge-based systems: Programs duplicating human knowledge. It's like capturing the knowledge of a human expert and making it accessible through a computer program.

Knowledge work system (KWS): Specialized information system used to create information in a specific area of expertise.

Knowledge worker: Person involved in the creation of information, such as an engineer and a scientist.

L

Label: Provides structure to a worksheet by describing the contents of the rows and columns. *See* Text entry.

Land: *See* Lands and pits.

Lands and pits: Flat and bumpy areas, respectively, that represent 1s and 0s on the optical disc surface to be read by a laser.

Language translator: Converts programming instructions into a machine language that can be processed by a computer.

Laptop computer: *See* Notebook computer and Notebook system unit.

Laser printer: Printer that creates dotlike images on a drum, using a laser beam light source.

Leopard: The next version of Apple's Mac OS operating system.

Levels: Generations or levels of programming languages ranging from "low" to "high." *See* Generations (of programming languages).

Light pen: A light-sensitive penlike device. Placing the pen against the monitor closes a photoelectric circuit and identifies the spot for entering or modifying data.

Link: A connection to related information.

Linux: Type of UNIX operating system initially developed by Linus Torvalds, it is one of the most popular and powerful alternatives to the Windows operating system.

Liquid crystal display (LCD): A technology used for flat-panel monitors.

Local area network (LAN): Network consisting of computers and other devices that are physically near each other, such as within the same building.

Location: For browsers to connect to resources, locations or addresses must be specified. Also known as uniform resource locators or URLs.

Logic error: Error that occurs when a programmer has used an incorrect calculation or left out a programming procedure.

Logic structure: Programming statements or structures called sequence, selection, or loop that control the logical sequence in which computer program instructions are executed.

Logical operation: Comparing two pieces of data to see whether one is equal to (=), less than (<), or greater than (>) the other.

Logical view: Focuses on the meaning and content of the data. End users and computer professionals are concerned with this view as opposed to the physical view, with which only specialized computer professionals are concerned.

Loop structure: Logic structure in which a process may be repeated as long as a certain condition remains true. This structure is called a "loop" because the program loops around or repeats again and again. There are two variations: DO UNTIL and DO WHILE.

Low bandwidth: *See* Voiceband.

Lower level: Programming language closer to the language the computer itself uses. The computer understands the 0s and 1s that make up bits and bytes.

M

Mac OS: Operating system designed for Macintosh computers.

Mac OS X: Macintosh operating system featuring a user interface called Aqua.

Machine language: Language in which data is represented in 1s and 0s. Most languages have to be translated into machine language for the computer to process the data. Either a compiler or an interpreter performs this translation.

Magnetic card reader: A card reader that reads encoded information from a magnetic strip on the back of a card.

Magnetic-ink character recognition (MICR): Direct-entry scanning devices used in banks. This technology is used to automatically read the numbers on the bottom of checks.

Magnetic tape: To find specific information, you will have to go through the tape sequentially until that data comes up. On the other hand, using an audio compact disc, select the song and the disc moves directly to that song. Tape may be slow, but it is effective and a commonly used tool for backing up data.

Magnetic tape reel: Typically $\frac{1}{2}$-inch wide and $\frac{1}{2}$-mile long, this type of magnetic tape is used by mainframe computers due to its massive storage capacity.

Magnetic tape streamer: Device that allows duplication (backup) of the data stored on a microcomputer hard disk.

Mainframe computer: This computer can process several million program instructions per second. Sizeable organizations rely on these room-size systems to handle large programs and a great deal of data.

Maintenance programmer: Programmers who maintain software by updating programs to protect them from errors, improve usability, standardize, and adjust to organizational changes.

Malware: Short for malicious software.

MAN: *See* Metropolitan area network.

Management information system (MIS): Computer-based information system that produces standardized reports in a summarized and structured form. Generally used to support middle managers.

Many-to-many relationship: In a network database, each child node may have more than one parent node and vice versa.

Marketing: The organizational department that plans, prices, promotes, sells, and distributes an organization's goods and services.

Markup language: *See* Formatting language.

Mass storage: Refers to the tremendous amount of secondary storage required by large organizations.

Mass storage devices: Devices such as file servers, RAID systems, tape libraries, optical jukeboxes, and more.

Master slide: A special slide that does not appear in a presentation but controls all the formats and placement of all slides in a presentation. The design template can be changed for an entire presentation using a master slide.

Mechanical mouse: Traditional and most widely used type of mouse. It has a ball on the bottom and is attached with a cord to the system unit.

Media: Media are the actual physical material that holds the data, such as a floppy disk, which is one of the important characteristics of secondary storage. Singular is medium.

Medium: *See* Media.

Medium band: Bandwidth of special leased lines, used mainly with minicomputers and mainframe computers.

Memory: Memory is contained on chips connected to the system board and is a holding area for data instructions and information (processed data waiting to be output to secondary storage). RAM, ROM, and CMOS are three types of memory chips.

Menu: List of commands.

Menu bar: Menus are displayed in a menu bar at the top of the screen.

Message: The content portion of e-mail correspondence.

Metasearch engine: Program that automatically submits your search request to several indices and search engines and then creates an index from received information. One of the best known is Dogpile.

Method: In an object-oriented database, description of how the data is to be manipulated.

Metropolitan area network (MAN): These networks are used as links between office buildings in a city.

Microcomputer: Small, low-cost computer designed for individual users. These include desktop, notebook, and personal digital assistant computers.

Microcomputer database: *See* Individual database.

Microprocessor: The central processing unit (CPU) of a microcomputer controls and manipulates data to produce information. The microprocessor is contained on a single integrated circuit chip and is the brains of the system.

Microwave: Communication using high-frequency radio waves that travel in straight lines through the air.

Middle management: Middle-level managers deal with control and planning. They implement the long-term goals of the organization.

MIDI: *See* Musical instrument digital interface.

Midrange computer: Also known as a minicomputer.

Minicomputer: Refrigerator-sized machines falling in-between microcomputers and mainframes in processing speed and data-storing capacity. Medium-sized companies or departments of large companies use minicomputers.

Mistaken identity: When the electronic profile of one person is switched with another.

Modem: Short for modulator-demodulator. It is a communication device that translates the electronic signals from a computer into electronic signals that can travel over telephone lines.

Modem card: Also known as an internal modem, a card that allows distant computers to communicate with one another by converting electronic signals from within the system unit into electronic signals that can travel over telephone lines and other types of connections.

Modulation: Process of converting digital signals to analog signals.

Module: *See* Program module.

Monitor: Output device like a television screen that displays data processed by the computer.

Morphing: Special effect in which one image seems to melt into another.

Motherboard: Also called a system board; the communications medium for the entire system.

Mouse: Device that typically rolls on the desktop and directs the cursor on the display screen.

Mouse pointer: Typically in the shape of an arrow. *See* Pointing device.

Multidimensional database: Data can be viewed as a cube having three or more sides consisting of cells. Each side of the cube is considered a dimension of the data; thus, complex relationships between data can be represented and efficiently analyzed. Sometimes called hyper cube and designed for analyzing large groups of records.

Multifunctional devices (MFD): Devices that typically combine the capabilities of a scanner, printer, fax, and copying machine.

Multimedia: Technology that can link all sorts of media into one form of presentation, such as video, music, voice, graphics, and text.

Multimedia authoring programs: Programs used to create multimedia presentations bringing together video, audio, graphics, and text elements into an interactive framework. Macromedia Director, Authorware, and Toolbook are examples of multimedia authoring programs.

Multitasking: Operating system that allows a single user to run several application programs at the same time.

Musical instrument digital interface (MIDI): A standard that allows musical instruments to connect to the system using MIDI ports.

N

Naive: People who underestimate the difficulty of changing computer systems or generating information.

National service provider: Internet service providers, such as America Online (AOL), that provide access through standard telephone or cable connections and allow users to access the Internet from almost anywhere within the country for a standard fee.

Natural language: Language designed to give people a more human connection with computers.

Network: The arrangement in which various communications channels are connected through two or more computers. The largest network in the world is the Internet.

Network adapter card: Connects the system unit to a cable that connects to other devices on the network.

Network administrator: Also known as network manager: Computer professional who ensures that existing information and communication systems are operating effectively and that new ones are implemented as needed. Also responsible for meeting security and privacy requirements.

Network architecture: Describes how networks are configured and how the resources are shared.

Network database: Database with a hierarchical arrangement of nodes, except that each child node may have more than one parent node. Also called many-to-many relationship.

Network gateway: Connection by which a local area network may be linked to other local area networks or to larger networks.

Network hub: The central unit in a star network where all computers and peripheral devices are linked. Typically a host computer or file server.

Network interface card (NIC): Also known as network adapter cards. They are used to connect a computer to one or more computers forming a communication network whereby users can share data, programs, and hardware.

Network operating system (NOS): Interactive software between applications and computers coordinating and directing activities between computers on a network. This operating system is located on one of the connected computers' hard disk, making that system the network server.

Network server: *See* Network operating system. This computer coordinates all communication between the other computers. Popular network operating systems include NetWare and Windows NT Server.

Network terminal: Low-cost alternative to intelligent terminal; relies on host computer or server for software. Also called network computer or thin client.

Node: Any device connected to a network. For example, a node is a computer, printer, or data storage device and each device has its own address on the network. Also, within hierarchical databases, fields or records are structured in nodes.

Notebook computer: Portable computer, also known as laptop computer, weighing between 4 and 10 pounds.

Notebook system unit: A small, portable system unit that contains electronic components, selected secondary storage devices, and input devices.

Numbered list: Sequence of steps or topics on a page organized by numbers.

Numeric entry: In a worksheet or spreadsheet; typically used to identify numbers or formulas.

Numeric keypad: Enters numbers and arithmetic symbols and is included on all computer keyboards.

O

Object: An element, such as a text box, that can be added to a workbook, which can be selected, sized, and moved. For example, if a chart (object) in an Excel workbook file (source file) is linked to a word document (destination file), the chart appears in the word document. In this manner, the object contains both data and instructions to manipulate the data.

Object code: Machine language code converted by a compiler from source code. Object code can be saved and run later.

Object-oriented database: A more flexible type of database that stores data as well as instructions to manipulate data and is able to handle unstructured data, such as photographs, audio, and video. Object-oriented databases organize data using objects, classes, entities, attributes, and methods.

Object-oriented programming (OOP): Methodology in which a program is organized into self-contained, reusable modules called objects. Each object contains both the data and processing operations necessary to perform a task.

Object-oriented software development: Software development approach that focuses less on the tasks and more on defining the relationships between previously defined procedures or objects.

Objectives: In programming, it is necessary to make clear the problems you are trying to solve to create a functional program.

Office automation system (OAS): System designed primarily to support data workers. It focuses on managing documents, communicating, and scheduling.

One Button Checkup: This program integrates several of the separate troubleshooting utilities from Norton Utilities.

One-to-many relationship: In a hierarchical database, each entry has one parent node, and a parent may have several child nodes.

Online: Being connected to the Internet is described as being online.

Online banking: A feature provided by banking institutions that allows customers to perform banking operations using a Web browser.

Online processing: *See* Real-time processing.

Online shopping: The buying and selling of a wide range of consumer goods over the Internet.

Online stock trading: Allows investors to research, buy, and sell stocks and bonds over the Internet.

Operating system: Software that interacts between application software and the computer, handling such details as running programs, storing and processing data, and coordinating all computer resources, including attached peripheral devices. It is the most important program on the computer. Windows XP, Windows Vista, and Mac OS X are examples of operating systems.

Operational feasibility: Making sure the design of a new system will be able to function within the existing framework of an organization.

Operational model: A decision model that helps lower-level managers accomplish the organization's day-to-day activities, such as evaluating and maintaining quality control.

Operators: Operators handle correcting operational errors in any programs. To do that, they need documentation, which gives them the understanding of the program, thus enabling them to fix any errors.

Optical-character recognition (OCR): Scanning device that uses special preprinted characters, such as those printed on utility bills, that can be read by a light source and changed into machine-readable code.

Optical disc: Storage device that can hold over 17 gigabytes of data, which is an equivalent of several million typewritten pages. Lasers are used to record and read data on the disc. The two basic types of optical discs are compact discs (CDs) and digital versatile or video discs (DVDs).

Optical disc drive: A disc is read by an optical disc drive using a laser that projects a tiny beam of light. The amount of reflected light determines whether the area represents a 1 or a 0.

Thermal printer: Printer that uses heat elements to produce images on heat-sensitive paper.

Thin client: *See* Network terminal.

Thin film transistor (TFT) monitor: Type of flat-panel monitor activating each pixel independently.

Third-generation language (3GL): *See* Procedural language.

Tiger: A name for the Mac OS X operating system.

Time-sharing system: System allowing several users to share resources in the host computer.

Toggle key: These keys turn a feature on or off like the CAP LOCK key.

Toolbar: Bar located typically below the menu bar containing icons or graphical representations for commonly used commands.

Top-down analysis method: Method used to identify top-level components of a system, then break these components down into smaller parts for analysis.

Top-down program design: Used to identify the program's processing steps, called program modules. The program must pass in sequence from one module to the next until the computer has processed all modules.

Top-level domain (TLD): Last part of an Internet address; identifies the geographical description or organizational identification. For example, using www.aol.com, the .com is the top a level domain code and indicates it is a commercial site. *Also see* Domain name.

Top management: Top-level managers are concerned with long-range (strategic) planning. They supervise middle management.

Topology: The configuration of a network. The four principal network topologies are *star, bus, ring,* and *hierarchical.*

Touch pad: Used to control pointer by moving and tapping your finger on the surface of a pad.

Touch screen: Monitor screen allowing actions or commands to be entered by the touch of a finger.

Track: Closed, concentric ring on a disk on which data is recorded. Each track is divided into sections called sectors.

Trackball: Device used to control the pointer by rotating a ball with your thumb. Also called a roller ball.

Traditional cookies: Intended to provide customized service. A program recording information on Web site visitors within a specific site. When you leave the site, the cookie becomes dormant and is reactivated when you revisit the site.

Traditional keyboard: Full-sized, rigid, rectangular keyboard that includes function, navigational, and numeric keys.

Transaction processing system (TPS): System that records day-to-day transactions, such as customer orders, bills, inventory levels, and production output. The TPS tracks operations and creates databases.

Transfer rate: Or transfer speed, is the speed at which modems transmit data, typically measured in bits per second (bps).

Transmission control protocol/Internet protocol (TCP/IP): TCP/IP is the standard protocol for the Internet. The essential features of this protocol involve (1) identifying sending and receiving devices and (2) reformatting information for transmission across the Internet.

Trojan horse: Program that is not a virus but is a carrier of virus(es). The most common Trojan horses appear as free computer games, screen savers, or antivirus programs. Once downloaded they locate and disable existing virus protection and then deposit the virus.

Troubleshooting program: A utility program that recognizes and corrects computer-related problems before they become serious. Also called diagnostic programs.

TV tuner card: Contains TV tuner card and video converter changing the TV signal into one that can be displayed on your monitor. Also known as video recorder cards and video capture cards.

U

Unicode: A 16-bit code designed to support international languages, like Chinese and Japanese.

Uniform resource locator (URL): For browsers to connect you to resources on the Web, the location or address of the resources must be specified. These addresses are called URLs.

Uninstall program: A utility program that safely and completely removes unwanted programs and related files.

Universal instant messenger: An instant messaging service that communicates with any other messaging service programs.

Universal Product Code (UPC): A barcode system that identifies the product to the computer, which has a description and the latest price for the product.

Universal serial bus (USB): Combines with a PCI bus on the system board to support several external devices without inserting cards for each device. USB buses are used to support high-speed scanners, printers, and video-capturing devices.

Universal serial bus (USB) port: Expected to replace serial and parallel ports. They are faster, and one USB port can be used to connect several devices to the system unit.

UNIX: An operating system originally developed for minicomputers. It is now important because it can run on many of the more powerful microcomputers.

Unstructured problem: A problem that requires the use of intuition, reasoning, and memory.

Uploading: Process of transferring information from the computer the user is operating to a remote computer.

USB drive: The size of a key chain, these hard drives connect to a computer's USB port enabling a transfer of files; has a capacity of 2GB.

User: Any individual who uses a computer. *See* End user.

User interface: Means by which users interact with application programs and hardware. A window is displayed with information for the user to enter or choose, and that is how users communicate with the program.

Utility: Performs specific tasks related to managing computer resources or files. Norton Utility for virus control and system maintenance is a good example of a utility. Also known as service programs.

Utility suite: A program that combines several utilities in one package to improve system performance. McAfee Office and Norton SystemWorks are examples.

V

Vector: Another common type of graphic file. A vector file contains all the shapes and colors, along with starting and ending points, necessary to recreate the image.

Vector illustration: *See* Vector image.

Vector image: Graphics file made up of a collection of objects such as lines, rectangles, and ovals. Vector images are more flexible than bitmaps because they are defined by mathematical equations so they can be stretched and resized. Illustration programs create and manipulate vector graphics. Also known as vector illustrations.

Very high-level languages: Problem-oriented languages that require little special training on the part of the user.

Video editing software: Allows you to reorganize, add effects, and more to your video footage.

Videoconferencing system: Computer system that allows people located at various geographic locations to have in-person meetings.

Virtual environment: *See* Virtual reality.

Virtual memory: Feature of an operating system that increases the amount of memory available to run programs. With large programs, parts are stored on a secondary device like your hard disk. Then each part is read in RAM only when needed.

Virtual reality: Interactive sensory equipment (headgear and gloves) allowing users to experience alternative realities generated in 3-D by a computer, thus imitating the physical world.

Virtual reality modeling language (VRML): Used to create real-time animated 3-D scenes.

Virtual reality wall: An immersive experience whereby you are viewing simulations on a virtual reality wall in stereoscopic vision.

Virus: Hidden instructions that migrate through networks and operating systems and become embedded in different programs. They may be designed to destroy data or simply to display messages.

Visual programming languages: A 5GL that provides a natural visual interface for program development, like intuitive icons, menus, and drawing tools for creating program code. Visual Basic is a visual programming language.

Voice over IP (VoIP): Transmission of telephone calls over networks. *See also* Telephony.

Voice recognition system: Using a microphone, sound card, and speciality software, the user can operate a computer and create documents using voice commands.

Voiceband: Bandwidth of a standard telephone line. Also known as low bandwidth.

Voltage surge (spike): Excess of electricity that may destroy chips or other electronic computer components.

VR: *See* Virtual reality.

W

WAN: *See* Wide area network.

Wand reader: Special-purpose handheld device used to read OCR characters.

Warm boot: Restarting your computer while the computer is already on and the power is not turned off.

Web: Introduced in 1992 and prior to the Web, the Internet was all text. The Web made it possible to provide a multimedia interface that includes graphics, animations, sound, and video.

Web auction: Similar to traditional auctions except that all transactions occur over the web; buyers and sellers seldom meet face-to-face.

Web authoring: Creating a Web site.

Web authoring program: Word processing program for generating Web pages. Also called HTML editor or Web page editor. Widely used Web authoring programs include Macromedia Dreamweaver and Microsoft FrontPage.

Web-based applications: By using the Web to connect with an application service provider (ASP), you can copy an application program to your computer system's memory and then run the application.

Web bug: Program hidden in the HTML code for a Web page or e-mail message as a graphical image. Web bugs can migrate whenever a user visits a Web site containing a Web bug or opens infected e-mail. They collect information on the users and report back to a predefined server.

Web database: Used by Web sites to record data collected from users and by Web search engines.

Web page: Browsers interpret HTML documents to display Web pages.

Web page editor: *See* Web authoring program.

Web utilities: Specialized utility programs making the Internet and the Web easier and safer. Some examples are plug-ins that operate as part of a browser and filters that block access and monitor use of selected Web sites.

Web log: A type of personal Web site where articles are regularly posted.

WebCam: Specialized digital video camera for capturing images and broadcasting to the Internet.

Webmaster: Develops and maintains Web sites and Web resources.

What-if analysis: Spreadsheet feature in which changing one or more numbers results in the automatic recalculation of all related formulas.

Wheel button: Some mice have a wheel button that can be rotated to scroll through information displayed on the monitor.

Wide area network (WAN): Countrywide and worldwide networks that use microwave relays and satellites to reach users over long distances.

Wi-Fi (wireless fidelity): Wireless standard also known as 802.11, used to connect computers to each other and to the Internet.

Window: A rectangular area containing a document or message.

Windows: An operating environment extending the capability of DOS.

Windows Update: A utility provided in the Windows platform that allows you to update the device drivers on your computer.

Windows Vista: The next version of Microsoft's Windows operating system, previously codenamed "Longhorn."

Windows XP: The most recent Windows operating system featuring a user interface called Luna.

Wireless keyboard: Transmits input to the system through the air, providing greater flexibility and convenience.

Wireless LAN (WLAN): Uses radio frequencies to connect computers and other devices. All communications pass through the network's centrally located wireless receiver or base station and are routed to the appropriate devices.

Wireless modem: Modem that connects to the serial port but does not connect to telephone lines. It receives through the air.

Wireless mouse: *See* Cordless mouse.

Wireless receiver: Or base station. The receiver interprets incoming radio frequencies from a wireless LAN and routes communications to the appropriate devices, which could be separate computers, a shared printer, or a modem.

Wireless revolution: A revolution that is expected to dramatically affect the way we communicate and use computer technology.

Wireless service provider: Provides Internet connections for computers with wireless modems and a wide array of wireless devices. They do not use telephone lines.

Word: The number of bits (such as 16, 32, or 64) that can be accessed at one time by the CPU.

Word processor: The computer and the program allow you to create, edit, save, and print documents composed of text.

Word wrap: Feature of word processing that automatically moves the cursor from the end of one line to the beginning of the next.

Workbook file: Contains one or more related worksheets or spreadsheets. *See* Spreadsheet.

Worksheet: Also known as a spreadsheet, or sheet; a rectangular grid of rows and columns used in programs like Excel.

Worksheet file: Is created by electronic spreadsheets to analyze things like budgets and to predict sales.

Worm: Virus that doesn't attach itself to programs and databases but fills a computer system with self-replicating information, clogging the system so that its operations are slowed or stopped.

Write-protection notch: When you slide the tile on a floppy disk so you can see through the hole, none of the information on that disk can be modified or deleted and the disk is write protected. If the hole is covered, you can save or change any material on the disk.

Credits

p. 167	© Royalty-Free/CORBIS	p. 219	Courtesy of RAIDking Technologies - www.raidking.com
p. 168	© Getty Images	p. 220	© Getty Images
p. 169 left top	Courtesy of Gateway, Inc.	p. 225	Courtesy of Apple Computer.
p. 169 bottom right	© Geostock/Getty Images	p. 221	Courtesy of Iomega Corporation.
p. 170 top left	Courtesy of AMD.	p. 223	Courtesy of Lexar Media, Inc.
p. 170 top right	Courtesy of Kingston Technology Company Inc.	p. 226	Courtesy of Lexar Media, Inc.
p. 171	Courtesy of Hauppauge Computer Works, Inc.	p. 227	Courtesy of Quantum Corporation.
p. 171	Courtesy of Hauppauge Computer Works, Inc.	p. 228	© Getty Images
p. 180 top center	© Royalty-Free/CORBIS	p. 229	© Royalty-Free/CORBIS
p. 180 right	Courtesy of Hewlett-Packard Company.	p. 230 left	© Keith Brofsky/Getty Images
p. 181 top center	© Bob Daemmrich/PhotoEdit	p. 231 bottom left	Courtesy of Iomega Corporation.
p. 181 bottom left	Courtesy of Hewlett-Packard Company.	p. 231 top right	IBM Corporate Archives
p. 181 bottom right	Courtesy of Sony Electronics Inc.	p. 231 bottom right	Courtesy of Toshiba America Information Systems, Inc.
p. 182 left	Courtesy of Adesso.	p. 232	© Getty Images
p. 182 right	Courtesy of Microsoft Corporation.	p. 240 top center	© Karen Moskowitz/Getty Images
p. 180 left & 183 top right	Courtesy of PalmOne, Inc.	p. 240 bottom left	© Stocktrek/CORBIS
p. 184 top left	Courtesy of Microsoft Corporation.	p. 240 bottom center	© Getty Images
p. 184 left center	© SuperStock	p. 240 bottom right	Courtesy of Novatel Wireless.
p. 184 left bottom	Courtesy of Hewlett-Packard Company.	p. 242	© Karen Moskowitz/Getty Images
p. 184 right	© PhotoDisc/Getty Images	p. 244 top	© Getty Images
p. 185 top	© Erik Dreyer/Getty Images	p. 240 bottom center	© Getty Images
p. 185 center	© Spencer Grant/PhotoEdit	p. 244 bottom	© Getty Images
p. 185 bottom	© Royalty-Free/CORBIS	p. 245 top	© Lester Lefkowitz/CORBIS
p. 186	Courtesy of Nokia, Inc.	p. 245 bottom	© Stocktrek/CORBIS
p. 187 top left	© David Young-Wolff/PhotoEdit	p. 246	Courtesy of Toyota Motor Sales, U.S.A., Inc.
p. 187 top right	Courtesy of Logitech.	p. 248 top center	Courtesy of Zoom Technologies, Inc.
p. 187 right	© Getty Images	p. 248 bottom left	Courtesy of USRobotics.
p. 187 bottom left	© David Young-Wolff/PhotoEdit	p. 248 bottom center	Courtesy of USRobotics.
p. 188	© Michael Newman/PhotoEdit	p. 248 bottom right	Courtesy of Novatel Wireless.
p. 189 left	Courtesy of Hewlett-Packard Company.	p. 264	© Tim Tadder/Corbis
p. 189 right	© Zigy Kaluzny/Getty Images	p. 265	© Reuters/CORBIS
p. 192 top	Courtesy of Sony Electronics Inc.	p. 266 left	© Karen Moskowitz/Getty Images
p. 192 bottom	© Jose Luis Pelaez, Inc./CORBIS	p. 266 right	© Stocktrek/CORBIS
p. 193	Courtesy of Sony Electronics Inc.	p. 267 top center	Courtesy of Zoom Technologies, Inc.
p. 194 left	Courtesy of Sony Electronics Inc.	p. 267 bottom left	Courtesy of USRobotics.
p. 194 right	© Mark Duncan/AP	p. 267 bottom center	Courtesy of USRobotics.
p. 195	© Bob Daemmrich/PhotoEdit	p. 267 bottom right	Courtesy of Novatel Wireless.
p. 196	© Robert Llewellyn/CORBIS	p. 276 top right	© Larry Dale Gordon/Getty Images
p. 197	Courtesy of Hewlett-Packard Company.	p. 276 bottom right	© Getty Images
p. 198	© Marianna Day Massey/Marianna Day Massey/ZUMA/Corbis	p. 277 top left	© Michael A. Keller Studios, Ltd./CORBIS
p. 199	Courtesy of Linksys.	p. 277 bottom center	© Eric Pearle/Getty Images
p. 200	© Charles Gupton/CORBIS	p. 277 top right	© Gabe Palmer/CORBIS
p. 201	© White Packert/Getty Images.	p. 278	© Getty Images
p. 202 left	Courtesy of Microsoft Corporation.	p. 290	© Larry Dale Gordon/Getty Images
p. 202 right	© Royalty-Free/CORBIS	p. 291 left	© Getty Images
p. 203 left	Courtesy of Hewlett-Packard Company.	p. 291 right	© Getty Images
p. 203 right	Courtesy of Sony Electronics Inc.	p. 294	© age fotostock/SuperStock
p. 204	© Bob Daemmrich/PhotoEdit	p. 295 left	© Michael A. Keller Studios, Ltd./CORBIS
p. 212 top left	Courtesy of Iomega Corporation.	p. 295 right	© Eric Pearle/Getty Images
p. 212 top right	© Getty Images	p. 297	© Gabe Palmer/CORBIS
p. 212 bottom center	Courtesy of Toshiba America Information Systems, Inc.	p. 298	© Royalty-Free/CORBIS
p. 213	Courtesy of Lexar Media, Inc.	p. 299	© Royalty-Free/CORBIS
p. 214	© Keith Brofsky/Getty Images	p. 301 left	© Getty Images
p. 215	Courtesy of Iomega Corporation.	p. 301 right	© Getty Images
p. 217 left	Courtesy of Iomega Corporation.	p. 310	© 1995-2006 FedEx. All rights reserved.
p. 217 right	Courtesy of Toshiba America Information Systems, Inc.	p. 311 left	© Getty Images
		p. 311 right	© Stockbyte/PunchStock
p. 218	IBM Corporate Archives	p. 312	© Colin Young-Wolff/PhotoEdit
		p. 314	© 1995-2006 FedEx. All rights reserved.

Subject Index

A

A6 Compiler, 335
AC adapters, 166
Accelerated graphics port (AGP), 164
Access, 278
Accuracy, 278
ACI, 137
ACID, 97
Acrobat Reader, 46, 47
Active-matrix monitor, 193
Ad-Aware, 283
Ad network cookie, 282
Add Printer Wizard, 133
Address, 32, 34
Adobe Illustrator, 96
Adobe PageMaker, 95
Adobe Photoshop, 95
ADSL, 249
Advance fee loans, 288
Advanced Research Project Agency Network
    (ARPANET), 30
Adware cookies, 282
Age of connectivity, 340–342
Agent, 81
AGP, 164
AI, 106–108
Air travel database, 308
Altair, 338
ALU, 155–156
Amazon, 45, 342
America Online (AOL), 31
America Online ISP, 32
Amerivault, 226
Analog, 152
Analog signals, 247
Analytical graphs, 70
Animations, 104
Anti-spyware programs, 283
Antitrust, 147
Antivirus programs, 128
AOL, 31
AOL Search, 41
Apology-B, 287
Apple Computer, 338–340, 342
Apple GarageBand, 97, 100
Apple iMovie, 97, 100
Apple iWork, 80
Applets, 33
AppleWorks, 79
Application software, 60–119
    artificial intelligence (AI), 106–108
    audio and video, 97

common features, 62–63
DBMS, 74–76
graphics, 94–97
integrated packages, 79
multimedia, 100–103
presentation graphics, 77–78
software suites, 80
spreadsheet, 69–73
Web authoring, 103–105
word processor, 66–68
Arial, 66
Arithmetic-logic unit (ALU), 155–156
Arithmetic operations, 155–156
ARPANET, 30, 337
Artificial intelligence (AI), 106–108
Artificial reality, 106
ASCII, 152, 153
Asimo robot, 107
Ask Jeeves, 41
Asymmetric digital subscriber line (ADSL), 249
Athlon 64, 156
ATM, 312
Attachments, 35
Auction fraud, 288
Auction house sites, 44, 45
Audio editing software, 97
Audio-input devices, 189–190
Audio-output devices, 197–199
Authorware, 102
AutoContent wizard, 77, 78
AutoCorrect, 68
Automated teller machine (ATM), 312
Autonomic computing, 137–138
Autonomic Computing Initiative (ACI), 137
AutoShapes, 70

B

Babbage, Charles, 334
Back and neck pain, 294
Backbone, 258
Backup, 129, 147, 292
Backup programs, 128
Bandwidth, 249–250
Banyan Vines, 260
Bar code, 187
Bar code readers, 187–188
Bar code scanner, 187
Base station, 254
Basic applications, 62
B2B e-commerce, 43
B2C e-commerce, 43–44
BD, 222

N

Naive, 315
Nanosecond, 156
Napster, 260–261, 274, 341
National Cristina Foundation, 298
National service providers, 31
Natural hazards, 289
Navigation keys, 183
Neck pain, 294
Net Nanny, 47
.NET platform, 342
Netscape Communications Corporation, 340
NetWare, 260
NetWare Lite, 261
Network, 251, 252. *See also* Communication and networks
Network adapter cards, 160
Network administration, 251
Network administrator, 264
Network architecture, 255–259
Network gateway, 253
Network hub, 255
Network interface card (NIC), 160, 251
Network operating system (NOS), 124, 251
Network server, 124
Network strategies, 260–262
Network terminal, 199
Network types, 253–254
New customer and supplier relationships, 314
New enterprises, 313–314
New products, 313
Newton MessagePad, 340
NIC, 160, 251
Node, 251
Noise, 295
Norton AntiVirus, 132
Norton CleanSweep, 132
Norton Internet Security Site, 80
Norton SystemWorks, 80, 132
Norton Utilities, 132
NOS, 124, 251
Notebook system units, 150, 176
Numbered lists, 66
Numeric entry, 69
Numeric keypad, 183

O

OCR, 188
Office grapevine, 321
OMR, 188
On the Web explorations
    artificial intelligence, 106
    Corel, 74
    encryption, 292
    ergonomic keyboard, 182
    ergonomics, 293
    eyestrain, 293
    flat-panel monitors, 193
    free e-mail service, 35
    graphics programs, 96
    HDTV, 194
    high-capacity hard disks, 216
    history of the Internet, 30

laser printer, 196
    Lotus, 77
    MFDs, 198
    microprocessor, 156
    Microsoft, 62
    multimedia authoring, 102
    multimedia presentation, 102
    privacy issues, 280
    system unit components, 153
    utility software, 132
    Web filtering programs, 47
One Button Checkup, 132
Online, 30
Online backup, 147
Online banking, 43–44
Online expert systems, 119
Online job search, 318–319, 331
Online shopping, 44, 50
Online stock trading, 44
OnlyMyEmailPersonal, 35
Operating system, 123–127
    categories, 124–125
    features, 123–124
    functions, 123
    Linux, 127
    MAC OS, 127
    UNIX, 127
    Windows, 125–126
Opteron, 156
Optical-character recognition (OCR), 188
Optical disc, 220–222
Optical disc drive, 220
Optical holography, 229
Optical-mark recognition (OMR), 188
Optical mouse, 184–185
Optical scanner, 186, 187
Organizational change, 320–321
Organizational Internet storage, 228
Organizational internets, 262–263
Organized crime, 286
Outlook Express, 34
Output, 192

P

Packets, 250
Page layout programs, 94
Paint Shop Pro, 95
Palm, 273
Parallel ports, 164
Parallel processing, 156
Passive-matrix monitor, 193
Password, 291
PayPal, 45
PC card, 161
PC Card hard disk, 217
PC Card modem, 248
PC World, 317
PCI, 164
PCI Express (PCIe), 165
PDA, 150, 151
PDA keyboards, 183
Peer-to-peer networks, 261–262

Pentium 4, 156
People, 4, 6
Perception system robots, 108
Peripheral component interconnect (PCI), 164
Person-to-person auction sites, 44, 45
Personal digital assistant (PDA), 150, 151
Personal firewalls, 307
Personal laser printers, 196
Personal software, 79
Personal suite, 80
Personal web site, 118
PersonalFirewall, 135
Photo editors, 95
Photo printers, 197
Physical health, 293–295
Physical security, 292
Picosecond, 156
Pirated software, 289
Pits, 220
Pixel, 95, 192
PKZip, 219
Plagiarism, 309
Platform, 125
Platform scanners, 187
Plotters, 197
Plug and Play, 160
Plug-ins, 46–47
Pod, 265
Pointer, 62, 123
Pointing devices, 184–185
Pointing stick, 184, 185
Polling, 255
Port, 164–166
Portable printers, 197
Portable scanner, 186, 187
Portable voice recognition system, 192
POST, 146
Power supply, 166
Power supply unit, 166
PowerPC, 156
Presence technology, 299
Presentation graphics, 77–78, 89
Presentation style, 78
Pretty Good Privacy, 291
Primary key, 75
Primary storage, 214
Printers, 194–197
Privacy, 278
    cookies, 280–282
    Internet, 280–286
    large databases, 278–280
    spyware, 283, 284–285
PrivacyService, 135
Proactive, 315–316
Procedures, 4
Processor, 155
Processor serial number (PSN), 178
Productivity suite, 80
Property, 278
Protocol, 32, 250

Proxy server, 263
PSN, 178
Pyra, 341

Q

QuarkXPress, 95
Query, 74, 76
QuickTime, 46, 47
QuickTime movies, 46
Qurb, 35
QXGA, 193

R

Radio frequency card reader, 187
Radio frequency identification (RFID), 187
RAID, 219
RAID systems, 228
RAM, 157–158
Random-access memory (RAM), 157–158
Range, 69
Raster images, 95
Read-only memory (ROM), 158
RealPlayer, 46, 47
Recalculation, 70
Records, 74, 75
Recycle, 297, 298
Redundant arrays of inexpensive disks (RAID), 219
Reformatting, 250
Refresh rate, 193
Relational database, 74
Removable hard disk and drive, 217
Repetitive motion injury, 294
Repetitive strain injury (RSI), 294
Report, 74, 76
Resolution
    monitor, 192–193
    printer, 195
Resolution standards, 193
Resume advice, 332
Retire-IT, 298
Reuniting sites, 38
Reverse directory, 278
RFID, 187
RFID tags, 157
Ribbons, 63
Ring network, 258
Robot, 107–109
Robotics, 107–108
Roller ball, 185
ROM, 158
Rows, 69
RSI, 294

S

Safe Eyes Platinum, 47
SATA, 165
Satellite, 245
Satellite/air connection services, 249
Saya robot, 109
Scam, 288
Scanner, 186

T

T1, T2, T3, T4 lines, 248
Table
  DBMS, 74, 75
  word processor, 68
Tablet PC, 150, 151
Tablet PC system units, 150–151
Tape cartridges, 227
Tape library, 228
TB, 158
TCP/IP, 250
Technical writer, 200
Technological failures, 290
Technology and organizations, 313–314
Technology and people, 314–316
Telephone lines, 244
Telephony, 199
Templates, 78
Terabyte (TB), 158
Terminal, 199
Terminal network, 260
Terrorism, 287, 289
Text entries, 69, 71
TFT monitors, 193
Theft, 289
Thermal printer, 196–197
Thesaurus, 66
Thin client, 199
Thin film transistor (TFT) monitors, 193
ThinkFree, 46
Three dimensional storing, 229
3G cellular networks, 249
Thus, 287
Tiger, 127
Tilting, 72
Time sharing system, 258
Times New Roman, 66
TLD, 32
Toggle keys, 183
Toolbars, 63
Toolbook, 102
Top-level domain (TLD), 32
Topology, 255
Torvalds, Linus, 340
Touch pad, 184, 185
Touch screen, 185
Track, 130, 131, 215
Trackball, 184, 185
Traditional cookies, 282
Traditional keyboard, 182
Transistor age, 336
Transmission control protocol/Internet protocol
  (TCP/IP), 250
Transfer rate, 247
Trojan horses, 288
Troubleshooting programs, 128
TV tuner cards, 160
TV tuner cards and video clips, 162–163, 176, 177
Twisted-pair cable, 244

U

Unicode, 152
Uniform resource locator (URL), 32
Uninstall programs, 128
UNIVAC, 335
Universal instant messenger, 38
Universal Product Code (UPC), 187
Universal serial bus (USB), 164
Universal serial bus (USB) ports, 164
UNIX, 127
UPC, 187
Upgrader's guide, 348–351
Uploading, 46
URL, 32
USB, 164
USB drives, 226
USB ports, 164
USB storage device, 237
User interface, 62, 123
Utilities, 46–48, 128–132
Utility suite, 80, 131–132
UXGA, 193

V

V Communications SystemSuite, 131
Vacation prize, 288
Vacuum tube age, 335
Vanquish vqME, 35
Vector, 96
Vector illustrations, 96
Vector image, 96
Video clips, 162–163, 176, 177
Video editing software, 97, 98–99, 117, 118
Virtual environments, 106
Virtual memory, 158, 177
Virtual reality, 106–107
Virtual reality modeling language (VRML), 106
Virtual reality wall, 107
Virus, 131, 134–135, 145, 146, 287, 288
Virus protection, 134–135, 145, 146, 288
VirusScan, 135
Voice over IP (VoIP), 199
Voice recognition, 209
Voice recognition systems, 192
Voiceband, 250
VoIP, 199
Voltage surge, 290
VR, 106

W

WAN, 254
Wand reader, 187, 188
Warm boot, 123
Wearable computers, 168
Web, 30. See also Internet
Web-accessibility refrigerators, 49
Web auctions, 44, 50
Web authoring, 103–105
Web-based applications, 46

Tips Index